DUNGEONS & DRAGONS®

COMPLETE ADVENTURER™

A Guide to Skillful Characters
of All Classes

Jesse Decker

CREDITS

DESIGN
Jesse Decker

ADDITIONAL DESIGN
Richard Baker, Michelle Lyons,
David Noonan, Stan!

DEVELOPMENT TEAM
Richard Baker, Andy Collins,
Andrew J. Finch

EDITORS
John D. Rateliff, Gary Sarli

ADDITIONAL EDITING
Jennifer Clarke Wilkes, Chris Thomasson

MANAGING EDITOR
Kim Mohan

DESIGN MANAGERS
Ed Stark, Christopher Perkins

DEVELOPMENT MANAGER
Andrew J. Finch

SENIOR ART DIRECTOR RPG
Stacy Longstreet

DIRECTOR OF RPG R&D
Bill Slavicsek

ART DIRECTOR D&D
Dawn Murin

COVER ARTIST
Matt Cavotta

INTERIOR ARTISTS
Steve Belledin, Mitch Cotie, Ed Cox,
Steve Ellis, Wayne England,
David Hudnut, Jeremy Jarvis, Doug Kovacs,
Chuck Lukacs, Jeff Miracola,
Monte Moore, William O'Connor,
Michael Phillippi, Ron Spencer,
Franz Vohwinkel

GRAPHIC DESIGNERS
Dee Barnett, Dawn Murin

CARTOGRAPHER
Todd Gamble

GRAPHIC PRODUCTION SPECIALIST
Angelika Lokotz

IMAGE TECHNICIAN
Candice Baker

PRODUCTION MANAGERS
Josh Fischer, Randall Crews

Resources: *Arms and Equipment Guide* by Eric Cagle, Jesse Decker, Jeff Quick, and James Wyatt; *Defenders of the Faith* by Rich Redman and James Wyatt; *Draconomicon* by Andy Collins, Skip Williams, and James Wyatt; *Epic Level Handbook* by Andy Collins, Bruce R. Cordell, and Thomas M. Reid; FORGOTTEN REALMS® Campaign Setting by Ed Greenwood, Sean K. Reynolds, Skip Williams, and Rob Heinsoo; *Magic of Faerûn* by Sean K Reynolds, Duane Maxwell, and Angel McCoy; *Masters of the Wild* by David Eckelberry and Mike Selinker; *Miniatures Handbook* by Michael Donais, Skaff Elias, Rob Heinsoo, and Jonathan Tweet; *Oriental Adventures* by James Wyatt; *Races of Faerûn* by Eric L. Boyd, Matt Forbeck, and James Jacobs; *Races of Stone* by Jesse Decker, Michelle Lyons, and David Noonan; *Song and Silence* by David Noonan and John D. Rateliff; *Sword and Fist* by Jason Carl; "Class Acts: The Nightsong Enforcer," by Monte Cook (DRAGON® Magazine #293); "Class Acts: The Nightsong Infiltrator," by Monte Cook (DRAGON #294); "Cloak & Dagger" by Eric Cagle and Evan Michael Jackson (DRAGON #316); "Silent Warriors," by Matthew Sernett (DRAGON #289); "Saying the Right Things" by Eric Cagle (DRAGON #303); "Spellbook Archive," various authors (www.wizards.com); "Pirates: Fact & Legend," (www.piratesinfo.com).

Based on the original DUNGEONS & DRAGONS® rules created by Gary Gygax and Dave Arneson and the new DUNGEONS & DRAGONS game designed by Jonathan Tweet, Monte Cook, Skip Williams, Richard Baker, and Peter Adkison.

U.S., CANADA, ASIA, PACIFIC,
& LATIN AMERICA
Wizards of the Coast, Inc.
P.O. Box 707
Renton WA 98057-0707
Questions? 1-800-324-6496

EUROPEAN HEADQUARTERS
Hasbro UK Ltd
Caswell Way
Newport, Gwent NP9 0YH
GREAT BRITAIN
Please keep this address for your records

620-17729000-001-EN
9 8 7 6 5 4 3
ISBN 978-0-7869-3651-9   First Printing: January 2005

Visit our website at **www.wizards.com/dnd**

Contents

Introduction

Complete Adventurer is a rules accessory for the Dungeons & Dragons® game. It is primarily a player resource focused on skills and other game elements that characters of any class can use. It looks at nearly every aspect of the D&D game with skills in mind, and it allows characters with the proper number of skill ranks access to new combat options, new spells, new equipment, and new classes. DMs can also use this book as a resource for creating or optimizing single creatures or even entire campaign worlds.

EVERYONE HAS SKILL

What does it mean to be a skilled character? Really, the term is just a matter of degree. Even a character who gets a measly 1 skill point for each new level he attains can become better at a particular skill than other characters he might encounter (or travel with). Much of this book is potentially relevant to any character—from new uses for skills to new equipment that can help even an unskilled character make a crucial skill check, *Complete Adventurer* provides exciting options even for characters with very low levels or very few skill points.

WHAT'S INSIDE

Complete Adventurer is structured similarly to its companion volumes *Complete Warrior, Complete Divine*, and *Complete Arcane*. It provides the same kinds of game information, emphasizing certain topics in a way that best suits the theme of the book.

For instance, a full chapter in *Complete Adventurer* is devoted to skills and feats, beginning with an extensive discussion of new applications for existing skills—the largest single expansion of the rules in Chapter 4 of the *Player's Handbook* that we've ever published. The chapter also includes a long list of new feats, many of which are suited to characters with a large number of skill points per level or a large number of ranks in a single skill.

Three new standard character classes—the deadly ninja, the masterful scout, and the versatile spellthief—provide players with new ways to approach highly skilled characters, and each class has a unique approach to combat as well.

The large number of prestige classes in this book is deliberate. Every character class (and nearly every character concept) is represented, each with a focus on skill use. Whether you're a spellcaster with a few levels of rogue or ninja, a fighter feeling a lack of skill points, or a highly skilled character looking to further specialize, you'll find exciting options and classes throughout these descriptions.

Many of the spells introduced in this book interact with skills—opening up new uses, providing special bonuses, or producing powerful effects for characters with the right skills. In addition, many of the spells focus on using existing abilities in unusual and interesting ways. These spells allow spellcasters to occupy a significant place in campaigns that emphasize skill use and give advantages to those characters with a large number of ranks in many skills.

The last chapter of this book provides information on several organizations open to player characters. Some are related to the prestige classes introduced earlier, while others stand on their own. Each organization has guidelines for membership, benefits for joining, and realistic reasons for adventurers to belong. Any one of these organizations could become the focus of a campaign, since each admits members from a diverse selection of character classes and concepts.

WHAT YOU NEED TO PLAY

Complete Adventurer makes use of the information in the three D&D core rulebooks—*Player's Handbook, Dungeon Master's Guide*, and *Monster Manual*. In addition, it includes references to material in the *Epic Level Handbook*, the *Expanded Psionics Handbook, Complete Warrior*, and *Complete Arcane*. Although possession of any or all of these supplements will enhance your enjoyment of this book, they are not strictly necessary.

SOURCES

This book includes material from other previously published work, including *Dragon Magazine* and earlier supplements such as *Defenders of the Faith* and *Song and Silence*. This material has been picked up and revised to v.3.5 based on feedback from thousands of D&D players comparing and debating the strengths and weaknesses of characters and options at gaming conventions, on message boards, on email lists, and over the counters of their friendly local gaming stores.

The changes we make to previously published material are intended to create an improved version of that material—to help out prestige classes that were formerly suboptimal choices, to adjust feats or spells that were simply too good, or take whatever steps the D&D v.3.5 revision made necessary for each individual class, feat, spell, or item. Of course, if you're playing with older material and it's working fine in your game, you shouldn't feel compelled to change.

Illus. by D. Kovacs

Since its inception, the latest edition of the DUNGEONS & DRAGONS roleplaying game has been about options, not restrictions. *Complete Adventurer* continues that theme, introducing new uses for old skills, new feats and equipment, and the new character classes presented in this chapter. Although every class participates in adventures and is worthy of the title "adventurer," the classes discussed here emphasize skill use and ingenuity, making them particularly appropriate for this book's emphasis on skills and adventure.

The three classes described in this chapter—ninja, scout, and spellthief—have access to a wide variety of class skills and gain 6 or more skill points per level. More important, however, is the way that these skills and the abilities unique to each class change the way an adventure feels. The scout and ninja both match the rogue's stealth and ability to find and bypass traps, but each of these classes approaches combat in a new way. The spellthief adds a modest progression of arcane spells. Although these abilities are potent, the most intriguing aspect of a spellthief is his ability to steal and replicate the abilities of his foes.

Each of these classes has a unique set of abilities, and each presents a new approach to a wide range of adventuring situations. The ninja, scout, and spellthief classes are especially interesting to groups who want to play in a campaign focused on espionage, politics, or intrigue.

NINJA

Ninjas move through the shadows, striking down the unwary and vanishing again with ease. Ninjas walk where others cannot. They blend their training in stealth and assassination with a focused mind. Their rigorous preparation sharpens their minds and bodies, giving them supernatural abilities of stealth and making them phantoms in the eyes of many. Although ninjas in battle lack the staying power of martial characters such as fighters or barbarians, they excel at making combat occur on their terms—appearing and disappearing seemingly at a whim.

Historically, ninjas came from clans of assassins and guerrilla warriors in feudal Japan. In a fantasy setting, they blend a gift for stealth and infiltration with devastating surprise attacks and supernatural means of avoiding blows. Although the specific abilities of the class differ from those attributed to the historical ninja, they mirror the ninja's fearsome reputation as a spy, assassin, and martial artist.

Adventures: Ninjas adventure for a variety of reasons. A loyal ninja might adventure at her lord's command, using her abilities of stealth and subterfuge to ferret out his enemies or recover powerful treasures to be used in his service. A mercenary ninja might seek only treasure and fame, while a more idealistic ninja might seek to thwart a growing evil. Most ninjas prefer anonymity to fame, and they go out of their way to disguise their profession and abilities. A rare few, however, revel in the mysterious reputation that surrounds ninjas and their training, making known their abilities and their role in a famous adventuring group. As ninjas grow in wealth and power, their goals often change, and their ability to uncover secrets and kill stealthily can shape the plans of entire nations. Rulers both fear and covet the skills of the ninja, and high-level ninjas whose identities are known often find adventures coming to them rather than the converse.

Characteristics: Highly skilled spies and assassins, ninjas can master a broad range of skills and combat techniques. Nearly every ninja perfects the arts of moving quietly and remaining hidden, and her secondary skills define her role in an adventuring party or a community. Many ninjas hone skills that help them become better spies, mastering the arts of social interaction and disguise. Others take on the role of cat burglars, practicing skills that help them find and bypass traps and locks.

In combat, a ninja can deal out devastating blows if her opponent doesn't know she's there, but she's not quite as adept as a rogue is at delivering such attacks in a prolonged battle.

Ninjas jump and climb farther and faster than members of most other classes, and they are skilled acrobats as well. Ninjas also receive special training in the use of poisons, and many ninjas employ poisonous weapons in combat.

Even with these impressive skills, a ninja's most dangerous and remarkable powers involve the ability to step briefly into the Ethereal Plane. By focusing her *ki*, a ninja can vanish from sight, walk through solid walls, and deal devastating attacks even when not physically present at the scene. As a ninja advances in level, she can turn this ability to defense, causing blows that would otherwise hit to pass harmlessly through her body.

Alignment: Although ninjas have a reputation as dangerous assassins and deceptive spies, they follow many different philosophies and ideals and can be of any alignment. For every dangerous mercenary who uses her ninja training to kill for money, an honest and loyal ninja stands guard over a just lord. Most ninjas follow their own beliefs rather than the dictates of a noble or magistrate, and therefore more ninjas are chaotic than lawful.

Religion: A ninja's religious beliefs follow those of her clan. In a fantasy game, ninjas can follow any god, although most clans devote themselves to deities of stealth or trickery. Neutral or mercenary ninjas might devote themselves to Olidammara (the god of thieves). Evil ninjas might revere Nerull (the god of death) or Erythnul (the god of slaughter).

Ninjas who have left or lost their clan follow any deity and often choose not to worship a deity.

Background: Many ninjas come from isolated clans that train in secret. They spend years perfecting the arts of stealth and subterfuge in distant villages and hidden training camps. These warriors, whether deployed in the service of an honorable lord or sent to serve as mercenary assassins, carefully conceal their identities and origins. These ninjas weave complicated webs of disguises, strike only from hiding, and deal through intermediaries whenever possible. Because of their strong ties to their clan, these ninjas must often put aside personal preferences or goals to serve their lord or clan, but in return they gain the support of a powerful political force and access to the clan's many safe houses and hideouts.

Although most ninjas come from such isolated clans, exceptions exist at every turn. Some ninjas receive specialized training from a single mentor, perhaps even a retired adventurer who wishes to pass along his skills. Others train alongside monks and other ascetics in a peaceful monastery. In some places, far-thinking nobles set up their own ninja training centers. One of these centers might consist merely of a single teacher with a handful of students; another might be a full-blown ninja school that progresses students through a rigid series of tests, ranks, and trials.

Races: Humans, halflings, half-elves, and half-orcs often have the combination of adaptability and ambition necessary to master the techniques of the ninja. Elves, both graceful and deadly, rarely become ninjas, but those who do often achieve great fame or notoriety. Such elf ninjas often attain the heights of ninja prowess, shaping the history of many human generations through their daring exploits. Dwarves and gnomes seldom train as ninjas. Not only is their social structure too open to

A ninja

Illus. by E. Cox

shelter hidden clans of ninjas, but their martial instincts run to more straightforward forms of combat.

Other Classes: Ninjas work best with rogues, scouts, or rangers. Although they appreciate the healing power of clerics and the sheer offensive might of fighters and barbarians, ninjas rely too much on stealth to completely embrace the idea of adventuring with other classes. Conversely, when traveling or not actively adventuring, ninjas who wish to go unnoticed benefit greatly from the presence of other classes. The less subtle and more visible her adventuring companions are, the easier it is for a ninja to remain in the background and disguise her own abilities.

Role: Depending on a ninja's skill selection and the mission that her party undertakes, the character's role in the group can vary dramatically. A ninja practiced in disguise and diplomacy might assume a false identity and act as the group's leader and front person. A stealthy ninja who has perfected the arts of infiltration might act as a scout or point, while a more cautious ninja might hang back, covering the group's rear. Whatever a ninja's role during routine dungeon exploration or other adventures, she is a dangerous and unpredictable combatant who can disable foes with poison, seemingly strike from nowhere, and escape almost any situation by using her supernatural abilities.

GAME RULE INFORMATION

Ninjas have the following game statistics.

Abilities: Ninjas benefit from a high Dexterity score, since it affects their most important skills, and many of their abilities require that they wear no armor. A high Dexterity also helps a ninja to act first in initiative and take advantage of her sudden strike ability. A ninja also appreciates a high Wisdom score, which improves her Armor Class, grants additional uses of her *ki* powers, and helps her locate foes with skills such as Listen and Spot.

Alignment: Any.

Hit Die: d6.

Starting Gold: 4d4×10 gp.

Class Skills

A ninja's class skills (and the key ability for each skill) are Balance (Dex), Bluff (Cha), Climb (Str), Concentration (Con), Craft (Int), Disable Device (Int), Disguise (Cha), Escape Artist (Dex), Gather Information (Cha), Hide (Dex), Jump (Str), Listen (Wis), Move Silently (Dex), Open Lock (Dex), Search (Int), Sense Motive (Wis), Sleight of Hand (Dex), Spot (Wis), Swim (Str), and Tumble (Dex).

Skill Points at 1st Level: (6 + Int modifier) × 4.

Skill Points at Each Additional Level: 6 + Int modifier.

Class Features

All of the following are class features of the ninja.

Weapon and Armor Proficiency: Ninjas are proficient with all simple weapons, plus the hand crossbow, kama, kukri, nunchaku, sai, shortbow, short sword, shuriken, and siangham. Ninjas are not proficient with any type of armor or shield.

AC Bonus (Ex): A ninja is highly trained at dodging blows, and she has a sixth sense that lets her avoid even unanticipated attacks. When unarmored and unencumbered, a ninja adds her Wisdom bonus (if any) to her Armor Class. This ability does not stack with the monk's AC bonus ability (a ninja with levels of monk does not add the bonus twice). In addition, a ninja gains a +1 bonus to AC at 5th level. This bonus increases by 1 for every five ninja levels thereafter (+2 at 10th, +3 at 15th, and +4 at 20th level).

These bonuses to AC apply even against touch attacks or when a ninja is flat-footed. The character loses these bonuses when she is immobilized or helpless, when she wears any armor, when she carries a shield, or when she carries a medium or heavy load.

Ki Power (Su): A ninja can channel her *ki* to manifest special powers of stealth and mobility. She can use her *ki* powers a number of times per day equal to one-half her class level (minimum 1) plus her Wisdom bonus (if any). *Ki* powers can be used only if a ninja is wearing no armor and is unencumbered.

As long as a ninja's *ki* pool isn't empty (that is, as long as she has at least one daily use remaining), she gains a +2 bonus on her Will saves.

A ninja's *ki* powers are ghost step, *ki* dodge, ghost strike, greater *ki* dodge, and ghost walk. Each power is described under a separate entry below.

Sudden Strike (Ex): If a ninja can catch an opponent when he is unable to defend himself effectively from her attack, she can strike a vital spot for extra damage. Whenever a ninja's target is denied a Dexterity bonus to Armor Class (whether the target actually has a Dexterity bonus or not), the ninja deals an extra 1d6 points of

damage with her attack. This extra damage increases by 1d6 points for every two ninja levels thereafter. A ninja can't use sudden strike when flanking an opponent unless that opponent is denied its Dexterity bonus to AC.

This damage also applies to ranged attacks against targets up to 30 feet away. Creatures with concealment, creatures without discernible anatomies, and creatures immune to extra damage from critical hits are all immune to sudden strikes. A ninja can't make a sudden strike while striking the limbs of a creature whose vitals are out of reach.

A ninja can't use sudden strike to deliver nonlethal damage. Weapons capable of dealing only nonlethal damage don't deal extra damage when used as part of a sudden strike.

The extra damage from the sudden strike ability stacks with the extra damage from sneak attack whenever both would apply to the same target.

Trapfinding (Ex): A ninja can use the Search skill to locate traps with a DC higher than 20, and she can use Disable Device to bypass a trap or disarm magic traps. See the rogue class feature, page 50 of the *Player's Handbook*.

Ghost Step (Su): Starting at 2nd level, a ninja can spend one daily use of her *ki* power to become invisible for 1 round. Using this ability is a swift action (see Swift Actions and Immediate Actions, page 137) that does not provoke attacks of opportunity.

At 10th level, a ninja can become ethereal when using ghost step instead of becoming invisible.

Poison Use (Ex): At 3rd level and higher, a ninja never risks accidentally poisoning herself when applying poison to a weapon.

Great Leap (Su): At 4th level and higher, a ninja always makes Jump checks as if she were running and had the Run feat, enabling her to make long jumps without a running start and granting her a +4 bonus on the jump (see the skill description, page 77 of the *Player's Handbook*). This ability can be used only if she is wearing no armor and is carrying no more than a light load.

Acrobatics (Ex): Starting at 6th level, a ninja gains a +2 bonus on Climb, Jump, and Tumble checks. This bonus increases to +4 at 12th level and +6 at 18th level.

Ki Dodge (Su): At 6th level and higher, a ninja can spend one daily use of her *ki* power to cause an attack against her to miss when it might otherwise hit. When a ninja activates this ability, her outline shifts and wavers, granting her concealment (20% miss chance) against all attacks for 1 round. Using this ability is a swift action that does not provoke attacks of opportunity.

SUDDEN STRIKE AND SNEAK ATTACK

For the purpose of qualifying for feats, prestige classes, and similar options that require a minimum number of sneak attack extra damage dice, treat the ninja's sudden strike ability as the equivalent of sneak attack.

TABLE 1–1: THE NINJA

Level	Base Attack Bonus	Fort Save	Ref Save	Will Save	AC Bonus	Special
1st	+0	+0	+2	+0	+0	*Ki* power, sudden strike +1d6, trapfinding
2nd	+1	+0	+3	+0	+0	Ghost step (invisible)
3rd	+2	+1	+3	+1	+0	Sudden strike +2d6, poison use
4th	+3	+1	+4	+1	+0	Great leap
5th	+3	+1	+4	+1	+1	Sudden strike +3d6
6th	+4	+2	+5	+2	+1	Acrobatics +2, *ki* dodge
7th	+5	+2	+5	+2	+1	Sudden strike +4d6, speed climb
8th	+6/+1	+2	+6	+2	+1	Ghost strike
9th	+6/+1	+3	+6	+3	+1	Sudden strike +5d6, improved poison use
10th	+7/+2	+3	+7	+3	+2	Ghost step (ethereal)
11th	+8/+3	+3	+7	+3	+2	Sudden strike +6d6
12th	+9/+4	+4	+8	+4	+2	Acrobatics +4, evasion
13th	+9/+4	+4	+8	+4	+2	Sudden strike +7d6
14th	+10/+5	+4	+9	+4	+2	Ghost mind
15th	+11/+6/+1	+5	+9	+5	+3	Sudden strike +8d6
16th	+12/+7/+2	+5	+10	+5	+3	Ghost sight
17th	+12/+7/+2	+5	+10	+5	+3	Sudden strike +9d6
18th	+13/+8/+3	+6	+11	+6	+3	Acrobatics +6, greater *ki* dodge
19th	+14/+9/+4	+6	+11	+6	+3	Sudden strike +10d6
20th	+15/+10/+5	+6	+12	+6	+4	Ghost walk

See invisibility has no effect on concealment granted by the *ki* dodge ability, but *true seeing* negates the miss chance. This concealment does not stack with that caused by other effects that grant concealment or by spells such as *blink* or *displacement*.

Speed Climb (Ex): A ninja of 7th level or higher can scramble up or down walls and slopes with great speed. She can climb at her speed as a move action with no penalty; however, she must begin and end the round on a horizontal surface (such as the ground or a rooftop). If she does not end her movement on a horizontal surface, she falls, taking falling damage as appropriate for her distance above the ground.

A ninja needs only one free hand to use this ability. This ability can be used only if a ninja is wearing no armor and is carrying no more than a light load.

Ghost Strike (Su): At 8th level and higher, a ninja can spend one daily use of her *ki* power to strike incorporeal and ethereal creatures as if they were corporeal. She also can use this ability to strike foes on the Material Plane normally while ethereal (for example, while using her ghost step ability).

Activating the ghost strike ability is a move action that does not provoke attacks of opportunity. It affects the next attack made by the ninja, as long as that attack is made before the end of her next turn.

Improved Poison Use (Ex): Starting at 9th level, a ninja can apply poison to a weapon as a move action. (Normally, applying a poison is a standard action, like applying an oil.)

Evasion (Ex): Beginning at 12th level, a ninja can avoid damage from certain attacks with a successful Reflex save. (See the monk class feature, page 41 of the *Player's Handbook*.) A ninja's use of evasion differs slightly from a monk's use in that a ninja can use evasion only if she is wearing no armor and is carrying no more than a light load.

Ghost Mind (Su): At 14th level, a ninja gains a special resistance to spells of the scrying subschool. To detect or see a ninja with such a spell, the caster must make a caster level check (DC 20 + the ninja's class level). In the case of scrying spells (such as *arcane eye*) that scan the ninja's area, a failed check indicates that the spell works but the ninja simply isn't detected. Scrying attempts targeted specifically at the ninja do not work at all if the check fails.

Ghost Sight (Su): At 16th level and higher, a ninja can see invisible and ethereal creatures as easily as she sees material creatures and objects.

Greater Ki Dodge (Su): Starting at 18th level, a ninja's *ki* dodge ability grants total concealment (50% miss chance).

Ghost Walk (Su): A 20th-level ninja can spend two daily uses of her *ki* power to enter the Ethereal Plane for an extended period of time. This ability functions as the *ethereal jaunt* spell with a caster level equal to the ninja's class level.

HUMAN NINJA STARTING PACKAGE

Armor: None (speed 30 feet).

Weapons: Kama (1d4, light, 2 lb., slashing).

Shortbow (1d6, crit ×3, range inc. 60 ft., 2 lb., piercing).

20 shuriken (1d2, range inc. 10 ft., 2 lb., piercing).

Skill Selection: Pick a number of skills equal to 7 + Int modifier.

Skill	Ranks	Ability	Armor Check Penalty
Balance	4	Dex	+0
Disable Device	4	Int	+0
Hide	4	Dex	+0
Listen	4	Wis	—
Move Silently	4	Dex	+0
Open Lock	4	Dex	—
Search	4	Int	—
Spot	4	Wis	—
Tumble	4	Dex	+0

Feat: Point Blank Shot.

Bonus Feat: Precise Shot.

Gear: Backpack with waterskin, one day's trail rations, bedroll, sack, flint and steel. Hooded lantern, 3 pints of oil. Quiver with 20 arrows.

Gold: 4d4 gp.

SCOUT

Any force on the move, whether it's an army or an adventuring group, needs information about what's ahead and what's behind and, more important, time to prepare for battle. A scout can navigate difficult terrain at good speed, and she specializes in seeing her foe before the opponent ever detects her presence. In a dungeon or in the wild, a scout is seen only when she wants to be.

Adventures: Scouts adventure for numerous reasons. Many have a role in a military organization. Whether serving as outriders for a large army or as foresters for a small border fort, these scouts venture into the wilderness under orders. Although more common than other scouts, those attached to the military are unlikely to have the time or permission necessary to undertake regular adventures. Instead, adventuring scouts come from rural villages, having honed their skills over a lifetime of wandering the woods. Others have left their military service behind and find themselves attracted to the adventuring lifestyle. Many adventuring scouts begin their careers as guides hired to lead other adventurers through the wilderness. Those who find the excitement and challenge of adventuring to their taste then seek out a group of their own.

Characteristics: A scout has some training in weapons and a unique combat style that favors fast movement and devastating attacks. She excels in performing during running battles, which allow her to maximize her special fighting techniques and high movement rate. Although a scout can hold her own in a fight, she's at her best before combat begins, when she can use her powers of stealth and observation to find an enemy and give her companions accurate information about what they face. The scout is a backcountry expert, exceeding even the ranger's ability to navigate rough terrain and lead a group of companions through the wilderness.

The scout also excels in a dungeon environment, and she can find and disable traps as well as any rogue. As a scout advances in level, her senses become amazingly acute, and she can eventually operate normally even in total darkness.

Alignment: Scouts can be of any alignment, and a scout's alignment is often shaped more by her personal background than from any training. The notable exceptions to this are the many scouts who receive their training in a military organization—such scouts are carefully and rigorously taught, and are almost always lawful in alignment. Outside of military organizations, more scouts are neutral than any other alignment, but every alignment and philosophy is represented within the class.

Religion: Scouts have varied and individual takes on religion, and no single religion stands out as typical of the class. Scouts occasionally pay homage to deities of nature, but these devotions are more a personal choice on the part of an individual than any outgrowth of their training. Scouts don't see nature as a force in its own right, and this belief is one of the most profound differences between the scout and the ranger classes. Where the ranger sees nature as something to be revered and protected, the scout sees it as the terrain over which she must do her job. Although a scout might love nature for its beauty or for the solitude she can find within it, she'll never draw power from nature the way a ranger does.

Background: Many scouts receive military training and serve for a time as outriders for an army. They perfect their techniques while trying to spot and hide from large groups of foes. The crucible of military service turns out tough, independent scouts accustomed to working on their own or in small groups. Such steady individuals make great additions to adventuring parties, and their expertise is often sought by members of other classes.

Other scouts come from a wide variety of backgrounds. Some train with foresters and rangers serving a rural lord, and others simply grow up among the common folk of the countryside, spending month after month exploring the wild in their leisure time. Scouts from such diverse backgrounds often take up adventuring to leave their home communities behind. Having exhausted the potential for exploration in their home region, they seek a wider variety of experience and wish to see a broader portion of the world.

Races: Humans make excellent scouts. Their adaptable nature allows them to perfect a wider variety of skills than most other races, and they make good use of the scout's many abilities. Elves and halflings are the most naturally gifted scouts; both races have produced nimble scouts with amazing abilities of stealth and observation. While halflings have more innate talent for sneaking than elves do, the greater speed of elf scouts gives them advantages of their own.

Dwarves and gnomes make respectable underground scouts, and the scout's bonuses to speed offset one of these races' greatest weaknesses. Combined with the dwarf's knack for operating in areas of earth and stone, scout training can turn dwarves into impressive underground explorers—although most dwarves prefer a more straightforward approach to combat and dislike the skirmish fighting style of the scout.

Other Classes: Scouts work well with members of almost any other class. Skilled and adaptable, they thrive when they can complement a slower and louder group of adventurers or soldiers. Scouts move ahead of such a group for brief periods, stealthily checking the next room or forest clearing for foes, and then circling back again to ensure that enemies are not sneaking up on the group from behind. When combat is joined, however, the group remains as a stable base to which a scout can fall back when pressed. Clerics, wizards, and others willing to cast spells that enhance a scout's mobility or stealth make her job easier, and are welcome companions in combat as well.

Conversely, a scout also welcomes a group made up entirely of stealthy characters such as rogues,

A scout

rangers, ninjas, and fellow scouts. This group moves much more quietly than a normal adventuring party, and it is seldom surprised.

Role: A scout plays several roles in most adventuring groups. First and foremost, a scout excels at detecting an enemy or creature before being detected herself. Whether moving well ahead of the group or guarding the rear, a scout is the character most likely to discover a potential threat and be ready to act in combat. Serving as a backup melee combatant or ranged expert in battle, she provides support for the more straightforward fighters in the group and confuses and distracts the enemy. A scout's stealth and trapfinding ability make her the natural choice for entering and searching dangerous areas.

GAME RULE INFORMATION
Scouts have the following game statistics.

Abilities: Dexterity helps scouts become stealthy and overcome their lack of access to heavy armor. Wisdom also is important because it affects many skills, especially Spot and Listen, that most scouts consider vital to their ability to survive in the wild and to detect enemies efficiently.

Alignment: Any. Scouts in military service are usually lawful.

Hit Die: d8.

Starting Gold: 5d4×10 gp.

Class Skills

A scout's class skills (and the key ability for each skill) are Balance (Dex), Climb (Str), Craft (Int), Escape Artist (Dex), Hide (Dex), Jump (Str), Knowledge (dungeoneering) (Int), Knowledge (geography) (Int), Knowledge (nature) (Int), Listen (Wis), Move Silently (Dex), Ride (Dex), Search (Int), Sense Motive (Wis), Speak Language (n/a), Spot (Wis), Survival (Wis), Swim (Str), Tumble (Dex), and Use Rope (Dex).

Illus. by J. Jarvis

TABLE 1–2: THE SCOUT

Level	Base Attack Bonus	Fort Save	Ref Save	Will Save	Special
1st	+0	+0	+2	+0	Skirmish (+1d6), trapfinding
2nd	+1	+0	+3	+0	Battle fortitude +1, uncanny dodge
3rd	+2	+1	+3	+1	Fast movement +10 ft., skirmish (+1d6, +1 AC), trackless step
4th	+3	+1	+4	+1	Bonus feat
5th	+3	+1	+4	+1	Evasion, skirmish (+2d6, +1 AC)
6th	+4	+2	+5	+2	Flawless stride
7th	+5	+2	+5	+2	Skirmish (+2d6, +2 AC)
8th	+6/+1	+2	+6	+2	Camouflage, bonus feat
9th	+6/+1	+3	+6	+3	Skirmish (+3d6, +2 AC)
10th	+7/+2	+3	+7	+3	Blindsense 30 ft.
11th	+8/+3	+3	+7	+3	Battle fortitude +2, fast movement +20 ft., skirmish (+3d6, +3 AC)
12th	+9/+4	+4	+8	+4	Bonus feat
13th	+9/+4	+4	+8	+4	Skirmish (+4d6, +3 AC)
14th	+10/+5	+4	+9	+4	Hide in plain sight
15th	+11/+6/+1	+5	+9	+5	Skirmish (+4d6, +4 AC)
16th	+12/+7/+2	+5	+10	+5	Bonus feat
17th	+12/+7/+2	+5	+10	+5	Skirmish (+5d6, +4 AC)
18th	+13/+8/+3	+6	+11	+6	Free movement
19th	+14/+9/+4	+6	+11	+6	Skirmish (+5d6, +5 AC)
20th	+15/+10/+5	+6	+12	+6	Battle fortitude +3, blindsight 30 ft., bonus feat

Skill Points at 1st Level: (8 + Int modifier) × 4.

Skill Points at Each Additional Level: 8 + Int modifier.

Class Features

All of the following are class features of the scout.

Weapon and Armor Proficiency: Scouts are proficient with all simple weapons, plus the handaxe, throwing axe, short sword, and shortbow. Scouts are proficient with light armor, but not with shields.

Skirmish (Ex): A scout relies on mobility to deal extra damage and improve her defense. She deals an extra 1d6 points of damage on all attacks she makes during any round in which she moves at least 10 feet. The extra damage applies only to attacks taken during the scout's turn. This extra damage increases by 1d6 for every four levels gained above 1st (2d6 at 5th, 3d6 at 9th, 4d6 at 13th, and 5d6 at 17th level).

The extra damage only applies against living creatures that have a discernible anatomy. Undead, constructs, oozes, plants, incorporeal creatures, and creatures immune to extra damage from critical hits are not vulnerable to this additional damage. The scout must be able to see the target well eough to pick out a vital spot and must be able to reach such a spot. Scouts can apply this extra damage to ranged attacks made while skirmishing, but only if the target is within 30 feet.

At 3rd level, a scout gains a +1 competence bonus to Armor Class during any round in which she moves at least 10 feet. The bonus applies as soon as the scout has moved 10 feet, and lasts until the start of her next turn. This bonus improves by 1 for every four levels gained above 3rd (+2 at 7th, +3 at 11th, +4 at 15th, and +5 at 19th level).

A scout loses this ability when wearing medium or heavy armor or when carrying a medium or heavy load. If she gains the skirmish ability from another class, the bonuses stack.

Trapfinding (Ex): A scout can use the Search skill to locate traps with a DC higher than 20, and she can use Disable Device to bypass a trap or disarm magic traps. See the rogue class feature, page 50 of the *Player's Handbook*.

Battle Fortitude (Ex): At 2nd level, a scout gains a +1 competence bonus on Fortitude saves and initiative checks. This bonus increases to +2 at 11th level and +3 at 20th level. A scout loses this bonus when wearing medium or heavy armor or when carrying a medium or heavy load.

Uncanny Dodge (Ex): Starting at 2nd level, a scout cannot be caught flat-footed and reacts to danger before her senses would normally allow her to do so. See the barbarian class feature, page 26 of the *Player's Handbook*.

Fast Movement (Ex): Starting at 3rd level, a scout's gains a +10 foot enhancement bonus to her base land speed. At 11th level, this bonus increases to +20 feet. See the monk class feature, page 41 of the *Player's Handbook*.

A scout loses this benefit when wearing medium or heavy armor or when carrying a medium or heavy load.

Trackless Step (Ex): Beginning at 3rd level, a scout cannot be tracked in natural surroundings. See the druid class feature, page 36 of the *Player's Handbook*.

Bonus Feats: At 4th level and every four levels thereafter (8th, 12th, 16th, and 20th level), a scout gains a bonus feat, which must be selected from the following list: Acrobatic, Agile, Alertness, Athletic, Blind-Fight, Brachiation†, Combat Expertise, Danger Sense†, Dodge, Endurance, Far Shot, Great Fortitude, Hear the Unseen†, Improved Initiative, Improved Swimming†, Iron Will, Lightning Reflexes, Mobility, Point Blank Shot, Precise Shot, Quick Draw, Quick Reconnoiter†, Rapid Reload, Shot on the Run, Skill Focus, Spring Attack, Track. She must meet all the prerequisites for the feat.

†New feat described in Chapter 3.

Evasion (Ex): Beginning at 5th level, a scout can avoid damage from certain attacks with a successful Reflex save. See the monk class feature, page 41 of the *Player's Handbook*.

Flawless Stride (Ex): Starting at 6th level, a scout can move through any sort of terrain that slows movement (such as undergrowth, rubble, and similar terrain) at her normal speed and without taking damage or suffering any other impairment.

This ability does not let her move more quickly through terrain that requires a Climb or Swim check to navigate, nor can she move more quickly through terrain or undergrowth that has been magically manipulated to impede motion.

A scout loses this benefit when wearing medium or heavy armor or when carrying a medium or heavy load.

Camouflage (Ex): Beginning at 8th level, a scout can use the Hide skill in any sort of natural terrain. See the ranger class feature, page 48 of the *Player's Handbook*. She loses this benefit when wearing medium or heavy armor or when carrying a medium or heavy load.

Blindsense (Ex): At 10th level, a scout gains the blindsense ability out to 30 feet. This ability functions as described on page 306 of the *Monster Manual*.

Hide in Plain Sight (Ex): Beginning at 14th level, a scout can use the Hide skill in natural terrain even while being observed. See the ranger class feature, page 48 of the *Player's Handbook*. A scout loses this benefit when wearing medium or heavy armor or when carrying a medium or heavy load.

Free Movement (Ex): At 18th level and higher, a scout can slip out of bonds, grapples, and even the effects of confining spells easily. This ability duplicates the effect of a *freedom of movement* spell, except that it is always active. A scout loses this benefit when wearing medium or heavy armor or when carrying a medium or heavy load.

Blindsight (Ex): A 20th-level scout gains the blindsight ability out to 30 feet. Her senses become so acute that she can maneuver and fight flawlessly even in total darkness. Invisibility, darkness, and most kinds of concealment are irrelevant, though the scout must have line of effect to a creature or object to discern it.

HALF-ELF SCOUT STARTING PACKAGE

Armor: Studded leather (+2 AC, armor check penalty –1, speed 30 feet, 20 lb.).

Weapons: Short sword (1d6, crit 19–20/×2, 1 lb., light, piercing).

Shortbow (1d6, crit ×3, range inc. 60 ft., 2 lb., piercing).

Skill Selection: Pick a number of skills equal to 8 + Int modifier.

Skill	Ranks	Ability	Armor Check Penalty
Balance	4	Dex	–1
Climb	4	Str	–1
Hide	4	Dex	–1
Jump	4	Str	–1
Knowledge (nature)	4	Int	—
Listen	4	Wis	—
Move Silently	4	Dex	–1
Search	4	Int	—
Spot	4	Wis	—
Survival	4	Wis	—
Swim	4	Str	–2

Feat: Track.

Gear: Backpack with waterskin, one day's trail rations, bedroll, sack, flint and steel. Hooded lantern, 3 pints of oil. Quiver with 20 arrows.

Gold: 5d4 gp.

SPELLTHIEF

Spellthieves use skill and arcane magic to drain the abilities of their opponents and turn their foes' own powers against them. Spellthieves love the challenges that adventure brings, and they relish finding unique and inventive ways to use their abilities. Because they have such a wide variety of abilities, spellthieves can adapt themselves to overcome nearly any challenge, but they have neither the overpowering arcane might of wizards nor the brute force of fighters. Spellthieves never cast two spells when one will do, and they excel at using misdirection and deception to overcome seemingly stronger opponents.

Good spellthieves use their skills and magic to entertain themselves, protect those less gifted than themselves, and occasionally serve a cause or nation as a spy. Evil spellthieves use their versatile skills to trick and deceive, or plague large cities as daring cat burglars.

Adventures: Spellthieves adventure because they love a challenge. They see each puzzle, trap, or monster as a new way to test their skills. This does not mean that they are all overconfident. Some are, but many simply have a healthy dose of curiosity and a keen interest in proving their own mastery. Because they have such versatile abilities, they know they have a chance to overcome nearly any kind of challenge. When confronted with a powerful physical foe, a spellthief often can't help wanting to know whether his stealth and cunning could overcome the foe's brute force. When confronted with a clever trap, a spellthief can't help wondering whether his speed and skill could overcome the trapmaker's ingenuity and preparation. Like other characters, spellthieves are attracted to the wealth that adventuring offers. Living an open, flamboyant (and therefore expensive) lifestyle suits many, if not all, spellthieves, and adventuring offers ready rewards both in gold and fame.

Characteristics: Spellthieves use an intuitive form of arcane magic to enhance their versatile talents. They have a broad skill selection and are capable of developing several sets of skills. Many spellthieves emphasize stealth and social abilities, perfecting the ability to surprise and deceive their opponents.

In combat, spellthieves use a combination of precise attacks and spells to steal abilities from their opponents. At lower levels, a spellthief concentrates on flanking foes and delivering sneak attacks. As a spellthief progresses in level, his ability to cast spells grows stronger, allowing him to magically augment his modest combat abilities. A spellthief's most potent ability allows him to temporarily steal spells, spell effects, and even energy resistances from his opponents.

Alignment: Most spellthieves are neutral. They view the world as a place full of challenges and interesting opportunities and rarely give much thought to morality. Even spellthieves with genuinely good intentions occasionally get caught up in the challenge of an adventure and fail to see (or decide to intentionally overlook) the moral implications of their actions.

Evil spellthieves are callous and cruel, using their abilities to trick, blackmail, or destroy anyone who has something they want or stands in the way of their personal agenda.

Religion: Most spellthieves prefer to rely on their own wits and skill rather than pay homage to a higher power. Occasionally, when planning a particularly daring raid, a spellthief makes a one-time offering or prayer to a deity with power over the night or thievery. Others sometimes seek divine protection before attempting to rob or raid a temple, but even these observances are more a chance for a spellthief to even the odds than a true attempt at devotion. Some particularly evil spellthieves devote themselves to Vecna (the god of secrets), using their abilities to wrest information from their opponents and exploit them for blackmail or more serious crimes.

Background: Spellthieves come from a wide variety of backgrounds. Although few places are devoted to the formal training of spellthieves, the ones that exist (usually military academies that train a capable corps of espionage agents) produce especially capable and loyal spellthieves. These agents of the crown are the exception rather than the rule, however; most spellthieves acquire their training from one or more solitary mentors.

These mentors are often spellthieves of varied backgrounds who wish to pass along their talents to a likely protégé. Others are rogues or sorcerers who only partially understand their disciple's unique mixture of skills, yet they provide enough guidance and encouragement for a young spellthief to develop his own skills. Spellthieves from these diverse backgrounds often pride themselves on their blend of skills and magic. They rarely take levels in other classes, viewing their mixture of abilities as something particularly suited to their talent and personality.

Races: Humans are more likely than members of other races to become spellthieves. Their flexible nature and varied interests make them well suited to the specialties of the spellthief. Elves also make excellent spellthieves, benefiting from their natural grace and affinity for arcane magic. Halflings and gnomes find the spellthief's combination of spellcasting abilities and skill selection a good match for their small size. Many gnomes, with their affinity for illusion magic, enjoy the versatility offered by the spellthief class, and they often use their combination of stealth and spellcasting to develop a formidable repertoire of practical jokes. Halflings, on the other hand, usually take advantage of the class's skill selection and stealth abilities, viewing their spells as a way to boost their ability to slip past dangerous traps and monsters.

Neither dwarves nor half-orcs make particularly good spellthieves, since most members of those races prefer physical power over skill or subterfuge. Dwarves who do become spellthieves often emphasize their ability to find and disable traps to the exclusion of other skills.

Other Classes: Spellthieves work well with members of almost any other class. Their spells and class skills help them play a variety of roles in an adventuring group. Because they're not suited to act as front-line melee combatants, they enjoy working with fighters and barbarians more than other classes.

Role: Spellthieves can fill any number of diverse roles in an adventuring group, depending on the skills and abilities of the other members of the party. They can at times function as a group's expert on arcane magic. With the right skill selection, a spellthief can act as a group's primary scout and its master of stealth. Because his abilities overlap with those of arcane spellcasters and rogues, a spellthief might have a hard time finding a niche in a group that already includes one character of each kind. In such a case, a spellthief usually concentrates on using his spells to augment his class abilities and combat prowess and ends up pairing with the rogue in most endeavors. The two can scout almost anywhere with little chance of being detected, and their ability to flank an opponent and both deal sneak attack damage makes them a deadly duo in combat.

GAME RULE INFORMATION

Spellthieves have the following game statistics.

Abilities: Charisma determines which spells a spellthief can cast and how hard those spells are to resist. Dexterity helps him avoid blows in combat despite his light armor. Spellthieves who prefer melee combat benefit from high Strength or Constitution scores.

Alignment: Any, although many spellthieves tend toward neutrality.

Hit Die: d6.

Starting Gold: 4d4×10 gp.

Class Skills

A spellthief's class skills (and the key ability for each skill) are Appraise (Int), Bluff (Cha), Concentration (Con), Craft (Int), Decipher Script (Int), Disable Device (Int), Escape Artist (Dex), Gather Information (Cha), Hide (Dex), Jump (Str), Knowledge (arcana) (Int), Knowledge (local) (Int), Listen (Wis), Move Silently (Dex), Open Lock (Dex), Search (Int), Speak Language (n/a), Spellcraft (Int), Spot (Wis), Swim (Str), Tumble (Dex), and Use Magic Device (Cha).

Skill Points at 1st Level: (6 + Int modifier) × 4.

Skill Points at Each Additional Level: 6 + Int modifier.

A spellthief

Class Features

All of the following are class features of the spellthief.

Weapon and Armor Proficiency: Spellthieves are proficient with all simple weapons and with light armor but not with shields. Because the somatic components required for spellthief spells are simple, a spellthief can cast spellthief spells while wearing light armor without incurring the normal arcane spell failure chance. However, a spellthief wearing medium or heavy armor or using a shield incurs a chance of arcane spell failure (see page 123 of the *Player's Handbook*) if the spell in question has a somatic component (most do). A multiclass spellthief still incurs the normal arcane spell failure chance for arcane spells received from other classes, including those stolen from arcane casters (see the steal spell ability, below).

Sneak Attack (Ex): A spellthief deals an extra 1d6 points of damage when flanking an opponent or at any time when the target would be denied its Dexterity bonus. This extra damage applies to ranged attacks only if the

Illus. by S. Belledin

target is within 30 feet. It increases to 2d6 points at 5th level, 3d6 points at 9th level, 4d6 points at 13th level, and 5d6 points at 17th level. See the rogue class feature, page 50 of the *Player's Handbook*. If a spellthief gets a sneak attack bonus from another source (such as rogue levels), the bonuses on damage stack.

Steal Spell (Su): A spellthief can siphon spell energy away from his target and use it himself. A spellthief who hits an opponent with a successful sneak attack can choose to forgo dealing 1d6 points of sneak attack damage and instead steal a spell, or the potential to cast a specific known spell, from his target. If the target is willing, a spellthief can steal a spell with a touch as a standard action.

The target of a steal spell attack loses one 0-level or 1st-level spell from memory if she prepares spells ahead of time, or one 0-level or 1st-level spell slot if she is a spontaneous caster. A spontaneous caster also loses the ability to cast the stolen spell for 1 minute. If the target has no spells prepared (or has no remaining spell slots, if she is a spontaneous caster), this ability has no effect. A spellthief can choose which spell to steal; otherwise, the DM determines the stolen spell randomly. If a spellthief tries to steal a spell that isn't available, the stolen spell (or spell slot) is determined randomly from among those the target has available.

For example, a 1st-level spellthief who uses this ability against a 1st-level sorcerer could choose to steal *magic missile*. Assuming the sorcerer knew that spell, a successful steal spell attack would eliminate one 1st-level spell slot and temporarily prevent her from casting *magic missile*. If the same spellthief stole *magic missile* from a wizard who had it prepared, the wizard would lose one prepared *magic missile* spell (but wouldn't lose any other *magic missile* spells she might also have prepared).

After stealing a spell, a spellthief can cast the spell himself on a subsequent turn. Treat the spell as if it were cast by the original owner of the spell for the purpose of determining caster level, save DC, and so forth. A spellthief can cast this spell even if he doesn't have the minimum ability score normally required to cast a spell of that level. The spellthief must supply the same components (including verbal, somatic, material, XP, and any focus) required for the stolen spell. Alternatively, a spellthief of 4th level or higher can use the stolen spell power to cast any spellthief spell that he knows of the same level or lower (effectively, this gives the spellthief one free casting of a known spell). A spellthief must cast a stolen spell (or use its energy to cast one of its own spells) within 1 hour of stealing

it; otherwise, the extra spell energy fades harmlessly away.

As a spellthief gains levels, he can choose to steal higher-level spells. At 4th level, he can steal spells of up to 2nd level, and for every two levels gained after 4th, the maximum spell level stolen increases by one (up to a maximum of 9th-level spells at 18th level).

At any one time, a spellthief can possess a maximum number of stolen spell levels equal to his class level (treat 0-level spells as 1/2 level for this purpose). For instance, a 4th-level spellthief can have two stolen 2nd-level spells, or one 2nd-level spell and two 1st-level spells, or any other combination of 0-level, 1st-level, and 2nd-level spells totaling four levels. If he steals a spell that would cause him to exceed this limit, he must choose to lose stolen spells sufficient to reduce his total number of stolen spell levels to no more than his maximum.

A spellthief can't apply metamagic feats or other effects to the stolen spell unless the specific spell stolen was prepared with such an effect. For example, a spellthief of 6th level or higher could steal a wizard's empowered *magic missile*, but only if he specifically chose to steal empowered *magic missile*. If he chose to steal an unmodified *magic missile*, he couldn't steal an empowered *magic missile*, a silent *magic missile*, or any other metamagic form of the spell. A spellthief couldn't steal an empowered *magic missile* from a sorcerer, since the sorcerer applies metamagic effects upon casting and thus has no prepared empowered *magic missile* spell.

This ability works only against spells. It has no effect on psionic powers or spell-like abilities (but see the steal spell-like ability class feature, below).

Trapfinding (Ex): A spellthief can use the Search skill to locate traps with a DC higher than 20, and he can use Disable Device to bypass a trap or disarm magic traps. See the rogue class feature, page 50 of the *Player's Handbook*.

Detect Magic (Sp): A spellthief of 2nd level or higher can use *detect magic* a number of times per day equal to his Charisma bonus, if any (minimum 1). His caster level is equal to his spellthief class level.

Spellgrace (Su): A spellthief of 2nd level or higher gains a +1 competence bonus on his saves against spells. This bonus improves to +2 at 11th level and to +3 at 20th level.

Steal Spell Effect (Su): Beginning at 2nd level, a spellthief can siphon an active spell effect from another creature. A spellthief who hits an opponent with a sneak attack can choose to forgo dealing 1d6 points of sneak attack damage and instead gain the effect of a single spell

Three adventurers team up for a better chance against their hulking foe

TABLE 1–3: THE SPELLTHIEF

Level	Base Attack Bonus	Fort Save	Ref Save	Will Save	Special	Spells per Day			
						1st	2nd	3rd	4th
1st	+0	+0	+0	+2	Sneak attack +1d6, steal spell (0 or 1st), trapfinding	—	—	—	—
2nd	+1	+0	+0	+3	*Detect magic,* spellgrace +1, steal spell effect	—	—	—	—
3rd	+2	+1	+1	+3	Steal energy resistance 10	—	—	—	—
4th	+3	+1	+1	+4	Steal spell (2nd)	0	—	—	—
5th	+3	+1	+1	+4	Sneak attack +2d6, steal spell-like ability	0	—	—	—
6th	+4	+2	+2	+5	Steal spell (3rd)	1	—	—	—
7th	+5	+2	+2	+5	Absorb spell	1	—	—	—
8th	+6/+1	+2	+2	+6	Steal spell (4th)	1	0	—	—
9th	+6/+1	+3	+3	+6	*Arcane sight,* sneak attack +3d6	1	0	—	—
10th	+7/+2	+3	+3	+7	Steal spell (5th)	1	1	—	—
11th	+8/+3	+3	+3	+7	Spellgrace +2, steal energy resistance 20	1	1	0	—
12th	+9/+4	+4	+4	+8	Steal spell (6th)	1	1	1	—
13th	+9/+4	+4	+4	+8	Discover spells, sneak attack +4d6	1	1	1	—
14th	+10/+5	+4	+4	+9	Steal spell (7th)	2	1	1	0
15th	+11/+6/+1	+5	+5	+9	Steal spell resistance	2	1	1	1
16th	+12/+7/+2	+5	+5	+10	Steal spell (8th)	2	2	1	1
17th	+12/+7/+2	+5	+5	+10	Sneak attack +5d6	2	2	2	1
18th	+13/+8/+3	+6	+6	+11	Steal spell (9th)	3	2	2	1
19th	+14/+9/+4	+6	+6	+11	Steal energy resistance 30	3	3	3	2
20th	+15/+10/+5	+6	+6	+12	Absorb spell (immediate casting), spellgrace +3	3	3	3	3

affecting the target. If the target is willing, a spellthief can steal a spell effect with a touch as a standard action.

The spellthief can choose which spell effect to steal; otherwise, the DM determines the stolen spell effect randomly. If a spellthief tries to steal a spell effect that isn't present, the stolen spell effect is determined randomly from among those currently in effect on the target. A spellthief can't steal a spell effect if its caster level exceeds his class level + his Charisma modifier.

Upon stealing a spell effect, a spellthief gains the stolen effect (and the original creature loses that effect) for 1 minute per class level (or until the spell's duration expires, whichever comes first). If the spell effect's duration hasn't expired by this time, the spell effect returns to the creature that originally benefited from it.

A spellthief can steal the effect of a spell only if the spell could be cast on him by the original caster. For example, a spellthief couldn't gain the effect of an *animal growth* spell (unless the spellthief is of the animal type) or the effect of a *shield* spell (since that spell's range is personal). If a spellthief tries to steal the effect of a spell not allowed to him, the effect is still suppressed on the original target of the spell for 1 minute per spellthief class level.

This ability does not work on spell effects that are immune to *dispel magic* (such as *bestow curse*).

Steal Energy Resistance (Su): Beginning at 3rd level, a spellthief can siphon off some or all of a target's resistance to an energy type (acid, cold, electricity, fire, or sonic). A spellthief who hits an opponent with a successful sneak attack can choose to forgo dealing 1d6 points of sneak attack damage and instead temporarily gain resistance 10 to an energy type to which his target is resistant (or immune). If the target is willing, a spellthief can steal energy resistance with a touch as a standard action.

Simultaneously, the target creature's resistance to that energy type is reduced by 10 (to a minimum of 0). A creature with immunity to an energy type retains that immunity.

If his target has more than one type of resistance to energy, a spellthief can choose which kind to steal; otherwise, the DM determines the stolen resistance randomly from among those possessed by the target. If a spellthief chooses to steal a type of resistance that the target doesn't possess, the stolen type of resistance is determined randomly from those possessed by the target.

The resistance a spellthief gains from using this ability lasts for 1 minute. If the resistance is derived from a temporary effect (such as a spell), the stolen resistance disappears when the effect expires.

A spellthief can use this ability multiple times, but its effects do not stack unless they apply to different types of energy. For example, throughout a long combat, a spellthief might use this ability to gain resistance to fire and resistance to cold, but he could not use it twice on a creature that is resistant to fire to gain twice as much resistance to fire (nor to reduce the creature's resistance to fire by twice as much).

At 11th level, a spellthief can steal resistance 20 to an energy type by using this ability, and at 19th level he can steal resistance 30 to an energy type.

Spells: Beginning at 4th level, a spellthief gains the ability to cast a small number of arcane spells, which are drawn from a subset of the sorcerer/wizard spell list (see below). He can cast any spell he knows without preparing it ahead of time, just as a sorcerer can (see page 54 of the *Player's Handbook*).

To learn or cast a spell, a spellthief must have a Charisma score equal to at least 10 + the spell level (Cha 11 for 1st-level spells, Cha 12 for 2nd-level spells, and so on). The DC for a saving throw against a spellthief's spell is 10 + spell level + spellthief's Cha modifier.

Like other spellcasters, a spellthief can cast only a certain number of spells of each spell level per day. His base daily spell allotment is given on Table 1–3: The Spellthief. In addition, he receives bonus spells per day if he has a high Charisma score (see Table 1–1, page 8 of the *Player's Handbook*). When Table 1–3 indicates that a spellthief gets 0 spells per day of a given spell level (for instance, 1st-level spells for a 4th-level spellthief), he gains only the bonus spells he would be entitled to based on his Charisma score for that spell level.

A spellthief's selection of spells is extremely limited. A spellthief begins play knowing no spells but gains one or more new spells at certain levels, as indicated on Table 1–4: Spellthief Spells Known. (Unlike spells per day, his Charisma does not affect the number of spells he knows; the numbers on Table 1–4 are fixed.) A spellthief can learn any sorcerer/wizard spell from the following schools: abjuration, divination, enchantment, illusion, and transmutation. No other sorcerer/wizard spells are on the spellthief's class spell list.

Upon reaching 12th level, and at every third spellthief level after that (15th and 18th), a spellthief can choose to learn a new spell in place of one he already knows. In effect, the spellthief "loses" the old spell in exchange for the new one. The new spell's level must be the same as that of the spell being exchanged, and it must be at least two levels lower than the highest-level spellthief spell that the spellthief can cast. For instance, upon reaching 12th level, a spellthief could trade in a single 1st-level spell for a different 1st-level spell. A spellthief can swap only a single spell at any given level, and he must choose whether or not to swap the spell at the same time that he gains new spells known for the level.

At 4th level and higher, a spellthief's caster level for spells is one-half his spellthief level.

TABLE 1–4: SPELLTHIEF SPELLS KNOWN

	Spells Known			
Level	1st	2nd	3rd	4th
1st	—	—	—	—
2nd	—	—	—	—
3rd	—	—	—	—
4th	2[1]	—	—	—
5th	2	—	—	—
6th	3	—	—	—
7th	3	—	—	—
8th	4	2[1]	—	—
9th	4	2	—	—
10th	4	3	—	—
11th	4	3	2[1]	—
12th	4	4	3	—
13th	4	4	3	—
14th	4	4	4	2[1]
15th	4	4	4	3
16th	4	4	4	3
17th	5	4	4	4
18th	5	5	4	4
19th	5	5	5	4
20th	5	5	5	5

1 Provided that the spellthief has sufficient Charisma to have a bonus spell of this level.

Steal Spell-Like Ability (Su): At 5th level and higher, a spellthief can use a sneak attack to temporarily steal a creature's spell-like ability. A spellthief who hits an opponent with a sneak attack can choose to forgo dealing 1d6 points of sneak attack damage and instead gain one use of one of the target's spell-like abilities. If the target is willing, a spellthief can steal a spell-like ability with a touch as a standard action.

This spell-like ability can originate from the target's class, race, template, or any other source, and can be of any level up to a maximum of one-third the spellthief's class level. A spellthief can select a specific spell-like ability to steal; otherwise, the DM chooses the ability at random. If the ability has a limited number of uses per day, the target must have at least one such use left, or the spellthief can't steal the ability. If the target can't use its ability at the present time (such as a summoned demon's summon ability), the spellthief can't steal it.

A spellthief can use a stolen spell-like ability once. For all purposes (caster level, save DC, and so on), treat the spell-like ability as if it were being used by the original possessor of the ability. A spellthief must use the stolen spell-like ability within 1 minute of acquiring it, or it is lost harmlessly. Until the spellthief uses the ability (or until the minute elapses), the target cannot use the stolen ability.

Absorb Spell (Su): Beginning at 7th level, if a spellthief makes a successful save against a spell that targets him, he can attempt to absorb the spell energy for later use. This ability affects only spells that have the spellthief as a target, not effect or area spells. A spellthief can't absorb a spell of a higher spell level than he could steal with his steal spell ability (see above).

To absorb a spell that targets him, a spellthief must succeed on a level check (1d20 + spellthief class level) against a DC of 10 + the spell's caster level. Failure indicates that the spell has its normal effect. Success means that the spellthief suffers no effect from the spell and can cast the spell later (or use its energy to cast one of his own spells known) as if he had stolen the spell with his steal spell ability. His normal limit of total spell levels stolen still applies.

At 20th level or higher, a spellthief can choose to use the stolen spell energy as an immediate action (see page 137), either to recast the original spell or to cast one of his own spells known using the stolen spell energy.

Arcane Sight (Sp): Beginning at 9th level, a spellthief can use *arcane sight* as a swift action (see page 137) a number of times per day equal to his Charisma modifier (minimum 1). His caster level is equal to his spellthief class level.

Discover Spells (Ex): A spellthief of 13th level or higher who steals a spell from a spellcaster with his steal spell ability automatically learns the names of all other spells prepared or known by the spellcaster that are of the same spell level as the stolen spell. This knowledge allows the spellthief to better choose which spells to steal on subsequent attacks.

For example, a 13th-level spellthief who steals *disintegrate* from an enemy sorcerer would also discover the names of all other 6th-level spells known by that sorcerer.

Steal Spell Resistance (Su): Beginning at 15th level, a spellthief can use a sneak attack to temporarily steal some or all of a creature's spell resistance. A spellthief who hits an opponent with a sneak attack can choose to forgo 3d6 points of sneak attack damage and instead reduce the target's spell resistance by 5. The spellthief also gains spell resistance equal to 5 + his class level (up to a maximum value equal to the original spell resistance of the target). If the target is willing, a spellthief can steal spell resistance with a touch as a standard action.

The stolen spell resistance benefits the spellthief for a number of rounds equal to the spellthief's Charisma modifier (minimum 1 round) and then returns to the target creature. If the spell resistance is derived from a temporary effect (such as a spell), the stolen spell resistance disappears when the effect elapses. A spellthief can't use this ability on the same creature again until the creature's stolen spell resistance returns.

HALFLING SPELLTHIEF STARTING PACKAGE

Armor: Studded leather (+2 AC, armor check penalty −1, speed 20 feet, 10 lb.).

Weapons: Light crossbow (1d6, crit 19–20/×2, range inc. 80 ft., 2 lb., piercing).

Spear (1d6, crit ×3, range inc. 20 ft., 3 lb., piercing).

Skill Selection: Pick a number of skills equal to 6 + Int modifier.

Skill	Ranks	Ability	Armor Check Penalty
Concentration	4	Con	—
Disable Device	4	Int	—
Hide	4	Dex	−1
Knowledge (any one)	4	Wis	—
Listen	4	Wis	—
Move Silently	4	Dex	−1
Open Lock	4	Dex	—
Search	4	Int	—
Spellcraft	4	Int	—
Spot	4	Wis	—
Tumble	4	Dex	−1

Feat: Improved Initiative.

Gear: Backpack with waterskin, one day's trail rations, bedroll, sack, flint and steel. Hooded lantern, 3 pints of oil. Case with 10 bolts.

Gold: 4d4 gp.

SPELLTHIEVES AND PSIONICS
A campaign that includes psionic characters, as described in the *Expanded Psionics Handbook*, would logically have room for psionic-themed spellthieves.

If psionics are common in your game, you have two options. The first is to allow spellthieves to affect both spells and psionic powers. The second is to create a new class, the psithief, that functions identically to the spellthief except that its special abilities affect psionic powers only.

In either case, a spellthief who can affect psionic powers treats psionic powers as if they were spells of the same level, allowing him to steal, absorb, or discover known psionic powers as normal for spells. A spellthief can't augment a stolen power, even if he has power points available of his own. Treat psi-like abilities as spell-like abilities for the purpose of a spellthief's stealing these abilities.

Illus. by D. Kovacs

his chapter presents a host of new prestige classes that provide skilled and often stealthy career choices for characters of every class. Spellcasters will find prestige classes that let them blend their spells and skills into deadly new abilities. Fighters and other combat-oriented characters will find ways to use their existing skills to improve their martial prowess. Rogues and other skill-focused characters will find ways to blend their already impressive abilities with those of other classes. Several of these prestige classes favor multiclass characters, accentuating the ideas of versatility and adventure that pervade this book.

PICKING A PRESTIGE CLASS

The easy part of looking for a prestige class involves comparing each class's requirements with the abilities and feats that you already have. Reading through this chapter and comparing the classes here to your current character or an NPC you're building is a good way to solidify your character concept at the same time that you look for new options. The more difficult part of

finding a suitable prestige class involves making sure that your character's new suite of abilities fulfills a needed role in the party. If your character is the primary trapfinder or scout, you'll want to make sure that the prestige class doesn't diminish those abilities while still providing you with interesting options in combat.

Good Guys/Bad Guys: Members of these groups define themselves by their alignment and their outlook on the world first, and their other abilities second. Their strengths reflect their alignment choices, and roleplaying one of these characters means putting attitude first.

Melee: A character belonging to one of these prestige classes is skilled at fighting in close quarters. In keeping with the skilled and stealthy themes of this book, the melee prestige classes described here typically depend on the sneak attack ability to deal the kind of damage found in high-level play. Many balance a good-sized Hit Die with armor selection or a high base attack bonus progression,

TABLE 2–1: ADVENTURER PRESTIGE CLASS GROUPINGS

Group	Prestige Classes
Bad guys	Dread pirate, ghost-faced killer
Good guys	Dread pirate, shadowbane inquisitor, shadowbane stalker, vigilante
Melee	Animal lord, daggerspell shaper, dread pirate, ghost-faced killer, nightsong enforcer, shadowbane inquisitor, streetfighter, tempest, wild plains outrider
Nature	Animal lord, beastmaster, bloodhound, Fochlucan lyrist, highland stalker, master of many forms, wild plains outrider
Special ability	Animal lord, beastmaster, bloodhound, exemplar, master of many forms, ollam, virtuoso
Spellcasting/psionics	Daggerspell mage, daggerspell shaper, Fochlucan lyrist, maester, shadowbane stalker, shadowmind, vigilante
Stealth	Daggerspell mage, dungeon delver, ghost-faced killer, highland stalker, nightsong enforcer, nightsong infiltrator, shadowbane stalker, shadowmind, spymaster, thief-acrobat

making their use in play involve much more than simply swinging away against the toughest foe present.

Nature: These characters are in their element when out in the wild. They generally have a good selection of wilderness-oriented class skills and can fend for themselves quite well.

Special Ability: Members of these prestige class take one special ability—such as bardic music, the druid's wild shape ability, or the ability to bond with an animal companion—to the extremes of power. Specialized and extremely effective, these classes provide entirely new types of abilities and innovative ways to use a character's existing abilities.

Spellcasting/Psionics: Spellcasters are rarely known for their selection of skills, since they often depend on spells to get them through the challenges they face. The classes described here, however, break that mold. Many of these prestige classes not only emphasize skill use but also provide new and interesting options for multiclass spellcasters. One prestige class, the shadowmind, expands the options for psionic characters (see the *Expanded Psionic Handbook*).

Stealth: The most roguelike of the prestige classes in this book, stealthy prestige classes not only provide Hide and Move Silently as class skills, but they emphasize the benefits of moving unseen through enemy territory or making surprise attacks.

ANIMAL LORD

For an animal lord, a humanoid form is simply an accident of birth. In spirit, he belongs with the wild pack of wolves, the running herd of horses, or the dancing school of fish. His nearly hairless, two-legged form is a hindrance to being one with his true kind, but it is a hindrance he can overcome.

Each animal lord forms a bond with one group of animals. Apelords, bearlords, birdlords, catlords, horselords, sharklords, snakelords, and wolflords all exist. Animals

in his selected group accept an animal lord as a kindred soul and a leader. They offer him their support, and he watches over them in turn.

Individual animal lords approach their calling in different ways. Some are simple defenders of their kind, content to live as part of the natural cycle of predator and prey. Others, believing that nature's creatures are meant to guard and ultimately improve this world, use their gifts to do good. Still others lead their animal brothers and sisters down a path of selfishness or vengeance.

Barbarians, rangers, and druids are the most likely characters to adopt this class. Barbarians prefer the more physically powerful options, including apelord, bearlord, and horselord. Rangers gravitate toward the stealthier selections, such as catlord and wolflord. Most birdlords are druids with the ability to use wild shape, but druids are equally likely to select any type of animal to bond with. Some scouts, rogues, and even rare monks find this path rewarding as well. Among the races, elves and half-elves are the most common examples of animal lords due to their close bond to nature.

A character can choose this prestige class more than once but must select a different group of associated animals and start at 1st level each time. Levels of different animal lord classes do not stack when determining level-based class features.

Adaptation: Customize this class for your campaign by associating each variety with a specific race or culture. Sahuagin (malenti) and evil aquatic elves make natural sharklords, for example, while plains-dwelling humans would be most appropriate as horselords. Eight animal lord types are presented here, but you can easily create others appropriate to your campaign, such as the sewer-dwelling ratlord, the gnoll hyenalord, or even the aquatic squidlord. Alternatively, you could subdivide existing groups (creating rival tigerlords and lionlords, for example). Use the examples below as templates when creating a new animal lord.

Hit Die: d10.

REQUIREMENTS

To qualify to become an animal lord, a character must fulfill all the following criteria.

Alignment: Neutral good, lawful neutral, neutral, chaotic neutral, or neutral evil.

Base Attack Bonus: +5.

Skills: Handle Animal 4 ranks, Knowledge (nature) 2 ranks, 4 ranks in the appropriate skill as follows. *Apelord:* Climb; *Bearlord:* Intimidate; *Birdlord:* Spot; *Catlord:* Move Silently; *Horselord:* Jump; *Sharklord:* Swim; *Snakelord:* Escape Artist; *Wolflord:* Survival.

Feats: Each kind of animal lord must have a specific feat as follows. *Apelord:* Toughness; *Bearlord:* Endurance; *Birdlord:* Improved Flight†; *Catlord:* Weapon Finesse; *Horselord:* Run; *Sharklord:* Improved Swimming†; *Snakelord:* Combat Reflexes; *Wolflord:* Track.

†New feat described on page 110.

CLASS SKILLS

The animal lord's class skills (and the key ability for each skill) are Climb (Str), Escape Artist (Dex), Handle Animal (Cha), Heal (Wis), Hide (Dex), Intimidate (Cha), Jump (Str), Knowledge (nature) (Int), Listen (Wis), Move Silently (Dex), Spot (Wis), Survival (Wis), and Swim (Str).

Skill Points at Each Level: 4 + Int modifier.

CLASS FEATURES

All of the following are class features of the animal lord prestige class.

Weapon and Armor Proficiency: Animal lords gain no proficiency with any weapon or armor.

Animal Bond (Ex): An animal lord develops a bond with animals of his selected group (see below). He gains a +4 bonus on Handle Animal and wild empathy checks made to influence animals from his chosen group. If an animal lord has the animal companion class feature, he adds his animal lord level to his effective druid level for the purpose of determining his animal companion's bonus Hit Dice, special abilities, and so forth.

The eight groups of animals included here, along with examples taken from the *Monster Manual*, are as follows.

Apelord: ape, baboon, dire ape, monkey.

Bearlord: black bear, brown bear, dire bear, polar bear.

Birdlord: eagle, giant eagle*, giant owl*, hawk, owl, raven.

Catlord: cat, cheetah, dire lion, dire tiger, leopard, lion, tiger.

Horselord: horse (all), pony, war-pony.

Sharklord: dire shark, shark (all).

Snakelord: constrictor, giant constrictor, viper (all).

Wolflord: dire wolf, wolf.

*These creatures are included even though they are not of the animal type.

Detect Animals (Sp): Beginning at 1st level, an animal lord can detect the presence of any animals of his selected group at will, as if using *detect animals or plants* with a caster level equal to his class level.

Wild Empathy (Ex): An animal lord can improve the attitude of an animal. See the druid class feature, page 35 of the *Player's Handbook*. If an animal lord has wild empathy from another class, his levels stack for determining the bonus.

First Totem: At 2nd level, an animal lord gains a +4 bonus on checks made with a specific skill, determined by his selected group as follows. *Apelord:* Climb; *Bearlord:* Intimidate; *Birdlord:* Spot; *Catlord:* Move Silently; *Horselord:* Jump; *Sharklord:* Swim; *Snakelord:* Escape Artist; *Wolflord:* Survival.

Low-Light Vision (Ex): At 2nd level, an animal lord gains low-light vision, allowing him to see twice as

Kozakh, an animal lord

Illus. by S. Ellis

far as a human in starlight, moonlight, torchlight, and similar conditions of shadowy illumination. He retains the ability to distinguish color and detail under these conditions.

If an animal lord already has low-light vision from another source (such as his race), his low-light vision improves, allowing him to see three times as far as a human in conditions of shadowy illumination.

Wild Aspect (Su): At 3rd level and higher, an animal lord can take on an aspect of the animals of his selected group. Assuming a wild aspect is a swift action that does not provoke attacks of opportunity (see Swift Actions and Immediate Actions, page 137). Unless otherwise noted, the effect lasts for 1 minute per level. An animal lord can use this ability once per day at 3rd level, plus one additional time per day for every three levels gained after 3rd (twice per day at 6th level and three times per day at 9th level).

When an animal lord reaches 7th level, his wild aspect becomes more powerful, as described below.

If an animal lord has the wild shape ability, he can spend one daily use of wild shape to assume his wild aspect instead (the duration is as normal for the wild aspect). If an animal lord already has a natural attack of the type gained by his wild aspect, use whichever damage figure is superior while the wild aspect is active. If an animal lord wields a weapon while using his wild aspect, he can use the natural attacks gained as natural secondary weapons if he uses his weapon as a primary attack, provided they are still available (an apelord couldn't use a secondary claw attack, for example, if he wields a two-handed weapon).

Apelord: An apelord gains two primary claw attacks. Each claw deals 1d4 points of damage (or 1d3 points for Small apelords). If an apelord hits an opponent with both claw attacks, he rends the foe for an additional 2d4 points of damage (or 2d3 points for Small apelords), plus 1-1/2 times his Strength bonus. At 7th level, the claw damage increases to 1d6 points (or 1d4 points for Small apelords) and the rend damage to 2d6 points (or 2d4 points for Small apelords).

Bearlord: A bearlord gains two primary claw attacks. Each claw deals 1d4 points of damage (or 1d3 points for Small bearlords). If a bearlord hits with a claw attack, he can attempt to start a grapple as a free action without provoking attacks of opportunity. The bearlord still follows all the other normal grappling rules. At 7th level, the claw damage increases to 1d6 points (or 1d4 points for Small bearlords).

Birdlord: A birdlord grows feathery wings, allowing him to fly at his base land speed (average maneuverability). At 7th level, the duration increases to 10 minutes per level.

Catlord: A catlord gains two primary claw attacks. Each claw deals 1d4 points of damage (or 1d3 points for Small catlords). If a catlord charges, he can attack with both claws at the end of his charge. At 7th level, the claw damage increases to 1d6 points (or 1d4 points for Small catlords).

Horselord: A horselord's speed, as well as the speed of any horse upon which he rides, improves by 10 feet for a duration of 1 hour per level. At 7th level, the speed increase improves to 20 feet.

Sharklord: A sharklord gains a devastating bite as a primary natural attack. The bite deals 1d8 points of damage (or 1d6 points for Small sharklords). A sharklord also gains the ability to breathe water while his wild aspect is active. At 7th level, the bite damage increases to 2d6 points (or 1d8 points for Small sharklords).

Snakelord: A snakelord gains a poisonous bite as a primary natural attack for 1 round per level. This bite deals 1d4 points of damage (or 1d3 points for Small snakelords). The poison's Fortitude save DC is 10 + animal lord level + Con modifier, and it deals initial and secondary damage of 1d3 points of Constitution. At 7th level, the bite damage increases to 1d6 points (or 1d4 points for Small snakelords), and the initial and secondary poison damage increases to 1d4 points of Constitution.

Wolflord: A wolflord gains the scent ability (see page 314 of the *Monster Manual*) for 10 minutes per level. At 7th level, the duration increases to 1 hour per level.

Speak with Animals (Sp): Beginning at 4th level, an animal lord can use *speak with animals* (as the spell) once per day to converse with animals of his selected group.

Summon Animal (Sp): Beginning at 5th level, an animal lord can summon one or more animals of his selected group once per day. This ability functions identically to *summon nature's ally V*, except that an animal lord can summon creatures only from his selected group, as detailed below. The duration of the effect is 1 minute per class level.

Apelord: 1d3 dire apes or 1d4+1 apes.

Bearlord: 1 polar bear, 1d3 brown bears, or 1d4+1 black bears.

Birdlord: 1d4+1 eagles, giant eagles¹, giant owls¹, hawks, ravens, or owls.

Catlord: 1 dire lion, 1d3 tigers, or 1d4+1 lions.

Horselord: 1d4+1 heavy horses, heavy warhorses, light horses, light warhorses, ponies, or warponies.

Sharklord: 1d3 Huge sharks[2] or 1d4+1 Large sharks[2].

Snakelord: 1 giant constrictor snake, 1d3 Huge vipers, or 1d4+1 constrictor snakes or Large vipers.

Wolflord: 1d4+1 dire wolves or wolves.

1 May be summoned only by nonevil birdlords.

2 May be summoned only into an aquatic or watery environment.

Second Totem: At 6th level, an animal lord gains a bonus feat related to his selected group, even if he doesn't meet the prerequisites. If the animal lord already has the feat, he can choose any other feat for which he meets the prerequisites. *Apelord:* Brachiation†; *Bearlord:* Improved Grapple; *Birdlord:* Flyby Attack (see page 303 of the *Monster Manual*); *Catlord:* Lightning Reflexes; *Horselord:* Trample; *Sharklord:* Improved Critical (bite); *Snakelord:* Improved Initiative; *Wolflord:* Improved Trip.

†New feat described on page 106.

Animal Growth (Sp): Once per day, an animal lord of 7th level or higher can use *animal growth* on a single animal from his selected group as a swift action (see Swift Actions and Immediate Actions, page 137) as a spellcaster of his class level. This ability otherwise functions just like the spell.

Animal Telepathy (Su): Beginning at 8th level, an animal lord can converse telepathically with any animal of his selected group that he can see within 100 feet.

Third Totem: At 10th level, an animal lord gains a permanent 2-point increase to one of his ability scores, determined by his chosen animal group as follows. *Apelord:* +2 Strength; *Bearlord:* +2 Constitution; *Birdlord:* +2 Wisdom; *Catlord:* +2 Dexterity; *Horselord:* +2 Constitution; *Sharklord:* +2 Strength; *Snakelord:* +2 Charisma; *Wolflord:* +2 Strength.

TABLE 2–2: THE ANIMAL LORD

Level	Base Attack Bonus	Fort Save	Ref Save	Will Save	Special
1st	+1	+2	+2	+0	Animal bond, *detect animals*, wild empathy
2nd	+2	+3	+3	+0	First totem, low-light vision
3rd	+3	+3	+3	+1	Wild aspect 1/day
4th	+4	+4	+4	+1	*Speak with animals*
5th	+5	+4	+4	+1	*Summon animal*
6th	+6	+5	+5	+2	Second totem, wild aspect 2/day
7th	+7	+5	+5	+2	*Animal growth*
8th	+8	+6	+6	+2	Animal telepathy
9th	+9	+6	+6	+3	Wild aspect 3/day
10th	+10	+7	+7	+3	Third totem

SAMPLE ANIMAL LORD

Kozakh: Male half-orc barbarian 5/apelord 3; CR 8; Medium humanoid (orc); HD 5d12+10 plus 3d10+6 plus 3; hp 73; Init +2; Spd 40 ft.; AC 18, touch 12, flat-footed 18; Base Atk +8; Grp +13; Atk +14 melee (1d12+7/×3, masterwork cold iron greataxe) or +13 melee (1d4+5, claw); Full Atk +14/+9 melee (1d12+7/×3, masterwork cold iron greataxe) or +13/+13 melee (1d4+5, claw); SA rage 2/day, wild aspect; SQ darkvision 60 ft., half-orc traits, improved uncanny dodge, low-light vision, uncanny dodge, trap sense +1, wild empathy +3 (+7 chosen group, –1 magical beasts); AL CN; SV Fort +9, Ref +6, Will +3; Str 20, Dex 14, Con 14, Int 8, Wis 12, Cha 6.

Skills and Feats: Climb +19, Handle Animal +5 (+9 with apes), Jump +19, Knowledge (nature) +1; Cleave, Power Attack, Toughness.

Languages: Common, Orc.

Animal Bond (Ex): Kozakh gains a +4 bonus on Handle Animal and wild empathy checks made to influence apes, baboons, dire apes, or monkeys.

Detect Animals (Sp): Kozakh can detect the presence of any apes, baboons, dire apes, or monkeys at will, as if casting *detect animals or plants*.

Half-Orc Traits: For all effects related to race, a half-orc is considered an orc.

Improved Uncanny Dodge (Ex): Kozakh cannot be flanked and can only be sneak attacked by a character who has at least 9 levels of rogue.

Rage (Ex): Twice per day, Kozakh can enter a state of fierce rage that lasts for 7 rounds. The following changes are in effect as long as he rages: hp increase by 16; AC 16, touch 10, flat-footed 14; Grp +15; Atk +16 melee (1d12+10/×3, masterwork cold iron greataxe) or +15 melee (1d4+7, claw); Full Atk +16/+11 melee (1d12+10/×3, masterwork cold iron greataxe) or +15/+15 melee (1d4+7, claw); SV Fort +11, Will +5; Str 24, Con 18; Climb +21, Jump +21. At the end of his rage, Kozakh is fatigued for the duration of the encounter.

Uncanny Dodge (Ex): Kozakh retains his Dexterity bonus to AC even when flat-footed or targeted by an unseen foe (he still loses his Dexterity bonus if paralyzed or otherwise immobile).

Wild Aspect (Su): Once per day, Kozakh can assume his wild aspect to gain two primary claw attacks (described in the statistics block above). If he hits an opponent with both claw attacks, he rends the foe for an additional 2d4+7 points of damage (or 2d4+10 while raging).

Possessions: +2 *chain shirt*, masterwork cold iron greataxe, *gauntlets of ogre power*, 2 *potions of cure moderate wounds*.

BEASTMASTER

A beastmaster feels more at home among the animals of nature than fellow sentient beings. Over time, these wanderers befriend a wide variety of animals, from mighty dire lions to tiny weasels. Eventually, a beastmaster takes on aspects of her animal companions, becoming almost as much animal as humanoid.

Druids and rangers are the most common beastmasters, thanks to those characters' natural link with the animal world. Some barbarians, fighters, or scouts also become beastmasters, particularly those with a strong affinity for nature (such as elves or halflings). Characters of other classes rarely pursue this path.

NPC beastmasters are typically loners, relying on their animal companions for friendship on their travels. Good-aligned beastmasters might use their powers to right injustices, even allying themselves with rural villages for a time. Evil-aligned beastmasters are often openly hostile to civilization, becoming reclusive xenophobes.

Adaptation: Beastmasters could belong to a widespread organization of like-minded individuals, each one dedicated to the bond between humanoid and animal. Rival factions might arise along alignment lines, or be divided by the choice of animal companions.

Hit Die: d10.

REQUIREMENTS

To qualify to become a beastmaster, a character must fulfill all the following criteria.

Skills: Handle Animal 8 ranks, Survival 4 ranks.
Feats: Skill Focus (Handle Animal).

CLASS SKILLS

The beastmaster's class skills (and the key ability for each skill) are Climb (Str), Handle Animal (Cha), Heal (Wis), Hide (Dex), Jump (Str), Knowledge (nature) (Int), Listen (Wis), Ride (Dex), Spot (Wis), Survival (Wis), and Swim (Str).

Skill Points at Each Level: 4 + Int modifier.

CLASS FEATURES

All of the following are class features of the beastmaster prestige class.

Weapon and Armor Proficiency: Beastmasters gain no proficiency with any weapon or armor.

Animal Companion (Ex): A beastmaster gains the service of a loyal animal companion. See the druid class feature, pages 35–36 of the *Player's Handbook*. Treat the beastmaster as a druid whose level is equal to the beastmaster's class level + 3. A beastmaster can select one of the animals available to a 1st-level druid and then apply the modifications as appropriate for a 4th-level druid's animal companion, or she can select a typical version of one of the animals available to a 4th-level druid.

As a beastmaster gains class levels, her animal companion gains Hit Dice and other special abilities just as a druid's animal companion does. Use the beastmaster's class level + 3 to determine the animal companion's special abilities.

If a beastmaster already has an animal companion from another class, her beastmaster class levels stack with class levels from all other classes that grant an animal companion. For example, a 5th-level druid/2nd-level beastmaster would be treated as a 10th-level druid for the purpose of improving the statistics of her animal companion (and which alternative animal companions she could select).

Wild Empathy (Ex): A beastmaster can improve the attitude of an animal. See the druid class feature, page 35 of the *Player's Handbook*. If a beastmaster has wild empathy from another class, her levels stack for determining the bonus.

Alertness: A beastmaster's senses grow keen as she

Illus. by J. Miracola

Leena of the mean streets, a beastmaster

TABLE 2–3: THE BEASTMASTER

Level	Base Attack Bonus	Fort Save	Ref Save	Will Save	Special
1st	+1	+2	+2	+0	Animal companion, wild empathy
2nd	+2	+3	+3	+0	Alertness
3rd	+3	+3	+3	+1	*Speak with animals* 1/day
4th	+4	+4	+4	+1	Extra animal companion (–3)
5th	+5	+4	+4	+1	Low-light vision
6th	+6	+5	+5	+2	*Speak with animals* 2/day
7th	+7	+5	+5	+2	Extra animal companion (–6)
8th	+8	+6	+6	+2	Scent
9th	+9	+6	+6	+3	*Speak with animals* 3/day
10th	+10	+7	+7	+3	Extra animal companion (–9)

learns some of the tricks of the animal kingdom. Accordingly, she gains Alertness as a bonus feat at 2nd level.

Speak with Animals (Sp): Starting at 3rd level, a beastmaster can use *speak with animals* once per day as the spell cast by a caster of her class level. She can use this ability twice per day at 6th level and three times per day at 9th level.

Extra Animal Companion (Ex): At 4th level, a beastmaster gains a second animal companion, chosen from the list of animal companions available to a 1st-level druid. Treat the beastmaster as a druid whose level is equal to the beastmaster's class level – 3 for the purpose of improving the animal companion's statistics (or of selecting an alternative companion at higher levels).

At 7th level, a beastmaster gains a third animal companion, chosen from the list of animal companions available to a 1st-level druid. Treat the beastmaster as a druid whose level is equal to the beastmaster's class level – 6 for the purpose of improving the animal companion's statistics (or of selecting an alternative companion at higher levels).

At 10th level, a beastmaster gains a fourth animal companion, chosen from the list of animal companions available to a 1st-level druid. Treat the beastmaster as a druid whose level is equal to the beastmaster's class level – 9 for the purpose of improving the animal companion's statistics (or of selecting an alternative companion at higher levels).

Other class levels in classes that offer an animal companion don't stack for the purpose of determining the power of a beastmaster's additional animal companions, nor do they allow her to choose additional animal companions from the alternative lists.

Low-Light Vision (Ex): At 5th level, a beastmaster gains low-light vision, allowing her to see twice as far as a human in starlight, moonlight, torchlight, and similar conditions of shadowy illumination. She retains the ability to distinguish color and detail under these conditions.

If she already has low-light vision from another source (such as her race), her low-light vision improves, allowing her to see three times as far as a human in conditions of shadowy illumination.

Scent (Ex): At 8th level, a beastmaster gains the scent ability (see page 314 of the *Monster Manual*).

SAMPLE BEASTMASTER

Leena of the Mean Streets: Female human ranger 5/ beastmaster 2; CR 7; Medium humanoid; HD 5d8+15 plus 2d10+6; hp 58; Init +5; Spd 30 ft.; AC 17, touch 11, flat-footed 16; Base Atk +7; Grp +11; Atk +12 melee (1d6+5/18–20, +1 *scimitar*); Full Atk +10/+5 melee (1d6+5/18–20, +1 *scimitar*) and +10 melee (1d6+2/19–20, masterwork short sword); SA favored enemy aberrations +2, favored enemy humanoids (humans) +4; SQ animal companion (dire rat), animal companion benefits, wild empathy +8 (+4 magical beasts); AL NG; SV Fort +10, Ref +8, Will +2; Str 18, Dex 13, Con 16, Int 10, Wis 12, Cha 8.

Skills and Feats: Climb +9, Handle Animal +12, Hide +7, Listen +12, Move Silently +7, Spot +12, Survival +9; Alertness[B], Endurance[B], Improved Initiative, Quick Draw, Skill Focus (Handle Animal), Track[B], Two-Weapon Defense, Two-Weapon Fighting[B].

Language: Common.

Animal Companion (Ex): Leena has a dire rat named Manster as an animal companion. Manster's abilities and characteristics are summarized below.

Animal Companion Benefits: Leena and Manster enjoy the link and share spells special qualities.

Link (Ex): Leena can handle Manster as a free action. She also gains a +4 circumstance bonus on all wild empathy checks and Handle Animal checks made regarding her dire rat.

Share Spells (Ex): Leena can have any spell she casts on herself also affect her animal companion if the latter is within 5 feet at the time. She can also cast a spell with a target of "You" on her dire rat.

Favored Enemy (Ex): Leena gains a +2 bonus on her Bluff, Listen, Sense Motive, Spot, and Survival checks when using these skills against aberrations. She gains the same bonus on weapon damage rolls.

Against humans, she gains a +4 bonus on these skill checks and on weapon damage rolls.

Ranger Spell Prepared (caster level 2nd): 1st—*longstrider*.

Possessions: +1 *chain shirt,* +1 *scimitar,* masterwork short sword, *gauntlets of ogre power.*

Manster, Dire Rat Companion: CR —; Small animal; HD 5d8+5; hp 27; Init +4; Spd 40 ft., climb 20 ft.; AC 19, touch 14, flat-footed 16; Base Atk +3; Grp +0; Atk or Full Atk +8 melee (1d4+1 plus disease, bite); SA disease; SQ bonus tricks (2), devotion, evasion, low-light vision, scent; AL N; SV Fort +4, Ref +6, Will +4; Str 12, Dex 19, Con 12, Int 1, Wis 12, Cha 4.

Skills and Feats: Climb +12, Hide +11, Listen +4, Move Silently +9, Spot +4, Swim +12; Alertness, Stealthy, Weapon Finesse[B].

Disease (Ex): Filth fever—bite, Fortitude DC 11, incubation period 1d3 days, damage 1d3 Dex and 1d3 Con. The save DC is Constitution-based.

Devotion (Ex): Manster's devotion to Leena is so complete that it gains a +4 morale bonus on Will saves against enchantment spells and effects.

Evasion (Ex): If Manster is exposed to any effect that normally allows it to attempt a Reflex saving throw for half damage, it takes no damage with a successful saving throw.

Tricks: Attack, seek, stay.

Skills: +8 racial bonus on Swim checks; +8 racial bonus on Climb checks and can always choose to take 10 on Climb checks, even if rushed or threatened. Manster uses its Dexterity modifier for Climb and Swim checks.

BLOODHOUND

A bandit king raids caravans on the road. An ogre pillages farms to the north. A sorcerer has kidnapped the mayor's son and hidden him somewhere in the marsh—and the soldiers of the king cannot seem to stem the tide. The terrified citizens have only one choice, and it isn't cheap. They call in a bloodhound.

A bloodhound tracks down wrongdoers and brings them to whatever justice awaits them. Low-level bloodhounds depend on their keen senses and careful training to hunt their targets. As they gain experience, their obsessive determination gives them supernatural abilities that make them nearly unstoppable.

Though some bloodhounds leave calling cards or even brands on their targets, most don't kill their quarry if they can help it. They prefer instead to subdue their targets and bring them in. For those of good alignment, this practice satisfies some deeply held belief in the cause of justice. For neutral and evil bloodhounds, it ensures a steady stream of income from catching the same targets over and over when they break out of jail.

Rangers and barbarians make the best bloodhounds, but rogues, bards, druids, and fighters can also excel in this role. Occasionally, a paladin shoulders the mantle, but never for money. Most bloodhounds are human, though elves and half-elves sometimes find this lifestyle satisfying. Some of the best bloodhounds are humanoids such as gnolls, hobgoblins, and bugbears.

Most NPC bloodhounds work for money (usually a lot of it), but some accept jobs for justice, revenge, or enjoyment. When a bloodhound accepts a job, he designates his target as a mark. Thereafter, he does not abandon the case until it is finished, which occurs when the mark is apprehended or when either the mark or the bloodhound dies.

Adaptation: The easiest way to adapt this class to your own campaign is to tie bloodhounds to one or more organizations of superlative trackers. The most obvious choice is the Bloodhounds, an organization described in Chapter 6 of this book. But you also might introduce a more localized group of bloodhounds—for example, a group of rangers and bloodhounds sworn to serve a small barony far to the north; funds earned by "the Brennmark Trackers" might be the major income of their tiny homeland.

Hit Die: d10.

REQUIREMENTS

To qualify to become a bloodhound, a character must fulfill all the following criteria.

Base Attack Bonus: +4.

Skills: Gather Information 4 ranks, Move Silently 4 ranks, Survival 4 ranks.

Feats: Endurance, Track.

CLASS SKILLS

The bloodhound's class skills (and the key ability for each skill) are Bluff (Cha), Climb (Str), Diplomacy (Cha), Disguise (Cha), Gather Information (Cha), Heal (Wis), Hide (Dex), Intimidate (Cha), Jump (Str), Listen (Wis), Move Silently (Dex), Open Lock (Dex), Ride (Dex), Search (Int), Sense Motive (Wis), Spot (Wis), Survival (Wis), Swim (Str), and Use Rope (Dex).

Skill Points at Each Level: 6 + Int modifier.

CLASS FEATURES

All of the following are class features of the bloodhound prestige class.

Weapon and Armor Proficiency: Bloodhounds are proficient with all simple and martial weapons, and with light armor.

Mark (Ex): A bloodhound can target, or mark, an individual humanoid or monstrous humanoid foe to better hunt that enemy. To do so, the bloodhound must focus on a foe who is present and visible, or on the depiction or description of one who is not, for 10 minutes. Any interruption ruins the attempt and forces the bloodhound to start the process again. Once this study is complete, that target is called a mark.

A bloodhound adds his bloodhound level as an insight bonus on all Gather Information, Listen, Search, Spot, and Survival checks made to determine the whereabouts of a mark. As a bloodhound gains levels, he gains additional abilities that can be used against a mark.

If a bloodhound chooses a new mark before apprehending an existing one, the latter becomes unmarked, and the bloodhound loses experience points equal to the amount he would have earned for defeating that creature. A bloodhound can choose a mark only once a week.

Initially, a bloodhound can have only one mark at a time. For every three bloodhound levels gained beyond 1st, a bloodhound can have one additional mark, but only if all the marks are chosen during the same process (see above). For example, a 4th-level bloodhound could mark two bugbears in the same group of prisoners, or the depictions of a bugbear and a hobgoblin if both were studied at the same time. If a bloodhound gives up on apprehending any of his marks, all remaining marked creatures become unmarked as described above.

Swift Tracker (Ex): A bloodhound can move at his normal speed while following tracks. See the ranger class feature, page 48 of the *Player's Handbook*.

Nonlethal Force (Ex): Starting at 2nd level, a bloodhound can use a melee weapon that deals lethal damage to deal nonlethal damage instead without taking the usual –4 penalty on his attack roll.

Ready and Waiting (Ex): Beginning at 2nd level, a bloodhound is ready for trickery at all times. He can ready an action against his mark, even outside of the initiative sequence. If the mark triggers the bloodhound's readied action at any point within the next 10 minutes, the bloodhound can carry out his readied action as if the two were engaged in combat (as long as the bloodhound is capable of carrying out that action). If the bloodhound is incapable of carrying out the action—for instance, if he is too far away to strike the mark with a readied melee attack—the readied action is lost.

Bring 'em Back Alive (Ex): At 3rd level and higher, a bloodhound can turn a potentially killing blow into an incapacitating one—all the better to bring a mark back for punishment. At the bloodhound's option, any melee attack that would reduce a foe to –2 or fewer hit points reduces the foe to –1 hit points instead. A bloodhound must choose to use this ability immediately upon reducing his foe to –2 or fewer hit points, and before making any other action (or even continuing a full attack). A raging bloodhound can't use this ability.

Tenacious Pursuit (Ex): At 3rd level and above, a bloodhound tracking a mark gains a +4 bonus on Constitution checks made to resist nonlethal damage from a forced march (see page 164 of the *Player's Handbook*).

In addition, a bloodhound tracking a mark can increase his own speed by 10 feet, up to a maximum value equal to the mark's speed. This bonus stacks with all other speed increases. At 6th level, the speed increase improves to 20 feet, and it goes up to 30 feet at 9th level.

Hunter's Dedication (Ex): Beginning at 4th level, a bloodhound adds his Constitution bonus (if any) to Will saves made to resist the special attacks or spells of his mark.

Move Like the Wind (Ex): Starting at 4th level, a bloodhound can move stealthily even at a quick pace. He no longer takes a –5 penalty

Ulfur, a bloodhound

Illus. by S. Belledin

on Hide and Move Silently checks when moving at any speed up to his normal speed, and he takes only a –10 penalty (instead of a –20 penalty) on Hide and Move Silently checks when running. (He takes the normal –20 penalty when attacking or charging.)

Crippling Strike (Ex): Starting at 5th level, a bloodhound can deliver strikes against his mark with such precision that each successful attack also deals 2 points of Strength damage to the mark. A bloodhound can deliver a crippling strike with a melee attack, or with a ranged attack from a distance of up to 30 feet. See the rogue class feature, page 51 of the *Player's Handbook*.

Track the Trackless (Su): Starting at 5th level, a bloodhound can track a creature moving under the influence of *pass without trace* or a similar effect, though he takes a –20 penalty on his Survival checks when doing so.

See Invisibility (Su): This ability, gained at 6th level, functions like a *see invisibility* spell, except that it is constantly in effect and it reveals only invisible marks.

Shielded Mind (Su): At 6th level, a bloodhound gains spell resistance against divination spells equal to 15 + his bloodhound level. This benefit does not stack with other forms of spell resistance.

Locate Creature (Sp): Once per day, a bloodhound of 7th level or higher can produce an effect identical to that of a *locate creature* spell with a caster level equal to the bloodhound's character level.

Freedom of Movement (Su): Starting at 8th level, a bloodhound can act normally regardless of magical effects that impede movement, as if he were affected by a *freedom of movement* spell. The effect lasts for a total time per day of 1 round per point of Wisdom bonus he possesses (minimum 1 round). The effect occurs automatically as soon as it is applied, lasts until it runs out or is no longer needed, and can be used multiple times per day (up to the total daily limit of rounds). The character's caster level is equal to his bloodhound level.

Scent (Ex): At 9th level, a bloodhound gains the scent ability (see page 314 of the *Monster Manual*).

Find the Path (Sp): A 10th-level bloodhound can use *find the path* twice per day as the spell. His caster level is equal to his bloodhound level.

SAMPLE BLOODHOUND

Ulfur: Male half-orc scout 4/fighter 1/bloodhound 3; CR 8; Medium humanoid (orc); HD 4d8+4 plus 4d10+4; hp 51; Init +4; Spd 40 ft.; AC 17 (18), touch 13 (14), flat-footed 17 (18); Base Atk +7; Grp +10; Atk +11 melee (1d6+4/19–20,

Level	Base Attack Bonus	Fort Save	Ref Save	Will Save	Special
1st	+1	+2	+2	+0	Mark (1), swift tracker
2nd	+2	+3	+3	+0	Nonlethal force, ready and waiting
3rd	+3	+3	+3	+1	Bring 'em back alive, tenacious pursuit (speed +10 ft.)
4th	+4	+4	+4	+1	Hunter's dedication, mark (2), move like the wind
5th	+5	+4	+4	+1	Crippling strike, track the trackless
6th	+6	+5	+5	+2	See invisibility, shielded mind, tenacious pursuit (speed +20 ft.)
7th	+7	+5	+5	+2	Locate creature, mark (3)
8th	+8	+6	+6	+2	Freedom of movement
9th	+9	+6	+6	+3	Scent, tenacious pursuit (speed +30 ft.)
10th	+10	+7	+7	+3	Find the path, mark (4)

Table 2–4: The Bloodhound

+1 *short sword*) or +12 ranged within 30 ft. (1d8+3/×3, +1 *composite longbow*); Full Atk +11/+6 melee (1d6+4/19–20, +1 *short sword*) or +12/+7 ranged (1d8+3/×3, +1 *composite longbow*); SA bring 'em back alive, nonlethal force, skirmish (+1 AC, +1d6 damage); SQ darkvision 60 ft., half-orc traits, mark (1), ready and waiting, swift tracker, tenacious pursuit, trackless step, trapfinding, uncanny dodge; AL N; SV Fort +8, Ref +10, Will +2; Str 17, Dex 16, Con 13, Int 10, Wis 10, Cha 6.

Skills and Feats: Climb +10, Gather Information +5, Hide +13, Jump +14, Move Silently +13, Search +10, Spot +10, Survival +10 (+12 following tracks); Endurance, Point Blank Shot, Precise Shot, Track, Weapon Focus (longbow).

Languages: Common, Orc.

Bring 'em Back Alive (Ex): At Ulfur's option, any melee attack that would reduce his foe to –2 or fewer hit points reduces the foe to –1 hit points instead. He must choose to use this ability immediately upon reducing the foe to –2 or fewer hit points, and before making any other action (or even continuing a full attack).

Half-Orc Traits: For all effects related to race, a half-orc is considered an orc.

Mark (Ex): Ulfur can target, or mark, an individual humanoid or monstrous humanoid foe, in order to better hunt that enemy. To do so, he must focus on a foe who is present and visible, or on the depiction or description of one who is not, for 10 minutes. Any interruption ruins the attempt and forces him to start the process again. Once this study is complete, that target is called a mark.

Ulfur gains a +3 insight bonus on all Gather Information, Listen, Search, Spot, and Survival checks made to determine the whereabouts of a mark.

Ulfur can have only one mark at a given time. If he chooses a new mark before apprehending an existing one, the latter becomes unmarked, and Ulfur loses experience points equal to the amount he would have earned for defeating that creature. Ulfur can choose a mark only once a week.

Nonlethal Force (Ex): Ulfur can use a melee weapon that deals lethal damage to deal nonlethal damage instead without taking the usual –4 penalty on his attack roll.

Ready and Waiting (Ex): Ulfur can ready an action against his mark, even outside of the initiative sequence. If the mark triggers his readied action at any point within the next 10 minutes, Ulfur can carry out his readied action as if the two were engaged in combat (as long as he is capable of carrying out that action). If he is incapable of carrying out the action—for instance, if he is too far away to strike the mark with a readied melee attack—the readied action is lost.

Skirmish (Ex): Ulfur gains a +1 competence bonus to AC and deals an extra 1d6 points of damage on all attacks during any round in which he moves at least 10 feet. The extra damage applies only to attacks taken during his turn. This damage also applies to ranged attacks against targets up to 30 feet away. Creatures with concealment, creatures without discernible anatomies, and creatures immune to extra damage from critical hits are all immune to this extra damage. Ulfur loses this ability when wearing medium or heavy armor or when carrying a medium or heavy load.

Swift Tracker (Ex): Ulfur can track at normal speed without taking the usual –5 penalty, or he can track at double speed at only a –10 penalty.

Tenacious Pursuit (Ex): When tracking a mark, Ulfur gains a +4 bonus on Constitution checks made to resist nonlethal damage from a forced march.

In addition, when tracking a mark Ulfur can increase his own speed by 10 feet, up to a maximum value equal to the mark's speed. This benefit stacks with all other speed increases.

Trackless Step (Ex): Ulfur leaves no trail in natural surroundings and cannot be tracked.

Trapfinding (Ex): Ulfur can find, disarm, or bypass traps with a DC of 20 or higher. He can use the Search skill to find, and the Disable Device skill to disarm, magic traps (DC 25 + the level of the spell used to create it). If his Disable Device result exceeds the trap's DC by 10 or more, he discovers how to bypass the trap without triggering or disarming it.

Uncanny Dodge (Ex): Ulfur retains his Dexterity bonus to AC even when flat-footed or targeted by an unseen foe (he still loses his Dexterity bonus if paralyzed or otherwise immobile).

Possessions: +2 *leather armor,* +1 *composite longbow* (+1 Str bonus) with 20 arrows, +1 *short sword,* masterwork manacles.

DAGGERSPELL MAGE

In a reclusive monastery in the heart of an ancient forest, a varied group of druids and arcane spellcasters train together. The adherents of this monastery work to perfect a unique fighting and spellcasting style that relies on wielding a pair of daggers at all times. Some of these students—known as daggerspell mages—blend the fighting style with arcane magic.

Daggerspell mages see the quick movements of their deadly daggers as an attendant part of their spellcasting. These sometimes reclusive figures remain spellcasters first and melee combatants second. Daggerspell mages, like their colleagues the daggerspell shapers, seek truth and justice, but they define such concepts in the heat of the moment. Daggerspell mages do not see morality as an absolute, and their ideals are guided by their sense of what is right and fair.

Daggerspell mages are closely related to the daggerspell shapers, the other half of the organization known as the Daggerspell Guardians (see page 167). Both preserve the work of good folk and balance the concerns of civilized communities against the sanctity of nature, but where a shaper is quiet and calculating, a daggerspell mage is wild and impulsive. The two halves of the organization work together amicably, but they have decidedly different approaches to most problems.

Almost every daggerspell mage begins his career as a wizard or sorcerer, taking a level or two of rogue after a few successful adventures. Drawn to the exotic fighting style and balanced ideas of the Daggerspell Guardians, these individuals enjoy the enigmatic reputation and unorthodox techniques of the guild. Although members of the guild are primarily spellcasters, some follow more complicated multiclass pathways that include fighter or paladin levels. These characters follow all precepts of the guild, but they are more likely to defend truth with the sharp points of their daggers than with the arcane power of their spells.

Adaptation: Although daggerspell shapers and daggerspell mages are related through their common organization, they need not be used together in every campaign. The mages, well suited for wizard/rogues of any alignment, could become a deadly group of dagger- and spell-wielding cultists.

Furthermore, in a campaign that includes psionics, the daggerspell mage makes an excellent class for psion/ rogues. Simply change the arcane spellcasting require- ment and progression to a similar psionic manifester level requirement and progression, and the daggerspell psion, the third branch of the Daggerspell Guardians, is ready for your campaign.

Hit Die: d6.

REQUIREMENTS

To qualify to become a daggerspell mage, a character must fulfill all the following criteria.

Alignment: Any nonevil.
Skills: Concentration 8 ranks.
Feats: Weapon Focus (dagger), Two-Weapon Fighting.
Special: Arcane caster level 5th.
Special: Sneak attack +1d6.

CLASS SKILLS

The daggerspell mage's class skills (and the key ability for each skill) are Balance (Dex), Climb (Str), Concentration (Con), Craft (Int), Handle Animal (Cha), Heal (Wis), Hide (Dex), Jump (Str), Knowledge (arcana) (Int), Listen (Wis), Move Silently (Dex), Profession (Wis), Ride (Dex), Spellcraft (Int), Spot (Wis), Survival (Wis), Swim (Str), and Tumble (Dex).

Skill Points at Each Level: 6 + Int modifier.

CLASS FEATURES

All of the following are class features of the daggerspell mage prestige class.

Weapon and Armor Proficiency: Daggerspell mages gain no proficiency with any weapon or armor.

Daggercast (Ex): Daggerspell mages seamlessly blend the use of their twin daggers with powerful spellcasting abilities. A daggerspell mage can cast a spell with somatic and material components even when holding a dagger in each hand. If a daggerspell mage holds anything other than a dagger, he must have at least one hand free to cast a spell with somatic or material components. Casting a spell in this way still provokes attacks of opportunity normally.

In addition, a daggerspell mage can deliver a touch spell with a dagger attack (either a melee touch attack or a normal melee attack, but not with a thrown dagger).

Invocation of the Knife (Su): Beginning at 2nd level, daggerspell mages develop a strong mystical connection between their arcane spellcasting abilities and the daggers that they wield. Whenever a daggerspell mage casts an arcane spell that deals energy damage, he can turn half of the damage dealt by the spell into magic slashing damage rather than energy damage. Energy resistance does not apply to this damage, but damage reduction might. This power does not affect a creature's ability to resist the affected spell with a saving throw or spell resistance.

Using this ability does not require an action; its use is part of the action required to cast the affected spell. Only spells with a duration of instantaneous can be modified by this ability.

Spells per Day/Spells Known: Beginning at 2nd level, a daggerspell mage gains new spells per day at each level (and spells known, if applicable) as if he had also gained a level in an arcane spellcasting class to which he belonged before adding the prestige class level. He does not, however, gain any other benefit a character of that class would have gained. If he had more than one arcane spellcasting class before becoming a daggerspell mage, he must decide to which class to add each level for the purpose of determin- ing spells per day and spells known.

Sneak Attack (Ex): Beginning at 3rd level, a dag- gerspell mage deals an extra 1d6 points of damage when flanking an opponent or at any time when the target would be denied its Dexterity bonus. This extra damage applies to ranged attacks only if the target is within 30 feet. It increases to 2d6 points at 6th level and 3d6 points at 9th level. See the rogue class feature, page 50 of the *Player's Handbook*. If a daggerspell mage gets a sneak attack bonus from another source (such as levels of rogue), the bonuses on damage stack.

Double Daggercast (Ex): As a daggerspell mage ad- vances in level, the connection between his spellcasting abilities and his two-dagger fighting style strengthens. At 5th level and higher, a mage can hold the charge for one touch spell for each dagger that he is holding in his hands. He must designate which dagger holds each touch spell at the time the spell is cast. If one of these daggers leaves the daggerspell mage's hands, the spell immedi- ately discharges harmlessly (unless the dagger is thrown by a mage with the arcane throw ability; see below).

Arcane Infusion (Su): At 7th level and higher, a daggerspell mage can infuse arcane spell power into his daggers, temporarily enabling them to deal extra energy damage. To use this ability, a mage must lose a prepared arcane spell from memory (or give up a potential spell slot for the day if he casts spells as a sorcerer). The dag- gerspell mage chooses one dagger that he is holding and an energy type (fire, cold, or electricity) when this ability is activated. The chosen dagger deals an extra 1d6 points

Table 2–5: The Daggerspell Mage

Level	Base Attack Bonus	Fort Save	Ref Save	Will Save	Special	Spells per Day/Spells Known
1st	+0	+0	+2	+2	Daggercast	—
2nd	+1	+0	+3	+3	Invocation of the knife	+1 level of existing arcane spellcasting class
3rd	+2	+1	+3	+3	Sneak attack +1d6	+1 level of existing arcane spellcasting class
4th	+3	+1	+4	+4	—	+1 level of existing arcane spellcasting class
5th	+3	+1	+4	+4	Double daggercast	+1 level of existing arcane spellcasting class
6th	+4	+2	+5	+5	Sneak attack +2d6	+1 level of existing arcane spellcasting class
7th	+5	+2	+5	+5	Arcane infusion	+1 level of existing arcane spellcasting class
8th	+6	+2	+6	+6	Arcane throw	+1 level of existing arcane spellcasting class
9th	+6	+3	+6	+6	Sneak attack +3d6	+1 level of existing arcane spellcasting class
10th	+7	+3	+7	+7	Daggerspell flurry	+1 level of existing arcane spellcasting class

of damage of the chosen energy type. This effect lasts for a number of rounds equal to the spell level sacrificed. Multiple uses of this ability on the same dagger don't stack, even if different energy types are chosen. If the dagger is thrown, the energy damage applies to that attack, but then the effect immediately dissipates.

Using this ability is a swift action that does not provoke attacks of opportunity (see Swift Actions and Immediate Actions, page 137).

Arcane Throw (Ex): At 8th level and higher, a daggerspell mage can imbue arcane spell power into his thrown daggers. The mage can deliver a touch spell with a thrown dagger just as if he were making a melee attack. If the dagger hits, the touch spell is discharged against the creature or object struck. If the dagger misses its intended target, the dagger returns to the mage just before his next turn (as if it had the returning special ability; see page 225 of the *Dungeon Master's Guide*) and retains the spell just as if the mage had missed with a melee attack.

Daggerspell Flurry (Ex): A 10th-level daggerspell mage can blend spellcasting with a flurry of dagger attacks. When using this ability, a daggerspell mage can quicken one spell as part of a full attack with his daggers. Doing this has no effect on the spell's effective level. A daggerspell mage must make at least one melee attack in any round in which he uses this ability, and he cannot make an attack with anything other than a dagger (although if a spell cast in conjunction with this ability requires an attack roll, he can still make the spell's attack).

A daggerspell mage can use this ability a number of times per day equal to his Dexterity modifier (minimum 1).

SAMPLE DAGGERSPELL MAGE

Vadamar Lyrr: Male elf wizard 5/rogue 2/daggerspell mage 7; CR 14; Medium humanoid; HD 5d4 plus 9d6; hp 48; Init +5; Spd 30 ft.; AC 20, touch 17, flat-footed 15; Base Atk +8; Grp +9; Atk +12 melee (1d4+3/19–20, +2 *dagger*) or +14 ranged (1d8/×3, longbow with masterwork arrow); Full Atk +12/+7 melee (1d4+3/19–20, +2 *dagger*) and +10 melee (1d4/19–20, adamantine dagger) or +14/+9 ranged (1d8/×3, longbow with masterwork arrow); SA arcane infusion, daggercast, double daggercast, invocation of the knife, sneak attack +3d6, spells; SQ elf traits, evasion, familiar (toad), familiar benefits, low-light vision, trapfinding; AL NG; SV Fort +3, Ref +14, Will +9 (+11 against enchantments); Str 13, Dex 20 (18 without *gloves of Dexterity* +2), Con 10, Int 16, Wis 10, Cha 8.

Skills and Feats: Climb +8, Concentration +15, Craft (armorsmith) +8, Craft (weaponsmith) +8, Disable Device +5, Hide +16, Jump +10, Knowledge (arcana) +11, Knowledge (the planes) +10, Listen +6, Move Silently +14, Search +7, Spellcraft +20, Spot +13, Tumble +18; Dodge, Mobility, Scribe Scroll[B], Spell Mastery[B] (*displacement, invisibility, vampiric touch*), Spring Attack, Two-Weapon Fighting, Weapon Focus (dagger).

Languages: Common, Elven, Draconic; Orc, Sylvan.

Arcane Infusion (Su): Vadamar can infuse arcane spellpower into his daggers, temporarily allowing them to deal extra energy damage. To use this ability, Vadamar must lose a prepared arcane spell from memory. He chooses one dagger that he is holding and a specific energy type (fire, cold, or electricity) when this ability is activated, and the chosen dagger deals an extra 1d6 points of damage of the chosen energy type. This effect lasts for a number of rounds equal to the spell level lost. Multiple uses of this ability on the same dagger don't stack, even if different energy types are chosen. If the dagger is thrown, the energy damage applies to that attack, but then the effect immediately dissipates. Using this ability is a swift action that does not provoke attacks of opportunity.

Daggercast (Ex): Vadamar can cast a spell with somatic and material components even when holding a dagger in each hand. If he holds anything other than a dagger, he must have at least one hand free to cast a spell with somatic or material components. Casting a spell in this way still provokes attacks of opportunity normally.

In addition, Vadamar can deliver a touch spell with a dagger attack (either a melee touch attack or a normal melee attack, but not with a thrown dagger).

Double Daggercast (Ex): Vadamar can hold the charge of one touch spell for each dagger that he is holding in his hands. He must designate which dagger holds each touch spell at the time the spell is cast. If one of these daggers leaves Vadamar's hands, the spell immediately discharges harmlessly.

Elf Traits: Elves have immunity to magic sleep effects. An elf who merely passes within 5 feet of a secret or concealed door is entitled to a Search check to notice it as if he were actively looking for it.

Evasion (Ex): If Vadamar is exposed to any effect that normally allows him to attempt a Reflex saving throw for half damage, he takes no damage with a successful saving throw.

Familiar: Vadamar's familiar is a toad named Berkich. The familiar uses the better of its own and Vadamar's base save bonuses. The creature's abilities and characteristics are summarized below.

Familiar Benefits: Vadamar gains special benefits from having a familiar. Berkich grants him +3 hit points (included in Vadamar's statistics). Berkich and Vadamar enjoy the empathic link and share spells special qualities.

Alertness (Ex): Berkich grants its master Alertness as long as it is within 5 feet.

Empathic Link (Su): Vadamar can communicate telepathically with his familiar at a distance of up to 1 mile. The master has the same connection to an item or a place that the familiar does.

Share Spells (Su): Vadamar can have any spell he casts on himself also affect Berkich if the latter is within 5 feet at the time. He can also cast a spell a target of "You" on his familiar.

Invocation of the Knife (Su): Whenever Vadamar casts an arcane spell that deals energy damage, he can turn half of the damage that the spell deals into magic slashing damage rather than energy damage. Energy resistance does not apply to the magic slashing damage caused by an affected spell, but damage reduction might. This power does not affect the target's ability to resist the affected spell with a saving throw or spell resistance. Using this ability does not require an action; its use is part of the action required to cast the affected spell. Only spells of instantaneous duration can be modified by this ability.

Sneak Attack (Ex): Vadamar deals an extra 3d6 points of damage on any successful attack against flat-footed or flanked targets, or against a target that has been denied its Dexterity bonus for any reason. This damage also applies to ranged attacks against targets up to 30 feet away. Creatures with concealment, creatures without discernible anatomies, and creatures immune to extra damage from critical hits are all immune to sneak attacks. Vadamar can choose to deliver nonlethal damage with his sneak attack, but only when using a weapon designed for that purpose, such as a sap (blackjack).

Trapfinding (Ex): Vadamar can find, disarm, or bypass traps with a DC of 20 or higher. He can use the Search skill to find, and the Disable Device skill to disarm, magic traps (DC 25 + the level of the spell used to create it). If his Disable Device result exceeds the trap's DC by 10 or more, he discovers how to bypass the trap without triggering or disarming it.

Wizard Spells Prepared (caster level 11th): 0—*dancing lights, critical strike†, detect magic, read magic, touch of fatigue* (+12 melee touch; DC 13); 1st—*mage armor, ray of enfeeblement* (+13 ranged touch), *shield, shocking grasp* (+12 melee touch); 2nd—*daggerspell stance† (2), invisibility, scorching ray* (+13 ranged touch), *touch of idiocy* (+12 melee touch); 3rd—*dispel magic, displacement, haste, lightning bolt* (DC 16), *vampiric touch* (+12 melee touch); 4th—*enervation* (+13 ranged touch), *shout* (DC 17), *stoneskin*; 5th—*cone of cold* (DC 18), *shadow form†*; 6th—*greater heroism*.

Spellbook: as above plus 0—all others; 1st—*burning hands, cause fear, swift expeditious retreat†, feather fall, identify, magic missile, magic weapon*; 2nd—*bear's endurance, bladeweave†, fox's cunning, Melf's acid arrow, spectral hand, summon monster II*; 3rd—*explosive runes, greater magic weapon, spectral weapon†, wind wall*; 4th—*Evard's black tentacles, summon monster IV, wall of fire*; 5th—*cloudkill, overland flight*; 6th—*cloak of the sea†, true seeing*.

† New spell described in Chapter 5.

Possessions: amulet of natural armor +3, ring of protection +2, +2 dagger, adamantine dagger, longbow with 20 masterwork arrows, *gloves of Dexterity +2, wand of magic missile* (9th level; 10 charges), *wand of invisibility* (16 charges), scroll of *haste*, spellbook, 16 gp.

Berkich, Toad Familiar: CR —; Diminutive magical beast; HD 5; hp 24; Init +1; Spd 5 ft.; AC 18, touch 15, flat-footed 17; Base Atk +0; Grp –17; Atk or Full Atk —; Space/Reach 1 ft./0 ft.; SA deliver touch spells; SQ amphibious, improved evasion, low-light vision, speak with master; AL N; SV Fort +3, Ref +10, Will +11; Str 1, Dex 12, Con 11, Int 8, Wis 14, Cha 4.

Skills and Feats: Hide +21, Listen +4, Spot +4; Alertness.

Deliver Touch Spells (Su): Berkich can deliver touch spells for its master (see Familiars, page 52 of the *Player's Handbook*).

Vadamar Lyrr, a
daggerspell mage

Zaadi Akanthas, a
daggerspell shaper

Improved Evasion (Ex): If Berkich is exposed to any effect that normally allows it to attempt a Reflex saving throw for half damage, it takes no damage with a successful saving throw and half damage if the saving throw fails.

Speak with Master (Ex): Berkich can communicate verbally with Vadamar. Other creatures do not understand the communication without magical help.

Skills: A toad's coloration gives it a +4 racial bonus on Hide checks.

DAGGERSPELL SHAPER

In a reclusive monastery in the heart of an ancient forest, a varied group of druids and arcane spellcasters train together. The adherents of this monastery work to perfect a unique fighting and spellcasting style that relies on wielding a pair of daggers at all times. Some of these students—known as daggerspell shapers—blend the fighting style with druid magic, spinning a deadly web of steel in front of them as they perform powerful feats of natural magic, or blending their daggers into the claws and talons of their wild-shaped forms.

Daggerspell shapers see the precise martial powers of their twin-dagger style and their magic as an extension of one powerful philosophy. The shapers seek truth in all things, believing that you can separate right from wrong and nature from corruption with the clean slice of a blade. Although never numerous, shapers are respected as judges, warriors, and defenders of the weak.

Daggerspell shapers are closely related to the other half of their guild, the daggerspell mages. Both preserve the work of good folk and balance the concerns of civilized communities against the sanctity of nature, but where a daggerspell mage is wild and impulsive, a shaper is quiet and calculating. The two halves of the Daggerspell Guardians organization (see page 167) work together amicably, but they have decidedly different approaches to most problems.

Almost every daggerspell shaper begins her career as a druid, taking a level or two of rogue or scout after a few successful adventures. These individuals are drawn to the exotic fighting style and balanced ideals of the guild. Although most daggerspell shapers are primarily spellcasters, some have more complicated multiclass pathways that include ranger or barbarian levels. These shapers follow all the precepts of the guild, but they are more likely to defend nature with the steel of their daggers than with their spells.

Adaptation: The daggerspell shapers and their colleagues, the daggerspell mages, form the two halves of the organization known as the Daggerspell Guardians. Although normally bound together through the guild, these groups need not be used together in every campaign. The shapers, well suited for druid/rogues of any alignment, can become a drastically different group with just a few changes. Adding neutral evil as an alignment requirement might change the shapers into a group of dagger-wielding fanatics dedicated to preserving the sanctity of nature by assassinating those who intrude into the wild.

Hit Die: d6.

REQUIREMENTS

To qualify to become a daggerspell shaper, a character must fulfill all the following criteria.

Alignment: Any nonevil.
Skills: Concentration 8 ranks.
Feats: Weapon Focus (dagger), Two-Weapon Fighting.
Special: Wild shape class feature.
Special: Either sneak attack +1d6 or skirmish +1d6.

CLASS SKILLS

The daggerspell shaper's class skills (and the key ability for each skill) are Balance (Dex), Climb (Str), Concentration (Con), Craft (Int), Handle Animal (Cha), Heal (Wis), Hide (Dex), Jump (Str), Knowledge (nature) (Int), Listen (Wis), Move Silently (Dex), Profession (Wis), Ride (Dex), Spellcraft (Int), Spot (Wis), Survival (Wis), Swim (Str), and Tumble (Dex).

Skill Points at Each Level: 6 + Int modifier.

CLASS FEATURES

All of the following are class features of the daggerspell shaper prestige class.

Weapon and Armor Proficiency: Daggerspell shapers gain no proficiency with any weapon or armor.

Daggercast (Ex): Daggerspell shapers seamlessly blend the use of their twin daggers with powerful spellcasting abilities. A daggerspell shaper can cast a spell with somatic and material components even when holding a dagger in each hand. If a daggerspell shaper holds anything other than a dagger, she must have at least one hand free to cast a spell with somatic or material components. Casting a spell in this way still provokes attacks of opportunity normally.

In addition, a daggerspell shaper can deliver a touch spell with a dagger attack (either a melee touch attack or a normal melee attack, but not with a thrown dagger).

Wild Shape (Su): A daggerspell shaper can change into a Small or Medium animal and back again, and can do so more often than most other characters with the wild shape

TABLE 2–6: THE DAGGERSPELL SHAPER

Level	Base Attack Bonus	Fort Save	Ref Save	Will Save	Special	Spells per Day/Spells Known
1st	+0	+0	+2	+2	Daggercast, wild shape (+1/day)	—
2nd	+1	+0	+3	+3	Dagger claws, wild shape (Tiny)	+1 level of existing divine spellcasting class
3rd	+2	+1	+3	+3	Sneak attack +1d6	+1 level of existing divine spellcasting class
4th	+3	+1	+4	+4	Wild shape (Large)	+1 level of existing divine spellcasting class
5th	+3	+1	+4	+4	Wild shape (+2/day)	+1 level of existing divine spellcasting class
6th	+4	+2	+5	+5	Sneak attack +2d6	+1 level of existing divine spellcasting class
7th	+5	+2	+5	+5	Fast wild shape	+1 level of existing divine spellcasting class
8th	+6	+2	+6	+6	Enhanced wild shape	+1 level of existing divine spellcasting class
9th	+6	+3	+6	+6	Sneak attack +3d6	+1 level of existing divine spellcasting class
10th	+7	+3	+7	+7	Daggerspell flurry, wild shape (+3/day)	+1 level of existing divine spellcasting class

ability. See the druid class feature, page 37 of the *Player's Handbook*. This ability lasts for 1 hour per class level or until she changes back. Levels of the daggerspell shaper prestige class stack with druid levels for the purpose of determining the maximum duration of the wild shape ability; they do not stack for any other purpose (such as the size and type of creature that a shaper can become).

A daggerspell shaper gains one additional daily use of her wild shape ability at 1st level, 5th level, and 10th level.

At 2nd level, a daggerspell shaper becomes able to use her wild shape ability to take the form of a Tiny animal. At 4th level, she can use wild shape to take the form of a Large animal.

Dagger Claws (Su): When a daggerspell shaper of 2nd level or higher uses wild shape, she adds any magical properties of daggers that she is holding in each hand into the natural attacks of her new form. The magic of a single dagger affects only the natural attacks made with the corresponding limb in the shaper's animal form, not all her attacks. For example, a 2nd-level daggerspell shaper holding a +1 *flaming dagger* in one hand and a +2 *keen dagger* in the other hand transforms into a leopard. The daggers affect the claw attacks of her new form as follows: One gains a +1 bonus on attack and damage rolls and also gains the flaming special ability, and the other gains a +2 bonus on attack and damage rolls and also gains the keen special ability. If the assumed form does not have a claw or slam attack with a limb that corresponds to the druid's natural limbs, this ability has no effect. The bonuses from this ability last for the duration of the wild shape effect. When a shaper uses this ability, her natural weapons in animal form overcome damage reduction exactly as do the daggers that she was holding when she transformed. In the example above, the shaper would be able to overcome a foe's damage reduction as if both of her natural weapons were magic.

Spells per Day/Spells Known: Beginning at 2nd level, a daggerspell shaper gains new spells per day at each level

(and spells known, if applicable) as if she had also gained a level in a divine spellcasting class to which she belonged before adding the prestige class level. She does not, however, gain any other benefit a character of that class would have gained. If she had more than one divine spellcasting class before becoming a daggerspell shaper, she must decide to which class to add each level for the purpose of determining spells per day and spells known.

Sneak Attack (Ex): Beginning at 3rd level, a daggerspell shaper deals an extra 1d6 points of damage when flanking an opponent or at any time when the target would be denied its Dexterity bonus. This extra damage applies to ranged attacks only if the target is within 30 feet. It increases to 2d6 points at 6th level and 3d6 points at 9th level. See the rogue class feature, page 50 of the *Player's Handbook*. If a daggerspell shaper gets a sneak attack bonus from another source (such as levels of rogue), the bonuses on damage stack.

Fast Wild Shape (Ex): Starting at 7th level, a daggerspell shaper can use her wild shape ability as a move action rather than as a standard action.

Enhanced Wild Shape (Su): Starting at 8th level, a daggerspell shaper can preserve the physical enhancements granted by her equipment even when in wild shape. Whenever the shaper uses wild shape, she retains any enhancement bonuses to Strength, Dexterity, or Constitution granted by any equipment she wears, even if the equipment can't be worn normally by her new form.

Daggerspell Flurry (Ex): A 10th-level daggerspell shaper can blend spellcasting with a flurry of dagger attacks. When using this ability, the shaper can quicken one spell as part of a full attack with her daggers. Doing this has no effect on the spell's effective level. A daggerspell shaper must make at least one melee attack in any round in which she uses this ability, and she cannot make an attack with anything other than a dagger (although if a spell cast in conjunction with this ability requires an attack roll, she can still make the spell's attack).

A daggerspell shaper can use this ability a number of times per day equal to her Dexterity bonus (minimum 1).

SAMPLE DAGGERSPELL SHAPER

Zaadi Akanthas: Female human druid 5/rogue 1/daggerspell shaper 4; CR 10; Medium humanoid; HD 5d8 plus 5d6; hp 43; Init +2; Spd 30 ft.; AC 15, touch 12, flat-footed 13; Base Atk +6; Grp +7; Atk +9 melee (1d4+2/17–20, *+1 keen dagger*) or +8 ranged (1d6/×3, short-bow); Full Atk +7/+2 melee (1d4+2/17–20, *+1 keen dagger*) and +7 melee (1d4+1/19–20, *+1 dagger*) or +8/+3 ranged (1d6/×3, shortbow); SA daggercast, daggerclaws, sneak attack +2d6, spells; SQ animal companion (cheetah), animal companion benefits, resist nature's lure, trackless step, trapfinding, wild empathy +8 (+4 magical beasts), wild shape 2/day, woodland stride; AL CN; SV Fort +5, Ref +9, Will +11; Str 13, Dex 15, Con 10, Int 8, Wis 16, Cha 12.

Skills and Feats: Concentration +8, Handle Animal +7, Heal +7, Hide +4, Knowledge (nature) +9, Listen +7, Move Silently +4, Spot +7, Survival +11 (+13 in natural terrain), Tumble +6; Dodge, Mobility, Spring Attack, Two-Weapon Fighting, Weapon Focus (dagger).

Languages: Common; Druidic.

Animal Companion (Ex): Zaadi has a cheetah named Rula as her animal companion (see *Monster Manual*, page 271). Its bonus trick is attack.

Animal Companion Benefits: Zaadi and Rula enjoy the link and share spells special qualities.

Link (Ex): Zaadi can handle Rula as a free action. She also gains a +4 circumstance bonus on all wild empathy checks and Handle Animal checks made regarding her cheetah.

Share Spells (Ex): Zaadi can have any spell she casts on herself also affect her animal companion if Rula is within 5 feet at the time. She can also cast a spell with a target of "You" on Rula.

Daggercast (Ex): Zaadi can cast a spell with somatic and material components even when holding a dagger in each hand. If she holds anything other than a dagger, she must have at least one hand free to cast a spell with somatic or material components as normal. Casting a spell in this way still provokes attacks of opportunity normally. In addition, Zaadi can deliver a touch spell with a dagger attack (either a melee touch attack or a normal melee attack, but not with a thrown dagger).

Daggerclaws (Su): If Zaadi uses her wild shape ability to assume animal form while holding her magic daggers, she incorporates the daggers' enhancement bonuses and special qualities into the natural attacks of her wild-shaped form. One of her claw attacks gains a +1 enhancement bonus and the keen special ability (from her *+1 keen dagger*), and the other claw gains a +1 enhancement bonus (from her *+1 dagger*). The benefits last for the duration of the wild shape effect.

Resist Nature's Lure (Ex): Zaadi gains a +4 bonus on saving throws against the spell-like abilities of fey.

Sneak Attack (Ex): Zaadi deals an extra 2d6 points of damage on any successful attack against flat-footed or flanked targets, or against a target that has been denied its Dexterity bonus for any reason. This damage also applies to ranged attacks against targets up to 30 feet away. Creatures with concealment, creatures without discernible anatomies, and creatures immune to extra damage from critical hits are all immune to sneak attacks. Zaadi can choose to deliver nonlethal damage with her sneak attack, but only when using a weapon designed for that purpose, such as a sap (blackjack).

Trackless Step (Ex): Zaadi leaves no trail in natural surroundings and cannot be tracked.

Trapfinding (Ex): Zaadi can find, disarm, or bypass traps with a DC of 20 or higher. She can use the Search skill to find, and the Disable Device skill to disarm, magic traps (DC 25 + the level of the spell used to create it). If her Disable Device result exceeds the trap's DC by 10 or more, she discovers how to bypass the trap without triggering or disarming it.

Wild Shape (Su): Twice per day, Zaadi can change into a Tiny to Large animal and back again, as per the *polymorph* spell. Her preferred forms are that of a lion and a cheetah. This ability lasts for 9 hours or until she changes back.

Woodland Stride (Ex): Zaadi can move through natural thorns, briars, overgrown areas, and similar terrain at her normal speed and without damage or other impairment. However, thorns, briars, and overgrown areas that are magically manipulated to impede motion still affect her.

Druid Spells Prepared (caster level 8th): 0—*cure minor wounds, detect magic, detect poison, guidance, light, read magic;* 1st—*charm animal* (DC 14), *entangle* (DC 14), *faerie fire, longstrider, obscuring mist;* 2nd—*bull's strength, flame blade* (+9 melee touch), *resist energy, summon swarm;* 3rd—*cure moderate wounds, dominate animal* (DC 16), *greater magic fang, poison* (+9 melee touch, DC 16); 4th—*flame strike* (DC 17), *freedom of movement.*

Possessions: +1 leather armor of light fortification, *+1 keen dagger, +1 dagger,* shortbow with 20 arrows, 2 *potions of barkskin* (+2), *potion of invisibility,* scroll of *bear's endurance,* scroll of *cat's grace,* 5 gp.

DREAD PIRATE

Thugs and cutthroats in every port lay claim to the title "pirate," but actually making a fortune through piracy is no easy task. A dread pirate, however, has mastered every aspect of larceny on the high seas. His network of contacts tells him when a particularly valuable cargo is shipping out. After a flawless ambush at sea, he swings aboard the target ship on a rope, rapier in hand. Once he and his shipmates have overpowered the prize vessel's crew, they liberate the cargo and make their escape. Later, the dread pirate meets representatives from the black market in an isolated cove and sells his newly acquired cargo for a handsome profit.

Some dread pirates accomplish their goals through fear, killing indiscriminately and ruling their ships at rapier-point. Others minimize bloodshed and exhibit a curious sort of chivalry, perhaps realizing that the captain and crew of a prize ship are more likely to surrender if they believe they will live to see port again. Now and then a dread pirate takes his chivalric streak a step farther and preys only on the ships of enemy nations—or even solely on other pirates.

A dread pirate's lifestyle is ideal for most rogues, because the job requires a number of skills that other classes don't have the time or inclination to learn. However, the class also attracts some spellcasters, who can use magic to conceal their ships or incapacitate a prize vessel's crew.

Adaptation: The dread pirate prestige class can be used to represent any powerful individual with great nautical skill. A famous admiral and a ruthless but honest privateer might not differ in abilities, but they will certainly differ in outlook and demeanor.

Hit Die: d8.

REQUIREMENTS

To qualify to become a dread pirate, a character must fulfill all the following criteria.

Alignment: Any nonlawful.

Base Attack Bonus: +4.

Skills: Appraise 8 ranks, Profession (sailor) 8 ranks, Swim 4 ranks, Use Rope 4 ranks.

Feats: Quick Draw, Weapon Finesse.

Special: The character must own a ship worth at least 10,000 gp. The method of acquisition—purchase, force of arms, or skullduggery—makes no difference, as long as he can freely operate it on the high seas.

CLASS SKILLS

The dread pirate's class skills (and the key ability for each skill) are Appraise (Int), Balance (Dex), Bluff (Cha), Climb (Str), Craft (Int), Gather Information (Cha), Intimidate (Cha), Jump (Str), Listen (Wis), Perform (Cha), Profession (Wis), Search (Int), Sense Motive (Wis), Sleight of Hand (Dex), Spot (Wis), Swim (Str), Tumble (Dex), and Use Rope (Dex).

Skill Points at Each Level: 6 + Int modifier.

CLASS FEATURES

All of the following are class features of the dread pirate prestige class.

Weapon and Armor Proficiency: Dread pirates are proficient with all simple weapons, with light martial weapons, and with the rapier. Dread pirates are proficient with light armor but not with shields.

Seamanship (Ex): A dread pirate adds his class level as an insight bonus on all Profession (sailor) checks. Allies within sight or hearing of a dread pirate add an insight bonus equal to half this number on their Profession (sailor) checks.

Two-Weapon Fighting: A dread pirate wearing light or no armor is treated as having the Two-Weapon Fighting feat, even if he does not have the prerequisites for the feat.

Fearsome Reputation (Ex): By the time he attains 2nd level, a dread pirate has developed a reputation on the high seas. At this point, he must choose whether to cultivate a reputation as an honorable pirate (avoiding undue bloodshed, honoring flags of truce, and the like) or as a dishonorable pirate (favoring mayhem and dire treatment of prisoners).

An honorable dread pirate gains a +2 circumstance bonus on Diplomacy checks, while a dishonorable one gains a +2 circumstance bonus on Intimidate checks. This bonus increases to +4 at 6th level and to +6 at 10th level. In addition, a dread pirate gains other abilities at higher levels based on his chosen reputation.

A dread pirate's actual activities or alignment need not match his reputation. However, a radical shift away from his reputation might negate or even reverse that reputation at the DM's option. Also, a dread pirate in disguise does not gain any effect granted by his reputation (including the special abilities described below that depend on the dread pirate's reputation).

Rally the Crew (Ex): Starting at 3rd level, an honorable dread pirate can inspire his allies (including himself) to great bravery in combat once per day. This inspiration grants them a +1 morale bonus on saving throws against charm and fear effects and a +1 morale bonus on attack rolls and weapon damage rolls. To be affected, an ally must be able to see or hear the dread pirate. The effect requires a free action to activate and lasts for 1 minute per class level, even if the dread pirate moves out of range or loses consciousness. This is a mind-affecting ability.

At 7th level, a dread pirate can use this ability twice per day, and the bonus increases to +2.

If a dread pirate has the inspire courage bardic music ability, he can add the morale bonus gained from that ability to the morale bonus gained from this ability to determine the total morale bonus granted. For example, an 8th-level bard/3rd-level dread pirate would provide a +3 morale bonus on attack rolls and weapon damage rolls.

Sneak Attack (Ex): Beginning at 3rd level, a dishonorable dread pirate deals an extra 1d6 points of damage when flanking an opponent or at any time when the target would be denied its Dexterity bonus. This extra damage applies to ranged attacks only if the target is within 30 feet. See the rogue class feature, page 50 of the *Player's Handbook*. The amount of extra damage dealt increases to 2d6 at 7th level. If a dishonorable dread pirate gets a sneak attack bonus from another source (such as levels of rogue), the bonuses on damage stack.

Acrobatic Charge (Ex): A dread pirate of 4th level or higher can charge over difficult terrain that normally slows movement or through the squares occupied by allies blocking his path. This ability enables him to charge across a cluttered ship's deck, leap down from a higher deck, or swing between two adjacent ships to get to his target. Depending on the circumstances, he might still need to make appropriate checks (such as Jump, Tumble,

*Daniel "the Daft" Simone,
a dread pirate*

or Use Rope checks) to successfully move over the terrain.

Steady Stance (Ex): At 4th level and higher, a dread pirate remains stable on his feet when others have difficulty standing. He is not considered flat-footed while balancing or climbing, and he adds his class level as a bonus on Balance or Climb checks to remain balancing or climbing when he takes damage.

Luck of the Wind (Ex): Once per day, an honorable dread pirate of 5th level or higher can reroll any failed attack roll, skill check, ability check, or saving throw. He must take the result of the reroll, even if it's worse than the original roll.

Scourge of the Seas (Ex): Starting at 5th level, a dishonorable dread pirate can instill fear into his enemies. When the character uses Intimidate to demoralize foes, the attempt affects all enemies within 30 feet who can see and hear him, and the effect lasts for a number of rounds equal to his Charisma modifier (minimum 1 round). Multiple uses of this ability don't stack. This is a mind-affecting ability.

Skill Mastery (Ex): At 8th level, a dread pirate becomes supremely confident of his mobility. He has mastered the skills Balance, Climb, Jump, and Tumble to the extent that he can take 10 with them even under stress.

Fight to the Death (Ex): At 9th level and higher, an honorable dread pirate can inspire his allies to carry on against tremendous odds. Each ally affected by the dread pirate's rally the crew ability (see above) also gains temporary hit points equal to 10 + the dread pirate's Cha bonus (minimum 10), gains a dodge bonus to Armor Class equal to the dread pirate's Cha bonus (minimum +1), and is treated as having the Diehard feat even if he doesn't meet the prerequisites. These effects are lost if the dread pirate loses consciousness.

Motivate the Scum (Ex): Once per day, a dishonorable dread pirate of 9th level or higher can motivate his allies by killing a helpless individual. All allies of the dread pirate who see the act gain a +2 morale bonus on damage rolls. This effect lasts for 24 hours.

Most dishonorable dread pirates don't care whether the victim is a prisoner or one of their own crew. In fact, if the slain individual is one of the dread pirate's crew, the morale bonus on damage rolls improves to +4, but the allies also take a –2 penalty on Will saves for the duration of the effect.

Pirate King (Ex): A 10th-level dread pirate's exploits have become so legendary that great numbers of able sailors are willing to sign on as his crew for no compensation other than a share of the booty. Treat this ability as the equivalent of the Leadership feat, except that only followers (and no cohorts) are gained.

SAMPLE DREAD PIRATE

Captain Daniel "the Daft" Simone: Male human bard 3/fighter 2/honorable dread pirate 4; CR 9; Medium humanoid; HD 3d6 plus 2d10 plus 4d8; hp 42; Init +4; Spd 30 ft.; AC 19, touch 14, flat-footed 14; Base Atk +8; Grp +9; Atk +13 melee (1d6+2/18–20, +1 *rapier*) or +13 ranged (1d4+1/19–20, masterwork dagger); Full Atk +11/+6 melee (1d6+2/18–20, +1 *rapier*) and +11 melee (1d4+1/19–20, masterwork dagger); or +13 ranged (1d4+1/19–20, masterwork dagger); SA spells; SQ acrobatic charge, bardic knowledge +4, bardic music 3/day (countersong, *fascinate*, inspire competence, inspire courage), fearsome reputation +2, rally the crew, seamanship +4 (+2 for allies), steady stance; AL CG; SV Fort +5, Ref +11, Will +4 (+7 against mind-affecting effects); Str 12, Dex 19, Con 10, Int 13, Wis 8, Cha 14.

Skills and Feats: Appraise +9, Balance +10, Bluff +8, Climb +5, Diplomacy +12, Disguise +2 (+4 acting in character), Escape Artist +10, Intimidate +4, Jump +13, Perform (oratory) +8, Profession (sailor) +11, Spot +7, Swim +9, Tumble +16, Use Rope +8 (+10 involving bindings);

Table 2–7: The Dread Pirate

Level	Base Attack Bonus	Fort Save	Ref Save	Will Save	Special
1st	+1	+0	+2	+0	Seamanship, two-weapon fighting
2nd	+2	+0	+3	+0	Fearsome reputation +2
3rd	+3	+1	+3	+1	Rally the crew +1 (1/day) or sneak attack +1d6
4th	+4	+1	+4	+1	Acrobatic charge, steady stance
5th	+5	+1	+4	+1	Luck of the wind or scourge of the seas
6th	+6	+2	+5	+2	Fearsome reputation +4
7th	+7	+2	+5	+2	Rally the crew +2 (2/day) or sneak attack +2d6
8th	+8	+2	+6	+2	Skill mastery
9th	+9	+3	+6	+3	Fight to the death or motivate the scum
10th	+10	+3	+7	+3	Fearsome reputation +6, pirate king

Combat Expertise, Combat Reflexes, Expert Tactician†, Force of Personality†, Improved Disarm, Quick Draw, Two-Weapon Fighting^B, Weapon Finesse.

† New feat described in Chapter 3.

Languages: Common; Elven.

Acrobatic Charge (Ex): Daniel can charge over difficult terrain that normally slows movement or allies blocking his path.

Bardic Music: Use bardic music three times per day. See the bard class feature, page 29 of the *Player's Handbook*.

Countersong (Su): Use music or poetics to counter magical effects that depend on sound.

Fascinate (Sp): Use music or poetics to cause one or more creatures to become fascinated with him.

Inspire Competence (Su): Use music or poetics to help an ally succeed at a task.

THE PIRATE CODE

Most pirate codes share a number of elements regarding the proper "etiquette" of piracy. Here are a few ideas that might be appropriate for your dread pirate's personal code:

- Everyone shall obey all orders.
- Everyone shall have a vote in major decisions. (This point is not necessarily limited to honorable dread pirates.)
- Everyone shall have a share of captured food and drink.
- Booty will be shared out as follows: one share to each among the crew; one and one-half shares each to the first mate, master carpenter, and boatswain; and two shares to the captain. (Some honorable captains might accept a smaller

share, but they will take no fewer than one and one-half shares.)
- Anyone not keeping his weapons clean and fit for an engagement shall be cut off from his share, and suffer other punishment as the captain deems fit.
- Anyone who strikes another among the crew shall receive forty lashes across his back.
- Anyone who attempts to desert or keep any secret from the company shall be marooned with one bottle of water and one weapon.
- Anyone who steals from a crewmate shall be marooned or run through. (The latter consequence is more appropriate for dishonorable dread pirates.)

Inspire Courage (Su): Use music or poetics to bolster his allies against fear and improve their combat abilities.

Rally the Crew (Ex): Once per day, Daniel can inspire his allies (including himself) to great bravery in combat, granting them a +2 morale bonus on saving throws against charm and fear effects and a +2 morale bonus on attack and weapon damage rolls. To be affected, an ally must be able to see or hear Daniel. The effect requires a free action to activate and lasts for 4 minutes, even if Daniel moves out of range or loses consciousness. This is a mind-affecting ability.

Steady Stance (Ex): Daniel is not considered flat-footed while balancing or climbing, and he gains a +4 bonus on Balance or Climb checks to remain balancing or climbing when he takes damage.

Bard Spells Known (3/2; caster level 3rd): 0—*dancing lights, daze* (DC 12), *ghost sound* (DC 12), *know direction, mage hand, message;* 1st—*animate rope, inspirational boost†, sleep* (DC 13).

Possessions: +2 studded leather armor, +1 rapier, masterwork dagger, *gloves of Dexterity +2,* sailing ship, 1,000 gp, 2,000 sp, 5,000 cp.

† New spell described on page 153.

DUNGEON DELVER

In many ways, the dungeon delver is the ultimate adventuring rogue. He's skilled at moving stealthily through all types of dungeon terrain, detecting and disarming inconvenient traps, bypassing locks, locating treasure, and filching protected items.

Since a dungeon delver frequently works alone, he must learn to think and act independently, relying upon no one but himself. Even when exploring a dungeon in the company of other adventurers, he often keeps to himself—scouting ahead, disarming traps a safe distance from the group, or seeking treasure while the others are distracted.

The typical dungeon delver has forsaken interaction skills to concentrate on the nuts and bolts of dungeon exploration and treasure retrieval. Rogues and scouts make excellent dungeon delvers, as do the rare few ninjas and spellthieves who choose to pursue this track. Multiclass rogue/rangers who favor the darkness of caverns to the light of the sky also make good dungeon delvers.

The best NPC dungeon delvers become legends and are sought after by anyone with a particularly inaccessible treasure to recover. Some even accept regular stipends from various nobles to leave their treasures alone. Only the best survive to make names for themselves, however—those who lack the necessary skill and savvy perish anonymously on unsuccessful expeditions, leaving behind their bones for some luckier compatriot to discover.

Adaptation: Some of the most interesting adaptations for the dungeon delver prestige class involve associating it with a certain race. Although dwarves and gnomes are natural choices because of their ties with underground life, dungeon delvers of less obvious races such as humans, dark elves, and halflings are interesting as well because such characters offer something other than the stereotypical depiction of their race. The dungeon delver and the nightsong infiltrator (see page 62) also serve as interesting roguelike prestige classes that do not rely on the sneak attack ability and might serve as a model for making similar prestige classes in your own campaign.

Hit Die: d6.

REQUIREMENTS

To qualify to become a dungeon delver, a character must fulfill all the following criteria.

Skills: Climb 10 ranks, Craft (stonemasonry) 5 ranks, Disable Device 10 ranks, Hide 5 ranks, Knowledge (dungeoneering) 5 ranks, Move Silently 5 ranks, Open Lock 10 ranks, Search 10 ranks.

Feats: Alertness, Blind-Fight.

Special: Trapfinding class feature.

Special: The character must survive a great trial underground. This trial usually takes one of three forms:

- A solo dungeon expedition that earns the character half of the experience points needed for advancement to the next level. (For example, a 7th-level character must earn 3,500 XP on such a solo run.) The character must complete the venture in one week, though he may leave the dungeon and return as often as desired during that time.
- Survival of a cave-in or other collapse (see page 66 of the *Dungeon Master's Guide*).
- Living for a year without seeing the light of the sun, usually among underground denizens such as the deep dwarves or drow.

CLASS SKILLS

The dungeon delver's class skills (and the key ability for each skill) are Appraise (Int), Balance (Dex), Climb (Str), Craft (Int), Disable Device (Int), Hide (Dex), Jump (Str), Knowledge (dungeoneering) (Int), Listen (Wis), Move Silently (Dex), Open Lock (Dex), Search (Int), Spot (Wis), Survival (Wis), Swim (Str), Tumble (Dex), Use Magic Device (Cha), and Use Rope (Dex).

Skill Points at Each Level: 8 + Int modifier.

CLASS FEATURES

All of the following are class features of the dungeon delver prestige class.

Weapon and Armor Proficiency: Dungeon delvers gain no proficiency with any weapon or armor.

Darkvision (Ex): A dungeon delver's long exposure to pitch-black subterranean surroundings enables him to develop darkvision out to 60 feet. If the character already has darkvision, the range increases by 30 feet.

Deep Survival (Ex): A dungeon delver's experience in deep, dark places grants him a great familiarity with that world. He adds his class level to Survival checks made in underground environments.

Trap Sense (Ex): A dungeon delver is adept at evading the effects of traps. See the barbarian class feature, page 26 of the *Player's Handbook*. The bonuses rise by 1 for every three additional dungeon delver levels gained (+2 at 4th level, +3 at 7th level, and +4 at 10th level) and stack with similar bonuses granted by other classes.

Reduce (Sp): A dungeon delver frequently finds it necessary to squeeze through narrow crevices, half-collapsed passages, prison bars, and other tight spots that would normally block a character of his size and bulk. Starting at 2nd level, a dungeon delver can use *reduce person* on himself three times per day (regardless of his creature type). His caster level is equal to his class level.

Morzul Darkhunter, a dungeon delver

Stonecunning (Ex): At 2nd level, a dungeon delver gains the stonecunning ability. This functions exactly as the dwarf racial trait of the same name (see page 15 of the *Player's Handbook*), except that the check modifiers are competence bonuses rather than racial bonuses. If a dungeon delver already has stonecunning because of his race, both sets of bonuses apply.

Augury (Sp): Beginning at 3rd level, a dungeon delver can foretell whether a particular action will bring good or bad results for him in the immediate future. Once per day, he can use *augury* as a free action; his caster level is equal to his class level. He can use this ability one additional time per day for every three additional class levels gained (2/day at 6th level and 3/day at 9th level).

Skill Mastery (Ex): At 3rd level, a dungeon delver becomes so confident in the use of certain skills that he can use them reliably even under adverse conditions. The character selects a number of skills equal to 3 + his Intelligence modifier. See the rogue class feature, page 51 of the *Player's Handbook*.

Evasion (Ex): Beginning at 4th level, a dungeon delver can avoid damage from certain attacks with a successful Reflex save. See the monk class feature, page 41 of the *Player's Handbook*.

If a dungeon delver already has evasion, he gains improved evasion instead, allowing him to avoid damage from certain attacks with a successful Reflex save and take only half damage on a failed save. See the monk class feature, page 42 of the *Player's Handbook*.

Blindsense (Ex): At 5th level, a dungeon delver gains the ability to activate an acute sensitivity to sounds, smells, movement, and other disturbances within 30 feet. This functions as described on page 306 of the *Monster Manual* and lasts for 1 minute per class level. A dungeon delver can use blindsense once per day at 5th level and twice per day at 10th level.

Passwall (Sp): Starting at 6th level, a dungeon delver can use *passwall* once per day as a caster of his class level. This ability comes in handy for bypassing small cave-ins or sneaking into vaults.

Find the Path (Sp): Starting at 8th level, a dungeon delver can use *find the path* twice per day as a caster of his class level. Typically, a delver uses this to find his way into and out of confounding mazes and dungeons. He can target only himself with the ability.

Phase Door (Sp): At 9th level, a dungeon delver gains the ability to use *phase door* once per day as an 18th-level caster. This ability enables him to bypass cave-ins, walk through dead ends and immovable obstructions, and make quick escapes through walls.

Illus. by S. Belledin

TABLE 2–8: THE DUNGEON DELVER

Level	Base Attack Bonus	Fort Save	Ref Save	Will Save	Special
1st	+0	+2	+2	+0	Darkvision, deep survival, trap sense +1
2nd	+1	+3	+3	+0	*Reduce*, stonecunning
3rd	+2	+3	+3	+1	*Augury* 1/day, skill mastery
4th	+3	+4	+4	+1	Evasion, trap sense +2
5th	+3	+4	+4	+1	Blindsense 1/day
6th	+4	+5	+5	+2	*Augury* 2/day, *passwall*
7th	+5	+5	+5	+2	Trap sense +3
8th	+6	+6	+6	+2	*Find the path*
9th	+6	+6	+6	+3	*Augury* 3/day, *phase door*
10th	+7	+7	+7	+3	Blindsense 2/day, trap sense +4

SAMPLE DUNGEON DELVER

Morzul Darkhunter: Male dwarf rogue 7/dungeon delver 3; Medium humanoid; CR 10; HD 10d6+30; hp 67; Init +8; Spd 20 ft.; AC 21, touch 15, flat-footed 21; Base Atk +7; Grp +9; Atk +12 melee (1d6+3/19–20, *+1 short sword*) or +12 ranged (1d8+1/19–20, masterwork light crossbow with *+1 bolt*); Full Atk +12/+7 melee (1d6+3/19–20, *+1 short sword*) or +12 ranged (1d8+1/19–20, masterwork light crossbow with *+1 bolt*); SA sneak attack +4d6; SQ *augury* 1/day, darkvision 90 ft., deep survival, dwarf traits, evasion, *reduce* 3/day, skill mastery, trap sense +3, trapfinding, uncanny dodge; AL NG; SV Fort +8* (+10 against poison), Ref +12*, Will +3*; Str 14, Dex 18, Con 16, Int 12, Wis 10, Cha 6.

Skills and Feats: Appraise +4 (+6 with metalwork, +8 with stonework), Climb^{SM} +12, Craft (stonemasonry) +8, Disable Device^{SM} +16, Escape Artist +9, Hide +17, Jump –4, Listen +2, Knowledge (dungeoneering) +6, Move Silently +17, Open Lock^{SM} +16, Search^{SM} +14, Spot +15, Survival +0 (+5 underground, +2 following tracks), Swim +5, Use Rope +7 (+9 with bindings); Alertness, Blind-Fight, Improved Initiative, Weapon Finesse.

Languages: Common, Dwarven; Undercommon.

Augury (Sp): Morzul can use *augury* once per day as a free action. Caster level 3rd.

Dwarf Traits: Dwarves have stonecunning, which grants them a +2 racial bonus on Search checks to notice unusual stonework. A dwarf who merely comes within 10 feet of it can make a Search check as if actively searching. Morzul adds his racial bonuses to his dungeon delver class bonuses to determine his total stonecunning bonuses.

When standing on the ground, dwarves are exceptionally stable and have a +4 bonus on ability checks made to resist being bull rushed or tripped. Dwarves have a +1 racial bonus on attack rolls against orcs and goblinoids

and a +4 racial bonus to Armor Class against giants. Their race also gives them a +2 bonus on Appraise or Craft checks that are related to stone or metal items.

*Dwarves have a +2 racial bonus on saving throws against spells and spell-like effects.

Evasion (Ex): If Morzul is exposed to any effect that normally allows him to attempt a Reflex saving throw for half damage, he takes no damage with a successful saving throw.

Reduce (Sp): Morzul can use *reduce person* (self only) three times per day. Caster level 3rd.

Skill Mastery (Ex): Morzul has mastered the skills Climb, Disable Device, Open Lock, and Search to the extent that he can take 10 with them even under stress. These skills are designated by ^{SM} in the statistics block.

Sneak Attack (Ex): Morzul deals an extra 4d6 points of damage on any successful attack against flat-footed or flanked targets, or against a target that has been denied its Dexterity bonus for any reason. This damage also applies to ranged attacks against targets up to 30 feet away. Creatures with concealment, creatures without discernible anatomies, and creatures immune to extra damage from critical hits are all immune to sneak attacks. Morzul can choose to deliver nonlethal damage with his sneak attack, but only when using a weapon designed for that purpose, such as a sap (blackjack).

Trapfinding (Ex): Morzul can find, disarm, or bypass traps with a DC of 20 or higher. He can use the Search skill to find, and the Disable Device skill to disarm, magic traps (DC 25 + the level of the spell used to create it). If his Disable Device result exceeds the trap's DC by 10 or more, he discovers how to bypass the trap without triggering or disarming it.

Uncanny Dodge (Ex): Morzul retains his Dexterity bonus to AC even when flat-footed or targeted by an unseen foe (he still loses his Dexterity bonus if paralyzed or otherwise immobile).

Possessions: *+2 mithral shirt*, *ring of protection +1*, *+1 short sword*, masterwork light crossbow, 25 *+1 bolts*, 10 silver bolts, 10 cold iron bolts, *gauntlets of Dexterity +2*, *Heward's handy haversack*, 4 *potions of cure light wounds*, 50-ft. coil of silk rope, grappling hook, masterwork thieves' tools.

EXEMPLAR

An exemplar is someone who believes that most individuals and creatures possess a wellspring of untapped talent and capability, and that the multiverse would be a better place if only they would all try to live up to their potential. To her mind, the best way to encourage this behavior in others is to exemplify it herself. An exemplar focuses her energy on improving the skills she possesses until she is able to perform them with fluidity, grace, and art. She believes that even the simplest action (such as climbing a tree or building a chair) can be done with such skill and flair as to inspire awe and stimulate a desire for self-betterment. No matter what area a particular exemplar excels in, be it walking a tightrope, deciphering forgotten languages, or remembering the names of every archfiend in the Abyss, she performs it with passion and joy.

Bards are the characters most likely to become exemplars, but wizards, rogues, rangers, and druids sometimes choose this path as well. All of these classes have a fair number of people who believe that their actions can be viewed as art, and like most artists they want to inspire others with their abilities. Clerics, paladins, and monks also choose this prestige class on rare occasions, but their dedication to promoting a philosophy or a higher power sometimes conflicts with the exemplar's belief that the best way to inspire others is simply to be a good role model.

NPC exemplars often are eccentric characters who travel the multiverse, stopping anywhere that catches their interest. Some might be nobles or members of rich merchant families who use their reputations to open doors at the courts of powerful and influential individuals, hoping that their example will help their hosts become wiser rulers. Other exemplars are mendicants or wandering sages, traveling among the common folk in the hopes of inspiring the people to improve their lots in life. The great majority of exemplars are just ordinary characters making livings as bakers, blacksmiths, merchants, or even adventurers. No matter what their jobs, though, at their hearts they are all educators, hoping to improve the multiverse by setting a good example.

Adaptation: The easiest way to customize the exemplar prestige class is to choose one skill that several exemplars specialize in and describe them as a separate class or organization. The exemplars of the Spot skill, for example, might become the Watchers of Ordoanai, a group of mercenary scouts and bodyguards. The exemplars of

the Tumble skill could be described as the Blue Circle Acrobats, a troupe of performers who work secretly as assassins and use their performance as a front.

Hit Die: d6.

REQUIREMENTS

To qualify to become an exemplar, a character must fulfill all the following criteria.

Skills: Diplomacy 6 ranks, any other skill 13 ranks.

Feat: Skill Focus (any).

CLASS SKILLS

All skills are class skills for an exemplar.

Skill Points at Each Level: 8 + Int modifier.

CLASS FEATURES

All of the following are class features of the exemplar prestige class.

Weapon and Armor Proficiency: Exemplars gain no proficiency with any weapon or armor.

Skill Artistry (Ex): An exemplar is particularly talented in the use of one of her skills. Choose one skill in which the exemplar has at least 13 ranks. She gains a +4 competence bonus on all checks involving that skill.

At 4th, 7th, and 10th levels, an exemplar gains this ability again. Each time she selects a different skill to receive the +4 competence bonus, provided she has at least 13 ranks in a skill that she has not yet chosen to benefit from this ability. If not, she gains no benefit from the ability until she has 13 ranks in another skill. She can then immediately apply the benefit of skill artistry to that skill.

Skill Mastery (Ex): An exemplar is so confident in the use of certain skills that she can use them reliably even under adverse conditions. She selects a number of skills equal to 1 + her Int modifier. When making a check with one of these skills, she can take 10 even if stress and distractions would normally prevent her from

Brieta Oestrow, an exemplar

Illus. by J. Miracola

doing so. Each time an exemplar gains a class level, she can add another skill to the list of skills with which she has mastery.

Lend Talent (Ex): Starting at 2nd level, an exemplar can lend some of her skill artistry to allies, allowing them to exceed their normal talents. By accepting a penalty on checks using a skill for which she has selected skill artistry, an exemplar grants a competence bonus on checks with that skill to all allies within 30 feet. The penalty can be any number that does not exceed the exemplar's class level, and the competence bonus is equal to one-half the penalty. Activating this ability is a full-round action, and the effect lasts for as long as the exemplar remains conscious and within range.

For example, a 4th-level exemplar who has selected skill artistry with Craft (armorsmithing) can accept a −4 penalty on Craft (armorsmithing) checks to grant all allies within 30 feet a +2 competence bonus on Craft (armorsmithing) checks for as long as she remains nearby.

At 8th level, the competence bonus granted by this ability becomes equal to the penalty accepted by the exemplar.

Bonus Feat: At 3rd, 6th, and 9th levels, an exemplar gains a bonus feat, which must be selected from the following list: Acrobatic, Agile, Alertness, Animal Affinity, Athletic, Blind-Fight, Combat Casting, Combat Expertise, Deceitful, Deft Hands, Diligent, Improved Initiative, Improved Swimming†, Investigator, Magical Aptitude, Negotiator, Nimble Fingers, Open Minded†, Persuasive, Self-Sufficient, Skill Focus, Stealthy, Track, or Versatile Performer†. The exemplar must meet all the prerequisites for the chosen feat.

† New feat described in Chapter 3.

Sustaining Presence (Su): Starting at 4th level, an exemplar knows how to call upon her force of personality to help keep herself alive in tense or dangerous situations. She adds her Charisma bonus (if any) to her Concentration checks and Fortitude saves.

Persuasive Performance (Ex): Starting at 5th level, an exemplar can use her skill artistry to improve the attitudes of NPCs. To do this, the NPCs must observe her using one of the skills to which she has applied skill artistry. Treat this as a Diplomacy check made to influence NPC attitudes (see pages 71–72 of the *Player's Handbook*), but replace the Diplomacy check with a check using the chosen skill.

The demonstration must be nonthreatening and intended to entertain and amuse the onlookers. Viewers must be within 30 feet of the exemplar, must be able to see her clearly, and must willingly pay attention to her

actions. This ability requires at least 1 minute to perform, and it can affect a particular creature only once every 24 hours.

Intellectual Agility (Su): Starting at 8th level, an exemplar can channel her intellect to more physical needs. She adds her Intelligence bonus (if any) to her initiative checks and Reflex saves.

Perfect Self: A 10th-level exemplar has tuned her body with skill to the point that she becomes a magical creature. Her type changes to outsider (native). See the monk class feature, page 42 of the *Player's Handbook*.

TABLE 2–9: THE EXEMPLAR

Level	Base Attack Bonus	Fort Save	Ref Save	Will Save	Special
1st	+0	+0	+0	+2	Skill artistry, skill mastery
2nd	+1	+0	+0	+3	Lend talent (one-half penalty)
3rd	+2	+1	+1	+3	Bonus feat
4th	+3	+1	+1	+4	Skill artistry, sustaining presence
5th	+3	+1	+1	+4	Persuasive performance
6th	+4	+2	+2	+5	Bonus feat
7th	+5	+2	+2	+5	Skill artistry
8th	+6	+2	+2	+6	Intellectual agility, lend talent (equal to penalty)
9th	+6	+3	+3	+6	Bonus feat
10th	+7	+3	+3	+7	Perfect self, skill artistry

SAMPLE EXEMPLAR

Brieta Oestrow: Female gnome bard 10/exemplar 4; CR 14; Small humanoid; HD 14d6; hp 51; Init +1; Spd 30 ft.; AC 18, touch 14, flat-footed 17; Base Atk +8; Grp +3; Atk +11 melee (1d4/18–20, *+1 rapier*) or +11 ranged (1d6/19–20, masterwork light crossbow); Full Atk +11/+6 melee (1d4/18–20, *+1 rapier*) or +11 ranged (1d6/19–20, masterwork light crossbow); SA spells, spell-like abilities; SQ bardic knowledge +12, bardic music 10/day (countersong, *fascinate*, inspire competence, inspire courage, inspire greatness, suggestion), gnome traits, lend talent, low-light vision, skill mastery; AL CG; SV Fort +9*, Ref +6*, Will +9*; Str 8, Dex 12, Con 10, Int 14, Wis 13, Cha 22.

Skills and Feats: Balance +16, Bluff^{SM} +23, Concentration^{SM} +19, Diplomacy +23, Gather Information +8, Hide^{SM} +5, Intimidate +8, Jump +21, Knowledge (local) +8, Listen +3, Perform (sing)^{SM} +26, Sense Motive^{SM} +13, Spot +9, Tumble^{SM} +22, Use Magic Device +23; Acrobatic^{B}, Combat Expertise, Disguise Spell†, Skill Focus (Perform [sing]), Versatile Performer†, Weapon Finesse.

† New feat described in Chapter 3.

Languages: Common, Gnome; Draconic, Dwarven.

Bardic Music: Use bardic music ten times per day. See the bard class feature, page 29 of the *Player's Handbook.*

Countersong (Su): Use music or poetics to counter magical effects that depend on sound.

Fascinate (Sp): Use music or poetics to cause one or more creatures to become fascinated with her.

Inspire Competence (Su): Use music or poetics to help an ally succeed at a task.

Inspire Courage (Su): Use music or poetics to bolster her allies against fear and improve their combat abilities.

Inspire Greatness (Su): Use music or poetics to inspire greatness in herself or an ally, granting her target extra fighting capability.

Suggestion (Sp): Use music or poetics to make a *suggestion* (as the spell) to a creature that she has already fascinated.

Gnome Traits: Gnomes have a +1 racial bonus on attack rolls against kobolds and goblinoids. Gnomes have a +4 racial bonus to Armor Class against giants.

*Gnomes have a +2 racial bonus on saving throws against illusions.

Spell-Like Abilities: 1/day—*dancing lights, ghost sound* (DC 16), *prestidigitation, speak with animals* (burrowing mammal only, duration 1 minute).

Lend Talent (Ex): By accepting a penalty on Perform (sing) or Tumble checks, Brieta grants a competence bonus on checks with those skills to all allies within 30 feet. The penalty can be up to –4, and the competence bonus is equal to one-half the penalty. Activating this ability is a full-round action, and the effect lasts for as long as she remains conscious and within range.

Skill Mastery (Ex): Brieta has mastered the skills Bluff, Concentration, Hide, Perform, Sense Motive, and Tumble to the extent that she can take 10 with them even under stress. These skills are designated by ᔆᴹ in the statistics block.

Bard Spells Known (3/5/5/3/1; caster level 10th): 0—*dancing lights, detect magic, ghost sound* (DC 16), *lullaby* (DC 16), *mage hand, read magic;* 1st—*accelerated movement†, animate rope, distort speech†* (DC 17), *feather fall;* 2nd—*bladeweave†* (DC 18), *silence* (DC 18), *suggestion* (DC 18), *swift invisibility†;* 3rd—*blink, glibness, sculpt sound, speechlink†;* 4th—*cure critical wounds, freedom of movement.*

† New spell described in Chapter 5.

Possessions: amulet of natural armor +1, bracers of armor +3, ring of protection +2, +1 rapier, masterwork light crossbow, 10 bolts, 10 cold iron bolts, *boots of striding and springing, cloak of Charisma +4,* gold ring with amethyst (1,700 gp), 26 pp.

FOCHLUCAN LYRIST

Warrior, thief, spy, poet, woodland champion—the Fochlucan lyrist is a legendary figure who serves as the herald and teacher to great kings, the champion of the common folk, and the keeper of lore long forgotten elsewhere. Only the best and brightest are invited to become Fochlucan lyrists, and those who eventually win the approval of the Fochlucan College's masters are remarkable individuals indeed, skilled in swordplay, magic, and diplomacy.

Those who aspire to join the Fochlucan College face a long and difficult road. The great bards who lead the school choose only individuals who have demonstrated skill at arms and stealth, learning and cleverness, superb talent with the lute and an ear for the stories of old. Finally, all applicants must first study the lore of the druids, learning the ways of growth and the hidden secrets of nature. Few indeed can stand up to the rigorous scrutiny of the Fochlucan masters.

Fochlucan lyrists adventure to gain information. They are spies and rumormongers, ever on the watch for news of events that may upset the balance they seek to preserve. A lyrist can serve as a diplomat, messenger, or assassin, as needed. The Fochlucans strongly believe in fostering the careers of other adventurers whose viewpoints align with their own, and many lyrists attach themselves to adventuring companies specifically for the purpose of guiding their comrades to oppose the right enemies and advance the interests of the Fochlucan College.

Adaptation: This class is a fusion of the druid and bard base classes. An interesting variation would be to adapt the class into a fusion of the druid and ranger base classes.

Hit Die: d6.

REQUIREMENTS

To qualify to become a Fochlucan lyrist, a character must fulfill all the following criteria.

Skills: Decipher Script 7 ranks, Diplomacy 7 ranks, Gather Information 7 ranks, Knowledge (nature) 7 ranks, Perform (string instruments) 13 ranks, Sleight of Hand 7 ranks, Speak Language (Druidic).

Alignment: Neutral good, neutral, chaotic neutral, or neutral evil.

Spells: Ability to cast 1st-level arcane and divine spells.

Special: Bardic knowledge and evasion abilities.

CLASS SKILLS

The Fochlucan lyrist's class skills (and the key ability for each skill) are Appraise (Int), Bluff (Cha), Concentration (Con), Craft (any) (Int), Decipher Script (Int), Diplomacy (Cha), Disguise (Cha), Gather Information (Cha), Handle Animal (Cha), Heal (Wis), Hide (Dex), Knowledge (all skills, taken individually) (Int), Listen (Wis), Move Silently (Dex), Perform (Cha), Profession (Wis), Ride (Dex), Sense Motive (Wis), Sleight of Hand (Dex), Speak Language (n/a), Spellcraft (Int), Survival (Wis), Swim (Str), and Use Magic Device (Cha).

Skill Points at Each Level: 6 + Int modifier.

CLASS FEATURES

All of the following are class features of the Fochlucan lyrist prestige class.

Weapon and Armor Proficiency: Fochlucan lyrists gain no proficiency with any weapon or armor.

Spells per Day/Spells Known: At each level, a Fochlucan lyrist gains new spells per day (and spells known, if applicable) as if she had also gained a level in any one arcane spellcasting class and any one divine spellcasting class to which she belonged before adding the prestige class level. She does not, however, gain any other benefit a character of that class would have gained. If she had more than one arcane spellcasting class or divine spellcasting class before becoming a Fochlucan lyrist, she must decide to which class to add each Fochlucan lyrist level for the purpose of determining spells per day, spells known, and overall caster level.

For example, a 2nd-level rogue/5th-level bard/4th-level druid/3rd-level Fochlucan lyrist can cast arcane spells as an 8th-level bard and divine spells as a 7th-level druid.

Bardic Knowledge (Ex): A Fochlucan lyrist can attempt to recall some relevant piece of information about local notable people, legendary items, or noteworthy places. See the bard class feature, page 28 of the *Player's Handbook*. She adds her Fochlucan lyrist class level to her bardic knowledge checks, so her bardic knowledge checks have a bonus equal to her bard level + her Fochlucan lyrist level + her Int modifier.

Bardic Music: A Fochlucan lyrist adds her lyrist level to her bard level to determine the number of times per day she can use her bardic music, the bardic music abilities she can employ, and the power of those abilities. For example, a 2nd-level rogue/5th-level bard/4th-level druid/3rd-level Fochlucan lyrist can use her bardic music eight times per day, can use any bardic music ability an 8th-level bard could use (assuming she meets the Perform skill rank requirements), and is treated as an 8th-level bard for adjudicating the effects of those abilities (such as number of targets, save DC, and so forth).

Unbound: A Fochlucan lyrist's druid oaths are relaxed, allowing her to wear light metal armor with no loss of spellcasting, supernatural, or spell-like abilities. A lyrist also suffers no experience point penalty for multiclassing.

SAMPLE FOCHLUCAN LYRIST

Tyrea Neylis: Female half-elf rogue 2/bard 4/druid 4/Fochlucan lyrist 2; CR 12; Medium humanoid (elf); HD 8d6 plus 4d8 plus 3; hp 45; Init +1; Spd 30 ft.; AC 18, touch 12, flat-footed 17; Base Atk +9; Grp +8; Atk +10 melee (1d6, +1 *spell storing quarterstaff*); Full Atk +10/+5 melee (1d6, +1 *spell storing quarterstaff*); SA sneak attack +1d6, spells; SQ animal companion (dire weasel), animal companion benefits, bardic knowledge +7, bardic music 6/day (countersong, *fascinate,* inspire courage, inspire competence), evasion, half-elf traits, low-light vision, resist nature's lure, trackless step, trapfinding, wild empathy +7, woodland stride; AL NG; SV Fort +8, Ref +12, Will +16 (+18 against enchantments); Str 8, Dex 13, Con 10, Int 12, Wis 20, Cha 16.

Skills and Feats: Climb +6, Concentration +14, Decipher Script +10, Diplomacy +14, Gather Information +14, Hide +10, Knowledge (nature) +13, Listen +14, Move Silently +15, Perform (string instruments) +16, Search +2, Sleight of Hand +10, Spot +6, Survival +7; Eschew Materials, Green Ear†, Scribe Scroll, Toughness, Weapon Focus (quarterstaff).

† New feat described on page 110.

Languages: Common, Elven; Druidic, Sylvan.

FOCHLUCAN BANDORE

In the same vein that most folk consider the Fochlucan College to be the most famous of the bardic colleges, the most well-known and most often encountered of all the famed instruments of the bards is the *Fochlucan bandore*. (This item and the other instruments of the bards are described in detail in *Complete Arcane*.)

This three-stringed masterwork lute grants a +2 circumstance bonus on Perform (string instruments) checks and a +1 compe-tence bonus on bardic music checks for countersong, *fascinate,* and suggestion. The instrument can be played by anyone to produce *light* once per day. Any character with at least 2 ranks in Perform (string instruments) can use the *bandore* to cast *flare, mending,* and *message* each once per day.

Faint transmutation, faint evocation; CL 3rd; Craft Wondrous Item, *flare, light, mending, message,* creator must be a bard; Price 1,900 gp; Weight 3 lb.

Sneak Attack (Ex): Tyrea deals an extra 1d6 points of damage on any successful attack against flat-footed or flanked targets, or against a target that has been denied its Dexterity bonus for any reason. This damage also applies to ranged attacks against targets up to 30 feet away. Creatures with concealment, creatures without discernible anatomies, and creatures immune to extra damage from critical hits are all immune to sneak attacks. Tyrea can choose to deliver nonlethal damage with her sneak attack, but only when using a weapon designed for that purpose, such as a sap (blackjack).

Animal Companion (Ex): Tyrea has a dire weasel named Fanger as an animal companion (see *Monster Manual*, page 65). Its bonus trick is defend.

Animal Companion Benefits: Tyrea and Fanger enjoy the link and share spells special qualities.

Link (Ex): Tyrea can handle Fanger as a free action. She also gains a +4 circumstance bonus on all wild empathy checks and

Tyrea Neylia, a Fochlucan lyrist

Handle Animal checks made regarding her dire weasel.

Share Spells (Ex): Tyrea can have any spell she casts on herself also affect Fanger if the latter is within 5 feet at the time. She can also cast a spell with a target of "You" on her animal companion.

Bardic Music: Use bardic music six times per day. See the bard class feature, page 29 of the *Player's Handbook.*

Countersong (Su): Use music or poetics to counter magical effects that depend on sound.

Fascinate (Sp): Use music or poetics to cause one or more creatures to become fascinated with her.

Inspire Competence (Su): Use music or poetics to help an ally succeed at a task.

Inspire Courage (Su): Use music or poetics to bolster her allies against fear and improve their combat abilities.

Evasion (Ex): If Tyrea is exposed to any effect that

Illus. by E. Cox

THE FOCHLUCAN COLLEGE

Perhaps the most famous of the bardic colleges, the Fochlucan College serves as a beacon of learning and diplomacy in a dark and restless land. Many have accused the Fochlucan masters of fomenting intrigues among the nearby kingdoms and using their famed neutrality to conceal the real extent of their meddling and manipulation. By advising mighty rulers and undertaking the tutoring of royal heirs, the Fochlucan bards turn the fate of kingdoms with nothing more than quiet words and whispered secrets.

The Fochlucan College itself is located on the shores of the misty Loch Firrnen, a few miles from the town of Oakenway. The College is a rambling old stone building that resembles something between a minor lord's manor house and a decrepit old monastery. Green ivy covers its walls, and old lanterns hanging from its eaves warm its chill, misty nights with golden light.

No more than a handful of its collegians are present at any given time—the strength of the organization lies in the learning and skill of its individual members, not in any muster of warriors. Members are welcome to stay as long as they like but are expected to contribute to the college's upkeep. The customary donation is 50 gp a month (for itinerant members) or 200 gp a month (for members living on the premises).

A small number of servants keep the College in order and prepare meals, but there are no guards or soldiers. Instead, its defense lies primarily in the reputation and influence of its members. Should trouble come anyway, the College is well defended by the handful of lyrists or guests who happen to be visiting at any given time. In case of serious trouble, the Fochlucans turn to the creatures of the surrounding forest. Through ancient pacts, the sylvan denizens of Loch Firrnen's forests are pledged to defend the bards' house against attack.

The College is governed by the Yew Circle, a small council composed of the five most senior Fochlucans currently enrolled in the order. All five are nominally equal, but if the Circle's opinion is divided on any important matter, the Eldest of the Circle—the Fochlucan who has served the longest in the college—decides the issue. Currently, the Eldest of Fochlucan is Yew Master Hurlich Stennarden, a half-elf who has belonged to the College for better than fifty years. The masters of the Yew Circle rarely meet, since they are not often at the College at the same time.

The Fochlucans are affiliated with several other bardic colleges in neighboring lands, including the College of Mac-Fuirmidh, the Doss School, and the High College of Anstruth, oldest and most knowledgeable of the colleges.

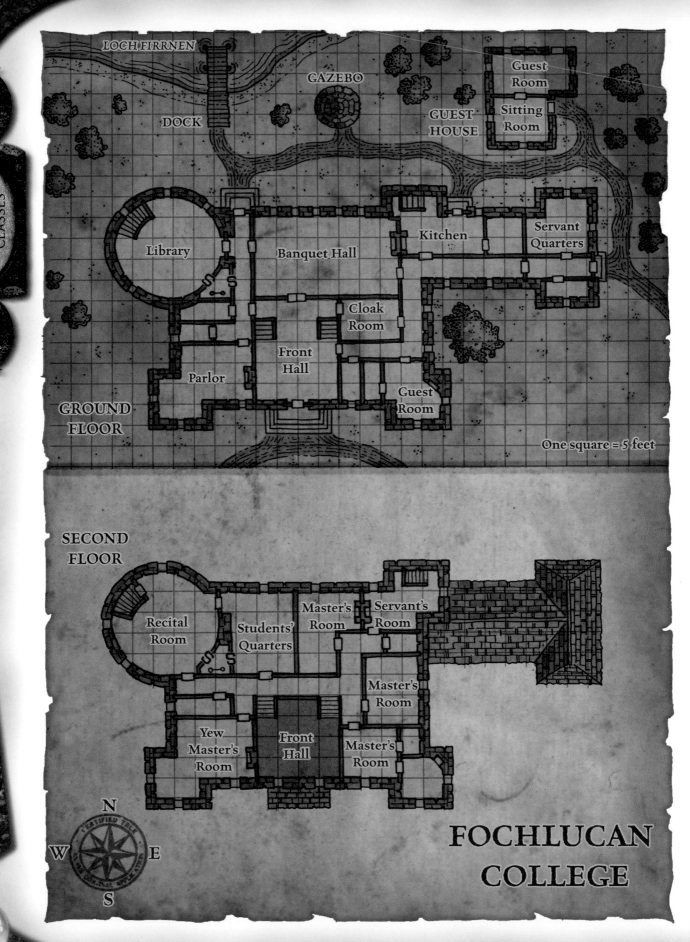

LOCH FIRRNEN

GAZEBO

DOCK

Guest Room

GUEST HOUSE

Sitting Room

Library

Banquet Hall

Kitchen

Servant Quarters

Cloak Room

Front Hall

Parlor

Guest Room

GROUND FLOOR

One square = 5 feet

SECOND FLOOR

Recital Room

Students' Quarters

Master's Room

Servant's Room

Master's Room

Yew Master's Room

Front Hall

Master's Room

N
W   E
S

FOCHLUCAN COLLEGE

TABLE 2–10: THE FOCHLUCAN LYRIST

Level	Base Attack Bonus	Fort Save	Ref Save	Will Save	Special	Spells per Day/Spells Known
1st	+1	+0	+2	+2	Bardic knowledge, bardic music, unbound	+1 level of existing arcane spellcasting class and +1 level of existing divine spellcasting class
2nd	+2	+0	+3	+3	—	+1 level of existing arcane spellcasting class and +1 level of existing divine spellcasting class
3rd	+3	+1	+3	+3	—	+1 level of existing arcane spellcasting class and +1 level of existing divine spellcasting class
4th	+4	+1	+4	+4	—	+1 level of existing arcane spellcasting class and +1 level of existing divine spellcasting class
5th	+5	+1	+4	+4	—	+1 level of existing arcane spellcasting class and +1 level of existing divine spellcasting class
6th	+6	+2	+5	+5	—	+1 level of existing arcane spellcasting class and +1 level of existing divine spellcasting class
7th	+7	+2	+5	+5	—	+1 level of existing arcane spellcasting class and +1 level of existing divine spellcasting class
8th	+8	+2	+6	+6	—	+1 level of existing arcane spellcasting class and +1 level of existing divine spellcasting class
9th	+9	+3	+6	+6	—	+1 level of existing arcane spellcasting class and +1 level of existing divine spellcasting class
10th	+10	+3	+7	+7	—	+1 level of existing arcane spellcasting class and +1 level of existing divine spellcasting class

normally allows her to attempt a Reflex saving throw for half damage, she takes no damage with a successful saving throw.

Half-Elf Traits: Half-elves have immunity to magic sleep effects. For all effects related to race, a half-elf is considered an elf.

Resist Nature's Lure (Ex): Tyrea gains a +4 bonus on saving throws against the spell-like abilities of fey.

Trackless Step (Ex): Tyrea leaves no trail in natural surroundings and cannot be tracked.

Trapfinding (Ex): Tyrea can find, disarm, or bypass traps with a DC of 20 or higher. She can use the Search skill to find, and the Disable Device skill to disarm, magic traps (DC 25 + the level of the spell used to create it). If her Disable Device result exceeds the trap's DC by 10 or more, she discovers how to bypass the trap without triggering or disarming it.

Woodland Stride (Ex): Tyrea can move through natural thorns, briars, overgrown areas, and similar terrain at her normal speed and without damage or other impairment. However, thorns, briars, and overgrown areas that are magically manipulated to impede motion still affect her.

Bard Spells Known (3/4/3 per day; caster level 6th): 0—*dancing lights, daze* (DC 13), *ghost sound* (DC 13), *lullaby* (DC 13), *mage hand, summon instrument;* 1st—*alarm, charm person* (DC 14), *disguise self, undetectable alignment;* 2nd—*detect thoughts* (DC 15), *invisibility, mirror image.*

Druid Spells Prepared (caster level 6th): 0—*create water, cure minor wounds, detect magic, know direction, purify food and drink;* 1st—*entangle* (DC 16), *longstrider, pass without trace, shillelagh, speak with animals;* 2nd—*animal messenger, cat's grace, spider climb, tree shape;* 3rd—*cure moderate wounds, sleet storm, speak with plants.*

Possessions: +2 *mithral chain shirt, ring of protection +1, +1 spell storing quarterstaff (poison),* masterwork shortbow with 20 arrows, *cloak of Charisma +2, periapt of Wisdom +2, boots of elvenkind,* divine scroll of *protection from energy,* masterwork lyre, 27 gp.

GHOST-FACED KILLER

From out of nothing the specter of death appears, an armored shadow with a brilliant blade held high. In a flash the katana falls, severing life from limb in a bloody arc. All around, screams of terror and shouts of fear erupt, as quaking hands draw blades to fight the masked murderer. His target dead, the ghost-faced killer walks calmly away as swords and fists pass harmlessly through his nearly transparent body.

Long ago, a persecuted clan of dangerous warriors sought a way to take revenge against their oppressors. Through sorcery, the spellcasters of the clan beseeched dark spirits to reveal a way that their clan might survive the coming strife and take revenge on the emperor who sought to crush them. The clan members struck a dark bargain, and the demon-spirits they had contacted provided the clan with a means to the bloody ends they desired. Donning terrifying masks to hide their identities, warriors of the clan crept into the imperial palace, and through the evil power of the pact they had made, passed invisibly and intangibly into the imperial household and murdered the entire imperial family, plunging the country into bloody civil war once again. No one ever discovered the clan's honorless actions, and to this day, no one knows what clan the ghost-faced killers came from.

Today ghost-faced killers act as assassins and spies for hire, a mercenary clan that hides behind a guise of open and honorable conduct. When on a mission, they wear porcelain demon-masks of ghostly white to hide their identities and as a symbol of the pact their clan made with the demon-spirits. Through training and discipline, ghost-faced killers learn the deadliest and most terrifying ways to attack foes, and through their mystic connection with spirits, ghost-faced killers learn to turn invisible, walk through walls, and even see with the eyes of the spirits themselves.

Most ghost-faced killers begin their careers as rangers or rogues, though ninjas are also common. Fighters are only slightly less common. Few monks, barbarians, or members of spellcasting classes choose to become ghost-faced killers, but such characters are not unknown.

NPC ghost-faced killers are members of the Ghost-Faced Killer clan of ninjas. This clan disguises itself as a normal samurai clan, loyal to the empire but unworthy of notice. Most of the time a ghost-faced killer simply pursues his responsibilities to the clan and the emperor, but when called by money or the clan daimyo the ghost-faced killer dons the mask that means death for his enemies.

Adaptation: Although the ghost-faced killers are described as a clan of samurai and ninjas, the class can easily lose these aspects of its flavor and become a group of assassins. When introduced as a force for good, the ghost-faced killer prestige class could be used to represent a clan of investigators or spies serving a good-aligned nation or faction.

Hit Die: d8.

*Qeng Yi,
a ghost-faced killer*

REQUIREMENTS

To qualify to become a ghost-faced killer, a character must fulfill all the following criteria:

Alignment: Any evil.

Base Attack Bonus: +5.

Skills: Hide 6 ranks, Concentration 4 ranks, Intimidate 8 ranks, Move Silently 6 ranks.

Feats: Improved Initiative, Power Attack.

CLASS SKILLS

The ghost-faced killer's class skills (and the key ability for each skill) are Bluff (Cha), Climb (Str), Concentration (Con), Hide (Dex), Intimidate (Cha), Jump (Str), Listen (Wis), Move Silently (Dex), Open Lock (Dex), Search (Int), Spot (Wis), Swim (Str), and Tumble (Dex).

Skill Points at Each Level: 4 + Int modifier.

CLASS FEATURES

All of the following are features of the ghost-faced killer prestige class.

Weapon and Armor Proficiency: Ghost-faced killers are proficient with all simple and martial weapons, and with light armor.

Ghost Step (Su): A ghost-faced killer can become invisible for 1 round once per day. Using this ability is a swift action (see Swift Actions and Immediate Actions, page 137) that does not provoke attacks of opportunity. A ghost-faced killer can use this ability one additional time per day for every three class levels gained above 1st (2/day at 4th level, 3/day at 7th level, and 4/day at 10th level).

At 6th level, a ghost-faced killer can become ethereal when using ghost step instead of becoming invisible.

Sudden Strike (Ex): If a ghost-faced killer of 2nd level or higher can catch an opponent when she is unable to defend herself effectively from his attack, he can strike a vital spot for extra damage. Whenever a ghost-faced killer's target is denied her Dexterity bonus to Armor Class (if any) against his attack, the ghost-faced killer deals an extra 1d6 points of damage with his attack. The bonus damage increases by 1d6 every three levels (+2d6 at 5th level, +3d6 at 8th level). This ability otherwise works like the ninja ability described on page 8.

Frightful Attack (Su): Beginning at 3rd level, a ghost-faced killer can panic onlookers and even frighten his victim to death by making a sudden strike attack. Once per day, a ghost-faced killer can designate a melee sudden strike attack as a frightful attack. The ghost-faced killer must use his Power Attack feat on the attack and must take a penalty of at least –1 to his attack roll. If the attack deals damage to the target, the victim must make a Will save (DC 10 + ghost-faced killer's class level + ghost-faced killer's Cha modifier). If the victim succeeds, she is shaken for 1 round per class level of the ghost-faced killer; if she fails, she instantly dies of fear. Creatures immune to mind-affecting effects, immune to fear, or with Hit Dice that exceed the ghost-faced killer's character level are immune to this frightful attack.

In addition, all creatures within 30 feet who see the frightful attack (not including the victim, the ghost-faced killer, or the ghost-faced killer's allies) become panicked (if their Hit Dice are less than the ghost-faced killer's class level + his Cha modifier) or shaken (if their Hit Dice equal or exceed the ghost-faced killer's class level + Cha modifier) for 1 round per class level of the ghost-faced killer. A successful Will save (DC 10 + ghost-faced killer's class level + ghost-faced killer's Cha modifier + damage bonus from Power Attack on the frightful attack) negates this effect.

A ghost-faced killer can use this ability one additional time per day for every three levels gained above 3rd (2/day at 6th level, 3/day at 9th level).

Ghost Sight (Su): Starting at 7th level, a ghost-faced killer can see ethereal and invisible creatures and objects as easily as he sees material creatures and objects.

Frightful Cleave (Su): If a 10th-level ghost-faced killer slays a foe with his frightful attack (either from the damage dealt or because of a failed save against its fear effect), he gets an immediate extra melee attack against another target within reach. If the new target is flat-footed, this extra attack is also a frightful attack, though it doesn't count against the ghost-faced killer's daily limit of frightful attacks. This ability otherwise functions exactly as the Cleave feat (see page 92 of the *Player's Handbook*.)

TABLE 2–11: THE GHOST-FACED KILLER

Level	Base Attack Bonus	Fort Save	Ref Save	Will Save	Special
1st	+1	+2	+0	+0	Ghost step 1/day
2nd	+2	+3	+0	+0	Sudden strike +1d6
3rd	+3	+3	+1	+1	Frightful attack 1/day
4th	+4	+4	+1	+1	Ghost step 2/day
5th	+5	+4	+1	+1	Sudden strike +2d6
6th	+6	+5	+2	+2	Frightful attack 2/day, ghost step (ethereal)
7th	+7	+5	+2	+2	Ghost sight, ghost step 3/day
8th	+8	+6	+2	+2	Sudden strike +3d6
9th	+9	+6	+3	+3	Frightful attack 3/day
10th	+10	+7	+3	+3	Frightful cleave, ghost step 4/day

SAMPLE GHOST-FACED KILLER

Qeng Yi: Male human rogue 2/fighter 4/ghost-faced killer 3; CR 9; Medium humanoid; HD 2d6+4 plus 4d10+8 plus 3d8+6; hp 63; Init +7; Spd 30 ft.; AC 18, touch 13, flat-footed 15; Base Atk +8; Grp +11; Atk +13 melee (2d6+7/19–20, +1 *greatsword*) or +12 ranged (1d8+3/×3, masterwork composite longbow); Full Atk +13/+8 melee (2d6+7/19–20, +1 *greatsword*) or +12/+7 ranged (1d8+3/×3, masterwork composite longbow); SA frightful attack 1/day, sneak attack +1d6, sudden strike +1d6; SQ evasion, ghost step 1/day, trapfinding; AL NE; SV Fort +10, Ref +9, Will +6; Str 16, Dex 16, Con 14, Int 10, Wis 12, Cha 8.

Skills and Feats: Balance +5, Climb +10, Concentration +6, Hide +9, Intimidate +8, Jump +8, Move Silently +9, Open Lock +11, Search +8, Spot +9, Survival +1 (+3 following tracks), Tumble +11; Dodge[B], Improved Initiative[B], Iron Will[B], Mobility, Power Attack[B], Spring Attack, Weapon Focus (greatsword), Weapon Specialization (greatsword).

Language: Common.

Evasion (Ex): If Qeng Yi is exposed to any effect that normally allows him to attempt a Reflex saving throw for half damage, he takes no damage with a successful saving throw.

Frightful Attack (Su): Once per day, Qeng Yi can designate a melee sudden strike attack as a frightful attack. He must use his Power Attack feat and take an attack roll penalty of at least –1. If the attack deals damage to the target, the victim must make a DC 12 Will save.

If the victim succeeds, she is shaken for 3 rounds; if she fails, she instantly dies of fear. Creatures immune to mind-affecting effects, immune to fear, or with 10 Hit Dice or more are immune to Qeng Yi's frightful attack.

All other creatures within 30 feet who see the frightful attack (not including Qeng Yi or his allies) become panicked (if of 1 Hit Die or less) or shaken (if of 2 Hit Dice or more) for 3 rounds (Will negates, DC 12 + damage bonus from Power Attack).

Ghost Step (Su): Qeng Yi can become invisible for 1 round once per day. This is a swift action that does not provoke attacks of opportunity (see Swift Actions and Immediate Actions, page 137).

Sneak Attack (Ex): Qeng Yi deals an extra 1d6 points of damage on any successful attack against flat-footed or flanked targets, or against a target that has been denied its Dexterity bonus for any reason. This damage also applies to ranged attacks against targets up to 30 feet away. Creatures with concealment, creatures without discernible anatomies, and creatures immune to extra damage from critical hits are all immune to sneak attacks. Qeng Yi can choose to deliver nonlethal damage with his sneak attack, but only when using a weapon designed for that purpose, such as a sap (blackjack).

Sudden Strike (Ex): Qeng Yi deals an extra 1d6 points of damage on any successful attack against a target that has been denied its Dexterity bonus for any reason. This extra damage stacks with extra damage from a sneak attack, so Qeng Yi deals an extra 2d6 points of damage against flat-footed foes, but only an extra 1d6 points of damage against flanked foes. See page 8 for details.

Trapfinding (Ex): Qeng Yi can find, disarm, or bypass traps with a DC of 20 or higher. He can use the Search skill to find, and the Disable Device skill to disarm, magic traps (DC 25 + the level of the spell used to create it). If his Disable device result exceeds the trap's DC by 10 or more, he discovers how to bypass the trap without triggering or disarming it.

Possessions: +2 studded leather, +1 greatsword, masterwork composite longbow (+3 Str bonus), 20 arrows, 10 silver arrows, gauntlets of ogre power, cloak of resistance +1, 2 potions of invisibility.

HIGHLAND STALKER

The mountains are unforgiving, and the ability to find food at high altitude often means the difference between survival and starvation. For those who live in such climes, hunters provide not only food but also clothing, shelter, and tools when they bring back animal skins and bones.

The best high-altitude hunters—highland stalkers—are consummate trackers with an instinctive knowledge of their mountainous territories.

Scouts (see page 10) are the most likely candidates to become highland stalkers, but rogues are well represented, and the prestige class attracts a fair number of multiclass barbarians and rangers who qualify.

NPC highland stalkers are found leading teams of four to six other hunters (typically scouts or rangers), often far from the tribe's base camp. Depending on how the game they're tracking is moving, they might stay away from camp for several days at a time.

Adaptation: This prestige class models a mountain warrior who favors stalking enemies and attacking from ambush—similar to the ranger, but with fewer skills and no spellcasting. Thus, it's easy to adapt for hunters beyond a mountain setting. A fighter's base attack bonus and the ability to make skirmish attacks is a compelling combination, so you don't need to load the prestige class with many other class features.

Hit Die: d8.

REQUIREMENTS

To qualify to become a highland stalker, a character must fulfill all the following criteria.

Base Attack Bonus: +5.

Skills: Listen 8 ranks, Spot 8 ranks, Survival 8 ranks.

Feats: Track.

Special: Skirmish or sneak attack class feature.

CLASS SKILLS

The highland stalker's class skills (and the key ability for each skill) are Balance (Dex), Climb (Str), Craft (Int), Hide (Dex), Jump (Str), Knowledge (geography) (Int), Knowledge (nature) (Int), Listen (Wis), Move Silently (Dex), Search (Int), Spot (Wis), and Survival (Wis).

Skill Points at Each Level: 4 + Int modifier.

CLASS FEATURES

All of the following are class features of the highland stalker prestige class.

Weapon and Armor Proficiency: Highland stalkers are proficient with light armor. They gain no proficiency with any weapon.

Mountain Stride (Ex): A highland stalker can move through scree and dense rubble at her normal speed. She can also move up steep slopes and stairs at her normal speed. See pages 89–92 of the *Dungeon Master's Guide* for descriptions of terrain types.

Skirmish (Ex): A highland stalker relies on mobility to deal extra damage and improve her defense. Starting at 2nd level, she deals an extra 1d6 points of damage on all attacks during any round in which she moves at least 10 feet. This extra damage applies only to attacks taken during her turn. It increases by an additional 1d6 for every four levels gained above 2nd (2d6 at 6th and 3d6 at 10th).

This extra damage only applies against living creatures that have a discernible anatomy. Undead, constructs, oozes, plants, incorporeal creatures, and creatures immune to extra damage from critical hits are not vulnerable to this extra damage. A highland stalker must be able to see the target well enough to pick out a vital spot and must be able to reach such a spot. Highland stalkers can apply this extra damage to ranged attacks made while skirmishing, but only if the target is within 30 feet.

At 4th level, a highland stalker gains a +1 competence bonus to Armor Class during any round in which she moves at least 10 feet. The bonus applies as soon as she has moved 10 feet, and lasts until the start of her next turn. It improves to +2 at 8th level.

A highland stalker loses this ability when wearing medium or heavy armor or when carrying a medium or heavy load. If she gains the skirmish ability from another class, the bonuses stack.

Swift Tracker (Ex): Beginning at 3rd level, a highland stalker can move at her normal speed while following tracks. See the ranger class feature, page 48 of the *Player's Handbook*.

Surefooted (Ex): Starting at 5th level, a highland stalker is well acquainted with the dangers of mountainous terrain. She can ignore DC modifiers on Balance, Move Silently, and Tumble checks derived from scree, light rubble, dense rubble, steep slopes, or stairs (see page 89 of the *Dungeon Master's Guide*). She also does not need to make a DC 10 Balance check when running or charging down a steep slope.

Camouflage (Ex): Beginning at 7th level, a highland stalker can use the Hide skill in any sort of natural terrain.

SAMPLE HIGHLAND STALKER

Egeth Darkhunter Kolae-Gileana: Female goliath ranger 5/highland stalker 3; CR 9; Medium monstrous humanoid; HD 8d8+24; hp 63; Init +4; Spd 30 ft.; AC 21, touch 15, flat-footed 16; Base Atk +8; Grp +14; Atk +11 melee (2d6+3, Large masterwork longspear) or +14 ranged (2d6+2/×3, Large masterwork composite longbow); Full Atk +11/+6 melee (2d6+3, Large masterwork longspear) or +12/+12/+7 ranged (2d6+2/×3, Large masterwork composite longbow); SA combat style (archery), favored enemy animals +2, favored enemy magical beasts +4, skirmish +1d6; SQ animal companion (wolf), animal companion benefits, goliath traits, mountain stride, swift tracker, wild empathy +4 (+0 magical beasts); AL CN; SV Fort +11, Ref +10, Will +5; Str 14, Dex 18, Con 16, Int 12, Wis 14, Cha 8.

Egeth Darkhunter Kolae-Gileana, a highland stalker

Skills and Feats: Climb +6, Hide +12, Jump +6, Knowledge (geography) +6, Knowledge (nature) +8, Listen +13, Move Silently +12, Sense Motive +4, Spot +13, Survival +13

TABLE 2–12: THE HIGHLAND STALKER

Level	Base Attack Bonus	Fort Save	Ref Save	Will Save	Special
1st	+1	+2	+0	+0	Mountain stride
2nd	+2	+3	+0	+0	Skirmish (+1d6)
3rd	+3	+3	+1	+1	Swift tracker
4th	+4	+4	+1	+1	Skirmish (+1d6, +1 AC)
5th	+5	+4	+1	+1	Surefooted
6th	+6	+5	+2	+2	Skirmish (+2d6, +1 AC)
7th	+7	+5	+2	+2	Camouflage
8th	+8	+6	+2	+2	Skirmish (+2d6, +2 AC)
9th	+9	+6	+3	+3	—
10th	+10	+7	+3	+3	Skirmish (+3d6, +2 AC)

Illus. by S. Ellis

(+15 to keep from getting lost or to avoid natural hazards, or in aboveground environments); Endurance[B], Point Blank Shot, Precise Shot, Rapid Shot[B], Track[B], Weapon Focus (longbow).

Languages: Common, Gol-Kaa; Giant.

Favored Enemy (Ex): Egeth gains a +2 bonus on her Bluff, Listen, Sense Motive, Spot, and Survival checks when using these skills against animals. She gains the same bonus on weapon damage rolls.

Against magical beasts, she gains a +4 bonus on these skill checks and on weapon damage rolls.

Skirmish (Ex): Egeth deals an extra 1d6 points of damage on all attacks during any round in which she moves at least 10 feet. This extra damage applies only to attacks taken during her turn. It also applies to ranged attacks against targets up to 30 feet away. Creatures with concealment, creatures without discernible anatomies, and creatures immune to extra damage from critical hits are all immune to additional extra damage. Egeth loses this ability when wearing medium or heavy armor or when carrying a medium or heavy load.

Animal Companion (Ex): Egeth has a wolf named Swiftrunner as an animal companion (see *Monster Manual*, page 283). Its bonus trick is attack.

Animal Companion Benefits: Egeth and Swiftrunner enjoy the link and share spells special qualities.

Link (Ex): Egeth can handle Swiftrunner as a free action. She also gains a +4 circumstance bonus on all wild empathy checks and Handle Animal checks made regarding her wolf.

Share Spells (Ex): Egeth can have any spell she casts on herself also affect her animal companion if the latter is within 5 feet at the time. She can also cast a spell with a target of "You" on her animal companion.

Goliath Traits (Ex): Egeth's physical stature lets her function in many ways as if she were one size category larger, including using weapons designed for a creature one size larger. Egeth can make standing long and high jumps as if they were running long and high jumps. She also can engage in accelerated climbing without taking a –5 penalty on the Climb check. Egeth is automatically acclimated to life at high altitudes and does not take the penalties for altitude described on page 90 of the *Dungeon Master's Guide*. (The goliath race is detailed in *Races of Stone*.)

Mountain Stride (Ex): Egeth can move through scree and dense rubble at her normal speed. She can also move up steep slopes and stairs at her normal speed.

Swift Tracker (Ex): Egeth can track at normal speed without taking the usual –5 penalty, or can track at double speed at only a –10 penalty.

Ranger Spell Prepared (caster level 5th): 1st—*longstrider.*

Possessions: +1 chain shirt, amulet of natural armor +1, ring of protection +1, Large masterwork composite longbow (+2 Str bonus), 50 Large arrows, Large masterwork longspear, gloves of Dexterity +2, cloak of resistance +1, wand of cure light wounds (50 charges), 10 pp.

MAESTER

Maesters are the master crafters of the gnome world, combining technical and magical expertise to create incredible marvels. They specialize in the creation of magic items, bending all their skill and ability toward the construction of items that are their art and livelihood.

Maesters are usually wizards, although sorcerers occasionally take up the class. Some bards also have been known to become maesters, but typically not until they have spent a number of years adventuring.

NPC maesters rarely stray from their laboratories, which makes them excellent patrons for groups of adventurers. Maesters often need rare minerals, unusual material components for spells, or other substances for the magic items they create, and it's usually too dangerous to fetch such materials alone. Maesters often hire bodyguards if they're undertaking a journey, paying their guards with magic items they have built. Other times, they simply send allies on a journey of acquisition, providing them with as much lore about their mission as possible.

Adaptation: While gnomes are renowned for their magical craftsmanship, they don't have a monopoly on the trade. This class would be appropriate for a secret organization of item-creating arcanists who are not necessarily gnomes. If you change the spell requirement to divine spells, it's also a good fit for clerics of deities who are known for their peerless magical craftings, such as Moradin.

Hit Die: d4.

REQUIREMENTS

To qualify to become a maester, a character must fulfill all the following criteria.

Race: Gnome.

Skills: Craft (any) 8 ranks, Use Magic Device 4 ranks.

Feats: Any two item creation feats.

Spells: Arcane caster level 5th.

CLASS SKILLS

The maester's class skills (and the key ability for each skill) are Appraise (Int), Concentration (Con), Craft (Int), Disable Device (Int), Knowledge (arcana) (Int), Knowledge (architecture and engineering) (Int), Spellcraft (Int), and Use Magic Device (Cha).

Skill Points at Each Level: 4 + Int modifier.

CLASS FEATURES

All of the following are class features of the maester prestige class.

Weapon and Armor Proficiency: Maesters gain no proficiency with any weapon or armor.

Bonus Feats: At 1st and 5th level, a maester receives a bonus item creation feat. He must meet the prerequisites for this feat.

Quick Crafting (Ex): A maester can craft magic items in half the normal time required (one day per 2,000 gp in the item's base price; minimum one day).

Pinker Bachin, a maester

Spells per Day/Spells Known: Beginning at 2nd level, a maester gains new spells per day (and spells known, if applicable) as if he had also gained a level in a spellcasting class to which he belonged before adding the prestige class level. He does not, however, gain any other benefit a character of that class would have gained. If he had more than one spellcasting class before becoming a maester, he must decide to which class to add each level for the purpose of determining spells per day and spells known.

Identification (Sp): A maester of 3rd level or higher can determine the magical properties of a magic item by handling it for 1 minute and making a successful Spellcraft check (DC 10 + the item's caster level). The maester can't take 10 on this check, nor can he retry the check (and thus he can't take 20). This ability otherwise functions as the *identify* spell.

SAMPLE MAESTER

Pinker Bachin: Male gnome wizard 5/maester 2; CR 7; Small humanoid; HD 7d4+14; hp 33; Init +0; Spd 20 ft.; AC 13, touch 12, flat-footed 13; Base Atk +3; Grp –3; Atk or Full Atk +1 melee (1d4–2, quarterstaff); SA spells, spell-like abilities; SQ familiar (rat), familiar benefits, gnome traits, low-light vision, quick crafting; AL LN; SV Fort +6*, Ref +2*, Will +10*; Str 6, Dex 10, Con 14, Int 16, Wis 14, Cha 14.

Illus. by F. Vohwinkel

TABLE 2–13: THE MAESTER

Level	Base Attack Bonus	Fort Save	Ref Save	Will Save	Special	Spells per Day/Spells Known
1st	+0	+0	+0	+2	Bonus feat, quick crafting	—
2nd	+1	+0	+0	+3	—	+1 level of existing spellcasting class
3rd	+1	+1	+1	+3	*Identification*	+1 level of existing spellcasting class
4th	+2	+1	+1	+4	—	+1 level of existing spellcasting class
5th	+2	+1	+1	+4	Bonus feat	+1 level of existing spellcasting class

Skills and Feats: Appraise +7 (+9 for alchemy items), Concentration +12, Craft (alchemy) +15, Knowledge (arcana) +12, Listen +4, Spellcraft +15 (+17 to decipher scrolls), Use Magic Device +7 (+9 involving scrolls); Brew Potion, Craft Magic Arms and Armor[B], Craft Wand[B], Craft Wondrous Item, Magical Aptitude, Scribe Scroll[B].

Languages: Common, Gnome; Draconic, Dwarven, Undercommon.

Spell-Like Abilities: 1/day—*dancing lights, ghost sound* (DC 12), *prestidigitation, speak with animals* (burrowing mammal only, duration 1 minute).

Familiar: Pinker's familiar is a rat named Wannbar. The familiar uses the better of its own and Pinker's base save bonuses. The rat's abilities and characteristics are summarized below.

Familiar Benefits: Pinker gains special benefits from having a familiar. Wannbar grants him a +2 bonus on Fortitude saves. Pinker and Wannbar enjoy the empathic link and share spells special qualities.

Alertness (Ex): Wannbar grants its master Alertness as long as it is within 5 feet.

Empathic Link (Su): Pinker can communicate telepathically with his familiar at a distance of up to 1 mile. The master has the same connection to an item or a place that the familiar does.

Share Spells (Su): Pinker can have any spell he casts on himself also affect Wannbar if the latter is within 5 feet at the time. He can also cast a spell a target of "You" on his familiar.

Gnome Traits: Gnomes have a +1 racial bonus on attack rolls against kobolds and goblinoids. Gnomes have a +4 racial bonus to Armor Class against giants.

*Gnomes have a +2 racial bonus on saving throws against illusions.

Quick Crafting (Ex): Pinker can craft magic items in half the normal time required (one day per 2,000 gp of the item's base price; minimum one day).

Wizard Spells Prepared (caster level 6th): 0—*detect magic, mending, message, read magic;* 1st—*comprehend languages, identify, magic missile, shield;* 2nd—*cat's grace, knock, mirror image, web* (DC 15); 3rd—*fireball* (DC 16), *fly, ray of exhaustion* (+4 ranged touch; DC 16).

Spellbook: as above plus 0—all others; 1st—*color spray, mage armor, ray of enfeeblement, shield;* 2nd—*levitate;* 3rd—*displacement.*

Possessions: bracers of armor +1, ring of protection +1, quarterstaff, *cloak of resistance +1,* 2 scrolls of *hold person,* scroll of *lightning bolt* (7th level), *wand of Melf's acid arrow* (21 charges), 3 pearls (100 gp each), 4 pp, 3 gp, 7 sp, 5 cp.

Wannbar, Rat Familiar: CR —; Tiny magical beast; HD 5; hp 16; Init +2; Spd 15 ft., climb 15 ft., swim 15 ft.; AC 17, touch 14, flat-footed 15; Base Atk +3; Grp –9; Atk +5 melee (1d3–4, bite); Full Atk +5 melee (1d3–4, bite); Space/Reach 2-1/2 ft./0 ft.; SA deliver touch spells; SQ improved evasion, low-light vision, scent, speak with master; AL N; SV Fort +2, Ref +4, Will +7; Str 2, Dex 15, Con 10, Int 12, Wis 12, Cha 2.

Skills and Feats: Balance +10, Climb +12, Hide +14, Move Silently +10, Swim +10; Weapon Finesse.

Deliver Touch Spells (Su): Wannbar can deliver touch spells for Pinker (see Familiars, page 52 of the *Player's Handbook*).

Improved Evasion (Ex): If Wannbar is exposed to any effect that normally allows it to attempt a Reflex saving throw for half damage, it takes no damage with a successful saving throw and half damage if the saving throw fails.

Speak with Master (Ex): Wannbar can communicate verbally with Pinker. Other creatures do not understand the communication without magical help.

MASTER OF MANY FORMS

A master of many forms has no shape that she calls her own. Instead, she occupies whatever body is most expedient for her at the time. While others base their identities largely on their external forms, a master of many forms actually comes closer to her true self through her transformations. Of necessity, her sense of self is based not on her outward form, but on her soul, which is truly the only constant about her. It is the inner strength of that soul that enables her to take on any shape and remain herself within.

The path of the master of many forms is ideal for a spellcaster of any race who has experienced shapechanging and yearns for more of it. Such a character can be a great force for either good or ill in the world. An evil master of many forms in particular poses a terrible threat, for she can appear anywhere, in any body. The same opponents may face her again and again, in one shape after another, never realizing that they are actually facing a single enemy.

NPC masters of many forms are typically loners, moving between communities of various creatures as suits their whims. They sometimes find work as spies or explorers.

The class description presented here is an updated version of the shifter prestige class that originally appeared in *Masters of the Wild*.

Adaptation: Masters of many forms can be introduced into a campaign in many ways. They might form an elite group of spies and scouts, they might be high-ranking members of a doppelganger-worshiping cult, or they might be a small group of druids who see beauty and power in all of nature's forms, not just animals and elementals.

Hit Die: d8.

REQUIREMENTS

To qualify to become a master of many forms, a character must fulfill all the following criteria.

Feats: Alertness, Endurance.

Special: Wild shape class feature.

CLASS SKILLS

The class skills of the master of many forms (and the key ability for each skill) are Climb (Str), Concentration (Con), Craft (any) (Int), Diplomacy (Cha), Disguise (Cha), Handle Animal (Cha), Hide (Dex), Jump (Str), Knowledge (nature) (Int), Listen (Wis), Spot (Wis), Swim (Str), and Survival (Wis).

Skill Points at Each Level: 4 + Int modifier.

CLASS FEATURES

All of the following are class features of the master of many forms prestige class.

Weapon and Armor Proficiency: Masters of many forms gain no proficiency with any weapon or armor.

Shifter's Speech (Ex): A master of many forms maintains her ability to speak normally (including verbal components of spells) regardless of the form she takes. Furthermore, she can communicate with other creatures of the same kind while in wild shape, as long as such creatures are normally capable of communicating with each other using natural methods.

Improved Wild Shape (Su): A master of many forms knows how to use her wild shape ability to assume a wider range of forms. At 1st level, she can assume a humanoid form with wild shape. She later gains the ability to assume the form of a giant (at 2nd level), a monstrous humanoid (at 3rd level), a fey (at 4th level), a vermin (at 5th level), an aberration (at 6th level), a plant (at 7th level), an ooze (at 8th level), an elemental (at 9th level), and a dragon (at 10th level).

The size limit of the shapes she can assume also increases as she gains levels. At 2nd level, she can assume the form of a Large creature; at 4th level, a Tiny creature; at 6th level, a Huge creature; at 8th level, a Diminutive creature; and at 10th level, a Gargantuan creature.

A master of many forms also gains one additional daily use of her wild shape ability per class level gained.

Fast Wild Shape (Ex): Starting at 3rd level, a master of many forms can use her wild shape ability as a move action, rather than as a standard action.

Extraordinary Wild Shape (Ex): Starting at 7th level, a master of many forms gains the extraordinary special qualities of any form she assumes with wild shape.

Evershifting Form: A 10th-level master of many forms has reached the pinnacle of her shapechanging abilities. She gains the shapechanger subtype and becomes immune to any transmutation effect unless she is willing to accept it.

Illus. by M. Moore

Galatea, a master of many forms

TABLE 2–14: THE MASTER OF MANY FORMS

Level	Base Attack Bonus	Fort Save	Ref Save	Will Save	Special
1st	+0	+2	+2	+0	Shifter's speech, improved wild shape (humanoid)
2nd	+1	+3	+3	+0	Improved wild shape (giant; Large)
3rd	+2	+3	+3	+1	Fast wild shape, improved wild shape (monstrous humanoid)
4th	+3	+4	+4	+1	Improved wild shape (fey; Tiny)
5th	+3	+4	+4	+1	Improved wild shape (vermin)
6th	+4	+5	+5	+2	Improved wild shape (aberration; Huge)
7th	+5	+5	+5	+2	Extraordinary wild shape, improved wild shape (plant)
8th	+6	+6	+6	+2	Improved wild shape (ooze; Diminutive)
9th	+6	+6	+6	+3	Improved wild shape (elemental)
10th	+7	+7	+7	+3	Evershifting form, improved wild shape (dragon; Gargantuan)

In addition, she no longer takes ability penalties for aging and is not subject to magical aging, though any aging penalties she already may have taken remain in place. Bonuses still accrue, and a master of many forms still dies of old age when her time is up.

SAMPLE MASTER OF MANY FORMS

Galatea: Female elf druid 5/master of many forms 2; CR 7; Medium humanoid; HD 7d8+7; hp 38; Init +2; Spd 20 ft.; AC 18, touch 12, flat-footed 16; Base Atk +4; Grp +5; Atk or Full Atk +6 melee (1d6+2, +1 scimitar) or +7 ranged (1d8+2, +1 composite longbow); SA spells; SQ animal companion (eagle), animal companion benefits, elf traits, improved wild shape (humanoid, giant; Large), low-light vision, resist nature's lure, shifter's speech, trackless step, wild empathy +4 (+0 magical beasts), wild shape 3/day, woodland stride; AL CN; SV Fort +8, Ref +6, Will +8 (+10 against enchantments); Str 12, Dex 15, Con 12, Int 10, Wis 18, Cha 8.

Skills and Feats: Knowledge (nature) +12, Listen +18, Search +2, Spot +18, Survival +16; Alertness, Endurance, Natural Spell.

Languages: Common, Elven; Druidic.

Animal Companion (Ex): Galatea has an eagle named Metrius as an animal companion. Metrius's abilities and characteristics are summarized below.

Animal Companion Benefits: Galatea and Metrius enjoy the link and share spells special qualities.

Link (Ex): Galatea can handle Metrius as a free action. She also gains a +4 circumstance bonus on all wild empathy checks and Handle Animal checks made regarding her eagle.

Share Spells (Ex): Galatea can have any spell she casts on herself also affect her animal companion if the latter is within 5 feet at the time. She can also cast a spell with a target of "You" on her eagle.

Elf Traits: Elves have immunity to magic sleep effects. An elf who merely passes within 5 feet of a secret or concealed door is entitled to a Search check to notice it as if she where actively looking for it.

Improved Wild Shape (Su): Galatea can assume humanoid or giant forms when she uses wild shape. She can also take the form of Large creatures.

Resist Nature's Lure (Ex): Galatea gains a +4 bonus on saving throws against the spell-like abilities of fey.

Shifter's Speech (Ex): Galatea can speak normally regardless of the form she takes, and she can communicate with creatures of whatever kind she transforms into.

Trackless Step (Ex): Galatea leaves no trail in natural surroundings and cannot be tracked.

Wild Shape (Su): Galatea can change into a Small, Medium, or Large animal, humanoid, or giant, and back again, as per the *polymorph* spell. This ability lasts for 5 hours or until she changes back.

Woodland Stride (Ex): Galatea can move through natural thorns, briars, overgrown areas, and similar terrain at her normal speed and without damage or other impairment. However, thorns, briars, and overgrown areas that are magically manipulated to impede motion still affect her.

Druid Spells Prepared (caster level 5th): 0—*cure minor wounds, detect magic, know direction, resistance, virtue;* 1st—*cure light wounds, endure elements, entangle (DC 15), magic fang;* 2nd—*barkskin, bear's endurance, cat's grace;* 3rd—*cure moderate wounds, greater magic fang.*

Possessions: +1 hide armor, +1 buckler, +1 composite longbow (+1 Str bonus) with 20 arrows, +1 scimitar, periapt of Wisdom +2, druid's vestment.

Metrius, Eagle Companion: CR —; Small animal; HD 3d8+3; hp 16; Init +3; Spd 10 ft., fly 80 ft. (average); AC 17, touch 14, flat-footed 14; Base Atk +2; Grp –2; Atk +6 melee (1d4, talons); Full Atk +6 (1d4, 2 talons); SQ bonus tricks (2), evasion, low-light vision; AL N; SV Fort +4, Ref +6, Will +3; Str 11, Dex 16, Con 12, Int 2, Wis 14, Cha 6.

Skills and Feats: Listen +2, Spot +16; Flyby Attack, Weapon Finesse.

Tricks: Attack, guard, seek.

Evasion (Ex): If Metrius is subjected to an attack that normally allows a Reflex saving throw for half damage, it takes no damage if it makes a successful saving throw.

NIGHTSONG ENFORCER

Throughout the city, even the vilest assassin does not command more respect than the nightsong enforcers. They could be anywhere—they could strike at any time. You cannot escape their uncanny senses. And worst of all, they often work in elite teams.

The enforcers of the Nightsong Guild (see page 177) focus on the stealth-centered combat training that rogues usually learn; they forgo some of the sleight of hand or fast-talking aspects of being a thief. However, nightsong enforcers are not mere thugs. They are deadly opponents who strike from hidden positions and move silently behind their foes. When in battle, their goal is to eliminate their enemies, not to fight. Thus, they strike quickly from the shadows. They do not worry about honor or fighting fair, scoffing at such ideals as childish.

Rogues most often become nightsong enforcers, although bards, fighters, and urban rangers are also known to undertake the class. On occasion a wizard or sorcerer will endure the intensive training required to join the enforcers' ranks.

When working with others, a nightsong enforcer is the linchpin. She is the very picture of fidelity when it comes to supporting teammates on a mission. It is common for an enforcer to lead a team composed of not only other enforcers, but fighters, spellcasters, or rogues.

Adaptation: Although described here as associated with the Nightsong Guild, the nightsong enforcer prestige class could have many different uses in a campaign. Enforcers could represent the members of an elite criminal organization, a well-funded private security force, or a highly trained branch of a nation's military. Emphasizing their training and group tactics can greatly shape an encounter or a character based around this prestige class.

Hit Die: d8.

REQUIREMENTS

To qualify to become a nightsong enforcer, a character must fulfill all the following criteria.

Base Attack Bonus: +5.

Skills: Hide 10 ranks, Move Silently 10 ranks.

Feats: Improved Initiative.

Special: Evasion class feature.

Special: The character must undergo intensive training and tests with the Nightsong Guild before she can gain the class abilities.

CLASS SKILLS

The nightsong enforcer's class skills (and the key ability for each skill) are Balance (Dex), Climb (Str), Disable Device (Int), Disguise (Cha), Escape Artist (Dex), Hide (Dex), Intimidate (Cha), Jump (Str), Listen (Wis), Move Silently (Dex), Open Lock (Dex), Profession (Wis), Ride (Dex), Search (Int), Spot (Wis), Swim (Str), and Tumble (Dex).

Skill Points at Each Additional Level: 4 + Int modifier.

CLASS FEATURES

All of the following are class features of the nightsong enforcer prestige class.

Weapon and Armor Proficiency: Nightsong enforcers are not proficient with any weapon. They are proficient with light armor but not with shields.

Sneak Attack (Ex): A nightsong enforcer deals an extra 1d6 points of damage when flanking an opponent or any time the target would be denied its Dexterity

Table 2–15: The Nightsong Enforcer

Level	Base Attack Bonus	Fort Save	Ref Save	Will Save	Special
1st	+1	+0	+2	+0	Sneak attack +1d6, teamwork (hear/see allies)
2nd	+2	+0	+3	+0	Agility training
3rd	+3	+1	+3	+1	Skill teamwork +2
4th	+4	+1	+4	+1	Sneak attack +2d6
5th	+5	+1	+4	+1	Flanking teamwork
6th	+6	+2	+5	+2	Opportunist
7th	+7	+2	+5	+2	Sneak attack +3d6, skill teamwork +4
8th	+8	+2	+6	+2	Improved evasion
9th	+9	+3	+6	+3	Teamwork (status)
10th	+10	+3	+7	+3	Sneak attack +4d6

bonus. This extra damage applies to ranged attacks only if the target is within 30 feet. It increases to 2d6 points at 4th level, 3d6 points at 7th level, and 4d6 points at 10th level. See the rogue class feature, page 50 of the *Player's Handbook*. If a nightsong enforcer gets a sneak attack bonus from another source (such as levels of rogue), the bonuses on damage stack.

Teamwork (Ex): Nightsong enforcers are trained to keep a close eye on teammates on a joint mission. A nightsong enforcer gains a +20 circumstance bonus on Listen and Spot checks to hear and see allies.

At 9th level, a nightsong enforcer's senses are honed so finely that she is aware of the location and status (as with the *status* spell) of all allies within 100 feet, even if they are not within sight.

Agility Training (Ex): Starting at 2nd level, a nightsong enforcer reduces the armor check penalty imposed on her by light armor by 2 (to a minimum of 0).

Skill Teamwork (Ex): At 3rd level and higher, a nightsong enforcer can use her training to improve the skill of those around her. All allies within 30 feet of the nightsong enforcer gain a +2 competence bonus on Balance, Climb, Escape Artist, Hide, Listen, Move Silently, and Spot checks. Allies must be able to see the nightsong enforcer to gain this bonus.

At 7th level, this bonus increases to +4.

Flanking Teamwork (Ex): When a nightsong enforcer of 5th level or higher flanks an opponent, the enforcer and all other allies who threaten the same opponent gain a +1 circumstance bonus on their attack rolls (in addition to the normal flanking bonus, if it applies).

Opportunist (Ex): Once per round, a nightsong enforcer of 6th level or higher can make an attack of opportunity against an opponent who has just been injured in melee by another character. See the rogue class feature, page 51 of the *Player's Handbook*.

Improved Evasion (Ex): If a nightsong enforcer of 8th level or higher is exposed to any effect that normally allows her to attempt a Reflex saving throw for half damage, she takes no damage with a successful saving throw and half damage if the saving throw fails.

SAMPLE NIGHTSONG ENFORCER

Karsta Longfist: Female half-orc monk 7/nightsong enforcer 3; CR 10; Medium humanoid (orc); HD 10d8+20; hp 68; Init +6; Spd 50 ft.; AC 18, touch 15, flat-footed 16; Base Atk +8; Grp +12; Atk +13 melee (1d8+4, unarmed); Full Atk +13/+8 melee (1d8+4, unarmed) or +12/+12/+8 melee (1d8+4, unarmed with flurry of blows); SA *ki* strike (magic), sneak attack +1d6; SQ AC bonus, agility training, darkvision 60 ft., evasion, half-orc traits, purity of body, skill teamwork, slow fall 30 ft., still mind, teamwork, wholeness of body 14 hp/day; AL LN; SV Fort +9, Ref +11, Will +8; Str 18, Dex 14, Con 14, Int 8, Wis 12, Cha 6.

Skills and Feats: Jump +12, Hide +15, Move Silently +15, Spot +14; Deflect Arrows[B], Dodge, Improved Initiative, Improved Trip[B], Mobility, Stunning Fist[B], Weapon Focus (unarmed strike).

Languages: Common, Orc.

Sneak Attack (Ex): Karsta deals an extra 1d6 points of damage on any successful attack against flat-footed or flanked targets, or against a target that has been denied its Dexterity bonus for any reason. This damage also applies to ranged attacks against targets up to 30 feet away. Creatures with concealment, creatures without discernible anatomies, and creatures immune to extra damage from critical hits are all immune to sneak attacks. Karsta can choose to deliver nonlethal damage with her sneak attack, but only when using a weapon designed for that purpose, such as a sap (blackjack).

Agility Training (Ex): The armor check penalty imposed on Karsta by light armor is reduced by 2 (to a minimum of 0).

Evasion (Ex): If Karsta is exposed to any effect that normally allows her to attempt a Reflex saving throw for half damage, she takes no damage with a successful saving throw.

Half-Orc Traits: For all effects related to race, a half-orc is considered an orc.

Purity of Body (Ex): Immune to all normal diseases. Magical and supernatural diseases still affect her.

Skill Teamwork (Ex): All allies within 30 feet of Karsta gain a +2 competence bonus on Balance, Climb, Escape Artist, Hide, Listen, Move Silently, and Spot checks. Allies must be able to see Karsta to gain this bonus.

Slow Fall (Ex): A monk within arm's reach of a wall can use it to slow her descent while falling. Karsta takes damage as if the fall were 30 feet shorter than it actually is.

Still Mind (Ex): +2 bonus on saves against spells and effects of the enchantment school.

Teamwork (Ex): Karsta gains a +20 circumstance bonus on Listen and Spot checks to hear and see allies.

Possessions: amulet of natural armor +1, bracers of armor +3, ring of protection +1, cloak of resistance +1, elixir of sneaking, elixir of hiding, elixir of vision, 2 potions of cure moderate wounds.

NIGHTSONG INFILTRATOR

An expert at breaking into "secure" areas, a nightsong infiltrator is the perfect thief and the perfect spy. Whether she is there to steal gold, information, jewels, or secrets, an infiltrator of the Nightsong Guild (see page 177) is trained to do her job quickly and efficiently. She practices extensively with locks and traps, focusing on doing her job under pressure and in unfavorable conditions. For example, nightsong infiltrators train extensively in climbing, since they often have to scale walls and reach high windows. They have little time to work on combat training and relegate such concerns to their companions, the nightsong enforcers (see the previous prestige class description).

Rogues most frequently and most easily become nightsong infiltrators. Bards, urban rangers, and intelligent fighters can make good members of the class as well. Rarer, but possible, are spellcasting nightsong infiltrators who use spells to get in and out of places. Woe to those wishing to protect their valuables from a Nightsong Guild member who can become invisible, walk through walls, or teleport.

Members of the Nightsong Guild rarely work alone. Usually they operate in teams, often in pairings of a nightsong infiltrator and a nightsong enforcer. (For a PC nightsong infiltrator, the other team member can be an adventuring ally.) When working as part of a team, a nightsong infiltrator works best as the advance scout and point person, while the other team members take care of threats that she is unable to deal with (guards, mostly).

Adaptation: Like their companions the nightsong enforcers, nightsong infiltrators can easily be used to represent a different group. Because its members are especially effective in small groups, the nightsong infiltrator prestige class makes an excellent choice for any organization that might form elite teams. Mercenary groups, intelligence organizations (private or governmental), or criminal groups can be represented by this prestige class with simple changes in the flavor.

Hit Die: d6.

REQUIREMENTS

To qualify to become a nightsong infiltrator, a character must fulfill all the following criteria.

Skills: Climb 10 ranks, Disable Device 5 ranks, Open Lock 5 ranks, Search 5 ranks.

Feats: Alertness.

Special: Evasion class feature.

Special: The character must undergo intensive training and tests with the Nightsong Guild before she can gain the class abilities.

CLASS SKILLS

The nightsong infiltrator's class skills (and the key ability for each skill) are Appraise (Int), Balance (Dex), Bluff (Cha), Climb (Str), Craft (Int), Decipher Script (Int), Diplomacy (Cha), Disable Device (Int), Disguise (Cha), Escape Artist (Dex), Forgery (Int), Gather Information (Cha), Hide (Dex), Jump (Str), Listen (Wis), Move Silently (Dex), Open Lock (Dex), Profession (Wis), Ride (Dex), Search (Int), Sleight of Hand (Dex), Spot (Wis), Swim (Str), Tumble (Dex), Use Magic Device (Cha), and Use Rope (Dex).

Skill Points at Each Level: 8 + Int modifier.

CLASS FEATURES

All of the following are class features of the nightsong infiltrator prestige class.

Weapon and Armor Proficiency: Nightsong infiltrators gain no proficiency with any weapon or armor.

Teamwork Trap Sense (Ex): A nightsong infiltrator has an intuitive sense that alerts her to danger from traps, giving her a +1 bonus on Reflex saves made to avoid traps and a +1 dodge bonus to Armor Class against attacks made by traps. All allies within 30 feet of the infiltrator also gain these bonuses (even if they already have trap sense from another class feature).

These bonuses increase to +2 at 4th level, to +3 at 7th level, and to +4 at 10th level.

Trapfinding (Ex): A nightsong infiltrator can find, disarm, or bypass traps with a DC of 20 or higher. She can use the Search skill to find, and the Disable Device skill to disarm, magic traps (DC 25 + the level of the spell used to create it). If her Disable Device result exceeds the trap's DC by 10 or more, she discovers how to bypass the trap without triggering or disarming it.

Karsta Longfist, a nightsong enforcer

Raelia Fennin, a nightsong infiltrator

Illus. by J. Miracola

Steady Stance (Ex): At 2nd level and higher, a nightsong infiltrator remains stable on her feet when others have difficulty standing. She is not considered flat-footed while balancing or climbing, and she adds her class level as a bonus on Balance or Climb checks to remain balancing or climbing when she takes damage.

Teamwork Infiltration (Ex): Starting at 2nd level, a nightsong infiltrator can study a small area (typically up to 10 feet square, such as a doorway or guard post) in order to prepare for infiltrating that area. If the infiltrator spends 1 hour studying the area from a distance of no more than 60 feet, she gains a +2 competence bonus on Balance, Climb, Disable Device, Hide, Move Silently, Open Lock, Search, and Tumble checks attempted in that area for the next 24 hours. All allies within 30 feet of the infiltrator gain the same bonus in that area. (The allies need not be present while the infiltrator studies the area.)

At 8th level, this bonus increases to +4.

Break Away (Ex): Skilled as she is, a nightsong infiltrator knows the sensibility of falling back from an unwinnable fight. Starting at 3rd level, she gains a +4 dodge bonus to Armor Class in any round during which she does nothing but move.

A nightsong infiltrator can grant this ability to an ally within 30 feet as a swift action (see Swift Actions and Immediate Actions, page 137). It lasts for 1 round.

Trackless Step (Ex): Beginning at 3rd level, a nightsong infiltrator cannot be tracked in natural surroundings. See the druid class feature, page 36 of the *Player's Handbook*.

At 7th level and higher, a nightsong infiltrator can share this ability with up to one additional ally per class level. Designating an ally for trackless step requires a standard action and lasts for 24 hours or until the infiltrator dismisses the effect (a standard action).

Detect Magic (Sp): Starting at 4th level, a nightsong infiltrator can use *detect magic* at will. See the spell, page 219 of the *Player's Handbook*.

Teamwork Sneak Attack (Ex): Beginning at 4th level, a nightsong infiltrator deals an extra 1d6 points of damage when flanking an opponent or any time the target would be denied its Dexterity bonus. Any ally of the infiltrator who is also flanking the infiltrator's opponent deals this extra damage as well. This extra damage applies to ranged attacks only if the target is within 30 feet. It increases to 2d6 points at 8th level. See the rogue class feature, page 50 of the *Player's Handbook*. If a nightsong infiltrator or her ally gets a sneak attack bonus from another source (such as levels of rogue), the bonuses on damage stack.

Defensive Roll (Ex): Starting at 5th level, a nightsong infiltrator can attempt to roll with a potentially lethal blow to take less damage from it than she otherwise would. See the rogue class feature, page 51 of the *Player's Handbook*.

Grant Move Action (Ex): Starting at 5th level, a nightsong infiltrator can direct and motivate her allies to act immediately. Once per day, as a standard action, she can grant an extra move action to any or all of her allies within 30 feet (but not herself). Each of the affected allies takes this extra move action immediately, acting in their current initiative order. This extra action does not affect the allies' initiative count; the round continues normally after the infiltrator's turn is over.

Starting at 9th level, a nightsong infiltrator can use this ability twice per day.

Improved Evasion (Ex): If a nightsong infiltrator of 6th level or higher is exposed to any effect that normally allows her to attempt a Reflex saving throw for half damage, she takes no damage with a successful saving throw and half damage if the saving throw fails.

Skill Mastery (Ex): At 6th level, a nightsong infiltrator has become so confident in the use of certain skills that she can use them reliably even under adverse conditions. When making a Climb, Disable Device, Open Lock, or Search check, she can take 10 even if stress and distractions would normally prevent her from doing so.

TABLE 2–16: THE NIGHTSONG INFILTRATOR

Level	Base Attack Bonus	Fort Save	Ref Save	Will Save	Special
1st	+0	+0	+2	+0	Teamwork trap sense +1, trapfinding
2nd	+1	+0	+3	+0	Steady stance, teamwork infiltration +2
3rd	+2	+1	+3	+1	Break away, trackless step (self)
4th	+3	+1	+4	+1	*Detect magic*, teamwork sneak attack +1d6, teamwork trap sense +2
5th	+3	+1	+4	+1	Defensive roll, grant move action 1/day
6th	+4	+2	+5	+2	Improved evasion, skill mastery, specialized tools
7th	+5	+2	+5	+2	Teamwork trap sense +3, trackless step (allies)
8th	+6	+2	+6	+2	Teamwork infiltration +4, teamwork sneak attack +2d6
9th	+6	+3	+6	+3	Grant move action 2/day
10th	+7	+3	+7	+3	Hide in plain sight, teamwork trap sense +4

Specialized Tools (Ex): After studying an area (see teamwork infiltration, above), a nightsong infiltrator of 6th level or higher can prepare a special tool for a job. Doing this requires 1 hour, a DC 15 Craft check (the specific type of Craft specialty required is up to the DM; blacksmithing, leatherworking, or woodworking are all likely candidates), and a set of artisan's tools for the Craft skill in question.

The tool prepared by the infiltrator grants a +4 circumstance bonus on all checks made with one of the following skills: Climb, Disable Device, Disguise, Escape Artist, Hide, Move Silently, Open Lock, Search, or Sleight of Hand. This bonus doesn't stack with the circumstance bonus granted by any other set of tools (such as a disguise kit or masterwork thieves' tools). The tool works only in the studied area, and it works only for 24 hours (though the infiltrator can rebuild the tool by following the same process).

Hide in Plain Sight (Ex): A 10th-level nightsong infiltrator can can use the Hide skill in natural terrain even while being observed. See the ranger class feature, page 48 of the *Player's Handbook*.

SAMPLE NIGHTSONG INFILTRATOR

Raelia Jaessin: Female elf rogue 7/nightsong infiltrator 3; CR 10; Medium humanoid; HD 10d6+10; hp 47; Init +4; Spd 30 ft.; AC 23, touch 15, flat-footed 23; Base Atk +7; Grp +9; Atk +13 melee (1d4+2/19–20, +1 *dagger* or 1d4+1/19–20, +1 *silver dagger*) or +13 ranged (1d4+2/19–20, +1 *dagger* or 1d4+1/19–20, +1 *silver dagger*); Full Atk +13/+8 melee (1d4+2/19–20, +1 *dagger* or 1d4+1/19–20, +1 *silver dagger*) or +13 ranged (1d4+2/19–20, +1 *dagger* or 1d4+1/19–20, +1 *silver dagger*); SA sneak attack +4d6; SQ break away, elf traits, evasion, low-light vision, steady stance, teamwork infiltration +2, teamwork trap sense +1, trackless step, trap sense +2, trapfinding, uncanny dodge; AL LN; SV Fort +5, Ref +13, Will +8 (+10 against enchantments); Str 14, Dex 18, Con 12, Int 10, Wis 12, Cha 8.

Skills and Feats: Climb +15, Disable Device +13, Hide +17, Move Silently +17, Listen +18, Open Lock +17, Search +15, Spot +18; Alertness, Improved Initiative, Weapon Finesse, Weapon Focus (dagger).

Languages: Common, Elven.

Sneak Attack (Ex): Raelia deals an extra 4d6 points of damage on any successful attack against flat-footed or flanked targets, or against a target that has been denied its Dexterity bonus for any reason. This damage also applies to ranged attacks against targets up to 30 feet away. Creatures with concealment, creatures without discernible anatomies, and creatures immune to extra damage

from critical hits are all immune to sneak attacks. Raelia can choose to deliver nonlethal damage with her sneak attack, but only when using a weapon designed for that purpose, such as a sap (blackjack).

Break Away (Ex): Raelia gains a +4 dodge bonus to AC on any round in which she does nothing but move. She can grant this ability to an ally within 30 feet as a swift action. It lasts for 1 round.

Elf Traits: Elves have immunity to magic sleep effects. An elf who merely passes within 5 feet of a secret or concealed door is entitled to a Search check to notice it as if she where actively looking for it.

Evasion (Ex): If Raelia is exposed to any effect that normally allows her to attempt a Reflex saving throw for half damage, she takes no damage with a successful saving throw.

Steady Stance (Ex): Raelia is not considered flat-footed while balancing or climbing, and she adds +3 to Balance or Climb checks to remain balancing or climbing when she takes damage.

Teamwork Infiltration (Ex): Raelia can study a small area (typically up to 10 feet square, such as a doorway or guard post) in order to prepare for infiltrating that area. If she spends 1 hour studying the area from a distance of no more than 60 feet, she gains a +2 competence bonus on Balance, Climb, Disable Device, Hide, Move Silently, Open Lock, Search, and Tumble checks attempted in that area for the next 24 hours. All allies within 30 feet of Raelia gain the same bonus in that area. (The allies need not be present while she studies the area.)

Teamwork Trap Sense (Ex): Raelia has a +1 bonus on Reflex saves made to avoid traps, and she adds a +1 dodge bonus to AC against attacks made by traps. All allies within 30 feet of Raelia also gain these same bonuses (even if they already have trap sense from another class feature).

Trackless Step (Ex): Raelia leaves no trail in natural surroundings and cannot be tracked.

Trapfinding (Ex): Raelia can find, disarm, or bypass traps with a DC of 20 or higher. She can use the Search skill to find, and the Disable Device skill to disarm, magic traps (DC 25 + the level of the spell used to create it). If her Disable Device result exceeds the trap's DC by 10 or more, she discovers how to bypass the trap without triggering or disarming it.

Uncanny Dodge (Ex): Raelia retains her Dexterity bonus to AC even when flat-footed or targeted by an unseen foe (she still loses her Dexterity bonus if paralyzed or otherwise immobile).

Possessions: +2 *studded leather, ring of protection +1, buckler +2, +1 dagger, +1 silver dagger, cloak of resistance +1.*

OLLAM

In Dwarven, the word "ollam" means teacher. The education of the dwarf people is considered a sacred duty, and those who are considered knowledgeable in dwarf history and legend—and thought to possess above-average common sense—are often called upon to take up the respected role of teacher in the community. While other cultures might see this as a job for young girls or old men, the dwarves see an ollam as a protector of their cherished culture. No one in the dwarf community takes that position lightly.

An ollam is granted a special position in the temple hierarchy—Moradin gives her spells that allow her not only to delve into the secrets of the universe but also to heal and keep an eye on her charges. While most ollams are clerics or bards, individuals of other classes are welcomed, as long as they possess the knowledge needed to teach the children properly.

Oviff Forigril, an ollam

NPC ollams are equally likely to be safely ensconced in the heart of a dwarf community, passing on the accumulated lore of their people, or wandering the lands, sharing their knowledge with dwarves and nondwarves alike. If there's something going on in a dwarf city, you can count on the ollams knowing about it first. They're uncommonly well connected with each clan and stratum of dwarf society.

Adaptation: One of the functions of the ollam prestige class is to give a few bardlike abilities to nonbards—without giving away so much that the prestige class steals the bard's thunder. Given different circumstances, it's easy to imagine ollams from other races and cultures.

Hit Die: d8.

REQUIREMENTS

To qualify to become an ollam, a character must fulfill all the following criteria.

Race: Dwarf.
Alignment: Lawful good.

Skills: Knowledge (history) 10 ranks, Knowledge (any other) 10 ranks, Perform (oratory) 5 ranks.

CLASS SKILLS

The ollam's class skills (and the key ability for each skill) are Concentration (Con), Craft (Int), Decipher Script (Int), Diplomacy (Cha), Gather Information (Cha), Heal (Wis), Knowledge (all skills, taken individually) (Int), Listen (Wis), Perform (Cha), Search (Int), Sense Motive (Wis), Speak Language (n/a), and Spellcraft (Int).

Skill Points at Each Level: 6 + Int modifier.

CLASS FEATURES

All of the following are class features of the ollam prestige class.

Weapon and Armor Proficiency: Ollams are proficient with all simple weapons, with all types of armor, and with shields.

Spells per Day/Spells Known: At 2nd, 3rd, and 4th level, an ollam gains new spells per day (and spells known, if applicable) as if she had also gained a level in a spellcasting class to which she belonged before adding the prestige class level. She does not, however, gain any other benefit a character of that class would have gained. If she had more than one spellcasting class before becoming an ollam, she must decide to which class to add each level for the purpose of determining spells per day and spells known.

If an ollam had no levels in a spellcasting class before taking the prestige class, at 2nd level she gains the spellcasting abilities of a cleric whose caster level is one lower than her class level.

Lore (Ex): An ollam has the ability to recall legends or information regarding various topics, just as a bard can with bardic knowledge. See the bardic knowledge class feature, page 29 of the *Player's Handbook*. An ollam adds her class level and her Intelligence modifier to her lore check. If the character has a similar ability from another class (such as bardic knowledge), her ollam levels stack with class levels from that other class to determine the success of the lore check.

Illus. by S. Belledin

TABLE 2-17: THE OLLAM

Level	Base Attack Bonus	Fort Save	Ref Save	Will Save	Special	Spells per Day/Spells Known
1st	+0	+0	+0	+2	Lore	—
2nd	+1	+0	+0	+3	—	+1 level of existing spellcasting class
3rd	+1	+1	+1	+3	Inspire competence	+1 level of existing spellcasting class
4th	+2	+1	+1	+4	—	+1 level of existing spellcasting class
5th	+2	+1	+1	+4	Inspire resilience	—

Inspire Competence (Su): An ollam of 3rd level or higher can use oratory to help an ally succeed at a task. The ally gets a +2 competence bonus on checks with a particular skill. If the ally is a dwarf, the competence bonus increases to +3. See the bardic music class feature, page 29 of the *Player's Handbook*.

If an ollam has the inspire competence bardic music ability, she can expend one daily use of her bardic music to increase the competence bonus to +4 (or +6 if the ally is a dwarf).

Inspire Resilience (Su): From an early age, dwarves learn to approach life with steadfast resolution and endurance. A 5th-level ollam can spend a standard action to use oratory to tap into this power, granting a single dwarf ally a +4 competence bonus on Constitution checks and Fortitude saves, as well as damage reduction 5/—. The ally must be within 30 feet and able to see and hear the ollam. The ollam must also be able to see the ally. The effect lasts for as long as the ollam orates and for 1 minute thereafter.

Allies who are not dwarves instead gain a +2 competence bonus on Constitution checks and Fortitude saves, gain no damage reduction, and are fatigued at the end of the duration. (Dwarves suffer no ill effect.)

SAMPLE OLLAM

Oviff Forigril: Female dwarf cleric 7/ollam 3; CR 10; Medium humanoid; HD 10d8+30; hp 76; Init +2; Spd 20 ft.; AC 20, touch 10, flat-footed 20; Base Atk +6; Grp +6; Atk +7 melee (1d8+1/×3, +1 *warhammer*) or +6 ranged (1d8/19–20, masterwork light crossbow); Full Atk +7/+2 melee (1d8+1/×3, +1 *warhammer*) or +6 ranged (1d8/19–20, masterwork light crossbow); SA turn undead 5/day (+4, 2d6+9, 7th); SQ darkvision 60 ft., dwarf traits, inspire competence, lore +4; AL LG; SV Fort +10* (+12 against poison), Ref +3*, Will +13*; Str 10, Dex 8, Con 16, Int 12, Wis 18, Cha 14.

Skills and Feats: Concentration +10, Gather Information +8, Knowledge (history) +11, Knowledge (religion) +11, Perform (oratory) +15; Lightning Reflexes, Martial Weapon Proficiency (warhammer), Obscure Lore†, Spell Penetration.

† New feat deescribed on page 111.

Languages: Common, Dwarven; Undercommon.

Dwarf Traits: Dwarves have stonecunning, which grants them a +2 racial bonus on Search checks to notice unusual stonework. A dwarf who merely comes within 10 feet of it can make a Search check as if actively searching.

When standing on the ground, dwarves are exceptionally stable and have a +4 bonus on ability checks made to resist being bull rushed or tripped. They have a +1 racial bonus on attack rolls against orcs and goblinoids. Dwarves have a +4 racial bonus to Armor Class against giants.

*Dwarves have a +2 racial bonus on saving throws against spells and spell-like effects.

Inspire Competence (Su): An ally within 30 feet who can see and hear Oviff gets a +2 competence bonus on checks with a particular skill for as long as he can hear her oratory. If the ally is a dwarf, the bonus increases to +3. Inspire competence lasts for up to 2 minutes.

Cleric Spells Prepared (caster level 9th): 0—*detect magic* (2), *light, mending, read magic, resistance*; 1st—*command* (DC 15), *comprehend languages, deathwatch, divine favor, protection from evil*[DG], *shield of faith*; 2nd—*bear's endurance, divine insight*†, *hold person* (DC 16), *remove paralysis, shield other*[D], *spiritual weapon*; 3rd—*dispel magic, magic vestment, protection from energy*[D], *searing light* (+5 ranged touch), *speak with dead*; 4th—*discern lies, divination, holy smite*[DG] (DC 18), *sending*; 5th—*dispel evil*[DG], *flame strike*.

D: Domain spell. *Domains:* Good (cast good spells [G] at caster level 10th), Protection (protective ward grants +7 resistance bonus on next save, 1/day).

† New spell described on page 147.

Possessions: +1 *full plate, ring of protection +1*, masterwork light wooden shield, +1 *warhammer*, masterwork light crossbow, 20 bolts, *cloak of Charisma +2, periapt of Wisdom +2, cloak of resistance +1*, incense (50 gp), 2 platinum rings (50 gp each), 150 gp.

SHADOWBANE INQUISITOR

Clad in bone-white armor and wreathed in righteous conviction, shadowbane inquisitors battle incessantly against evil in whatever form it takes. Every shadowbane inquisitor belongs to a fellowship of religious knights called the Order of Illumination (see page 179). The order advocates merciless aggression against evil, and its members train to detect and destroy evil creatures and individuals. Filled with fervor, an inquisitor knows only one solution to an infestation of evil: the sword. The purifying flame and the clean cut of a holy blade are his tools.

Along with their comrades (as members of the order refer to one another) the shadowbane stalkers, inquisitors find and confront evil wherever it hides. Unlike shadowbane stalkers, however, inquisitors emphasize purging evil rather than finding it. Their relentless zeal and their overwhelming belief in their own righteousness allow shadowbane inquisitors to root out evil cleanly, even if it costs the lives of a few good creatures, without the moral doubt that other knights might feel. The Order of Illumination expounds that it is better to sacrifice a village that hides a powerful demon than it is to risk letting the demon escape or the evil spread. Although inquisitors remain devoted to the cause of good, this conviction allows them to use their abilities against enemies regardless of their alignment.

Inquisitors must watch shadowbane stalkers carefully to make sure they do not slip into darkness—stalkers are willing to use subterfuge to find evil where it hides, and subtlety and stealth are tools of evil. This situation occasionally puts the two branches of the Order of Illumination at odds, but the order as a whole remains zealously dedicated to good.

Almost all shadowbane inquisitors were once paladins who took a few levels of rogue to better understand and combat the subtle forces of evil. This unusual class combination gives the inquisitor a remarkable ability to resist the manipulations of evil creatures and confront them without fear. Some cleric/rogues become inquisitors, sacrificing their study of divine magic in order to perfect their combat abilities.

Adaptation: Shadowbane inquisitors can easily be added to a campaign as part of a less extreme organization by portraying them as good-aligned detectives with solid combat abilities and distinctive special powers. Although most martial characters have difficulty participating in detective work or social encounters, the inquisitors shine in both areas. On the other hand, simply removing the alignment requirement from the class and renaming it to fit a neutral or evil order of knights makes the inquisitor into a much more overt entry class for the blackguard prestige class.

Hit Die: d10.

REQUIREMENTS

To qualify to become a shadowbane inquisitor, a character must fulfill all the following criteria.

Alignment: Lawful good.
Base Attack: +5.
Skills: Gather Information 4 ranks, Knowledge (religion) 2 ranks, Sense Motive 8 ranks.
Feats: Power Attack.
Special: Detect evil class feature or ability to cast *detect evil* as a divine spell.
Special: Turn undead class feature.
Special: Sneak attack class feature.

CLASS SKILLS

The shadowbane inquisitor's class skills (and the key ability for each skill) are Climb (Str), Concentration (Con), Craft (Int), Decipher Script (Int), Gather Information (Cha), Heal (Wis), Hide (Dex), Jump (Str), Knowledge (religion) (Int), Move Silently (Dex), Profession (Wis), Search (Int), Sense Motive (Wis), and Swim (Str).

Skill Points at Each Level: 4 + Int modifier.

CLASS FEATURES

All of the following are class features of the shadowbane inquisitor prestige class.

Weapon and Armor Proficiency: Shadowbane inquisitors are proficient with all simple and martial weapons, with all types of armor, and with shields (except tower shields).

Absolute Conviction (Ex): Should a shadowbane inquisitor's alignment ever change from lawful good for any reason, he may not take additional levels in this prestige class, but he does not lose any class abilities from levels already attained.

Pierce Shadows (Su): A shadowbane inquisitor can spend one of his daily uses of his turn undead ability to shed a holy radiance. This light brightly illuminates an area in a radius of 20 feet plus 5 feet per class level of the inquisitor. The light is centered on the inquisitor and sheds no shadowy illumination beyond its border. This radiance lasts for 10 minutes per inquisitor class level.

Sacred Stealth (Su): Starting at 2nd level, a shadowbane inquisitor can channel some of his divine spell power to become stealthier. To do this, he must lose a prepared divine spell from memory (or give up a potential spell slot for the day if he casts spells as a sorcerer). He gains a +4 sacred bonus on Hide and Move Silently checks for a number of minutes equal to his Charisma bonus (if any) plus the level of spell given up in this manner.

At 7th level, the bonus increases to +8.

Using this ability is a swift action that does not provoke attacks of opportunity (see Swift Actions and Immediate Actions, page 137).

Smite (Su): Once per day, a shadowbane inquisitor of 2nd level or higher can attempt to smite a creature that he judges to be corrupt with one normal melee attack. He adds his Charisma bonus (if any) to his attack roll and deals an extra 1 point of damage per inquisitor class level. Unlike with a paladin's smite evil ability, an inquisitor relies only on his own judgment when determining what creatures to use this ability against. How an inquisitor uses this ability exemplifies his outlook on the world. The more suspicious and uncompromising an inquisitor is, the more likely he is to feel that a creature should be struck down.

An inquisitor can use this ability twice per day at 6th level and three times per day at 10th level.

Improved Sunder: At 3rd level, a shadowbane becomes accomplished at shattering the weapons of his foes and tainted magic items. He gains the Improved Sunder feat as a bonus feat.

Sneak Attack (Ex): Beginning at 4th level, a shadowbane inquisitor deals an extra 1d6 points of damage when flanking an opponent or any time the target would be denied its Dexterity bonus. This extra damage applies to ranged attacks only if the target is within 30 feet. It increases to 2d6 points at 7th level and 3d6 points at 10th level. See the rogue class feature, page 50 of the *Player's Handbook*. If a shadowbane inquisitor gets a sneak attack bonus from another source (such as levels of rogue), the bonuses on damage stack.

Merciless Purity (Su): Beginning at 5th level, a shadowbane inquisitor benefits when his enemies perish. Upon the death of a creature that the inquisitor has designated as corrupt, he gains a +1 sacred bonus on his Fortitude and Reflex saves for the next 24 hours. An inquisitor designates a creature as corrupt in his eyes by using his smite ability (see above) as part of a melee attack against the creature. The inquisitor need not kill the creature himself. An inquisitor can benefit from this ability only once per day; subsequent deaths of creatures that he has designated as corrupt grant no special benefit.

Righteous Fervor (Su): When an inquisitor of 8th level or higher designates a creature as corrupt, he gains

a +1 sacred bonus on attack and damage rolls against that creature for the rest of the encounter. The inquisitor designates a creature as corrupt by using his smite ability (see above) as part of a melee attack against the creature. This bonus does not apply to the smite attempt itself, only to subsequent attacks against the same creature made in that encounter.

Burning Light (Su): At 9th level and higher, an inquisitor can spend one of his daily uses of his turn undead ability to deal damage to creatures around him. To do this, he must already have his pierce shadows ability active. All creatures within the illuminated area (except for the inquisitor) take 4d6 points of damage. This damage results directly from divine power and is not subject to being reduced by energy resistance. Using this ability requires a standard action.

Multiclassing Note: A paladin can multiclass as a shadowbane inquisitor without losing his ability to take additional levels of paladin. In addition, he can multiclass freely between the paladin and rogue classes and may even gain additional rogue levels. He must still remain lawful good in order to retain his paladin abilities and take paladin levels.

TABLE 2–18: THE SHADOWBANE INQUISITOR

Level	Base Attack Bonus	Fort Save	Ref Save	Will Save	Special
1st	+1	+2	+0	+0	Absolute conviction, pierce shadows
2nd	+2	+3	+0	+0	Sacred stealth (+4), smite 1/day
3rd	+3	+3	+1	+1	Improved Sunder
4th	+4	+4	+1	+1	Sneak attack +1d6
5th	+5	+4	+1	+1	Merciless purity
6th	+6	+5	+2	+2	Smite 2/day
7th	+7	+5	+2	+2	Sacred stealth (+8), sneak attack +2d6
8th	+8	+6	+2	+2	Righteous fervor
9th	+9	+6	+3	+3	Burning light
10th	+10	+7	+3	+3	Smite 3/day, sneak attack +3d6

FALLEN INQUISITORS

Like paladins, shadowbane inquisitors occasionally fall into darkness and evil. The light of self-righteousness burns strongly within an inquisitor, and he never faces the self-doubt or moral dilemmas that heroes of less conviction must deal with. It is this overwhelming confidence in his own ability to define what is right and wrong, however, that sometimes leads an inquisitor into darkness. The path of the inquisitor is long and dangerous, and those who complete it are among the most powerful and persistent opponents of evil. But those

Illus. by M. Phillippi

who fall, having known the heights of purity, become evil beyond reckoning.

Convinced of their own moral purity, fallen inquisitors pursue their vile agenda without ever feeling doubt, and they are often charismatic enough to draw others into their wicked plans. Should an inquisitor who also has paladin levels ever gain levels in the blackguard class, his shadowbane inquisitor levels stack with his paladin levels when determining the number of extra abilities that the blackguard gains for having paladin levels. For example, if a 5th-level paladin/1st-level rogue/5th-level shadowbane inquisitor takes a level of blackguard, he gains extra blackguard class abilities as if he were a fallen paladin of 10th level.

SAMPLE SHADOWBANE INQUISITOR

Kalva: Male human rogue 2/paladin 4/shadowbane inquisitor 2; CR 8; Medium humanoid; HD 2d6+4 plus 6d10+10; hp 60; Init +0; Spd 20 ft.; AC 20, touch 10, flat-footed 20; Base Atk +7; Grp +10; Atk +12 melee (1d10+5/19–20, *+1 greatsword*); Full Atk +12/+7 melee (1d10+5/19–20, *+1 greatsword*); SA smite 1/day, smite evil 1/day, sneak attack +1d6, turn undead 5/day (+4, 2d6+3, 1st); SQ absolute conviction, aura of courage, aura of good, *detect evil*, divine grace, divine health, evasion, lay on hands 8/day, pierce shadows, sacred stealth, trapfinding; AL LG; SV Fort +12, Ref +7, Will +5; Str 16, Dex 10, Con 14, Int 8, Wis 12, Cha 14.

Skills and Feats: Diplomacy +4, Disable Device +3, Gather Information +6, Hide +5, Listen +8, Knowledge (religion) +4, Move Silently +5, Search +3, Sense Motive +9, Spot +9; Cleave, Devoted Inquisitor†, Power Attack, Stealthy, Weapon Focus (greatsword).

† New feat described on page 107.

Language: Common.

Smite (Su): Kalva can attempt to smite a creature he judges to be corrupt with one normal melee attack. He adds 2 to his attack roll and deals an extra 2 points of damage.

Smite Evil (Su): Once per day, Kalva can attempt to smite evil with one normal melee attack. He adds 2 to his attack roll and deals an extra 4 points of damage.

Sneak Attack (Ex): Kalva deals an extra 1d6 points of damage on any successful attack against flat-footed or flanked targets, or against a target that has been denied its Dexterity bonus for any reason. This damage also applies to ranged attacks against targets up to 30 feet away. Creatures with concealment, creatures without discernible anatomies, and creatures immune to extra damage from critical hits are all immune to sneak attacks. Kalva

can choose to deliver nonlethal damage with his sneak attack, but only when using a weapon designed for that purpose, such as a sap (blackjack).

Absolute Conviction (Ex): Kalva does not lose any shadowbane inquisitor class abilities if he changes alignment.

Aura of Courage (Su): Immune to fear, and each ally within 10 feet gains a +4 morale bonus on saving throws against fear effects.

Detect Evil (Sp): Kalva can use *detect evil* at will. See the spell, page 218 of the *Player's Handbook*.

Divine Health (Ex): Immunity to disease.

Evasion (Ex): If Kalva is exposed to any effect that normally allows him to attempt a Reflex saving throw for half damage, he takes no damage with a successful saving throw.

Pierce Shadows (Su): Kalva can spend one of his daily uses of his turn undead ability to brightly illuminate an area with a 30-foot radius centered on himself. This radiance lasts for 20 minutes.

Sacred Stealth (Su): Kalva can lose a prepared divine spell from memory to gain a +4 sacred bonus on Hide and Move Silently checks for a number of minutes equal to 2 plus the level of spell given up in this manner.

Trapfinding (Ex): Kalva can find, disarm, or bypass traps with a DC of 20 or higher. He can use the Search skill to find, and the Disable Device skill to disarm, magic traps (DC 25 + the level of the spell used to create it). If his Disable Device result exceeds the trap's DC by 10 or more, he discovers how to bypass the trap without triggering or disarming it.

Paladin Spell Prepared (caster level 2nd): 1st—*bless weapon.*

Possessions: +2 full plate, +1 greatsword, cloak of resistance +1, scroll of bless weapon, 2 *scrolls of iron silence†, scroll of lesser restoration.*

† New spell described on page 153.

SHADOWBANE STALKER

Those they name as heretics or servants of evil call them zealots. Those they protect from darkness call them saviors and defenders of the truth. Whatever their label, shadowbane stalkers rank as some of the most feared individuals wherever they go.

All shadowbane stalkers belong to the Order of Illumination (see page 179), a fellowship of holy knights dedicated to finding and rooting out hidden evil. The Order of Illumination hunts evil—from liars and petty con artists to mind flayer cabals hidden in the heart of a

Kalva, a
shadowbane
inquisitor

Farsi, a shadowbane stalker

decadent empire—in its most secret lair, and shadowbane stalkers lead the search.

Although many think it restrictive and insensitive, the Order of Illumination is a powerful force for good. Shadowbane stalkers do their part to find evil hidden within the midst of civilized areas so that the martial arm of the order, led by the shadowbane inquisitors (see the previous prestige class), can spearhead the attack against the corruption. Shadowbane stalkers usually work alone or with small groups of independent adventurers, but it is also common for a stalker and an inquisitor to adventure together as partners. Their skills and abilities complement each other, and they know that the other members of the order are some of the few beings they can trust implicitly.

Almost all shadowbane stalkers are clerics who took a few levels of rogue. This unorthodox career path gives a character the divine spellcasting power and martial training necessary to deal with powerful and subtle evils, as well as giving her the broad expertise in skills and stealth required to find and ambush the hidden evils that she seeks.

Adaptation: The Order of Illumination might be too zealous for some campaigns. Its members are so thoroughly dedicated to good that they can sometimes stray into intolerance or unfounded accusations. But by leaving the game mechanics unchanged and simply removing the flavor elements of zealotry and suspicion, the shadowbane stalkers become a small group of dedicated cleric/rogues who are extremely skilled at finding evil monsters. This order probably would consist of clerics from several different churches and would welcome characters who have the right skills. Alternatively, a single shadowbane stalker might run into more than she can handle in the course of an investigation and turn to the PCs for help. In this way, the shadowbane stalkers could become a steady source of adventure leads and staunch allies as the campaign progresses.

Hit Die: d8.

REQUIREMENTS

To qualify to become a shadowbane stalker, a character must fulfill all the following criteria.

Alignment: Lawful good.

Skills: Gather Information 8 ranks, Search 4 ranks, Sense Motive 4 ranks.

Special: Detect evil class feature or ability to cast *detect evil* as a divine spell.

Special: Sneak attack +1d6.

CLASS SKILLS

The shadowbane stalker's class skills (and the key ability for each skill) are Appraise (Int), Balance (Dex), Climb (Str), Concentration (Con), Craft (Int), Decipher Script (Int), Disable Device (Int), Escape Artist (Dex), Gather Information (Cha), Heal (Wis), Hide (Dex), Jump (Str), Knowledge (history) (Int), Knowledge (nature) (Int), Knowledge (religion) (Int), Knowledge (the planes) (Int), Listen (Wis), Move Silently (Dex), Open Lock (Dex), Profession (Wis), Search (Int), Sense Motive (Wis), Sleight of Hand (Dex), Spellcraft (Int), Spot (Wis), Tumble (Dex), Use Magic Device (Cha), and Use Rope (Dex).

Skill Points at Each Level: 6 + Int modifier.

CLASS FEATURES

All of the following are class features of the shadowbane stalker prestige class.

Weapon and Armor Proficiency: Shadowbane stalkers gain no proficiency with any weapon or armor.

Spells per Day/Spells Known: A shadowbane stalker continues training in divine spellcasting as well as learning. At each level gained in the shadowbane stalker class except for 4th and 9th, she gains new spells per day (and spells known, if applicable) as if she had also gained a level in a divine spellcasting class she belonged to before adding the prestige class level. She does not, however, gain any other benefit a character of that class would have gained. If she had more than one divine spellcasting class before becoming a shadowbane stalker, she must decide to which class to add each level for the purpose of determining spells per day and spells known.

Detect Evil (Sp): A shadowbane stalker can use *detect evil* at will. See the spell, page 218 of the *Player's Handbook*.

Sacred Stealth (Su): A shadowbane stalker can channel some of her divine spellpower to become stealthier. To do this, she must lose a prepared divine spell from memory (or give up a potential spell slot for the day if she casts spells as a sorcerer). She gains a +4 sacred bonus on Hide and Move Silently checks for a number of minutes equal to her Charisma bonus (if any) plus the level of spell given up in this manner.

At 7th level, the bonus increases to +8.

Using this ability is a swift action that does not provoke attacks of opportunity.

Discover Subterfuge (Ex): A shadowbane stalker trains diligently to detect subterfuge and the misdirection of others. At 2nd level and higher, she gains a +2 competence bonus on Search and Sense Motive checks. This bonus increases to +4 at 5th level and +6 at 8th level.

TABLE 2–19: THE SHADOWBANE STALKER

Level	Base Attack Bonus	Fort Save	Ref Save	Will Save	Special	Spells per Day/Spells Known
1st	+0	+0	+2	+2	*Detect evil*, sacred stealth +4	+1 level of existing divine spellcasting class
2nd	+1	+0	+3	+3	Discover subterfuge +2	+1 level of existing divine spellcasting class
3rd	+2	+1	+3	+3	Sneak attack +1d6	+1 level of existing divine spellcasting class
4th	+3	+1	+4	+4	Sacred defense	—
5th	+3	+1	+4	+4	Discover subterfuge +4	+1 level of existing divine spellcasting class
6th	+4	+2	+5	+5	Sneak attack +2d6	+1 level of existing divine spellcasting class
7th	+5	+2	+5	+5	Sacred stealth +8	+1 level of existing divine spellcasting class
8th	+6	+2	+6	+6	Discover subterfuge +6	+1 level of existing divine spellcasting class
9th	+6	+3	+6	+6	Sneak attack +3d6	—
10th	+7	+3	+7	+7	Sacred strike	+1 level of existing divine spellcasting class

Sneak Attack (Ex): Beginning at 3rd level, a shadowbane stalker deals an extra 1d6 points of damage when flanking an opponent or any time the target would be denied its Dexterity bonus. This extra damage applies to ranged attacks only if the target is within 30 feet. It increases to 2d6 points at 6th level and 3d6 points at 9th level. See the rogue class feature, page 50 of the *Player's Handbook*. If a shadowbane stalker gets a sneak attack bonus from another source (such as levels of rogue), the bonuses on damage stack.

Sacred Defense (Su): At 4th level and higher, a shadowbane stalker can channel some of her divine spellpower to help her avoid the attacks of enemies. To do this, she must lose a prepared divine spell from memory (or give up a potential spell slot for the day if she casts spells as a sorcerer). The stalker gains a +4 sacred bonus to Armor Class for a number of rounds equal to the level of the divine spell given up in this manner.

Using this ability is a swift action that does not provoke attacks of opportunity.

Sacred Strike (Su): At 10th level, a shadowbane stalker can channel her divine spellpower to deal extra damage. To do this, she must lose a prepared divine spell from memory (or give up a potential spell slot for the day if she casts spells as a sorcerer). The stalker can add an extra 1d6 points of damage per level of the spell lost, up to the number of her sneak attack damage dice. This ability affects the next attack she makes in the same round that she uses this ability.

Creatures immune to sneak attacks are immune to extra damage from this ability. If the affected attack misses, the sacred strike is lost with no effect.

Using this ability is a swift action that does not provoke attacks of opportunity.

SAMPLE SHADOWBANE STALKER

Farsi: Female human rogue 3/cleric 2/shadowbane stalker 3; CR 8; Medium humanoid; HD 3d6+3 plus 4d8+4; hp 43; Init +7; Spd 30 ft.; AC 21, touch 13, flat-footed 18; Base Atk +5; Grp +7; Atk or Full Atk +9 melee (1d8+3, +1 heavy mace); SA sneak attack +3d6, turn undead 3/day; SQ aura of good, aura of law, *detect evil*, discover subterfuge +2, evasion, sacred stealth, trap sense +1, trapfinding, turn undead 3/day (+0, 2d6+2, 2nd); AL LG; SV Fort +6, Ref +9, Will +9; Str 14, Dex 16, Con 12, Int 8, Wis 14, Cha 10.

Skills and Feats: Bluff +4, Gather Information +8, Hide +13, Listen +13, Knowledge (religion) +4, Move Silently +13, Search +6, Sense Motive +8, Spot +13; Dodge, Improved Initiative, Mobility, Weapon Focus (heavy mace).

Language: Common.

Sneak Attack (Ex): Farsi deals an extra 3d6 points of damage on any successful attack against flat-footed or flanked targets, or against a target that has been denied its Dexterity bonus for any reason. This damage also applies to ranged attacks against targets up to 30 feet away. Creatures with concealment, creatures without discernible anatomies, and creatures immune to extra damage from critical hits are all immune to sneak attacks. Farsi can choose to deliver nonlethal damage with her sneak attack, but only when using a weapon designed for that purpose, such as a sap (blackjack).

Detect Evil (Sp): Farsi can use *detect evil* at will. See the spell, page 218 of the *Player's Handbook*.

Evasion (Ex): If Farsi is exposed to any effect that normally allows her to attempt a Reflex saving throw for half damage, she takes no damage with a successful saving throw.

Sacred Stealth (Su): Farsi can lose a prepared divine spell from memory to gain a +4 sacred bonus on Hide and Move Silently checks for a number of minutes equal to the level of spell given up in this manner.

Trapfinding (Ex): Farsi can find, disarm, or bypass traps with a DC of 20 or higher. She can use the Search skill to find, and the Disable Device skill to disarm, magic traps (DC 25 + the level of the spell used to create it). If her Disable Device result exceeds the trap's DC by 10 or more, she discovers how to bypass the trap without triggering or disarming it.

Cleric Spells Prepared (caster level 5th): 0—*create water, detect magic, light, mending, resistance*; 1st—*bless, detect chaos, doom* (DC 13), *protection from chaos*[DL], *shield of faith*; 2nd—*align weapon, hold person* (DC 14), *shatter*[D] (DC 13), *silence* (DC 13); 3rd—*magic circle against chaos*[DL], *summon monster III*.

D: Domain spell. *Domains*: Destruction (smite 1/day, +4 on attack, extra 2 damage), Law (cast lawful [L] spells at caster level 6th).

Possessions: +1 mithral breastplate, +1 light shield, +1 heavy mace, triple weapon capsule retainer†, ghostblight capsule†, quickspark capsule†.

† New equipment detailed in Chapter 5.

SHADOWMIND

A specter in the thoughts of the unwary, the shadowmind moves through the twisting pathways of the mind as easily as she slides through the dark alleyways of the city. A shadowmind blends psionic powers and uncanny stealth into an effective whole. Although they can be capable spies or thieves, shadowminds view themselves as much more. Shadowminds see their training and psychic powers as an extension of a deep self-examination process that requires the knowledge of the innermost goals and motivations of others.

While a few shadowminds are trained in secret by governments, covert cabals, and the like, most train at a distant monastery. These ascetics forsake many of the worldly goals they had before joining the shadowmind monastery, instead devoting themselves to peering inside the minds and secrets of others. The rigorous training stresses the need to see the faults and secrets of others as extensions of the shadowmind's own experiences. To a shadowmind, enlightenment and true understanding come from using the secret motivations of others as a means of self-awareness.

Most shadowminds begin their careers as psions and later diversify their skills and abilities by taking a level of rogue. Psychic warriors also find the class appealing, although they are more likely to multiclass as a ranger or ninja than as a rogue. Although wilders can qualify for the class as easily as psions, few wilders become shadowminds. (For full information about psionic classes and psionic powers, see the *Expanded Psionics Handbook*.)

Adaptation: With their excellent skill selection and steady progression of psionic powers, shadowminds can be recast easily to fill almost any niche. Simply change the powers that a shadowmind learns for free to match the desired flavor of the class. Two examples appear below. The powers noted in the examples replace the shadowmind's 1st-level ability *read thoughts*, the 3rd-level ability *cloud mind*, and the 9th-level ability *mass cloud mind*.

Cerebral infiltrator (psionic spy): 1st—*distract*, 3rd—*forced sense link*, 9th—*mind probe*.

Thought killer (psionic assassin): 1st—*conceal thoughts*, 3rd—*energy stun*, 9th—*personal mind blank*.

Hit Die: d6.

REQUIREMENTS

To qualify to become a shadowmind, a character must fulfill all the following criteria.

Base Attack Bonus: +3.

Skills: Hide 5 ranks, Move Silently 5 Ranks, Sleight of Hand 3 ranks.

Special: Manifester level 3rd.

Special: Able to manifest *concealing amorpha*.

CLASS SKILLS

A shadowmind's class skills (and the key ability for each skill) are Autohypnosis* (Wis), Bluff (Cha), Concentration* (Con), Craft (Int), Disable Device (Int), Escape Artist (Dex), Hide (Dex), Jump (Str), Knowledge (psionics)* (Int), Listen (Wis), Move Silently (Dex), Open Lock (Dex), Psicraft* (Int), Search (Int), Sense Motive (Wis), Sleight of Hand (Dex), Spot (Wis), and Tumble (Dex).

*New skill or skill use described in the *Expanded Psionics Handbook*.

Skill Points at Each Level: 4 + Int modifier.

CLASS FEATURES

All the following are class features of the shadowmind prestige class.

Weapon and Armor Proficiency: Shadowminds gain no proficiency with any weapon or armor.

Powers Known: At every level indicated on the accompanying table, a shadowmind gains additional power points per day and access to new discovered powers as if she had also gained a level in whatever psionic manifesting class she belonged to before she added the prestige class. She does not, however, gain any other benefit a character of that class would have gained. If a character had more than one psionic class before becoming a shadowmind, she must decide to which class to add the new level of shadowmind for the purpose of determining power points per day, powers known, and manifester level.

Read Thoughts (Ps): At 1st level, a shadowmind adds *read thoughts* to her repertoire (if she doesn't already know it). Once per day, she can manifest *read thoughts* at a reduced power point cost. The cost of *read thoughts* is reduced by the shadowmind's class level, to a minimum of 1 power point. The effect of this power is still restricted by the shadowmind's manifester level.

Sneak Attack (Ex): Beginning at 2nd level, a shadowmind deals an extra 1d6 points of damage when flanking an opponent or any time the target would be denied its Dexterity bonus. This extra damage applies to ranged attacks only if the target is within 30 feet. It increases to 2d6 points at 5th level and 3d6 points at 8th level. See the rogue class feature, page 50 of the *Player's Handbook*. If a shadowmind gets a sneak attack bonus from another source (such as levels of rogue), the bonuses on damage stack.

Cloud Mind (Ps): At 3rd level, a shadowmind adds *cloud mind* to her repertoire (if she doesn't already know it). Once per day, she can manifest *cloud mind* at a reduced power point cost. The cost of *cloud mind* is reduced by the shadowmind's class level, to a minimum of 1 power point. The effect of this power is still restricted by the shadowmind's manifester level.

Mass Cloud Mind (Ps): At 9th level, a shadowmind adds *mass cloud mind* to her repertoire (if she doesn't already know it). Once per day, she can manifest *mass cloud mind* at a reduced power point cost. The cost of *mass cloud mind* is reduced by the shadowmind's level, to a minimum of 1 power point. The effect of this power is still restricted by the shadowmind's manifester level.

Mind Stab (Su): A 10th-level shadowmind can combine a precise blow with a burst of mental energy, removing her presence from the mind and memory of her victim even as she stabs him. Once per round as a free action, immediately after successfully dealing sneak attack damage to an opponent, a shadowmind can manifest *cloud mind* against that opponent.

Mysk, a shadowmind

Illus. by M. Moore

TABLE 2–20: THE SHADOWMIND

Level	Base Attack Bonus	Fort Save	Ref Save	Will Save	Special	Powers Known
1st	+0	+0	+2	+2	*Read thoughts*	+1 level of existing manifesting class
2nd	+1	+0	+3	+3	Sneak attack +1d6	—
3rd	+2	+1	+3	+3	*Cloud mind*	+1 level of existing manifesting class
4th	+3	+1	+4	+4	—	+1 level of existing manifesting class
5th	+3	+1	+4	+4	Sneak attack +2d6	—
6th	+4	+2	+5	+5	—	+1 level of existing manifesting class
7th	+5	+2	+5	+5	—	+1 level of existing manifesting class
8th	+6	+2	+6	+6	Sneak attack +3d6	—
9th	+6	+3	+6	+6	*Mass cloud mind*	+1 level of existing manifesting class
10th	+7	+3	+7	+7	Mind stab	+1 level of existing manifesting class

Manifesting *cloud mind* in this way uses a reduced power point expenditure as described under the *cloud mind* ability above.

SAMPLE SHADOWMIND

Mysk: Human female rogue 1/psion (seer) 6/shadowmind 3; CR 10; Medium humanoid; HD 6d4+6 plus 4d6+4; hp 39; Init +6; Spd 30 ft.; AC 15, touch 13, flat-footed 13; Base Atk +5; Grp +4; Atk or Full Atk +6 melee (1d4+1, 19–20, dagger); SA psionics, sneak attack +2d6; SQ trapfinding; AL N; SV Fort +4, Ref +9, Will +10; Str 12, Dex 14, Con 13, Int 19, Wis 10, Cha 8.

Skills and Feats: Balance +4, Bluff +3, Disable Device +16, Escape Artist +6, Gather Information +5, Hide +7, Knowledge (local) +11, Knowledge (psionics) +13, Knowledge (the planes) +8, Move Silently +7, Open Lock +14, Psicraft +19, Search +13, Sleight of Hand +6, Spot +4, Survival +0 (+2 following tracks or on other planes), Tumble +12; Force of Will*, Greater Power Penetration*, Improved Diversion†, Improved Initiative, Iron Will, Mind over Body*, Power Penetration*.

*Feat described in the *Expanded Psionics Handbook*.

† New feat described on page 110.

Languages: Common; Draconic, Dwarven, Elven, Orc.

Psionic Powers Known (power points 72; manifester level 8th): 1st—*conceal thoughts, destiny dissonance, dissipating touch, mind thrust* (DC 15), *precognition*; 2nd—*cloud mind* (DC 16), *concealing amorpha, concussion blast, id insinuation* (DC 16), *object reading, read thoughts* (DC 16); 3rd—*body adjustment, energy burst, mental barrier, mind trap*; 4th—*aura sight, psionic freedom of movement, mindwipe* (DC 18), *remote viewing* (DC 18).

Sneak Attack (Ex): Mysk deals an extra 2d6 points of damage on any successful attack against flat-footed or flanked targets, or against a target that has been denied its Dexterity bonus for any reason. This damage also applies to ranged attacks against targets up to 30 feet away. Creatures with concealment, creatures without discernible anatomies, and creatures immune to extra damage from critical hits are all immune to sneak attacks. Mysk can choose to deliver nonlethal damage with her sneak attack, but only when using a weapon designed for that purpose, such as a sap (blackjack).

Trapfinding (Ex): Mysk can find, disarm, or bypass traps with a DC of 20 or higher. She can use the Search skill to find, and the Disable Device skill to disarm, magic traps (DC 25 + the level of the spell used to create it). If her Disable Device result exceeds the trap's DC by 10 or more, she discovers how to bypass the trap without triggering or disarming it.

Possessions: bracers of armor +2, ring of protection +1, headband of intellect +2, cloak of resistance +1, 2 potions of cure moderate wounds, potion of cat's grace, dagger, 100 gp.

SPYMASTER

Some adventurers glory in their reputations—the wider their exploits are known, the happier they are. By contrast, the spymaster prefers to avoid attention. She does her work quietly and in private, keeping well away from public scrutiny. To allay suspicions, she often maintains a cover identity by pretending to be a member of some other class—typically the one in which she began her career.

Spymasters are rarely popular, but so long as nation distrusts nation there will be work for those who can gather information that others wish to keep hidden. Many a ruler who publicly claims to abhor spymasters secretly employs a stable of them, if only to protect his own secrets from the spymasters of other nations. This set of circumstances, plus the secrecy inherent in the profession of spymaster and its high mortality rate, makes it impossible to determine how many spymasters are active in a setting at any given time.

Rogues make excellent spymasters because of their generous skill allotments and their propensity for sneakiness. Likewise, rangers have an edge when operating as spymasters in outdoor surroundings. However, a character of any class can become a spymaster—the more unlikely the combination may seem, the better the cover it provides. Some wizards and sorcerers use their spell ability as a cover for subterfuge, and some barbarians are far more subtle than they seem. Spymasters can be of any alignment. They range from self-serving information brokers who sell their services to the highest bidder to high-minded moles who penetrate and destroy corrupt organizations.

It's important for a spymaster to keep her personal emotions distinct from her professional attachments. She must be ready to liquidate someone she has come to like without a moment's thought if so ordered. Betrayal is her business, and her loyalty is always to her mission, not to the people she encounters while carrying it out.

Occasionally, a spymaster may find it expedient to infiltrate an adventuring party heading for the area where her real mission lies. In such a case, she behaves in all ways as a loyal party member until her goals and those of her companions diverge.

Adaptation: Nearly undetectable and constantly covering their tracks, spymasters are easily included in a campaign as single NPCs or villains. Spymasters work best on their own or with a small group of adventuring companions of other classes, so incorporating them into a campaign doesn't usually involve creating spymaster-specific organizations. Rather, spymasters serve as the eyes and ears of many organizations. Several of the organizations described in Chapter 6 of this book might make use of one or more high-level spymasters to train other members, keep tabs on rival organizations, and undertake special missions not suitable for the talents of their regular members. Every kingdom has or wants as many spymasters in its employ as possible, and many who have the talent for such work find themselves carefully watched and encouraged by agents of the crown.

Hit Die: d6.

REQUIREMENTS

To qualify to become a spymaster, a character must fulfill all the following criteria.

Skills: Bluff 8 ranks, Diplomacy 4 ranks, Disguise 8 ranks, Forgery 4 ranks, Gather Information 4 ranks, Sense Motive 4 ranks.

Feat: Skill Focus (Bluff).

CLASS SKILLS

The spymaster's class skills (and the key ability for each skill) are Appraise (Int), Balance (Dex), Bluff (Cha), Climb (Str), Decipher Script (Int), Diplomacy (Cha), Disable Device (Int), Disguise (Cha), Escape Artist (Dex), Forgery (Int), Gather Information (Cha), Hide (Dex), Intimidate (Cha), Jump (Str), Knowledge (geography) (Int), Knowledge (history) (Int), Knowledge (local) (Int), Knowledge (nobility and royalty) (Int), Listen (Wis), Move Silently (Dex), Open Lock (Dex), Search (Int), Sense Motive (Wis), Sleight of Hand (Dex), Speak Language (n/a), Spot (Wis), Swim (Str), Tumble (Dex), Use Magic Device (Cha), and Use Rope (Dex).

Skill Points at Each Level: 8 + Int modifier.

CLASS FEATURES

All of the following are class features of the spymaster prestige class.

Weapon and Armor Proficiency: Spymasters are proficient with all simple and martial weapons and with light and medium armor.

Cover Identity (Ex): A spymaster has one specific cover identity (such as "Murek, the tailor from Sumberton"). While operating in that identity, she gains a +4 circumstance bonus on Disguise checks and a +2 circumstance bonus on Bluff and Gather Information checks.

A spymaster can add an additional cover identity to her repertoire at 4th level and another at 7th level.

Should a spymaster wish to "retire" a cover identity and develop a new one, she must spend one week rigorously practicing subtle vocal intonations and body language before she earns the bonuses. Cover identities do not in themselves provide the spymaster with additional skills, proficiencies, or class features that others might expect of the professions pretended. Thus, a spymaster must be careful to choose identities that can withstand ordinary scrutiny.

Illus. by S. Ellis

Gilifar, a spymaster

Undetectable Alignment (Ex): The web of different identities and agendas inside a spymaster's mind makes it impossible for others to detect her alignment by means of any form of divination. This ability functions like an *undetectable alignment* spell, except that it is always active.

Quick Change (Ex): By 2nd level, a spymaster has become adept at quickly switching from one identity to another. She now can don a disguise in one-tenth the normal time (1d3 minutes) and don or remove armor in one-half the normal time.

Scrying Defense (Ex): Starting at 2nd level, a spymaster adds her class level to Will saves against divination (scrying) spells, as well as to Spot checks made to notice the sensors created by such spells.

Magic Aura (Sp): At 3rd level, a spymaster gains the ability to use *Nystul's magic aura* at will with a caster level equal to her class level. Most spymasters use this ability to shield their own magic items from detection.

Sneak Attack (Ex): Beginning at 3rd level, a spymaster deals an extra 1d6 points of damage when flanking an opponent or any time the target would be denied its Dexterity bonus. This extra damage applies to ranged attacks only if the target is within 30 feet. It increases to 2d6 points at 6th level. See the rogue class feature, page 50 of the *Player's Handbook*. If a spymaster gets a sneak attack bonus from another source (such as levels of rogue), the bonuses on damage stack.

Slippery Mind (Ex): Starting at 4th level, a spymaster has a second chance to wriggle free from any enchantment spells and effects. See the rogue class feature, page 51 of the *Player's Handbook*.

Dispel Scrying (Su): At 5th level and higher, a spymaster can dispel a scrying sensor as if casting a targeted *greater dispel magic*. Her caster level is equal to her class level + 10. She can use this ability a number of times per day equal to 3 + her Intelligence modifier.

Deep Cover (Ex): At 7th level, a spymaster becomes able to quiet her mind and completely immerse herself in her cover identity. While she operates under deep cover, divination spells detect only information appropriate to her cover identity; they reveal nothing relating to her spymaster persona.

SAMPLE SPYMASTER

Gilifar: Female half-elf rogue 5/spymaster 3; CR 8; Medium humanoid (elf); HD 8d6+8; hp 35; Init +7; Spd 30 ft.; AC 18, touch 14, flat-footed 18; Base Atk +5; Grp +4; Atk or Full Atk +8 melee (1d6–1/18–20, +1 *rapier*); SA

TABLE 2–21: THE SPYMASTER

Level	Base Attack Bonus	Fort Save	Ref Save	Will Save	Special
1st	+0	+0	+2	+0	Cover identity, undetectable alignment
2nd	+1	+0	+3	+0	Quick change, scrying defense
3rd	+2	+1	+3	+1	*Magic aura*, sneak attack +1d6
4th	+3	+1	+4	+1	Cover identity, slippery mind
5th	+3	+1	+4	+1	Dispel scrying
6th	+4	+2	+5	+2	Sneak attack +2d6
7th	+5	+2	+5	+2	Cover identity, deep cover

sneak attack +4d6; SQ cover identity, evasion, half-elf traits, low-light vision, *magic aura*, quick change, scrying defense, trap sense +1, trapfinding, uncanny dodge, undetectable alignment; AL N; SV Fort +4, Ref +9, Will +3; Str 8, Dex 16, Con 12, Int 10, Wis 13, Cha 14.

Skills and Feats: Balance +5, Bluff +15, Diplomacy +18, Disguise +12 (+14 acting), Forgery +13, Gather Information +14, Hide +14, Intimidate +3, Jump +1, Listen +4, Move Silently +14, Search +3, Sense Motive +11, Sleight of Hand +16, Spot +4 (+7 to notice scrying sensors), Tumble +14; Improved Initiative, Skill Focus (Bluff), Weapon Finesse.

Languages: Common, Elven.

Sneak Attack (Ex): Gilifar deals an extra 4d6 points of damage on any successful attack against flat-footed or flanked targets, or against a target that has been denied its Dexterity bonus for any reason. This damage also applies to ranged attacks against targets up to 30 feet away. Creatures with concealment, creatures without discernible anatomies, and creatures immune to extra damage from critical hits are all immune to sneak attacks. She can choose to deliver nonlethal damage with her sneak attack, but only when using a weapon designed for that purpose, such as a sap (blackjack).

Cover Identity (Ex): Gilifar has adopted a cover identity of Falimet, a pitiful beggar who asks for coins near the city gate.

Evasion (Ex): If Gilifar is exposed to any effect that normally allows her to attempt a Reflex saving throw for half damage, she takes no damage with a successful saving throw.

Half-Elf Traits: Half-elves have immunity to magic sleep effects. For all effects related to race, a half-elf is considered an elf.

Magic Aura (Sp): Gilifar can use *Nystul's magic aura* at will.

Quick Change (Ex): Gilifar can don a disguise in 1d3 minutes and don or remove armor in one-half the normal time.

Scrying Defense (Ex): Gilifar gains a +3 bonus on Will saves against divination (scrying) spells and a +3 bonus on Spot checks made to notice the sensors created by such spells.

Trapfinding (Ex): Gilifar can find, disarm, or bypass traps with a DC of 20 or higher. She can use the Search skill to find, and the Disable Device skill to disarm, magic traps (DC 25 + the level of the spell used to create it). If her Disable Device result exceeds the trap's DC by 10 or more, she discovers how to bypass the trap without triggering or disarming it.

Uncanny Dodge (Ex): Gilifar retains her Dexterity bonus to AC even when flat-footed or targeted by an unseen foe (she still loses her Dexterity bonus if paralyzed or otherwise immobile).

Undetectable Alignment (Ex): Gilifar's alignment is concealed as by an always active *undetectable alignment* spell.

Possessions: +2 leather armor, ring of protection +1, +1 rapier, cloak of resistance +1.

STREETFIGHTER

Streetfighters have found a place, and even some small amount of fame, among the shadowy and dangerous regions of the world's great cities. Some leave their homes, putting their skills to the test against dangerous monsters in lost tombs or fighting for sport in front of the nobility, but they always remember the lessons of the streets.

Streetfighters never rest easy. They have seen violence and depravity to rival any dungeon adventurer, and they have survived because they never let their guard down. Rather than leaving a streetfighter suspicious or spent, this experience has forged his mind and body into that of a lean, quick-thinking combatant capable of seizing any advantage in battle.

Most streetfighters are fighter/rogues who have had to survive in dangerous urban environments their entire lives. Perhaps the strangest streetfighters are barbarians and rangers who adopt urban environments as their chosen homes. These wild men and women seek the challenges of the back alleys as a way of testing themselves and their experience in the wider world against the street smarts and tough talk of the city. Very few spellcasters have the bravado or the melee skill to become streetfighters.

Adaptation: With a few simple changes, the streetfighter prestige class can be used to represent any group of opportunistic fighters. Just change the description of the class, and it might be associated with a school of gladiatorial training in a city's elite urban patrol. Adding the Weapon Focus or Weapon Finesse feats to the requirements can also bring about large changes in the feel of the class. Weapon Focus (dagger) turns a streetfighter into a knife fighter, while Weapon Focus (rapier) makes the class well suited to a school of fencers from an urban environment.

Hit Die: d8.

REQUIREMENTS

To qualify to become a streetfighter, a character must fulfill all the following criteria.

Base Attack Bonus: +5.

Skills: Bluff 5 ranks, Intimidate 5 ranks, Knowledge (local) 5 ranks.

Feats: Combat Expertise, Improved Feint.

CLASS SKILLS

The streetfighter's class skills (and the key ability for each skill) are Bluff (Cha), Climb (Str), Disable Device (Int), Hide (Dex), Intimidate (Cha), Jump (Str), Knowledge (local) (Int), Listen (Wis), Move Silently (Dex), Open Lock (Dex), Ride (Dex), Search (Int), Spot (Wis), and Tumble (Dex).

Skill Points at Each Level: 4 + Int modifier.

CLASS FEATURES

All of the following are class features of the streetfighter prestige class.

Weapon and Armor Proficiency: Streetfighters gain no proficiency with any weapon or armor.

Always Ready (Ex): A streetfighter knows that an attack can come from any quarter, and that an innocuous conversation can turn into a deadly fight in an instant. Accordingly, he gains a +1 competence bonus on initiative checks. This bonus increases to +2 at 3rd level and to +3 at 5th level.

Streetwise (Ex): A streetfighter knows how to survive in dangerous urban areas; he gains a +2 competence bonus on Gather Information and Knowledge (local) checks.

Stand Tough (Ex): A streetfighter's toughness has been honed by years of hard living and dirty fighting. Starting at 2nd level, a streetfighter can stand tough once per day. When he would be damaged in combat (from a weapon or some other blow, but not from a spell or special ability), he can attempt to shake off the damage.

TABLE 2–22: THE STREETFIGHTER

Level	Base Attack Bonus	Fort Save	Ref Save	Will Save	Special
1st	+1	+2	+0	+0	Always ready +1, streetwise
2nd	+2	+3	+0	+0	Stand tough 1/day
3rd	+3	+3	+1	+1	Always ready +2, sneak attack +1d6
4th	+4	+4	+1	+1	Stand tough 2/day
5th	+5	+4	+1	+1	Always ready +3, uncanny dodge

To do this, he must attempt a Fortitude saving throw against a DC equal to the number of points of damage dealt. If the save succeeds, he takes no lethal damage from the blow, instead taking nonlethal damage equal to half the amount of damage the blow would have dealt. If the save fails, he takes damage normally. A streetfighter need not be aware of the impending attack to use this ability.

Starting at 4th level, a streetfighter can use this ability twice per day.

Sneak Attack (Ex): Beginning at 3rd level, a streetfighter deals an extra 1d6 points of damage when flanking an opponent or any time the target would be denied its Dexterity bonus. This extra damage applies to ranged attacks only if the target is within 30 feet. See the rogue class feature, page 50 of the *Player's Handbook*. If a streetfighter gets a sneak attack bonus from another source (such as levels of rogue), the bonuses on damage stack.

Uncanny Dodge (Ex): At 5th level, a streetfighter cannot be caught flat-footed and reacts to danger before his senses would normally allow him to do so. See the barbarian class feature, page 26 of the *Player's Handbook*.

If a streetfighter already has uncanny dodge from a different class, he gains improved uncanny dodge instead. See the barbarian class feature, page 26 of the *Player's Handbook*.

SAMPLE STREETFIGHTER

Barsh "The Red" Merryweather: Male halfling fighter 3/rogue 3/streetfighter 3; CR 9; Small humanoid; HD 3d10+6 plus 3d6+6 plus 3d8+6; hp 63; Init +6; Spd 20 ft.; AC 23, touch 16, flat-footed 19; Base Atk +8; Grp +4; Atk +14 melee (1d4+1/19–20, +1 *short sword*) or +15 ranged (1d3, masterwork sling); Full Atk +14/+9 melee (1d4+1/19–20, +1 *short sword*) or +15 ranged (1d3, masterwork sling); SA sneak attack +3d6; SQ always ready +2, evasion, stand tough 1/day, streetwise, trap sense +1, trapfinding; AL CN; SV Fort +11, Ref +11, Will +6 (+8 against fear); Str 10, Dex 18, Con 14, Int 13, Wis 8, Cha 11.

Skills and Feats: Balance +6, Bluff +13, Climb +8, Gather Information +4, Hide +13, Intimidate +14, Jump +4, Knowledge (local) +6, Listen +8, Move Silently +10, Spot +6, Tumble +11; Alertness, Combat Expertise[B], Improved Feint[B], Iron Will, Persuasive, Weapon Finesse.

Languages: Common, Halfling; Goblin.

Always Ready (Ex): Barsh gains a +2 competence bonus on initiative checks.

Evasion (Ex): If Barsh is exposed to any effect that normally allows him to attempt a Reflex saving throw for half damage, he takes no damage with a successful saving throw.

Sneak Attack (Ex): Barsh deals an extra 3d6 points of damage on any successful attack against flat-footed or flanked targets, or against a target that has been denied its Dexterity bonus for any reason. This damage also applies to ranged attacks against targets up to 30 feet away. Creatures with concealment, creatures without discernible anatomies, and creatures immune to extra damage from critical hits are all immune to sneak attacks. Barsh can choose to deliver nonlethal damage with his sneak attack, but only when using a weapon designed for that purpose, such as a sap (blackjack).

Stand Tough (Ex): Once per day, Barsh can attempt to shake off the damage from a single blow. To do this, he must attempt a Fortitude saving throw against a DC equal to the number of points of damage dealt. If the

Barsh "the Red" Merryweather, a streetfighter

save succeeds, he takes no lethal damage from the blow, instead taking nonlethal damage equal to half the amount of the damage that the blow would have dealt. If the save fails, he takes damage normally.

Streetwise (Ex): Barsh gets a +2 competence bonus on Gather Information and Knowledge (local) checks.

Trapfinding (Ex): Barsh can find, disarm, or bypass traps with a DC of 20 or higher. He can use the Search skill to find, and the Disable Device skill to disarm, magic traps (DC 25 + the level of the spell used to create it). If his Disable device result exceeds the trap's DC by 10 or more, he discovers how to bypass the trap without triggering or disarming it.

Possessions: +1 studded leather, amulet of natural armor +1, ring of protection +1, +1 short sword, masterwork sling, 2 potions of bear's endurance, 2 potions of cat's grace, 3 potions of cure light wounds, 70 pp.

TEMPEST

A tempest is the point of calm within a whirling barrier of deadly blades. Poets use colorful terms such as "dancing" to describe the movement of a tempest and her two blades, but mastery of this fighting style is not about dancing, nor is it about impressing anyone—least of all poets. A tempest focuses on learning the secrets of two-weapon fighting for a single purpose: the destruction of her enemies.

Typically hardy individualists, tempests rarely learn their skills through formal training. Instead, they master their art through constant application of its disciplines and experimentation on their foes. Similarly, no matter how famous a tempest becomes, it's rare for one to take on students. Their art, they say, is one that can be learned but never taught.

This prestige class is open to all classes and races. Though tempests are rare, every humanoid race has boasted at least a few. Even members of the smaller races can find the tempest's path appealing. Elves make nimble, clever tempests whose Dexterity works to their advantage. Dwarves are the least likely to become tempests, perhaps because they favor heavy armor and heavy weapons, but some do exist.

Adaptation: Elite two-weapon fighters could be trained in many schools and kingdoms. An interesting way to incorporate tempests into a campaign world involves having several groups of tempests specialize in different pairs of weapons. Elf war leaders might train to perfect their grace and effectiveness with two short swords, while an exotic group of human warriors might prefer a handaxe and a kukri.

Hit Die: d10.

REQUIREMENTS

To qualify to become a tempest, a character must fulfill all the following criteria.

Base Attack Bonus: +6.

Feats: Dodge, Improved Two-Weapon Fighting, Mobility, Spring Attack, Two-Weapon Fighting.

CLASS SKILLS

The tempest's class skills (and the key ability for each skill) are Balance (Dex), Climb (Str), Craft (Int), Jump (Str), Sleight of Hand (Dex), and Tumble (Dex).

Skill Points at Each Level: 2 + Int modifier.

CLASS FEATURES

All of the following are class features of the tempest prestige class.

Weapon and Armor Proficiency: Tempests gain no proficiency with any weapon or armor.

Tempest Defense (Ex): When wielding a double weapon or two weapons (not including natural weapons or unarmed strikes), a tempest gains a +1 bonus to Armor Class. This bonus increases to +2 at 3rd level and +3 at 5th level. The character loses this ability when fighting in medium or heavy armor.

Ambidexterity (Ex): For a tempest of 2nd level or higher, her attack penalties for fighting with two weapons are lessened by 1 (from −4 to −3, or from −2 to −1 if the off-hand weapon is a light weapon). At 4th level, the attack penalties are lessened by another 1 (from −3 to −2, or to +0 if the off-hand weapon is a light weapon). The character loses this ability when fighting in medium or heavy armor. See Table 8–10: Two-Weapon Fighting Penalties, page 160 of the *Player's Handbook*.

Two-Weapon Versatility (Ex): When a tempest of 3rd level or higher fights with two weapons, she can apply

TABLE 2–23: THE TEMPEST

Level	Base Attack Bonus	Fort Save	Ref Save	Will Save	Special
1st	+1	+2	+0	+0	Tempest defense +1
2nd	+2	+3	+0	+0	Ambidexterity (−3/−1)
3rd	+3	+3	+1	+1	Tempest defense +2, two-weapon versatility
4th	+4	+4	+1	+1	Ambidexterity (−2/+0)
5th	+5	+4	+1	+1	Tempest defense +3, two-weapon spring attack

the effects of certain feats from one weapon to the other weapon as well, as long as those effects can be applied legally. She can use this ability only with the following feats: Greater Weapon Focus, Greater Weapon Specialization, Improved Critical, Weapon Focus, and Weapon Specialization. For example, a tempest who wields a longsword and a short sword and who has the Weapon Focus (longsword) feat can apply the effect of Weapon Focus to her short sword as well as to her longsword. If a tempest already has the feat with both weapons, she gains no additional effect.

Two-Weapon Spring Attack (Ex): When a 5th-level tempest makes a spring attack, she can attack once each with two different weapons as an attack action. The character loses this ability when fighting in medium or heavy armor.

Illus. by M. Cotie

SAMPLE TEMPEST

Dwotia Keenaxe:
Female dwarf fighter 6/tempest 3; CR 9; Medium humanoid; HD 9d10+27; hp 76; Init +3; Spd 20 ft.; AC 21, touch 16, flat-footed 18; Base Atk +9; Grp +12; Atk +14 melee (1d10+6/19–20/×3, +1 dwarven waraxe) or +12 ranged (1d8+3/×3, composite longbow); Full Atk +14/+9 melee (1d10+6/19–20/×3, +1 dwarven waraxe) and +13 melee (1d6+4/19–20/×3, +1 handaxe), or +12/+7 ranged (1d8+3/×3, composite longbow); SA ambidexterity, two-weapon versatility; SQ darkvision 60 ft., dwarf traits, tempest defense +2; AL CG; SV Fort +11* (+13* against poison), Ref +6*, Will +4*; Str 16, Dex 16, Con 16, Int 8, Wis 12, Cha 8.

Dwotia Keenaxe, a tempest

Skills and Feats: Climb +6, Jump +7, Tumble +7; Dodge[B], Improved Critical (dwarven waraxe), Improved Two-Weapon Fighting[B], Mobility[B], Spring Attack[B], Two-Weapon Fighting, Weapon Focus (dwarven waraxe), Weapon Specialization (dwarven waraxe).

Languages: Common, Dwarven.

Ambidexterity (Ex): Dwotia's attack penalties for fighting with two weapons are lessened by 1.

Two-Weapon Versatility (Ex): When Dwotia fights with two weapons, her Improved Critical (dwarven waraxe), Weapon Focus (dwarven waraxe), and Weapon Specialization (dwarven waraxe) feats apply to her second weapon as well as to her dwarven waraxe.

Dwarf Traits: Dwarves have stonecunning, which grants them a +2 racial bonus on Search checks to notice unusual stonework. A dwarf who merely comes within 10 feet of it can make a Search check as if actively searching. When standing on the ground, dwarves are exceptionally stable and have a +4 bonus on ability checks made to resist being bull rushed or tripped. They have a +1 racial bonus on attack rolls against orcs and goblinoids. Dwarves have a +4 racial bonus to Armor Class against giants. Their race also gives them a +2 bonus on Appraise or Craft checks that are related to stone or metal items.

*Dwarves have a +2 racial bonus on saving throws against spells and spell-like effects.

Possessions: +1 chain shirt, ring of protection +1, +1 dwarven waraxe, +1 handaxe, composite longbow (+3 Str bonus) with 20 arrows, gauntlets of ogre power, 2 potions of cure light wounds, 20 gp.

THIEF-ACROBAT

A thief-acrobat excels in getting in and getting out. If every street-level entrance to the Jewelers' Guildhouse is locked and well guarded, a thief-acrobat simply jumps atop the building from the roof of a nearby inn, throws a grappling hook to the highest minaret, runs up the attached rope to a shuttered window, and quickly picks the lock. Should a thief-acrobat's escape go awry once she has the goods, her gymnastic combat style keeps her out of harm's way.

Most thief-acrobats are rogues who worked their way up through the ranks of the local thieves guild before learning the second-story trade from more experienced burglars. Characters of other classes—particularly barbarians and illusionists—often find that the acrobatics and climbing skills of the thief-acrobat prestige class complement their abilities nicely.

Adventuring parties often encounter an NPC thief-acrobat in the middle of committing a crime. Sometimes, however, thief-acrobats hire adventurers to help them with particularly dangerous capers, or even to create diversions while they work.

Adaptation: Guilds of thieves large and small could have an elite cadre of cat burglars and second-story people. Changing the class's name slightly can have a great impact on how the prestige class is perceived in your game. Despite its name, members of the thief-acrobat class might have nothing to do with thievery. Labeling the class "adventuring acrobat" or something similar gives the class a reason to exist that has little to do with high-level burglaries.

Hit Die: d6.

REQUIREMENTS

To qualify to become a thief-acrobat, a character must fulfill all the following criteria.

Skills: Balance 8 ranks, Climb 8 ranks, Jump 8 ranks, Tumble 8 ranks.

Special: Evasion class feature.

CLASS SKILLS

The thief-acrobat's class skills (and the key ability for each skill) are Appraise (Int), Balance (Dex), Climb (Str), Craft (Int), Disable Device (Int), Escape Artist (Dex), Hide (Dex), Jump (Str), Move Silently (Dex), Open Lock (Dex), Perform (Cha), Search (Int), Tumble (Dex), and Use Rope (Dex).

Skill Points at Each Level: 6 + Int modifier.

TABLE 2–24: THE THIEF-ACROBAT

Level	Base Attack Bonus	Fort Save	Ref Save	Will Save	Special
1st	+0	+0	+2	+0	Fast acrobatics, kip up, steady stance
2nd	+1	+0	+3	+0	Agile fighting +1/+2, slow fall 20 ft.
3rd	+2	+1	+3	+1	Acrobatic charge, defensive roll 1/day
4th	+3	+1	+4	+1	Agile fighting +2/+3, skill mastery, slow fall 30 ft.
5th	+3	+1	+4	+1	Defensive roll 2/day, improved evasion

CLASS FEATURES

All of the following are class features of the thief-acrobat prestige class.

Weapon and Armor Proficiency: Thief-acrobats are proficient with all simple weapons.

Fast Acrobatics (Ex): A thief-acrobat can avoid the normal penalties for accelerated movement while using her acrobatic talents. She ignores the normal –5 penalty when making a Balance check while moving at her full normal speed. She can climb at half her speed as a move action without taking a –5 penalty on her Climb check. Finally, she can tumble at her full speed without taking the normal –10 penalty on her Tumble check.

Kip Up (Ex): A thief-acrobat can stand up from a prone position as a free action that doesn't provoke attacks of opportunity. This ability works only if the thief-acrobat wears light or no armor and carries no more than a light load.

Steady Stance (Ex): A thief-acrobat remains stable on her feet when others have difficulty standing. She is not considered flat-footed while balancing or climbing, and she adds her class level as a bonus on Balance or Climb checks to remain balancing or climbing when she takes damage.

Agile Fighting (Ex): A whirling, spinning thief-acrobat is a devilishly difficult target. Starting at 2nd level, a thief-acrobat gains a +1 dodge bonus to Armor Class. When fighting defensively or using total defense, this bonus becomes +2. At 4th level, these bonuses increase by 1 (to +2 and +3, respectively).

In addition, a thief-acrobat takes no penalty to her Armor Class or on her melee attack rolls when kneeling, sitting, or prone.

This ability works only if a thief-acrobat wears light or no armor and carries no more than a light load.

Diana, a thief-acrobat

Illus. by W. O'Connor

Slow Fall (Ex): Beginning at 2nd level, a thief-acrobat reduces the effective distance of falls by 20 feet. At 4th level, this improves to reduce the effective distance of falls by 30 feet. See the monk class feature, page 41 of the *Player's Handbook*. If a thief-acrobat has this ability from another class, the distances stack to determine the effective reduction of the falling distance.

Acrobatic Charge (Ex): Starting at 3rd level, a thief-acrobat can charge in situations where others cannot. She can charge over difficult terrain that normally slows movement or through allies blocking her path. This ability enables her to charge across a cluttered battlefield, leap down from a ledge, or swing across a chasm to get to her target. Depending on the circumstance, she may still need to make appropriate checks (such as Jump, Tumble, or Use Rope checks) to successfully move over the terrain.

Defensive Roll (Ex): Beginning at 3rd level, once per day a thief-acrobat can roll with a potentially lethal blow to take less damage from it than she otherwise would. See the rogue class feature, page 51 of the *Player's Handbook*.

At 5th level, a thief-acrobat can use this ability twice per day.

Skill Mastery (Ex): At 4th level, a thief-acrobat has become so confident in the use of certain skills that she can use them reliably even under adverse conditions. When making a Balance, Climb, Jump, or Tumble check, she can take 10 even if stress and distractions would normally prevent her from doing so.

Improved Evasion (Ex): A 5th-level thief-acrobat can avoid damage from certain attacks with a successful Reflex save and takes only half damage on a failed save. See the monk class feature, page 42 of the *Player's Handbook*.

SAMPLE THIEF-ACROBAT

Diana: Female halfling rogue 5/thief-acrobat 4; CR 9; Small humanoid; HD 9d6+18; hp 52; Init +4; Spd 30 ft.; AC 19, touch 15, flat-footed 19; Base Atk +6; Grp +3; Atk +9 melee (1d6+2, +1 *spear*) or +11 ranged (1d6, light crossbow); Full Atk +9/+4 melee (1d6+2, +1 *spear*) or +11 ranged (1d6, light crossbow); SA acrobatic charge, agile fighting +2/+3, sneak attack +3d6; SQ defensive roll 1/day, evasion, fast acrobatics, kip up, skill mastery, slow fall 30 ft., steady stance, trap sense +1, trapfinding, uncanny dodge; AL N; SV Fort +5, Ref +13, Will +3 (+5 against fear); Str 12, Dex 18, Con 14, Int 12, Wis 10, Cha 8.

Skills and Feats: Balance[SM] +18, Climb[SM] +15, Escape Artist +16, Hide +20, Jump[SM] +22, Listen +10, Move Silently +18, Spot +8, Tumble[SM] +18, Use Rope +4; Dive for Cover†, Dodge, Mobility, Spring Attack.

† New feat described on page 108.

Languages: Common, Halfling; Gnome.

Acrobatic Charge (Ex): Diana can charge over difficult terrain that normally slows movement or through allies blocking her path.

Agile Fighting (Ex): Diana gains a +2 dodge bonus to AC. When fighting defensively or using total defense, this bonus becomes +3. In addition, she takes no penalty to her AC or on her melee attack rolls when kneeling, sitting, or prone.

Sneak Attack (Ex): Diana deals an extra 3d6 points of damage on any successful attack against flat-footed or flanked targets, or against a target that has been denied its Dexterity bonus for any reason. This damage also applies to ranged attacks against targets up to 30 feet away. Creatures with concealment, creatures without discernible anatomies, and creatures immune to extra damage from critical hits are all immune to sneak attacks. Diana can choose to deliver nonlethal damage with her sneak attack, but only when using a weapon designed for that purpose, such as a sap (blackjack).

Defensive Roll (Ex): Diana can attempt to roll with the damage when on the receiving end of an attack from a weapon that would reduce her to 0 or fewer hit points. On a successful Reflex save (DC equal to damage from that attack), she takes only half damage. Diana can only react to attacks she is aware of; if she is denied her Dexterity bonus to AC for any reason, she cannot use this ability. Evasion does not apply to defensive rolls.

Evasion (Ex): If Diana is exposed to any effect that normally allows her to attempt a Reflex saving throw for half damage, she takes no damage with a successful saving throw.

Fast Acrobatics (Ex): Diana ignores the normal –5 penalty when making a Balance check while moving at her full normal speed. She can climb at half her speed as a move action without taking a –5 penalty on her Climb check. Finally, she can tumble at her full speed without taking the normal –10 penalty on her Tumble check.

Kip Up (Ex): Diana can stand up from a prone position as a free action that doesn't provoke attacks of opportunity.

Skill Mastery (Ex): Diana has mastered the skills Balance, Climb, Jump, and Tumble to the extent that she can take 10 with them even under stress. These skills are designated by ^{SM} in the statistics block.

Slow Fall (Ex): A thief-acrobat within arm's reach of a wall can use it to slow her descent while falling. Diana takes damage as if the fall were 30 feet shorter than it actually is.

Steady Stance (Ex): Diana is not considered flat-footed while balancing or climbing, and she adds +4 to Balance or Climb checks to remain balancing or climbing when she takes damage.

Trapfinding (Ex): Diana can find, disarm, or bypass traps with a DC of 20 or higher. She can use the Search skill to find, and the Disable Device skill to disarm, magic traps (DC 25 + the level of the spell used to create it). If her Disable Device result exceeds the trap's DC by 10

or more, she discovers how to bypass the trap without triggering or disarming it.

Uncanny Dodge (Ex): Diana retains her Dexterity bonus to AC even when flat-footed or targeted by an unseen foe (she still loses her Dexterity bonus if paralyzed or otherwise immobile).

Possessions: +1 studded leather, +1 spear, light crossbow with 20 bolts, boots of striding and springing, rope of climbing.

VIGILANTE

Some vigilantes have suffered personally at the hands of criminals and are bent on revenge. Others have lost loved ones to knives in the alleyway. Still others are atoning for the time they spent on the wrong side of the law. But they all have one thing in common: a burning desire to solve crimes and bring criminals to justice.

The vigilante combines magical and mundane investigative techniques to assess a crime scene. He is adept at learning "the word on the street" about a crime, analyzing clues, and identifying likely suspects. Once on the trail, he relentlessly tails, apprehends, and interrogates a suspect until the truth comes out. Many vigilantes work for the local ruler or the city guard; others are independent detectives-for-hire. Some even take to the streets by night to stop crimes in progress—or to keep would-be criminals from striking in the first place.

A bard or rogue can quickly pick up the variety of skills a vigilante needs. Rangers find the class appealing because it allows them to engage in urban hunts with criminals as their prey, but they must typically multiclass as bards or rogues to qualify. Some would-be vigilantes add one or more levels of fighter or paladin to aid their combat prowess.

An NPC vigilante might turn up just in time to save the player characters from becoming crime victims themselves. However, if they break the law on a vigilante's home turf, they may find themselves under his unwelcome scrutiny.

Adaptation: Although members of this class usually work alone, that need not be the case in every campaign. Any highly trained group of professional adventurers, bounty hunters, or even assassins could include members of the vigilante class, especially if you remove the alignment restriction.

Hit Die: d8.

REQUIREMENTS

To qualify to become a vigilante, a character must fulfill all the following criteria.

Alignment: Any nonevil.

Base Attack Bonus: +4.

Skills: Gather Information 8 ranks, Intimidate 4 ranks, Knowledge (local) 8 ranks, Search 4 ranks, Sense Motive 8 ranks.

Feats: Alertness.

CLASS SKILLS

The vigilante's class skills (and the key ability for each skill) are Balance (Dex), Climb (Str), Craft (Int), Disable Device (Int), Disguise (Cha), Escape Artist (Dex), Gather Information (Cha), Hide (Dex), Intimidate (Cha), Jump (Str), Knowledge (local) (Int), Move Silently (Dex), Open Lock (Dex), Perform (Cha), Search (Int), Sense Motive (Wis), Tumble (Dex), and Use Rope (Dex).

Skill Points at Each Level: 6 + Int modifier.

CLASS FEATURES

All of the following are class features of the vigilante prestige class.

Weapon and Armor Proficiency: Vigilantes are proficient with all simple and martial weapons, plus the net. They are not proficient with any type of armor or shields.

Detect Evil (Sp): A vigilante can use *detect evil* at will. See the spell, page 218 of the *Player's Handbook*.

Spells per Day: A vigilante has the ability to cast a small number of arcane spells. To cast a vigilante spell, a vigilante must have a Charisma score of at least 10 + the spell's level, so if he has a Charisma of 10 or lower, he cannot cast these spells. Bonus spells are based on Charisma, and saving throws against these spells have a DC of 10 + spell level + the vigilante's Cha modifier. When a vigilante gets 0 spells per day of a given level (for instance, 1st-level spells at 1st level), he gains only the bonus spells he would be entitled to based on his Charisma score for that spell level. The vigilante spell list appears below. A vigilante casts spells just as a bard does.

A vigilante's selection of spells is extremely limited. A vigilante begins play knowing two 1st-level spells of his choice. At most new vigilante levels, he gains one or more new spells known as indicated on Table 2–25: Vigilante Spells Known. (Unlike spells per day, the number of spells a vigilante knows is not affected by his Charisma score.)

Upon reaching 6th level, and at every even-numbered level after that, a vigilante can choose to learn a new spell in place of one he already knows. This works identically to the bard's ability to learn new spells in the place of old ones (see page 28 of the *Player's Handbook*).

A vigilante's spell list includes all spells from the bard spell list that belong to the following schools: abjuration, divination, illusion, necromancy, and transmutation. The spell list below includes all spells from the *Player's Handbook* and this book that qualify. (Treat 0-level bard spells as 1st-level vigilante spells.)

Streetwise (Ex): A vigilante knows how to survive in dangerous urban areas. He gains a +2 competence bonus on Gather Information and Knowledge (local) checks.

At 7th level, this bonus improves to +4.

Smite the Guilty (Su): Starting at 2nd level, a vigilante can attempt to smite someone whom he has personally witnessed committing a crime in his home city. He can use this ability once per day. He adds his Charisma bonus (if any) to his melee attack roll and deals an extra 1 point of damage per vigilante level.

The smite attack must occur within three days of the crime; otherwise, the benefits of this ability no longer apply. A vigilante can use this ability multiple times against the same miscreant and in response to the same incident, so long as all such uses occur within the time limit. Should a vigilante mistakenly try to punish someone who is not guilty of the crime witnessed, the benefits do not apply, but the attempt still counts against the number allowed per day.

A vigilante can use this ability twice per day at 6th level and three times per day at 10th level.

TABLE 2–25: THE VIGILANTE

Level	Base Attack Bonus	Fort Save	Ref Save	Will Save	Special	Spells per Day			
						1st	2nd	3rd	4th
1st	+0	+0	+2	+2	*Detect evil*, streetwise +2	0	—	—	—
2nd	+1	+0	+3	+3	Smite the guilty 1/day	1	—	—	—
3rd	+2	+1	+3	+3	Quick search	2	0	—	—
4th	+3	+1	+4	+4	*Speak with dead*	3	1	—	—
5th	+3	+1	+4	+4	Quick hide	3	2	0—	
6th	+4	+2	+5	+5	Smite the guilty 2/day	3	3	1—	
7th	+5	+2	+5	+5	Streetwise +4	3	3	20	
8th	+6	+2	+6	+6	*Dimensional anchor*	3	3	31	
9th	+6	+3	+6	+6	Mettle	3	3	32	
10th	+7	+3	+7	+7	Smite the guilty 3/day	3	3	33	

Illus. by D. Hudnut

Beasley "the Nightstalker" Bigums,
a vigilante

hudnut

Quick Search (Ex): Starting at 3rd level, a vigilante can search a 5-foot-by-5-foot area or a volume of goods 5 feet on a side as a move action, rather than as a full-round action.

Speak with Dead (Sp): Starting at 4th level, a vigilante can use *speak with dead* once per day. His caster level equals his class level.

Quick Hide (Ex): At 5th level and higher, a vigilante can use Bluff to create a diversion to hide as a move action, rather than as a standard action. He gains a +4 bonus on Bluff checks made for this purpose.

Dimensional Anchor (Sp): Starting at 8th level, a vigilante can use *dimensional anchor* once per day. His caster level equals his class level.

Mettle (Ex): Starting at 9th level, a vigilante's grim determination allows him to shrug off magical effects that would otherwise harm him. If a vigilante makes a successful Will or Fortitude saving throw that would normally reduce the spell's effect (such as any spell with a saving throw entry of Will partial or Fortitude half), he instead negates the effect. An unconcsious or sleeping vigilante does not gain the benefit of mettle.

VIGILANTE SPELL LIST

1st Level: *accelerated movement†, alarm, animate rope, cause fear, comprehend languages, detect magic, detect secret doors, disguise self, distort speech†, erase, expeditious retreat, swift expeditious retreat†, feather fall, ghost sound, identify, joyful noise†, know direction, mage hand, magic mouth, master's touch†, mending, message, Nystul's magic aura, obscure object, open/close, prestidigitation, read magic, remove fear, resistance, silent image, undetectable alignment, ventriloquism.*

2nd Level: *alter self, bladeweave†, blindness/deafness, blur, cat's grace, detect thoughts, eagle's splendor, swift fly†, fox's cunning, hypnotic pattern, invisibility, swift invisibility†, iron silence†, locate object, minor image, mirror image, misdirection, pyrotechnics, scare, silence, sonic weapon†, tactical precision†, tongues, whispering wind.*

3rd Level: *allegro†, blink, clairaudience/clairvoyance, dispel magic, displacement, fear, gaseous form, glibness, haste, illusory script, invisibility sphere, major image, remove curse, scrying, sculpt sound, secret page, see invisibility, slow, speak with animals, speechlink†.*

4th Level: *break enchantment, detect scrying, freedom of movement, hallucinatory terrain, greater invisibility, legend lore, listening coin†, locate creature, rainbow pattern, repel vermin, shadow conjuration, speak with plants, spectral weapon†, zone of silence.*

† New spell described in Chapter 5.

88

TABLE 2–26: VIGILANTE SPELLS KNOWN

Level	Spells Known			
	1st	2nd	3rd	4th
1st	2*	—	—	—
2nd	3	—	—	—
3rd	3	2*	—	—
4th	4	3	—	—
5th	4	3	2*	—
6th	4	4	3	—
7th	4	4	3	2*
8th	4	4	4	3
9th	4	4	4	3
10th	4	4	4	4

*Provided the vigilante has a high enough Charisma to have a bonus spell of this level.

SAMPLE VIGILANTE

Beasley "the Nightstalker" Bigums: Male halfling rogue 3/fighter 2/vigilante 5; CR 10; Small humanoid; HD 3d6+3 plus 2d10+2 plus 5d8+5; hp 56; Init +6; Spd 30 ft.; AC 19, touch 13, flat-footed 17; Base Atk +7; Grp +3; Atk +11 melee (1d4+1/19–20, +1 short sword) or +12 ranged (1d4/×3, masterwork throwing axe); Full Atk +11/+6 melee (1d4+1/19–20, +1 short sword) or +12 ranged (1d4/×3, masterwork throwing axe); SA smite the guilty 1/day, sneak attack +2d6; SQ *detect evil*, evasion, quick hide, quick search, *speak with dead* 1/day, streetwise +2, trap sense +1, trapfinding; AL LN; SV Fort +7, Ref +10, Will +7 (+9 against fear); Str 10, Dex 15, Con 12, Int 12, Wis 12, Cha 14.

Skills and Feats: Balance +6, Bluff +9, Climb +6, Diplomacy +6, Disable Device +3, Disguise +4, Gather Information +14, Hide +16, Intimidate +14, Jump +14, Knowledge (local) +11, Listen +6, Move Silently +10, Search +5, Sense Motive +9, Spot +11, Tumble +9; Alertness, Improved Initiative[B], Persuasive, Point Blank Shot, Stealthy, Weapon Finesse[B].

Languages: Common, Halfling; Orc.

Detect Evil (Sp): Beasley can use *detect evil* at will. See the spell, page 218 of the *Player's Handbook*.

Evasion (Ex): If Beasley is exposed to any effect that normally allows him to attempt a Reflex saving throw for half damage, he takes no damage with a successful saving throw.

Quick Hide (Ex): Beasley can use Bluff to create a diversion to hide as a move action, rather than as a standard action. He gains a +4 bonus on Bluff checks made for this purpose.

Quick Search (Ex): Beasley can search a 5-foot-by-5-foot area or a volume of goods 5 feet on a side as a move action, rather than as a standard action.

Smite the Guilty (Su): Once per day, Beasley can attempt to smite someone whom he has personally witnessed committing a crime in his home city. He adds 2 to his melee attack roll and deals an extra 5 points of damage.

Sneak Attack (Ex): Beasley deals an extra 2d6 points of damage on any successful attack against flat-footed or flanked targets, or against a target that has been denied its Dexterity bonus for any reason. This damage also applies to ranged attacks against targets up to 30 feet away. Creatures with concealment, creatures without discernible anatomies, and creatures immune to extra damage from critical hits are all immune to sneak attacks. Beasley can choose to deliver nonlethal damage with his sneak attack, but only when using a weapon designed for that purpose, such as a sap (blackjack).

Speak with Dead (Sp): Beasley can use *speak with dead* once per day as a 5th-level caster.

Trapfinding (Ex): Beasley can find, disarm, or bypass traps with a DC of 20 or higher. He can use the Search skill to find, and the Disable Device skill to disarm, magic traps (DC 25 + the level of the spell used to create it). If his Disable Device result exceeds the trap's DC by 10 or more, he discovers how to bypass the trap without triggering or disarming it.

Vigilante Spells Known (4/3; caster level 5th): 1st—*accelerated movement†, cause fear* (DC 13), *feather fall, ventriloquism* (DC 13); 2nd—*blur, swift fly†, invisibility.*

† New spell described in Chapter 5.

Possessions: +1 *studded leather,* +1 *buckler,* +1 *short sword,* masterwork throwing axe, *rope of climbing, hat of disguise, cloak of elvenkind, eyes of the eagle, boots of striding and springing,* 2 *potions of cure light wounds,* 2 tanglefoot bags, 2 smokesticks, 2 thunderstones, 43 pp.

VIRTUOSO

The roar of the crowd, the praise of spectators after a truly great performance, the showers of gifts from attractive admirers—why would anyone trade all that for sleeping in the woods or poking around in smelly old dungeons? The virtuoso leaves creeping down dark corridors and matching wits against deadly traps to others. His place is on the stage, surrounded by adoring fans. Fortunately for him, every place he goes becomes a stage, and so long as there's anyone around for him to impress, he's in the spotlight.

The typical virtuoso is outgoing, charismatic, and gregarious. He loves to be around people and is quick to win friends with his charming manner. Some might call him a temperamental egomaniac, yet everyone feels a little better in his presence. Many virtuosos are musicians; others are accomplished dancers or actors. Still others choose to specialize in obscure and unusual forms of entertainment, such as stage magic or juggling.

Bards are most often drawn to this prestige class, although multiclass rogue/sorcerers or rogue/clerics can also excel in it. Bards tend to perform as musicians or actors, rogues as either dancers or sleight-of-hand artists, sorcerers as stage magicians, and clerics as orators. Characters of most other classes are either not outgoing enough to enjoy being virtuosos, or they find other outlets for their extroverted tendencies.

Since entertainers are often on the road, an NPC virtuoso can be encountered anywhere, incorporating as much adventuring into his journeys as he wishes. Because of his talent for winning admirers, he usually remains above suspicion should anything underhanded take place in a town he is visiting on tour.

Adaptation: The virtuoso prestige class can play many different roles in a campaign. In one world, members of a specific bardic college might all be members of the class. In another, virtuosos might be dedicated to magic, not music.

Hit Die: d6.

REQUIREMENTS

To qualify to become a virtuoso, a character must fulfill all the following criteria.

Skills: Diplomacy 4 ranks, Intimidate 4 ranks, Perform (any) 10 ranks.

Spells: Arcane caster level 1st

CLASS SKILLS

The virtuoso's class skills (and the key ability for each skill) are Balance (Dex), Bluff (Cha), Concentration (Con), Craft (Int), Diplomacy (Cha), Disguise (Cha), Escape Artist (Dex), Gather Information (Cha), Intimidate (Cha), Jump (Str), Perform (Cha), Spellcraft (Int), and Tumble (Dex).

Skill Points at Each Level: 6 + Int modifier.

CLASS FEATURES

All of the following are class features of the virtuoso prestige class.

Weapon and Armor Proficiency: Virtuosos gain no proficiency with any weapon or armor.

Bardic Music: Virtuoso levels stack with bard levels for the purpose of determining the virtuoso's daily uses of his bardic music abilities (if any) and the value of the bonus granted by inspire courage (if the virtuoso has that bardic music ability). For example, a 10th-level bard/4th-level virtuoso could use bardic music fourteen times per day, and his inspire courage ability would grant a +3 morale bonus on the appropriate rolls.

A virtuoso also gains the *fascinate* bardic music ability, if he doesn't already have it. He can use his performance to cause one or more creatures to become fascinated with him. See the bard class feature, page 29 of the *Player's Handbook*.

*Master flutist
Tevaldo Mordani,
a virtuoso*

Virtuoso Performance (Su): A virtuoso can use his Perform skill to create magical effects on those around him. He can use this ability once per day per virtuoso level. He can use any form of performance as part of this ability. Although many of the names refer to musical performances, a virtuoso isn't actually so limited—for example, an actor could perform a "sustaining soliloquy" or "sustaining dance" rather than a sustaining song. Each ability requires both a minimum virtuoso level and a minimum number of ranks in any Perform skill to qualify. If a virtuoso does not have the required number of ranks in at least one Perform skill, he does not gain the virtuoso performance ability until he acquires the needed ranks.

Starting a virtuoso performance effect is a standard action. Some virtuoso performance abilities require concentration, which means that the virtuoso must take a standard action each round to maintain the ability. Unlike with bardic music, virtuoso performance doesn't restrict a virtuoso's spellcasting or magic item activation. If a virtuoso's performance requires sound, a deaf virtuoso has a 20% chance to fail when attempting to use virtuoso performance. If he fails, the attempt still counts against his daily limit.

If a virtuoso has the bardic music class

TABLE 2–27: THE VIRTUOSO

Level	Base Attack Bonus	Fort Save	Ref Save	Will Save	Special	Spells per Day/Spells Known
1st	+0	+0	+0	+2	Bardic music (*fascinate*), virtuoso performance (persuasive song)	—
2nd	+1	+0	+0	+3	—	+1 level of existing arcane spellcasting class
3rd	+1	+1	+1	+3	Virtuoso performance (sustaining song)	+1 level of existing arcane spellcasting class
4th	+2	+1	+1	+4	—	+1 level of existing arcane spellcasting class
5th	+2	+1	+1	+4	Virtuoso performance (jarring song)	+1 level of existing arcane spellcasting class
6th	+3	+2	+2	+5	—	+1 level of existing arcane spellcasting class
7th	+3	+2	+2	+5	Virtuoso performance (song of fury)	+1 level of existing arcane spellcasting class
8th	+4	+2	+2	+6	—	+1 level of existing arcane spellcasting class
9th	+4	+3	+3	+6	Virtuoso performance (*mindbending melody*)	+1 level of existing arcane spellcasting class
10th	+5	+3	+3	+7	Virtuoso performance (revealing melody)	+1 level of existing arcane spellcasting class

feature, he can spend two daily uses of bardic music to deliver a virtuoso performance.

Persuasive Song (Ex): A virtuoso with at least 11 ranks in a Perform skill can deliver a performance that sways the attitude of his audience. Treat this as a Diplomacy check made to influence NPC attitudes (see pages 71–72 of the *Player's Handbook*), but replace the Diplomacy check with a Perform check. Viewers must be within 30 feet of the virtuoso, be able to see and hear him clearly, and be willingly paying attention to his actions. This ability requires at least 10 consecutive rounds of concentration to take effect, and it can affect a particular creature only once per day. Hostile audience members can't be influenced with this ability.

Sustaining Song (Su): A virtuoso of 3rd level or higher with at least 13 ranks in a Perform skill can sustain his dying allies, assisting their recovery. Each round that the song continues, all allies within 30 feet of him automatically become stable (if dying) or regain 1 hit point (if stable and between –1 and –9 hit points). A sustaining song has no effect on enemies or on allies with 0 or more hit points. A virtuoso can keep up his sustaining song for 5 minutes. This is a mind-affecting ability.

Jarring Song (Su): A virtuoso of 5th level or higher with at least 15 ranks in a Perform skill can inhibit spellcasting. Any enemy within 30 feet attempting to cast a spell during a jarring song must make a Concentration check with a DC equal to the virtuoso's Perform check to avoid losing the spell. A virtuoso can keep up his jarring song for 10 rounds.

Song of Fury (Su): A virtuoso of 7th level or higher with at least 17 ranks in a Perform skill can use his performance

to turn his allies into furious berserkers. Each ally within 30 feet who can see and hear the virtuoso can choose to enter a rage on her turn. This functions identically to a barbarian's rage, except that it ends automatically if the virtuoso stops performing. If the ally already has the ability to rage, she can choose to apply the full effect of her own rage, without spending one of her daily uses of rage. A virtuoso can't use song of fury on himself. This is a mind-affecting ability.

Mindbending Melody (Sp): A virtuoso of 9th level or higher with at least 19 ranks in a Perform skill can dominate a humanoid that he has already fascinated. This ability functions like a *dominate person* spell with a caster level equal to the virtuoso's class level. The target can make a Will save (DC 10 + virtuoso's class level + virtuoso's Cha modifier) to negate the effect. A mindbending melody is a mind-affecting, language-dependent, enchantment (compulsion) ability.

Revealing Melody (Su): A 10th-level virtuoso with at least 20 ranks in a Perform skill can use his performance to reveal all things as they actually are. All allies within 30 feet who can see and hear the virtuoso's performance are affected as if by a *true seeing* spell with a caster level equal to the virtuoso's class level. The effect lasts as long as the virtuoso performs.

Spells per Day/Spells Known: Beginning at 2nd level, a virtuoso gains new spells per day (and spells known, if applicable) as if he had also gained a level in an arcane spellcasting class to which he belonged before adding the prestige class level. He does not, however, gain any other benefit a character of that class would have gained. If he had more than one arcane spellcasting class before becoming a virtuoso, he must decide to which class to add each level for the purpose of determining spells per day and spells known.

SAMPLE VIRTUOSO

Master Flutist Tevaldo Mordani: Male gnome bard 7/virtuoso 3; CR 10; Small humanoid; HD 10d6+30; hp 67; Init +2; Spd 20 ft.; AC 17, touch 13, flat-footed 15; Base Atk +6; Grp +1; Atk +10 melee (1d4/18–20, +1 *ghost touch rapier*) or +10 ranged (1d4/×3, shortbow with masterwork arrow); Full Atk +10/+5 melee (1d4/18–20, +1 *ghost touch rapier*) or +10/+5 ranged (1d4/×3, shortbow with masterwork arrow); SA spells, spell-like abilities; SQ bardic music 10/day (countersong, *fascinate*, inspire competence, inspire courage +2, suggestion), bardic knowledge +10, gnome traits, low-light vision, virtuoso performance 3/day (persuasive song, sustaining song); AL CG; SV Fort +6*, Ref +8*, Will +7*; Str 8, Dex 14, Con 16, Int 13, Wis 8, Cha 18.

Skills and Feats: Bluff +9, Concentration +11, Craft (alchemy) +8, Diplomacy +13, Disguise +8 (+10 act in character), Intimidate +10, Knowledge (history) +6, Knowledge (local) +6, Listen +6, Perform (dance) +7, Perform (wind instruments) +17 (+19 with masterwork flute), Perform (sing) +12, Sense Motive +4, Spellcraft +4 (+6 decipher spells on scrolls), Tumble +10, Use Magic Device +9; Combat Expertise, Improved Feint, Quick Draw, Weapon Finesse.

Languages: Common, Gnome; Elven.

Spell-Like Abilities: 1/day—*dancing lights, ghost sound* (DC 14), *prestidigitation, speak with animals* (burrowing mammal only, duration 1 minute).

Bardic Music: Tevaldo can use bardic music ten times per day. See the bard class feature, page 29 of the *Player's Handbook.*

Countersong (Su): Use music or poetics to counter magical effects that depend on sound.

Fascinate (Sp): Use music or poetics to cause one or more creatures to become fascinated with him.

Inspire Competence (Su): Use music or poetics to help an ally succeed at a task.

Inspire Courage (Su): Use music or poetics to bolster his allies against fear and improve their combat abilities.

Suggestion (Sp): Use music or poetics to make a suggestion (as the spell) to a creature that he has already fascinated.

Gnome Traits: Gnomes have a +1 racial bonus on attack rolls against kobolds and goblinoids. Gnomes have a +4 racial bonus to Armor Class against giants.

*Gnomes have a +2 racial bonus on saving throws against illusions.

Virtuoso Performance (Su): Tevaldo can deliver a virtuoso performance three times per day. See the virtuoso class features for details.

Persuasive Song (Ex): Use the Perform skill instead of the Diplomacy skill to influence the attitudes of creatures within 30 feet.

Sustaining Song (Su): Dying allies automatically become stable, while stable allies between –1 and –9 hit points regain 1 hit point.

Bard Spells Known (3/4/4/3; caster level 9th): 0—*dancing lights, detect magic, ghost sound* (DC 14), *lullaby* (DC 14), *read magic, summon instrument;* 1st—*charm person* (DC 15), *expeditious retreat, Tasha's hideous laughter* (DC 15), *undetectable alignment;* 2nd—*hold person* (DC 16), *invisibility, mirror image, silence* (DC 16); 3rd—*confusion* (DC 17), *good hope, haste.*

Possessions: mithral shirt, +1 *ghost touch rapier*, shortbow with 16 masterwork arrows, *cloak of Charisma +2, hat of disguise, wand of cure light wounds* (25 charges), scroll of *cat's grace*, masterwork flute, entertainer's outfit, 10 gp.

WILD PLAINS OUTRIDER

The wild plains demand constant vigilance from those who wander their spaces. While moving through such areas, groups of nomads, adventurers, and even armies call upon the services of specially trained outriders. These scouts and wanderers work tirelessly to keep the plains as safe as such remote places can be.

The many dangers of the plains necessitate trust between mount and rider, and the two must move as one—whether on a week-long trek covering hundreds of miles or in a short, bloody combat against a group of goblins. The wild plains outriders, a group of powerful rangers and druids who have gathered together to protect the plains and those who cross them, work to perfect this bond between mount and rider.

Joining the wild plains outriders requires a special bond with a mount of some kind, so all outriders must have at least a few levels of druid, ranger, or paladin. Beyond that requirement, the life of an outrider demands survival, tracking, and combat skills that appeal more to rangers than to members of other classes. Although barbarians and scouts must multiclass before gaining levels in the outrider prestige class, they often find the class appealing. Barbarians are drawn to the class because of an outrider's ability to travel great distances with a trusted mount and because of their strong survival skills; scouts find that the outrider's skills and abilities mesh well with their own expertise.

Adaptation: The wild plains outrider prestige class can be tailored easily to fit a specific campaign, race, culture, or organization. Simply add a minor aspect to the requirements. For example, specifying that an outrider's animal companion or special mount must have a fly speed and changing the name of the class to the "Skythunder outrider" makes it a better fit for a reclusive but powerful tribe of goblins called the Skythunder tribe. Similar changes can make the class fit dwarf rangers on dire boars, elf foresters on giant lizards, or human nomads on wild horses.

Hit Die: d8.

REQUIREMENTS

To qualify to become a wild plains outrider, a character must fulfill all the following criteria.

Skills: Ride 9 ranks.

Feats: Mounted Combat, Track.

Special: Animal companion large enough to serve as a mount, or a paladin's special mount.

CLASS SKILLS

The wild plains outrider's class skills (and the key ability for each skill) are Balance (Dex), Handle Animal (Cha), Jump (Str), Knowledge (nature) (Int), Listen (Wis), Move Silently (Dex), Ride (Dex), Spot (Wis), Survival (Wis), and Swim (Str).

*Joran Vhask,
a wild plains outrider*

Skill Points at Each Level: 4 + Int modifier.

CLASS FEATURES

All of the following are class features of the wild plains outrider prestige class.

Weapon and Armor Proficiency: Wild plains outriders gain no proficiency with any weapon or armor.

Animal Companion/Special Mount: A wild plains outrider adds his outrider class levels to his effective druid level (his actual druid level or one-half his ranger level) to determine the capabilities of his animal companion. Alternatively, he can add his outrider class levels to his effective paladin level to determine the capabilities of his special mount. However, he can only use one of these abilities. The choice must be made when the character enters the wild plains outrider class and can never be changed.

Ride Bonus (Ex): A wild plains outrider gains a competence bonus equal to his class level on all Ride checks, as well as on Handle Animal checks made in conjunction with his animal companion mount or special mount.

Wild Plains Stalker (Ex): A wild plains outrider knows how to move a mount stealthily through nearly any terrain. His mount uses the outrider's skill ranks, rather than its own, to make Hide and Move Silently checks. The mount still uses its own size, Dexterity, armor check penalty, and other applicable modifiers when making such checks.

Wild Plains Swiftness (Ex): A wild plains outrider knows how to draw every bit of speed possible from a mount. At 2nd level and higher, a wild plains outrider (while mounted) increases his mount's base speed by 10 feet. This increase affects every movement mode the mount has, including fly, climb, and swim speeds.

Wild Plains Offensive (Ex): Starting at 3rd level, a wild plains outrider can make a full attack with a melee weapon as long as his mount takes only a single move.

Multiclassing Note: A paladin can multiclass as a wild plains outrider without losing her ability to take additional levels in paladin.

Illus. by S. Elès

TABLE 2–28: THE WILD PLAINS OUTRIDER

Level	Base Attack Bonus	Fort Save	Ref Save	Will Save	Special
1st	+1	+2	+0	+0	Animal companion/special mount, ride bonus, wild plains stalker
2nd	+2	+3	+0	+0	Wild plains swiftness
3rd	+3	+3	+1	+1	Wild plains offensive

SAMPLE WILD PLAINS OUTRIDER

Joran Vhask: Male human ranger 6/wild plains outrider 3; CR 9; Medium humanoid; HD 9d8+9; hp 51; Init +2; Spd 30 ft.; AC 17, touch 12, flat-footed 15; Base Atk +9; Grp +12; Atk +13 melee (1d8+4/19–20, +1 longsword) or +13 ranged (1d6+4/×3, +1 composite shortbow with +1 arrow); Full Atk +13/+8 melee (1d8+4/19–20, +1 longsword) or +11/+11/+6 ranged (1d6+4/×3, +1 composite shortbow with +1 arrow and Rapid Shot feat); SA favored enemy goblinoids +4, favored enemy orcs +2, wild plains offensive; SQ animal companion (heavy warhorse), animal companion benefits, wild empathy +5 (+1 magical beasts), wild plains swiftness; AL NG; SV Fort +10, Ref +9, Will +6; Str 16, Dex 14, Con 12, Int 10, Wis 14, Cha 8.

Skills and Feats: Concentration +6, Handle Animal +7 (+10 for animal companion), Heal +7, Knowledge (geography) +5, Knowledge (nature) +6, Jump +5, Listen +9, Move Silently +5, Ride +19, Search +4, Spot +9, Survival +7 (+9 avoid getting lost or avoid hazards, +9 in aboveground natural environments), Swim +6, Use Rope +6; Endurance[B], Manyshot[B], Mounted Archery, Mounted Combat, Point Blank Shot, Precise Shot, Rapid Shot[B], Ride-By Attack, Track[B].

Language: Common.

Animal Companion (Ex): Joran has a heavy warhorse named Ji'ikala as an animal companion. Ji'ikala's abilities and characteristics are summarized below.

Animal Companion Benefits: Joran and his warhorse enjoy the link and share spells special qualities.

Link (Ex): Joran can handle Ji'ikala as a free action. He also gains a +4 circumstance bonus on all wild empathy checks and Handle Animal checks made regarding his warhorse.

Share Spells (Ex): Joran can have any spell he casts on himself also affect his animal companion if the latter is within 5 feet at the time. He can also cast a spell with a target of "You" on his animal companion.

Favored Enemy (Ex): Joran gains a +4 bonus on his Bluff, Listen, Sense Motive, Spot, and Survival checks when using these skills against goblinoids. He gains the same bonus on weapon damage rolls.

Against orcs, he gains a +2 bonus on these skill checks and on weapon damage rolls.

Wild Plains Offensive (Ex): As long as his mount takes only a single move, Joran can make a full attack with a melee weapon.

Wild Plains Swiftness (Ex): While mounted, Joran increases his mount's base speed by 10 feet.

Ranger Spell Prepared (caster level 3rd): 1st—longstrider.

Possessions: +1 chain shirt, +1 longsword, +1 composite shortbow (+3 Str bonus) with 50 +1 arrows, masterwork short sword, cloak of resistance +1, 2 potions of cure moderate wounds, Quaal's feather token (bird), traveler's outfit, cold weather outfit, trail rations (10 days), 50-foot hemp rope, 22 gp.

Ji'ikala, Heavy Warhorse Companion: CR —; Large animal; HD 8d8+24; hp 60; Init +2; Spd 35 ft. (45 ft. when ridden by Joran); AC 22, touch 11, flat-footed 20; Base Atk +6; Grp +15; Atk +10 melee (1d6+5, hoof); Full Atk +10 melee (1d6+5, 2 hooves) and +5 melee (1d4+2, bite); Space/Reach 10 ft./5 ft.; SQ bonus tricks (3), devotion, evasion, low-light vision, scent, wild plains stalker; AL N; SV Fort +7, Ref +6, Will +2; Str 20, Dex 15, Con 17, Int 2, Wis 13, Cha 6.

Skills and Feats: Hide –2, Listen +7, Move Silently +2, Spot +6; Alertness, Endurance, Run.

Carrying Capacity: A light load for a heavy warhorse is up to 300 pounds; a medium load 301–600 pounds; and a heavy load, 601–900 pounds. A heavy warhorse can drag 4,500 pounds.

Tricks: Attack, defend, guard, heel.

Devotion (Ex): Ji'ikala's devotion to Joran is so complete that it gains a +4 morale bonus on Will saves against enchantment spells and effects.

Evasion (Ex): If Ji'ikala is subjected to an attack that normally allows a Reflex saving throw for half damage, it takes no damage if it makes a successful saving throw.

Wild Plains Stalker (Ex): Ji'ikala uses Joran's skill ranks, rather than its own, to make Hide and Move Silently checks.

Possessions: Masterwork chainmail barding, military saddle, 4 saddlebags, bit and bridle.

Illus. by D. Kovacs

It takes more than just muscle or the ability to sling a spell to survive life as an adventurer. Regardless of how swiftly or accurately you swing a sword, or how devastatingly powerful your spells are, adventures invariably pose problems and challenges that require quick thinking, versatile abilities, and a little luck to survive. This chapter explores alternate uses for many skills, providing many new ways in which characters can use existing skill ranks to overcome different challenges.

Skills, although one of the main focuses of this book, are but part of a character's many abilities. The feats in this chapter speak to the versatility of the accomplished adventurer. Whether you're a fighter wanting to handle tasks other than a toe-to-toe melee or a rogue looking to boost your combat ability, these new feats help shape a character into a more versatile, more durable adventurer. Many of the feats emphasize skill use, opening up new ways to use existing skill ranks that would be too powerful to simply give to every character. Others focus on the rogue's, ninja's, and scout's special attack forms. Finally, subsets of feats offer expanded uses for existing character abilities such as bardic music or the druid's wild shape.

SKILLS

Skill use is essential to every adventurer's career, from the burly fighter who specializes only in climbing to the genius-intellect wizard with ranks in every Knowledge skill.

COMBINING SKILL ATTEMPTS

Teamwork is an oft-overlooked element of the D&D game. It's all too easy for the fighter to pay attention only when it's time to swing his sword, or for the cleric to tune out during the rogue's attempt to bluff the party past a guard post, but these characters are ignoring valuable opportunities to contribute to the group's success. In addition to the aid another rule (see page 65 of the *Player's Handbook*), this section describes some new ways for characters to help their friends succeed.

Individual Events

Even in some cases where several characters attempt the same action, with each succeeding or failing as a result of separate checks, characters can assist one another. By offering advice, guidance, or simply leading by example, a character can effectively share some of her expertise with her comrades. However, this activity comes at a cost, since the character's concentration is split between multiple tasks (and thus she isn't as capable at the task as she would normally be).

A character with 5 or more ranks in a skill who is engaged in a task using that skill can voluntarily accept a –4 penalty on the check in order to grant a +2 circumstance bonus on the same skill checks made by nearby allies engaged in the same task. For example, Lidda the 2nd-level rogue can help her allies sneak through a dungeon. By accepting a –4 penalty on her Hide and Move Silently checks, Lidda grants Jozan, Tordek, and Mialee each a +2 circumstance bonus on the same checks. While Lidda isn't as quiet and hidden as she'd normally be, the group overall is more stealthy than they would be without her help.

At higher levels, a character can grant more assistance, but at a greater cost. A character with 15 or more ranks in a skill can accept a –10 penalty on the check to grant a +5 circumstance bonus on the same skill checks made by nearby allies engaged in the same task.

An ally must be within 30 feet of you to gain the bonus, and you must be able to see and hear each other. Using the previous example, if Lidda were invisible, she couldn't grant the bonus to any character who couldn't see her; if Mialee were invisible, Lidda couldn't grant her the bonus unless she could see invisible creatures (but she could still grant the bonus to the other characters).

Typically, only the following skills can be assisted in this manner: Balance, Bluff, Climb, Craft, Diplomacy, Escape Artist, Handle Animal, Hide, Move Silently, Ride, Search, Survival, and Swim. In special circumstances, the DM may rule that other skills can benefit from this assistance, or that characters can't benefit from this form of assistance even when using the skills described above.

Aid Another

The *Player's Handbook* describes how a character can help another character achieve success by aiding him with a skill check of the same type; a successful DC 10 check by the first character grants a +2 circumstance bonus on the second character's check to use the same skill (see pages 65–66 of the *Player's Handbook*). This section expands on that rule by allowing more skilled characters to grant greater assistance.

When a character with 5 or more ranks in a skill uses the aid another action to assist another character's skill check, he can grant a higher bonus than that described in the *Player's Handbook*. For every 10 points of the helper's check result above 10, the circumstance bonus increases by 1. Thus, a result of 10–19 would grant a +2 circumstance bonus (as normal), a result of 20–29 would grant a +3 circumstance bonus, a result of 30–39 a +4 circumstance bonus, and so on. (To determine the circumstance bonus quickly, simply divide the helper's check result by 10, round down, and add 1.)

This higher bonus is available only to helpers with at least 5 ranks in the skill being used. Only experienced characters have the ability to provide the extra assistance offered by this rule.

At the DM's option, this rule can also be extended to using the aid another action in combat to improve an ally's attack roll or AC. Any character with a base attack bonus of +5 or higher can grant a greater bonus on an ally's attack roll or AC as described above. This rule rewards the tactic of experienced combatants helping each other in a fight (often the best option when fighting a monster with an extremely high AC or attack bonus).

Skill Synergy

In addition to helping a character's own skill checks, skill synergies can be used to aid the checks of allies as well. A character with 5 or more ranks in a skill that offers a bonus on another skill due to synergy can make a check using the first skill to aid the skill that would normally receive the bonus from synergy. For example, Soveliss the 2nd-level ranger could make a Handle Animal check to aid Jozan's Ride check (using the aid another rules described above and in the *Player's Handbook*), because a character with 5 ranks in Handle Animal gains a +2 bonus on Ride checks due to synergy. See Table 4–5: Skill Synergies, page 66 of the *Player's Handbook*.

The normal rules for aiding another still apply. For instance, even if Krusk the barbarian had 5 ranks in Handle Animal, he couldn't use it to aid Vadania the druid's wild empathy check, because Krusk can't make a wild empathy check himself. Some combinations may be difficult to imagine, but the DM should allow any synergistic aid another attempt that seems reasonable. For instance, it might seem odd at first glance for Mialee to use Spellcraft to assist Lidda's Use Magic Device check when reading a scroll—until you imagine the wizard leaning over the rogue's shoulder, helping her sound out the tougher words.

EXPANDED SKILL DESCRIPTIONS

The section below outlines new and clarified uses for some of the skills in the D&D game. The new and expanded actions described in this section are available to any characters who can normally use the skill unless otherwise noted.

APPRAISE (INT)

Whether performing a daring burglary or a hasty act of espionage, adventurers don't always have time to carefully study the value of potential loot. Characters can use the Appraise skill to make a quick but rough estimation of an item's value.

Check: You can appraise an item quickly, but the DC is higher. Failing the check means that you cannot estimate the item's value.

Item (Examples)	DC
Common	15
Trade goods (spices, food stuffs, raw materials, etc.), mundane items, livestock	
Rare	20
Fine clothing, precious metals (unworked), gems, artwork	
Exotic	25
Unusual gems (strange colorings, unusual to the region, unusually large or pure), spell components, jewelry, obscure religious items	
Unique	30+
Masterpiece artwork, royal jewels, crowns, or other adornments	

Action: Appraising an item quickly takes 1 round.

Try Again: You can try to appraise an item normally (requires 1 minute), but you cannot try to appraise the item quickly again. You can try to appraise an item normally whether or not you successfully appraise the item quickly.

Special: The Appraise Magic Value feat enables you to use the Appraise skill to determine a magic item's properties; see the feat description on page 103.

BALANCE (DEX)

You can run across narrow surfaces or resist being tripped.

Resist Trip: If you have 10 or more ranks in Balance, you can make a Balance check in place of a Strength or Dexterity check to avoid being tripped by an opponent. You take a –10 penalty on your Balance check. If you succeed on this check, you are not tripped. When you succeed on a Balance check to resist being tripped, you may not attempt to trip your opponent.

Sprinting Balance: You can try to run across a narrow surface by accepting a –20 penalty on your Balance check.

CLIMB (STR; ARMOR CHECK PENALTY)

Skilled climbers can climb much more quickly than others or even fight effectively while climbing. The rapid climb option first appeared in the *Epic Level Handbook*, but the following uses of Climb are open to characters of any level provided that they are willing to accept the appropriate penalty.

Rapid Climb: You can climb more quickly than normal. By accepting a –20 penalty on your Climb check, you can move your speed (instead of one-quarter your speed).

Combat Climb: You can move freely enough to avoid blows while climbing. By accepting a –20 penalty on your Climb check, you can retain your Dexterity bonus to AC while climbing.

CRAFT (INT)

By voluntarily raising the difficulty of the task before you, you can craft items more quickly than normal. This option first appeared in the *Epic Level Handbook*, but this use of the Craft skill is open to characters of any level provided that they are willing to accept the appropriate penalty.

Task	DC
Quick creation	+10 or more to DC

Quick Creation: You can voluntarily increase the DC of crafting an item by any multiple of 10. This tactic allows you to create an item more quickly (since you'll be multiplying this higher DC by your check result to determine progress). You must decide the increase before you make the check.

Craft (Poisonmaking): The fine art of refining raw materials into effective poisons requires both patience and care (not to mention discretion, in areas where poisons are outlawed). Making poisons with the Craft (poisonmaking) skill follows the rules in the *Player's Handbook* for all Craft skills, with the following exceptions.

Price: The cost of raw materials varies widely depending on whether the character has access to the active ingredient—that is, the venom or plant that actually provides the toxin. If a supply is readily available, the raw materials cost one-sixth of the market price, not

TABLE 3–1: CRAFT (POISONMAKING) DCs

Poison	DC to Create	Price	Type	DC to Resist	Initial Damage	Secondary Damage
Arsenic	15	120 gp	Ingested	13	1 Con	1d8 Con
Black adder venom	15	120 gp	Injury	12	1d6 Con	1d6 Con
Black lotus extract	35	4,500 gp	Contact	20	3d6 Con	3d6 Con
Bloodroot	15	100 gp	Injury	12	0	1d4 Con + 1d3 Wis
Blue whinnis	15	120 gp	Injury	14	1 Con	Unconsciousness
Burnt othur fumes	25	2,100 gp	Inhaled	18	1 Con*	3d6 Con
Carrion crawler brain juice	15	200 gp	Contact	13	Paralysis	0
Dark reaver powder	25	300 gp	Ingested	18	2d6 Con	1d6 Con +1d6 Str
Deathblade	25	1,800 gp	Injury	20	1d6 Con	2d6 Con
Dragon bile	30	1,500 gp	Contact	26	3d6 Str	0
Drow poison	15	75 gp	Injury	13	Unconsciousness	Unconsciousness 2d4 hr.
Giant wasp poison	20	210 gp	Injury	14	1d6 Dex	1d6 Dex
Greenblood oil	15	100 gp	Injury	13	1 Con	1d2 Con
Id moss	15	125 gp	Ingested	14	1d4 Int	2d6 Int
Insanity mist	20	1,500 gp	Inhaled	15	1d4 Wis	2d6 Wis
Large scorpion venom	20	200 gp	Injury	14	1d4 Con	1d4 Con
Lich dust	20	250 gp	Ingested	17	2d6 Str	1d6 Str
Malyss root paste	20	500 gp	Contact	16	1 Dex	2d4 Dex
Medium spider venom	15	150 gp	Injury	12	1d4 Str	1d4 Str
Nitharit	20	650 gp	Contact	13	0	3d6 Con
Oil of taggit	15	90 gp	Ingested	15	0	Unconsciousness
Purple worm poison	20	700 gp	Injury	25	1d6 Str	2d6 Str
Sassone leaf residue	20	300 gp	Contact	16	2d12 hp	1d6 Con
Shadow essence	20	250 gp	Injury	17	1 Str*	2d6 Str
Small centipede poison	15	90 gp	Injury	10	1d2 Dex	1d2 Dex
Striped toadstool	15	180 gp	Ingested	11	1 Wis	2d6 Wis + 1d4 Int
Terinav root	25	750 gp	Contact	16	1d6 Dex	2d6 Dex
Ungol dust	20	1,000 gp	Inhaled	15	1 Cha	1d6 Cha, +1 Cha*
Wyvern poison	25	3,000 gp	Injury	17	2d6 Con	2d6 Con

*Ability drain, not ability damage.

one-third. Otherwise, the raw materials cost at least three-quarters of the market price—assuming the substance in question is for sale at all.

Amount: To figure out how much poison you are able to create in a week, make a Craft (poisonmaking) check at the end of the week. If the check is successful, multiply the check result by the DC for the check. That result is how many gp worth of poison you created that week. When your total gp created equals or exceeds the market price of one dose of the poison, that dose is finished. (You may sometimes be able to create more than one dose in a week, depending on your check result and the market price of the poison.) If you fail the check by 4 or less, you make no progress that week. If you fail the check by 5 or more, you ruin half the raw materials and have to buy them again.

DECIPHER SCRIPT (INT)

You can use the Decipher Script skill to create a private cipher. This code system allows you (or anyone with the proper key) to record information without the risk of others reading it. Any document you create using your private cipher can be read only by you or someone who has the proper decoding information. Other characters with ranks in the Decipher Script skill can attempt to decipher

the code. The DC for such a decoding attempt is 10 + your total skill modifier at the time that you create the cipher. (In effect, you "take 10" on a skill check to create the cipher, and those attempting to decode it make a Decipher Script check opposed by your take 10 result.)

Action: Creating a cipher takes a week of uninterrupted work. The first attempt to decipher a code system created by the Decipher Script skill requires a day of uninterrupted work, and subsequent retries each take a week's time.

Try Again: You can attempt to decipher a private cipher more than once, but you must spend a great deal of time on each retry attempt. Each attempt to decipher a code beyond your first attempt takes a week's worth of uninterrupted work. The first attempt to decipher a code system requires only one day's work.

DIPLOMACY (CHA)

You can haggle over prices with a merchant or mediate between disagreeing groups, finding a solution to a diplomatic or legal matter that is satisfactory to everyone regardless of background.

Haggle: You can use the Diplomacy skill to bargain for goods or services, including those of a magical nature.

When discussing the sale of an item or service, you can attempt to lower the asking price with a Diplomacy check made to influence NPC attitudes (see the sidebar on page 72 of the *Player's Handbook*). If you manage to adjust the vendor's attitude to helpful (most vendors begin as indifferent), the vendor lowers the asking price by 10%. Add the vendor's Diplomacy check modifier to the DC needed to achieve the result. For example, to adjust the attitude of an indifferent vendor with a Diplomacy modifier of +3 to friendly, you must achieve a result of 33 or higher on your Diplomacy check (a base chance of 30, +3 for target's Diplomacy modifier). If you worsen the vendor's attitude, the vendor refuses to sell anything to you at this time. The DM is the final arbiter of any sale of goods and should discourage abuse of this option if it is slowing the game down too much.

Action: Haggling requires at least 1 full minute, as normal for a Diplomacy check.

Try Again: You can't retry a Diplomacy check to haggle.

Mediate: In order to mediate a disagreement, you must succeed in adjusting each group's attitude to friendly or better toward the other party in the negotiation. Make a Diplomacy check as normal for influencing NPC attitudes, but add the group leader's Diplomacy check modifier to the DC needed to achieve the result. For example, to adjust the attitude of an unfriendly group led by an individual with a Diplomacy modifier of +7 to friendly, you would need to roll a result of 32 or higher on your Diplomacy check (a base chance of 25, +7 for target's Diplomacy modifier). If your check result is less than 12 (a base chance of less than 5, +7 for target's Diplomacy modifier), the target's attitude worsens to hostile. The DC increases by 5 if the two parties are of different cultures or races.

Action: Mediation is a long process and cannot often be rushed successfully. Each check requires a full day of game time. You can take a –10 penalty on the check if you wish to attempt a mediation in an hour instead of a day (such as staving off an impending battle).

Try Again: As long as both sides aren't hostile (that is, as long as at least one side remains unfriendly or better), you can retry a Diplomacy check made to mediate a disagreement. If both parties become hostile at any time after the first check is made, you can't retry the check.

DISABLE DEVICE (INT)

You can reduce the amount of time it takes to disable a device or add a bypass element to an existing trap.

Bypass Trap: You try to incorporate a bypass element enabling you to avoid a trap's effects if you encounter it again later. Doing this imposes a –10 penalty on your Disable Device check. If you succeed, you can not only bypass a trap without disarming it (just as if you had beat the trap's DC by 10 or more—see page 72 of the *Player's Handbook*) but also add a bypass element allowing you or your companions to avoid triggering the trap again later. For example, you could insert a wedge that blocks the gears of a mechanical trap, or pick out a narrow path between the pressure plates that trigger poison darts from the wall.

Quick Disable: You can try to disable a device more quickly than normal. To reduce the time required to disable any device to a full-round action, add +20 to the DC. For example, a trap that normally requires a DC 20 check and 2d4 rounds to disarm could be disabled in 1 round with a successful DC 40 check.

ESCAPE ARTIST (DEX)

You can slip out of confining spell effects, bonds, or grapples much more quickly than

No bonds can hold a talented escape artist

Illus. by J. Miracola

normal, but you must voluntarily accept a penalty on your skill check.

Quick Escape: Making a quick Escape Artist check increases the required DC by 10. Escaping from rope bindings, manacles, or other restraints (except a grappler) takes only 5 rounds of work. Escaping from a net or an *animate rope, command plants, control plants,* or *entangle* spell with the quick escape option is a standard action. Escaping from a grapple or pin with the quick escape option is a move action. Squeezing through a tight space takes half the time that it normally would (DM's discretion, at least 5 rounds).

FORGERY (INT)

Official documents can provide an excellent means of proving yourself and reinforcing your point. With properly forged documents—created with a normal use of the Forgery skill and opposed by the viewer's Forgery check (or an Intelligence check for those without ranks in Forgery)—you can gain special bonuses to certain skills due to synergy.

At the DM's discretion, you can forge documents that grant a +2 circumstance bonus on a specific Bluff, Diplomacy, or Intimidate check. These false credentials become, in effect, the perfect tool for the job and provide a bonus much like the bonuses provided to other skills by masterwork tools. Unlike other bonuses, these apply only when you present the documents and the creature you are interacting with does not detect the forgery. If you present forged documents and they are detected as a forgery, the check you were attempting to use the documents for automatically fails. The DM is also free to rule that there are other repercussions in such situations.

HANDLE ANIMAL (CHA)

Teach an Animal a Trick: In addition to the tricks found on pages 74–75 of the *Player's Handbook,* the following tricks can be taught to an animal with a successful Handle Animal check (DCs noted below). Some tricks require that the animal already know an existing trick.

Assist Attack (DC 20): The animal aids your attack or that of another creature as a standard action. You must designate both the recipient of the aid and a specific opponent when commanding the animal to perform the task. The animal uses the aid another combat action (see page 154 of the *Player's Handbook*), attempting to grant a bonus on the recipient's next attack roll against the designated opponent. It also flanks the designated opponent, if it can do so without provoking attacks of opportunity. An

animal must know the attack trick (*Player's Handbook,* page 74) before it can learn this trick.

Assist Defend (DC 20): The animal aids your defense or that of another creature as a standard action. You must designate both the recipient of the aid and a specific opponent when commanding the animal to perform the task. The animal uses the aid another combat action, attempting to grant a bonus on the recipient's AC against the designated opponent's next attack. An animal must know the defend trick (*Player's Handbook,* page 75) before it can learn this trick.

Assist Track (DC 20): The animal aids your attempt to track. The animal must be present as you attempt a Survival check to track another creature; if the animal succeeds on a DC 10 Survival check, you gain a +2 circumstance bonus on your Survival check made to track. An animal must have the scent ability and know the track trick (*Player's Handbook,* page 75) before it can learn this trick.

Hold (DC 20): The animal initiates a grapple attack and attempts to hold a designated enemy in its arms, claws, or teeth. An animal with the improved grab ability uses that ability in the attempt; otherwise, the attack provokes attacks of opportunity. An animal must know the attack trick (*Player's Handbook,* page 74) before it can learn this trick.

Home (DC 20): The animal returns to the location where it was trained to perform this trick, traveling overland as required.

Hunt (DC 15): The animal attempts to hunt and forage for food for you using its Survival skill. See page 83 of the *Player's Handbook* for details on how to use Survival to hunt and forage for food. While any animal automatically knows how to hunt and forage for its own needs, this trick causes it to return with food rather than simply eating its fill of what it finds.

Stalk (DC 20): The animal follows a designated target, doing its best to remain undetected, until the target is wounded or resting, and then attacks. An animal must know the attack trick (*Player's Handbook,* page 74) before it can learn this trick.

Steal (DC 20): The animal grabs an object in the possession of a target creature, wrests it away, and brings it to you. If multiple objects are available, the animal attempts to steal a random one. An animal must know the fetch trick (*Player's Handbook,* page 75) before it can learn this trick.

Subdue (DC 20): The animal attacks a designated target creature to deal nonlethal damage, taking a −4 penalty on its attack roll. The animal stops its attack when the target creature lapses into unconsciousness. An animal must know the attack trick (*Player's Handbook*, page 74) before it can learn this trick.

Warn (DC 20): The animal reacts to new creatures coming near, even without any command being given, regardless of whether the animal sees the newcomer, or hears it, or detects the creature with scent. The exact warning sound given (hiss, growl, squawk, bark) varies depending on animal type and the training; this sound is chosen at the time of training and cannot be changed. If the newcomer does not stop after this warning, the animal attacks. As part of the training, the animal can be trained to ignore specific creatures (such as the trainer's allies). An animal must know the guard trick (*Player's Handbook*, page 75) before it can learn this trick.

Train an Animal for a Purpose: The general purposes described here expand on those presented in the *Player's Handbook*. To be trained for a purpose, an animal must have an Intelligence of 2.

Advanced Fighting (DC 20): An animal trained for advanced fighting knows the tricks assist attack, attack, down, hold, stay, and subdue. Training an animal for advanced fighting takes five weeks. You can also "upgrade" an animal trained for fighting to one trained for advanced fighting by spending two weeks and making a successful DC 20 Handle Animal check. The new general purpose and tricks completely replace the animal's previous purpose and any tricks it once knew.

Defensive Guarding (DC 20): An animal trained for defensive guarding knows the tricks defend, down, guard, hold, subdue, and warn. Training an animal for defensive guarding takes six weeks. You can also "upgrade" an animal trained for guarding to one trained for defensive guarding by spending three weeks and making a successful DC 20 Handle Animal check. The new general purpose and tricks completely replace the animal's previous purpose and any tricks it once knew.

Thievery (DC 20): An animal trained for thievery knows the tricks fetch, heel, home, seek, steal, and work. Training an animal for thievery takes six weeks.

HEAL (WIS)

You can use the Heal skill to determine what killed a dead creature. The difficulty of this task depends on the nature of the death itself, as shown on the table below.

Cause of Death	DC
Physical wounds	0
Environmental (fire, suffocation, etc.)	5
Spell with visible effects	10
Poison	15
Spell with no visible effects	20

Each day that passes between the time of the creature's death and the time the examination is made increases the DC of the Heal check to determine the cause of death by 5.

Action: Making a Heal check to determine the cause of a creature's death takes 10 minutes.

Try Again: Yes, but it takes 10 more minutes for each check.

HIDE (DEX)

You can blend into a crowd, slip between areas of cover or concealment to maintain secrecy, sneak up on a foe, or tail a target.

Blend into a Crowd: You can use the Hide skill to blend into a crowd, but doing so conceals you only from someone scanning the area to find you. You remain visible to everyone around you, and if they happen to be hostile they're likely to point you out.

Move between Cover: If you're already hiding (thanks to cover or concealment) and you have at least 5 ranks in Hide, you can make a Hide check (with a penalty) to try to move across an area that does not offer cover or concealment without revealing yourself. For every 5 ranks in Hide you possess, you can move up to 5 feet between one hiding place and another. For every 5 feet of open space you must cross between hiding places, you take a –5 penalty on your Hide check. If you move at more than one-half your speed, you also take the normal penalty

---

TRICK CAPACITY

Most creatures with an Intelligence lower than 3 can learn three tricks for every point of Intelligence. Trained animals and special mounts can learn more by taking the Extra Tricks feat, described below. DMs should feel free to introduce special stables or trainers that specialize in producing animals with the Extra Tricks feat and unique selections of tricks.

Extra Tricks

A creature with this feat can learn more tricks than normal.

Prerequisites: Animal or magical beast with Int 1 or 2, must know at least one trick.

Benefit: The creature can learn three more tricks than normal.

Normal: Without this feat, animals and magical beasts can learn a maximum of three tricks per point of Intelligence.

Special: This feat can be taken multiple times. Each time it is taken, the creature can learn up to three more tricks.

on Hide checks when moving quickly (–10 for moving faster than normal speed, or –5 for moving between half speed and normal speed).

You can also use this option to sneak up on someone from a hiding place. For every 5 feet of open space between you and the target, you take a –5 penalty on your Hide check. If your Hide check succeeds, your target doesn't notice you until you attack or make some other attention-grabbing action. Such a target is treated as being flat-footed with respect to you.

For example, Lidda the 2nd-level rogue could attempt to dash across a 5-foot-wide doorway without revealing her presence to the orcs inside. Even though the open doorway provides no cover or concealment, she can attempt a Hide check as normal, opposed by the orcs' Spot checks. She takes a –5 penalty on her check because of the distance involved. If she moved at more than half her speed, she would take an additional –5 or –10 penalty on the check depending on how fast she moved (see above).

Tail Someone: You can try to follow someone while remaining unseen. If you stay at least 60 feet away from your quarry, you must succeed on a Hide check (opposed by your quarry's Spot check) once every 10 minutes. At a distance of less than 60 feet, you must make a Hide check each round. Extraordinary actions on your part (such as spellcasting or attacking) may disrupt this attempt even if you do not fail a check.

Tailing someone still requires cover or concealment, as normal for attempting a Hide check. A moderately crowded street provides sufficient cover and concealment to accomplish this goal. Alternatively, you can duck between areas of cover or concealment, as described in Move between Cover (see above).

Even if you fail a Hide check while tailing someone or you are spotted while moving too great a distance between hiding places, you can attempt a Bluff check opposed by your quarry's Sense Motive check to look innocuous. Success means your quarry sees you but doesn't realize you're tailing him; failure alerts him that you're actually following. A modifier may apply to the Sense Motive check, depending on how suspicious your quarry is. The table below provides Sense Motive modifiers for particular situations.

SENSE MOTIVE

Your Quarry . . .	DC Modifier
Is sure nobody is following	–5
Has no reason to suspect anybody is following	+0
Is worried about being followed	+10
Is worried about being followed and knows you're an enemy	+20

OPEN LOCK (DEX)

You can rush an Open Lock attempt, reducing the amount of time it takes to perform the attempt.

Quick Lockpick: You can try to open a lock more quickly than normal. To reduce the time required to open any lock to a move action, add 20 to the DC. For example, opening an average lock normally requires a DC 25 check and requires a full-round action. To open the lock as a move action requires a DC 45 check.

SENSE MOTIVE (WIS)

You can assess the combat prowess of an opponent, identifying particularly dangerous or vulnerable foes.

Assess Opponent: As a standard action, you can use Sense Motive to ascertain how tough a challenge an opponent poses for you, based on your level and your opponent's CR. This skill check is opposed by the opponent's Bluff check. To attempt this task, your opponent must be visible to you and within 30 feet. If you have seen the opponent in combat, you gain a +2 circumstance bonus on the check.

The accuracy of the assessment depends on the amount by which your Sense Motive check result exceeds the opposed Bluff check result. On a successful Sense Motive opposed check, you can gain the following information:

Opponent's CR	Assess Opponent Result
4 or more less than your level/HD	A pushover
1, 2, or 3 less than your level/HD	Easy
Equal to your level/HD	A fair fight
Equal to your level/HD plus 1, 2, or 3	A tough challenge
Exceeds your level/HD by 4 or more	A dire threat

A successful assessment reveals that your foe belongs in one of two adjacent categories (for example, "Easy" or "A fair fight"). If your Sense Motive check result exceeds the opposed Bluff check result by 10 or more, you can narrow the result down to a single category.

By contrast, if the target's Bluff check result equals or slightly exceeds your Sense Motive check result, you gain no useful information. If the target's Bluff check result exceeds your Sense Motive check result by 5 or more, you may (at the DM's option) gain a false impression, believing your opponent to be much stronger or weaker than he really is (equal chance of either). If the target's Bluff check result exceeds your Sense Motive check result by 10 or more, your assessment is off by at least two categories (for example, a dire threat might be assessed as a fair fight).

Special: The Combat Intuition feat (see page 106) grants a +4 bonus on Sense Motive checks made to assess opponents. It also enables you to narrow your assessment of your opponent's combat capabilities to a single category. Finally, it allows you to accomplish this task as a free action.

An opponent that is particularly vulnerable to your typical attack routine (for example, a vampire facing a high-level cleric of Pelor) registers as one category less challenging; one who is resistant to your typical attack routine (for example, a golem opposing a rogue who relies heavily on sneak attacks) registers as one category more challenging.

Try Again: You can use this skill on a different opponent each round.

SURVIVAL (WIS)

You can blaze a trail through the wilderness, improving your and your allies' overland speed.

Trailblazing: When traveling in poor conditions or difficult terrain, you can attempt a Survival check to hasten your group's progress.

On a check result of 15 or better, you increase the movement modifier for overland movement by 1/4, to a maximum of ×1 (see Table 9–5: Terrain and Overland Movement, page 164 of the *Player's Handbook*). For example, you could increase your movement rate through trackless jungle from ×1/4 to ×1/2 your normal overland movement rate. With a result of 25 or higher, you can increase the movement modifier by 1/2 (and thus could travel through trackless jungle at ×3/4 your normal rate). In either case the ×1 maximum still applies—that is, you can improve up to but not exceed your normal movement rate by this means.

You can guide a group of up to four individuals (including yourself) at no penalty. However, for each three additional people (rounded up) in the group being guided, apply a –2 penalty to the trailblazing attempt. Thus, a group of five to seven (yourself and four to six others) would incur a –2 penalty, a group of eight to ten a –4 penalty, and so forth.

This ability applies only to long-distance overland movement—it has no effect on tactical movement.

SWIM (STR; ARMOR CHECK PENALTY)

You can swim more quickly than normal.

Accelerated Swimming: You try to swim more quickly than normal. By accepting a –10 penalty on your Swim check, you can swim at up to your speed as a full-round action (rather than half your speed or

at half your speed as a move action (rather than one-quarter).

TUMBLE (DEX; ARMOR CHECK PENALTY)

You can fall from significant heights without taking damage, stand up more quickly than normal, or tumble at a full sprint.

Free Stand: With a DC 35 Tumble check result, you can stand up from prone as a free action (instead of as a move action). This use of the skill still provokes attacks of opportunity as normal.

Ignore Falling Damage: For every 15 points of your Tumble check result, you can treat a fall as if it were 10 feet shorter than it really is when determining damage. A check result of 15–29 treats a fall as 10 feet shorter than it is, 30–44 as 20 feet shorter, 45–59 as 30 feet shorter, and so forth.

Sprinting Tumble: You can try to tumble past or through an opponent's space while running by accepting a –20 penalty on your Tumble check.

USE ROPE (DEX)

You can tie knots more quickly than normal.

Quick Knot-Tying: You can try to tie a knot, a special knot, or a rope around yourself more quickly than normal. By accepting a –10 penalty on your Use Rope check, you can accomplish any one of these tasks as a move action (rather than a full-round action).

FEATS

Feats are the cornerstone of any adventurer's abilities. They define an adventurer's abilities by providing new uses for skills, enhancing class features, or providing entirely new combat options. The feats in this section stress skill use, provide options for multiclass characters, open up new options for the bardic music ability, and accentuate the abilities of highly skilled characters such as rogues, bards, rangers, scouts, spellthieves, and ninjas.

APPRAISE MAGIC VALUE

Your ability to determine an item's worth and your knowledge of magic allow you to determine the exact properties of a magic item without the use of the *identify* spell or similar magic.

Prerequisites: Appraise 5 ranks, Knowledge (arcana) 5 ranks, Spellcraft 5 ranks.

Benefit: If you know that an item is magical, you can

Table 3–2: Feats

General Feats	Prerequisites	Benefit
Appraise Magic Value	Appraise 5 ranks, Knowledge (arcana) 5 ranks, Spellcraft 5 ranks	Use Appraise to determine magic item properties
Ascetic Hunter	Improved Unarmed Strike, favored enemy	Monk and ranger levels stack for unarmed strike damage, favored enemy bonus improves stunning DC
Ascetic Knight	Improved Unarmed Strike, smite evil	Monk and paladin levels stack for unarmed strike and smite evil damage
Ascetic Mage	Improved Unarmed Strike, spontaneous 2nd-level arcane spells	Monk and sorcerer levels stack for AC bonus (Cha-based), sacrifice spell to gain bonus on unarmed strike
Ascetic Rogue	Improved Unarmed Strike, sneak attack	Monk and rogue levels stack for sneak attack damage, unarmed strike sneak attack gains improved stunning DC
Brachiation	Climb 4 ranks, Jump 4 ranks	Swing through trees at normal land speed
Brutal Throw[B]	—	Use Str rather than Dex to attack rolls with thrown weapons
Power Throw[B]	Str 13, Brutal Throw, Power Attack	Power Attack with thrown weapons
Combat Intuition[B]	Sense Motive 4 ranks, base attack bonus +5	+1 to attack opponent you engaged in the preceding round
Danger Sense	Improved Initiative	Reroll initiative once per day
Death Blow	Improved Initiative, base attack bonus +2	Coup de grace as a standard action
Deft Opportunist	Dex 15, Combat Reflexes	+4 bonus on attack rolls on attacks of opportunity
Deft Strike	Int 13, Spot 10 ranks, Combat Expertise, sneak attack	Ignore armor and natural armor
Devoted Inquisitor	Smite evil, sneak attack	Use smite evil and sneak attack together to daze a foe
Devoted Performer	Bardic music, smite evil	Paladin and bard levels stack for smite evil and bardic music
Devoted Tracker	Track, smite evil, wild empathy	Special mount becomes animal companion, and paladin and ranger levels stack for smite evil and wild empathy
Disguise Spell	Perform 9 ranks, bardic music	Cast spells unobtrusively as part of a performance
Dive for Cover	Base Reflex save +4	Make one retry on failed Reflex save, but end up prone
Dual Strike[B]	Improved Two-Weapon Fighting, Two-Weapon Fighting	Attack once with each hand as a standard action
Expert Tactician	Dex 13, Combat Reflexes, base attack bonus +2	All allies gain +2 attack and damage bonus for a round against a target you've hit with an attack of opportunity
Extra Music	Bardic music	Gain four extra uses per day of bardic music
Extraordinary Concentration	Concentration 15 ranks	Concentrate on a spell as a move action or swift action
Extraordinary Spell Aim	Spellcraft 15 ranks	Exclude one creature from spell area
Force of Personality	Cha 13	Add Cha modifier, rather than Wis modifier, to Will saves
Goad[B]	Cha 13, base attack bonus +1	Cause target to attack only you
Green Ear	Perform 10 ranks, bardic music	Affect plants with your bardic music ability
Hear the Unseen	Listen 5 ranks, Blind-Fight	Pinpoint a target's location by sound, not sight
Improved Diversion[B]	Bluff 4 ranks	Use Bluff to create a diversion, then Hide as a move action
Improved Flight	Ability to fly	Flight maneuverability improves by one step
Improved Swimming	Swim 6 ranks	Double your swimming speed
Insightful Reflexes	—	Add Int modifier, rather than Dex modifier, to Reflex saves
Jack of All Trades	Int 13	Use any skill, even "Trained Only" ones
Leap Attack	Jump 8 ranks, Power Attack	Doubles damage by Power Attack on successful charge
Lingering Song	Bardic music	Extend the duration of your bardic music effects
Mobile Spellcasting	Concentration 8 ranks	Cast a spell and move at the same time
Natural Bond	Animal companion	Add +3 to effective druid level when determining animal companion's abilities
Obscure Lore	Bardic music or lore	Gain +4 bonus on bardic knowledge or lore checks
Open Minded	—	Immediately gain 5 skill points
Oversized Two-Weapon Fighting[B]	Str 13, Two-Weapon Fighting	Treat one-handed weapon in off hand as if light weapon
Quick Reconnoiter	Listen 5 ranks, Spot 5 ranks	Spot and Listen as free actions, +2 on initiative checks
Razing Strike	Ability to cast 3rd-level arcane or divine spells, sneak attack	Spend a spell use to gain attack and damage bonuses against constructs or undead
Staggering Strike	Base attack bonus +6, sneak attack	Limit target to a single action for 1 round
Subsonics	Perform 10 ranks, Bardic music	Produce bardic music effects very softly
Tactile Trapsmith	—	Add Dex modifier, rather than Int modifier, to Search and Disable Device checks
Versatile Performer	Perform 5 ranks	Treat number of Perform skills as if they had ranks equal to your highest Perform rank

Table 3–2: Feats (cont.)

Bardic Music Feats	Prerequisites	Benefit
Chant of Fortitude	Bardic music, Concentration 8 ranks, Perform 8 ranks	Bardic music keeps allies conscious at negative hit points
Ironskin Chant	Bardic music, Concentration 12 ranks, Perform 12 ranks	Use bardic music to gain DR 5/—
Lyric Spell	Bardic music, arcane spellcaster level 6th, Perform 9 ranks	Spend bardic music uses to cast extra spells

Wild Feats	Prerequisites	Benefit
Blindsense	Wild shape, Listen 4 ranks	Spend wild shape use to gain blindsense 30 ft.
Climb Like an Ape	Wild shape	Spend wild shape use to gain climb movement mode
Cougar's Vision	Wild shape, Spot 2 ranks	Spend wild shape use to gain low-light vision
Hawk's Vision	Wild shape, Spot 4 ranks	Spend wild shape use to gain +8 to Spot checks and cut range increment penalties in half
Savage Grapple	Wild shape, sneak attack	Deal sneak attack damage when grappling in wild shape
Scent	Wild shape	Spend wild shape use to gain scent

B: A fighter may select this feat as one of his fighter bonus feats.

use the Appraise skill to identify the item's properties. This use of the Appraise skill requires 8 hours of uninterrupted work and consumes 25 gp worth of special materials. The DC of the Appraise check is 10 + the caster level of the item.

ASCETIC HUNTER

You have gone beyond the bounds of your monastic training to incorporate new modes of bringing the unlawful to justice. Although many of your fellow monks frown on your methods, none can doubt that your diverse training has added to your ability to strike precisely and bring down your foes quickly

Prerequisites: Improved Unarmed Strike, favored enemy.

Benefit. When you use an unarmed strike to deliver a stunning attack against a favored enemy, you can add one-half your favored enemy bonus on damage rolls to the DC of your stunning attempt.

If you have levels in ranger and monk, those levels stack for the purpose of determining your unarmed strike damage. For example, a human 7th-level ranger/1st-level monk would deal 1d10 points of damage with her unarmed strike.

In addition, you can multiclass freely between the monk and ranger classes. You must still remain lawful in order to retain your monk abilities and take monk levels. You still face the normal XP penalties for having multiple classes more than one level apart.

ASCETIC KNIGHT

You belong to a special order of religious monks that teaches its adherents that self-enlightenment and honorable service grow from the same well of purity. As a student of this philosophy, you have blended your training as a paladin and as a monk into one seamless whole.

Prerequisite: Improved Unarmed Strike, ability to smite evil.

Benefit: Your paladin and monk levels stack for the purpose of determining your unarmed strike damage. For example, a human 3rd-level paladin/1st-level monk would deal 1d8 points of damage with her unarmed strike.

Your paladin and monk levels also stack when determining the extra damage dealt by your smite evil ability.

In addition, you can multiclass freely between the paladin and monk classes. You must still remain lawful good in order to retain your paladin abilities and take paladin levels, and you must remain lawful in order to continue advancing as a monk. You still face the normal XP penalties for having multiple classes more than one level apart.

ASCETIC MAGE

You practice an unusual martial art that mixes self-taught spellcasting and melee attacks to great effect.

Prerequisites: Improved Unarmed Strike, ability to spontaneously cast 2nd-level arcane spells.

Benefit: As a swift action that doesn't provoke attacks of opportunity, you can sacrifice one of your daily allotment of spells to add a bonus to your unarmed strike attack rolls and damage rolls for 1 round. The bonus is equal to the level of the spell sacrificed. The spell is lost as if you had cast it.

If you have levels in sorcerer and monk, those levels stack for the purpose of determining your AC bonus. For example, a human 4th-level sorcerer/1st-level monk would have a +1 bonus to AC as if she were a 5th-level monk. If you would normally be allowed to add your Wisdom bonus to AC (such as for a unarmored, unencumbered monk), you instead add your Charisma bonus (if any) to your AC.

In addition, you can multiclass freely between the sorcerer and monk classes. You must still remain lawful in order to continue advancing as a monk. You still face the normal XP penalties for having multiple classes more than one level apart.

ASCETIC ROGUE

You have gone beyond the bounds of your monastic training to incorporate new modes of stealthy combat. Although your fellow monks may frown on your methods, none can doubt that your diverse training has improved your ability to strike precisely and bring down your foes quickly.

Prerequisites: Improved Unarmed Strike, sneak attack.

Benefit: When you use an unarmed strike with a sneak attack to deliver a stunning attack, you add 2 to the DC of your stunning attempt.

If you have levels in rogue and monk, those levels stack for the purpose of determining your unarmed strike damage. For example, a human 5th-level rogue/1st-level monk would deal 1d8 points of damage with her unarmed strike.

In addition, you can multiclass freely between the monk and rogue classes. You must still remain lawful in order to retain your monk abilities and take monk levels. You still face the normal XP penalties for having multiple classes more than one level apart.

BRACHIATION

You can swing through trees like a monkey.

Prerequisites: Climb 4 ranks, Jump 4 ranks.

Benefit: You can move through wooded areas at your base land speed, ignoring any effects on movement due to terrain. You must be at least 20 feet from the ground to use this ability. This ability works only in medium and dense forests (see page 87 of the *Dungeon Master's Guide*).

BRUTAL THROW

You have learned how to hurl weapons to deadly effect.

Benefit: You can add your Strength modifier (instead of your Dexterity modifier) to attack rolls with thrown weapons.

Normal: A character attacking with a ranged weapon adds his Dexterity modifier to the attack roll.

Special: A fighter may select Brutal Throw as one of his fighter bonus feats.

COMBAT INTUITION

Your keen understanding of your opponent's moves and your instinctive feel for the flow of combat enable you to shrewdly assess your opponent's combat capabilities.

Prerequisites: Sense Motive 4 ranks, base attack bonus +5.

Benefit: As a free action, you can use Sense Motive to assess the challenge presented by a single opponent in relationship to your own level/Hit Dice (see the assess opponent option under the Sense Motive skill, page 102). You gain a +4 bonus on such checks and narrow the result to a single category.

In addition, whenever you make a melee attack against a creature that you made a melee attack against during the previous round, you gain a +1 insight bonus on your melee attack rolls against that creature.

Special: A fighter may select Combat Intuition as one of his fighter bonus feats.

DANGER SENSE

You are one twitchy individual.

Prerequisite: Improved Initiative.

Benefit: Once per day, you can reroll an initiative check you have just made. You use the better of your two rolls. You must decide to reroll before the round starts.

DEATH BLOW

You waste no time in dealing with downed foes.

Prerequisites: Improved Initiative, base attack bonus +2.

Benefit: You can perform a coup de grace attack against a helpless defender as a standard action. Doing this still provokes attacks of opportunity as normal.

Normal: Performing a coup de grace is a full-round action.

DEFT OPPORTUNIST

You are prepared for the unexpected.

Prerequisites: Dex 15, Combat Reflexes.

Benefit: You get a +4 bonus on attack rolls when making attacks of opportunity.

DEFT STRIKE

You can place attacks at weak points in your opponent's defenses.

Prerequisites: Int 13, Combat Expertise, Spot 10 ranks, sneak attack.

Benefit: As a standard action, you can attempt to find a weak point in a visible target's armor. This requires a Spot check against a DC equal to your target's Armor Class. If you succeed, your next attack against that target (which must be made no later than your next turn) ignores the target's armor bonus and natural armor bonus to AC (including any enhancement bonuses to armor or natural armor). Other AC bonuses still apply normally.

If you use a ranged weapon to deliver the attack, your opponent must be within 30 feet of you in order for you to benefit from this feat.

DEVOTED INQUISITOR

Your faithful service to your patron deity involves training and methods that many paladins consider questionable. By using the unconventional methods of rogues and assassins, you have learned to deliver devastating sneak attacks against evil foes.

Prerequisite: Smite evil, sneak attack.

Benefit: When you successfully use your sneak attack ability and your smite evil ability against the same foe in a single attack, you can potentially daze your foe. An opponent affected by both abilities must make a Will saving throw (DC 10 + 1/2 your character level + your Cha modifier) or be dazed for 1 round.

In addition, you can multiclass freely between the paladin and rogue classes. You must still remain lawful good in order to retain your

Combat Intuition helps this paladin overcome an orc

paladin abilities and take paladin levels. You still face the normal XP penalties for having multiple classes more than one level apart.

DEVOTED PERFORMER

You have foregone the pursuit of frivolous musical talents, instead entering religious training in service of honor and justice.

Prerequisite: Bardic music, smite evil.

Benefit: If you have levels in paladin and bard, those levels stack for the purpose of determining the bonus damage dealt by your smite evil ability and determining the number of times per day that you can use your bardic music. This feat does not allow additional daily uses of smite evil or bardic music abilities beyond what your class levels would normally allow.

In addition, you can multiclass freely between the paladin and bard classes and may even gain additional bard levels regardless of your lawful alignment. You must still remain lawful good in order to retain your paladin abilities and take paladin levels. You still face the normal XP penalties for having multiple classes more than one level apart.

Illus. by D. Hudnut

hudnut

DEVOTED TRACKER

You have found a balance between your woodland training and your devotion to religious training, blending these two aspects into one seamless whole.

Prerequisite: Track, smite evil, wild empathy.

Benefit: If you have levels in paladin and ranger, those levels stack for the purposes of determining the extra damage dealt by your smite evil ability and determining the bonus for your wild empathy class feature. This feat does not allow additional daily uses of smite evil.

If you have both the special mount and animal companion class features, you can designate your special mount as your animal companion. The mount gains all the benefits of being both your special mount and your animal companion. For instance, a 5th-level paladin/6th-level ranger's special mount would have 4 bonus Hit Dice, a +6 natural armor adjustment, +2 Strength, +1 Dexterity, two bonus tricks, and Intelligence 6, as well as the empathic link, improved evasion, share spells, share saving throws, and link special abilities.

In addition, you can multiclass freely between the paladin and ranger classes. You must still remain lawful good in order to retain your paladin abilities and take paladin levels. You still face the normal XP penalties for having multiple classes more than one level apart.

DISGUISE SPELL

You can cast spells without observers noticing.

Prerequisite: Perform (any) 9 ranks, bardic music.

Benefit: You can cast spells unobtrusively, mingling verbal and somatic components into your performances. To disguise a spell, make a Perform check as part of the action used to cast the spell. Onlookers must match or exceed your check result with a Spot check to detect that you're casting a spell (your performance is obvious to everyone in the vicinity, but the fact that you are casting a spell isn't). Unless the spell visibly emanates from you, or observers have some other means of determining its source, they don't know where the effect came from.

A disguised spell can't be identified with a Spellcraft check, even by someone who realizes you're casting a spell. The act of casting still provokes attacks of opportunity as normal.

DIVE FOR COVER

You can dive behind cover or drop to the ground quickly enough to avoid many area effects.

Prerequisite: Base Reflex save bonus +4.

Benefit: If you fail a Reflex saving throw, you can immediately attempt the saving throw again. You must take the second result, whether it succeeds or fails. You become prone immediately after attempting the second roll.

Dive for Cover

DUAL STRIKE

You are an expert skirmisher skilled at fighting with two weapons. Your extensive training with two weapons allows you to attack with both while moving through a chaotic combat or fighting a running battle.

Prerequisites: Improved Two-Weapon Fighting, Two-Weapon Fighting.

Benefit: As a standard action, you can make a melee attack with your primary weapon and your off-hand weapon. Both attacks use the same attack roll to determine success, using the worse of the two weapons' attack modifiers. If you are using a one-handed or light weapon in your primary hand and a light weapon in your off hand, you take a –4 penalty on this attack roll; otherwise you take a –10 penalty.

Each weapon deals its normal damage. Damage reduction and other resistances apply separately against each weapon attack.

Special: When you make this attack, you apply precision-based damage (such as from sneak attack) only once. If you score a critical hit, only the weapon in your primary hand deals extra critical hit damage; your off-hand weapon deals regular damage.

A fighter may select Dual Strike as one of his fighter bonus feats.

EXPERT TACTICIAN

Your tactical skills work to your advantage.

Prerequisites: Dex 13, Combat Reflexes, base attack bonus +2.

Benefit: If you hit a creature with an attack of opportunity, you and all your allies gain a +2 circumstance bonus on melee attack rolls and damage rolls against that creature for 1 round.

EXTRA MUSIC

You can use your bardic music more often than you otherwise could.

Prerequisite: Bardic music.

Benefit: You can use your bardic music four extra times per day.

Normal: Bards without the Extra Music feat can use bardic music once per day per bard level.

Special: You can gain this feat multiple times. Its effects stack.

EXTRAORDINARY CONCENTRATION

Your mind is so focused that you can cast spells even while concentrating on another spell.

Prerequisite: Concentration 15 ranks.

Benefit: When concentrating to maintain a spell, you can make a Concentration check (DC 25 + spell level) to maintain concentration with just a move action. If you beat the DC by 10 or more, you can maintain concentration on the spell as a swift action (see Swift Actions and Immediate Actions, page 137). Using this ability is a free action, but if you fail the Concentration check, you lose concentration on the maintained spell and its effect ends. This feat does not give you the ability to maintain concentration on more than one spell at a time.

Normal: Concentrating on a spell is a standard action.

EXTRAORDINARY SPELL AIM

You can shape a spell's area to exclude one creature from its effects.

Prerequisite: Spellcraft 15 ranks.

Benefit: Whenever you cast a spell with an area, you can attempt to shape the spell's area so that one creature within the area is unaffected by the spell. To accomplish this, you must succeed on a Spellcraft check (DC 25 + spell level).

Casting a spell affected by the Extraordinary Spell Aim feat requires a full-round action unless the spell's normal casting time is longer, in which case the casting time is unchanged.

FORCE OF PERSONALITY

You have cultivated an unshakable belief in your self-worth. Your sense of self and purpose are so strong that they bolster your willpower.

Prerequisite: Cha 13.

Benefit: You add your Charisma modifier (instead of your Wisdom modifier) to Will saves against mind-affecting spells and abilities.

GOAD

You are skilled at inducing opponents to attack you.

Prerequisites: Cha 13, base attack bonus +1.

Benefit: As a move action, you can goad an opponent that threatens you, has line of sight to you, can hear you, and has an Intelligence of 3 or higher. (The goad is a mind-affecting ability.) When the goaded opponent starts its next turn, if it threatens you and has line of sight to you, it must make a Will saving throw (DC 10 + 1/2 your character level + your Cha modifier). If the opponent fails its save, you are the only creature it can make melee attacks against during this turn. (If it kills you, knocks you unconscious, loses sight of you, or otherwise is unable to make melee attacks against you, it may make any remaining melee attacks against other foes, as normal.) A goaded creature can still cast spells, make ranged attacks, move, or perform other actions normally. The use of this feat restricts only melee attacks.

Special: A fighter may select Goad as one of his fighter bonus feats.

GREEN EAR

Your bardic music can affect plant creatures.

Prerequisite: Perform (any) 10 ranks, bardic music.

Benefit: You can alter any of your mind-affecting bardic music abilities (or similar Perform-based abilities from other classes) so that they influence only plant creatures instead of other creatures. However, plants receive a +5 bonus on Will saves against any of these effects.

Normal: Plants are normally immune to all mind-affecting spells and abilities.

HEAR THE UNSEEN

Your sense of hearing is so acute that you can partially pinpoint an opponent's location by sound, allowing you to strike even if the opponent is concealed or displaced.

Prerequisites: Listen 5 ranks, Blind-Fight.

Benefit: As a move action that does not provoke attacks of opportunity, you can attempt a DC 25 Listen check. If successful, you can pinpoint the location of all foes within 30 feet, as long as you have line of effect to them. This benefit does not eliminate the normal miss chance for fighting foes with concealment, but it ensures that you can target the correct square with your attacks.

If you are deafened or within an area of *silence*, you can't use this feat. If an invisible or hidden opponent is attempting to move silently, your Listen check is opposed by your opponent's Move Silently check, but your opponent gains a +15 bonus on this check. This feat does not work against perfectly silent opponents, such as incorporeal creatures.

IMPROVED DIVERSION

You can create a diversion to hide quickly and with less effort.

Prerequisite: Bluff 4 ranks.

Benefit: You can use Bluff to create a diversion to hide (see page 68 of the *Player's Handbook*) as a move action. You gain a +4 bonus on Bluff checks made for this purpose.

Normal: Without this feat, creating a diversion to hide using the Bluff skill requires a standard action.

Special: A fighter may select Improved Diversion as one of his fighter bonus feats.

IMPROVED FLIGHT

You gain greater maneuverability when flying than you would normally have.

Prerequisite: Ability to fly (naturally, magically, or through shapechanging).

Benefit: Your maneuverability class while flying improves by one step—clumsy to poor, poor to average, average to good, or good to perfect.

IMPROVED SWIMMING

You can swim faster than you normally could.

Prerequisite: Swim 6 ranks.

Benefit: You can swim half your speed as a move action or your speed as a full-round action.

Normal: You swim at one-quarter your speed as a move action or at half your speed as a full-round action.

INSIGHTFUL REFLEXES

Your keen intellect allows you an uncanny knack for evading dangerous effects.

Benefit: You add your Intelligence modifier (instead of your Dexterity modifier) to Reflex saves.

JACK OF ALL TRADES

You have picked up a smattering of even the most obscure skills.

Prerequisite: Int 13.

Benefit: You can use any skill as if you had 1/2 rank in that skill. This benefit allows you to attempt checks with skills that normally don't allow untrained skill checks (such as Decipher Script and Knowledge). If a skill doesn't allow skill checks (such as Speak Language), this feat has no effect.

Normal: Without this feat, you can't attempt some skill checks (Decipher Script, Disable Device, Handle Animal, Knowledge, Open Lock, Profession, Sleight of Hand, Speak Language, Spellcraft, Tumble, and Use Magic Device) unless you have ranks in the skill.

LEAP ATTACK

You can combine a powerful charge and a mighty leap into one devastating attack.

Prerequisites: Jump 8 ranks, Power Attack.

Benefit: You can combine a jump with a charge against an opponent. If you cover at least 10 feet of horizontal distance with your jump, and you end your jump in a square from which you threaten your target, you can double the extra damage dealt by your use of the Power Attack feat. If you use this tactic with a two-handed weapon, you instead triple the extra damage from Power Attack.

This attack must follow all the normal rules for using the Jump skill and for making a charge, except that you ignore rough terrain in any squares you jump over.

LINGERING SONG

Your inspirational bardic music stays with the listeners long after the last note has died away.

Prerequisite: Bardic music.

Benefit: If you use bardic music to inspire courage, inspire greatness, or inspire heroics, the effect lasts for 1 minute after an inspired ally stops hearing you play.

Normal: Inspire courage, inspire greatness, and inspire heroics last as long as an ally hears the bard sing plus an additional 5 rounds thereafter.

MOBILE SPELL-CASTING

Your focused concentration allows you to move while casting a spell.

Prerequisite: Concentration 8 ranks.

Benefit: You can make a special Concentration check (DC 20+ spell level) when casting a spell. If the check succeeds, you can cast the spell and move up to your speed as a single standard action. (You can't use this ability to cast a spell that takes longer than 1 standard action to cast.) If the check fails, you lose the spell and fail to cast it, just as if you had failed a Concentration check to cast the spell defensively.

You still provoke attacks of opportunity for casting spells from any creatures who threaten you at any point of your movement. You can cast defensively while using this feat, but doing so increases the Concentration DC to 25 + spell level.

NATURAL BOND

Your bond with your animal companion is exceptionally strong.

Prerequisite: Animal companion.

Benefit: Add three to your effective druid level for the purpose of determining the bonus Hit Dice, extra tricks, special abilities, and other bonuses that your animal companion receives (see page 36 of the *Player's Handbook*). This bonus can never make your effective druid level exceed your character level.

OBSCURE LORE

You are a treasure trove of little-known information.

Prerequisite: Bardic knowledge or lore class feature.

Benefit: You gain a +4 insight bonus on checks using your bardic knowledge or lore class feature.

OPEN MINDED

You are naturally able to reroute your memory and skill expertise.

Benefit: You immediately gain 5 skill points. Spend these skill points as normal. You cannot exceed the normal maximum ranks for your level in any skill.

Special: You can gain this feat multiple times. Each time, you immediately gain another 5 skill points.

OVERSIZED TWO-WEAPON FIGHTING

You are adept at wielding larger than normal weapons in your off hand

Prerequisite: Str 13, Two-Weapon Fighting.

Benefit: When wielding a one-handed weapon in your off hand, you take penalties for fighting with two weapons as if you were wielding a light weapon in your off hand (see page 160 of the *Player's Handbook*).

Special: A fighter may select Oversized Two-Weapon Fighting as one of his fighter bonus feats.

POWER THROW

You have learned how to hurl weapons to deadly effect.

Prerequisite: Str 13, Brutal Throw, Power Attack.

Benefit: On your turn, before making any attack rolls, you can choose to subtract a number from all thrown weapon attack rolls and add the same number to all thrown weapon damage rolls. This number may not exceed your base attack bonus. The penalty on attack rolls and the bonus on damage rolls applies until your next turn.

Special: A fighter may select Power Throw as one of his fighter bonus feats.

Leap Attack

Illus. by R. Spencer

QUICK RECONNOITER

You can learn a lot of information from just a quick scan of an area or object.

Prerequisite: Listen 5 ranks, Spot 5 ranks.

Benefit: You can make one Spot check and one Listen check each round as a free action.

You also gain a +2 bonus on initiative checks.

Normal: Using Spot or Listen in a reactive fashion is a free action, but actively trying to make a Spot check or Listen check requires a move action.

RAZING STRIKE

You have mastered the art of delivering precise strikes against nonliving creatures while channeling spell energy through your melee attacks.

Prerequisite: Sneak attack, caster level 5th.

Benefit: To activate this feat, you must sacrifice one of your daily allotment of spells (minimum spell level 1st). Doing this is a swift action that doesn't provoke attacks of opportunity.

In exchange, you gain an insight bonus on your melee attack rolls and damage rolls for 1 round. The bonus on attack rolls equals the level of the spell sacrificed. The bonus on damage rolls is 1d6 points per level of the spell sacrificed, plus any extra damage based on your sneak attack ability.

These bonuses apply against only one type of creature, depending on the type of spell sacrificed. If you sacrifice an arcane spell, they apply against constructs; if the sacrificed spell is divine, the bonuses apply against undead.

Example: A 5th-level wizard/1st-level rogue activates this feat, sacrificing a prepared *web* spell. She gains a +2 insight bonus on her melee attack rolls against constructs for 1 round, and also adds 3d6 points of damage to successful attacks against constructs during that round (2d6 for the 2nd-level spell, plus 1d6 for her sneak attack damage).

This feat does not allow you to deliver critical hits or sneak attacks against constructs or undead.

STAGGERING STRIKE

You can deliver a wound that hampers an opponent's movement.

Prerequisite: Base attack bonus +6, sneak attack.

Benefit: If you deal damage with a melee sneak attack, you can also deliver a wound that limits your foe's mobility. For 1 round (or until the target is the beneficiary of a DC 15 Heal check or any magical healing that restores at least 1 hit point, whichever comes

first), your target is treated as if it were staggered, even if its nonlethal damage doesn't exactly equal its current hit points. A target can resist this effect by making a successful Fortitude save (DC equal to damage dealt). Multiple staggering strikes on the same creature do not stack. This feat has no effect on creatures not subject to sneak attack damage.

SUBSONICS

Your music can affect even those who do not consciously hear it.

Prerequisite: Perform (any) 10 ranks, bardic music.

Benefit: You can produce music or poetics so subtly that opponents do not notice it, yet your allies still gain all the usual benefits from your bardic music. Similarly, you can affect opponents within range with your music, but unless they can see you performing or have some other means of discovering it, they cannot determine the source of the effect.

TACTILE TRAPSMITH

You can rely on your rapid reflexes and nimble fingers instead of your intellect when searching a room or when disabling a trap.

Benefit: You add your Dexterity bonus (rather than your Intelligence bonus) on all Search and Disable Device checks.

In addition, you receive no penalty on these checks for darkness or blindness.

VERSATILE PERFORMER

You are skilled at many kinds of performances.

Prerequisite: Perform (any) 5 ranks.

Benefit: Pick a number of Perform categories equal to your Intelligence bonus (minimum 1). For the purpose of making Perform checks, you are treated as having a number of ranks in those skills equal to the highest number of ranks you have in any Perform category. You cannot change these categories once you have picked them, but your score in them automatically increases if you later add additional ranks in your highest-ranked Perform category. You gain new categories of your choice if your Intelligence bonus permanently increases.

In addition, you gain a +2 bonus on a combined Perform check when using two or more forms of performance at the same time, such as a bard strumming a lyre while singing. In such cases, add the bonus to the higher of your two Perform skill modifiers.

BARDIC MUSIC FEATS

Bardic music feats, as the name suggests, require the bardic music ability and cost daily uses of the bardic music ability to activate. All bardic music feats require that the character be able to produce music to use the feat, even those that only require free actions and those that require no action at all.

Class features that resemble bardic music, such as the war chanter's war chanter music (see *Complete Warrior*) or a seeker of the song's seeker music abilities (see *Complete Arcane*) can be substituted for the bardic music prerequisite of a bardic music feat.

CHANT OF FORTITUDE [BARDIC MUSIC]

You can channel the power of your bardic music to sustain your allies, allowing them to function even after receiving wounds that would cause others to falter.

Prerequisites: Bardic music, Concentration 9 ranks, Perform 9 ranks.

Benefit: You can expend one daily use of your bardic music ability as an immediate action to provide all allies (including yourself) the benefit of the Diehard feat (see page 93 of the *Player's Handbook*) until the end of your next turn. You can use this feat multiple times consecutively to keep yourself and your allies conscious. Even while this feat is active, you or your allies die if reduced to –10 hit points or lower.

This feat does not function in an area of magical *silence*.

IRONSKIN CHANT [BARDIC MUSIC]

You can channel the power of your bardic music to enable yourself to ignore minor injuries.

Prerequisites: Bardic music, Concentration 12 ranks, Perform 12 ranks.

Benefit: As a swift action that does not provoke attacks of opportunity, you can expend one daily use of your bardic music ability to provide damage reduction of 5/— to yourself or to one ally within 30 feet who can hear you until the start of your next turn.

This feat does not function in an area of magical *silence*.

LYRIC SPELL [BARDIC MUSIC]

You can channel the power of your bardic music into your magic, allowing you to expend uses of your bardic music ability to cast spells.

Prerequisites: Bardic music, Perform 9 ranks, ability to spontaneously cast 2nd-level arcane spells.

Benefit: You can expend daily uses of your bardic music to cast any arcane spell that you know and can cast spontaneously. You must still use an action to cast the spell (following the normal rules for casting time), but using the Lyric Spell feat counts as part of the spellcasting action. Casting a spell requires one use of your bardic music ability, plus one additional use per level of the spell. For example, casting a 3rd level spell requires four daily uses of your bardic music ability.

Special: Any spell that you cast using the Lyric Spell feat gains your instrument as an additional arcane focus, if you use one.

You cannot use Lyric Spell to cast a spell improved by the Silent Spell metamagic feat.

Ironskin Chant

WILD FEATS

All wild feats have as a prerequisite the wild shape class feature. Thus, they are open to druids of 5th level or higher, as well as any character who has gained wild shape or a similar class feature from a prestige class.

Each use of a wild feat generally costs you one daily use of your wild shape ability. If you don't have any uses of wild shape left, you can't use a wild feat. Changing form with wild shape is a standard action (unless you have a special ability that says otherwise); these wild feats likewise take a standard action to activate unless otherwise noted. You can activate only one wild feat (or use the wild shape ability to change form once) per round, though overlapping durations may allow you the benefits of more than one wild feat at a time.

Illus. by M. Cotie

Activating a wild feat is a supernatural ability and does not provoke attacks of opportunity unless otherwise specified in the feat description. Activating a wild feat is not considered an attack unless the feat's activation could be the direct cause of damage to a target.

BLINDSENSE [WILD]

You can sense creatures that you cannot see.

Prerequisites: Wild shape class feature, Listen 4 ranks.

Benefit: You can expend one daily use of wild shape to gain blindsense for 1 minute per Hit Die, enabling you to pinpoint the location of a creature within 30 feet if you have line of effect to that creature (see page 306 of the *Monster Manual*). You retain this benefit regardless of what form you are in.

CLIMB LIKE AN APE [WILD]

You can improve your climbing ability.

Prerequisites: Wild shape.

Benefit: You can expend one daily use of wild shape to gain a climb speed equal to your base land speed for 10 minutes per Hit Die. This feat also grants you a +8 racial bonus on Climb checks and allows you to take 10 on Climb checks, even if rushed or threatened.

COUGAR'S VISION [WILD]

You can see in the dark like a cat.

Prerequisites: Wild shape, Spot 2 ranks.

Benefit: You can expend one daily use of wild shape to gain low-light vision for 1 hour per Hit Die. In addition, you gain a +4 bonus on all Spot checks. You retain these benefits regardless of what form you are in.

HAWK'S VISION [WILD]

You can improve your visual acuity.

Prerequisites: Wild shape, Spot 4 ranks.

Benefit: You can expend one of your daily uses of wild shape to gain a +8 bonus on your Spot checks for 1 hour per Hit Die. While this benefit is in effect, you take only half the normal penalty for range increment (–1 on ranged attacks per range increment instead of –2), and you take a –1 penalty on Spot checks per 20 feet of distance (rather than

per 10 feet). You retain these benefits regardless of what form you are in.

SAVAGE GRAPPLE [WILD]

While transformed into the shape of a wild animal, you can savagely tear at any creature that you manage to grapple.

Prerequisites: Wild shape, sneak attack.

Benefit: While you are in a wild shape, any time you make a successful grapple check to damage a creature with which you are already grappling, you can add your sneak attack damage as well. Creatures not subject to sneak attacks don't take this extra damage.

SCENT [WILD]

You can sharpen your sense of smell.

Prerequisites: Wild shape.

Benefit: You can expend one daily use of wild shape to gain the scent ability (see page 314 of the *Monster Manual*) for 1 hour per Hit Die. While this benefit is in effect, you can detect opponents within 30 feet by sense of smell.

In addition, if you have the Track feat, you can track creatures by scent. You retain this benefit regardless of what form you are in.

Savage Grapple

Illus. by D. Kovacs

hether humble thieves' tools or elaborate alchemical substances or magic items, an adventurer relies on his equipment to see him through. Adventurers are often defined as much by their gear as by their abilities.

NEW WEAPONS

The weapons found on Table 4–1: Weapons are described below, along with any special options the wielder has for their use. More variations on existing weapons than entirely new weapons, these exotic weapons allow wielders to apply certain feats to their use.

Dagger, Barbed: Barbed daggers, as their name implies, look like normal daggers with long barbs covering the blade. The design makes the weapon more difficult to wield properly than a normal dagger, but it allows those skilled in the weapon's use to deal more damage with a well-placed attack.

If you have 5 or more ranks in Sleight of Hand and use a barbed dagger, you gain a +2 bonus on damage rolls on any successful sneak attack made with the weapon as it twists in the wound. This bonus also applies (and

is therefore doubled) on successful critical hits with the weapon.

Characters proficient with the barbed dagger can treat it as a dagger for the purpose of any of the following feats: Greater Weapon Focus, Greater Weapon Specialization, Improved Critical, Weapon Focus, and Weapon Specialization.

Longaxe: A longaxe looks like a greataxe with an elongated haft. This feature makes the weapon awkward to wield by those unfamiliar with its use, but those proficient with the weapon can use the haft's extra length to attack foes more than 5 feet away as long as they are willing to forgo precision in favor of dealing extra damage.

If you are proficient with the longaxe, you can treat it as a reach weapon any time you use the Power Attack feat to shift 3 or more points of your attack bonus from attack to damage. When you use a longaxe in this manner, you can strike opponents 10 feet away with it, but you cannot use it against an adjacent foe. Because you determine the use of the Power Attack feat for an entire turn, you must wield the longaxe

TABLE 4–1: WEAPONS

Exotic Weapons	Cost	Dmg (S)	Dmg (M)	Critical	Range Increment	Weight[1]	Type
Light Melee Weapons							
Dagger, barbed	35 gp	1d3	1d4	19–20/×2	—	1 lb.	Piercing
Sword, short, broadblade	75 gp	1d4	1d6	19–20/×2	—	3 lb.	Piercing
One-Handed Melee Weapons							
Rapier, quickblade	75 gp	1d4	1d6	18–20/×2	—	3 lb.	Piercing
Two-Handed Melee Weapons							
Longaxe	35 gp	1d10	1d12	×3	—	15 lb.	Slashing
Longstaff	15 gp	1d4/1d4	1d6/1d6	×2	—	6 lb.	Bludgeoning

1 Weight figures are for Medium weapons. A Small weapon weighs half as much, and a Large weapon weighs twice as much.

as either a reach weapon or a normal weapon until the beginning of your next turn once you make the decision. You cannot wield it as both a reach weapon and a normal weapon in the same turn.

Characters proficient with the longaxe can treat it as a greataxe for the purpose of any of the following feats: Greater Weapon Focus, Greater Weapon Specialization, Improved Critical, Weapon Focus, and Weapon Specialization.

Longstaff: As its name implies, the longstaff is a longer version of the quarterstaff. The extra length makes the weapon much more difficult to use, but those skilled in its use are better able to protect themselves from multiple attackers when fighting cautiously.

If you are proficient with the longstaff and you fight defensively or employ the total defense combat maneuver, you cannot be flanked for the rest of the round. This benefit also applies if you are proficient in the weapon, have the Combat Expertise feat, and shift at least 2 points of your attack bonus to AC for the round.

A longstaff is a double weapon. You can fight with it as if fighting with two weapons, but if you do, you incur all the normal attack penalties associated with fighting with two weapons, just as if you were fighting with a one-handed weapon and a light weapon (see Two-Weapon Fighting, page 160 of the *Player's Handbook*). You can also strike with either end singly. A creature wielding a longstaff in one hand can't use it as a double weapon—only one end of the weapon can be used in any given round.

The longstaff is a special monk weapon. This designation gives a monk wielding a longstaff special options (see the flurry of blows description, page 40 of the *Player's Handbook*).

Characters proficient with the longstaff can treat it as a quarterstaff for the purpose of any of the following feats: Greater Weapon Focus, Greater Weapon Specialization, Improved Critical, Weapon Focus, and Weapon Specialization.

Rapier, Quickblade: Quickblade rapiers are longer and thinner than normal rapiers, with specially tapered blades and carefully balanced pommels. The design makes the weapon more difficult to wield properly than a normal rapier, but it allows those skilled in the weapon's use to disarm opponents more easily and to feint more effectively in combat. Most quickblade rapiers are at least masterwork in quality.

EXOTIC WEAPONS FROM COMPLETE WARRIOR

Complete Warrior introduced several exotic weapons that could benefit from allowing those specialized in the use of similar weapons to apply the benefit of certain feats (specifically, Greater Weapon Focus, Greater Weapon Specialization, Improved Critical, Weapon Focus, and Weapon Specialization) to an exotic weapon's use as well. Just as the barbed dagger in this book is similar enough to the dagger that it allows a character to treat it as one for the purpose of several feats, consider expanding this benefit to the following weapons.

Weapon	Treat as . . .
Blowgun, greater	Blowgun
Bolas, barbed	Bolas
Greatbow	Longbow
Greatspear	Longspear
Pick, dire	Pick, heavy
Poleaxe, heavy	Halberd
Warmace	Mace, heavy

Illus. by D. Kovacs

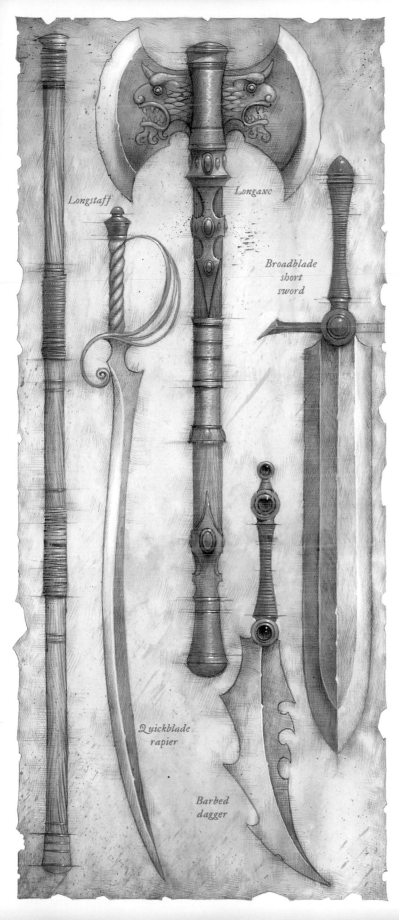

Longstaff

Longaxe

Broadblade
short
sword

Quickblade
rapier

Barbed
dagger

Illus. by W. England

If you are proficient with the quickblade rapier, you gain a +2 bonus on opposed attack rolls made to disarm an enemy (including the roll to avoid being disarmed if such an attempt fails). You also gain a +2 circumstance bonus on Bluff checks made to feint in combat.

You can use the Weapon Finesse feat (see page 102 of the *Player's Handbook*) to apply your Dexterity modifier instead of your Strength modifier to attack rolls with a quickblade rapier sized for you. You can't use a quickblade rapier in two hands to apply 1-1/2 times your Strength modifier to damage.

Characters proficient with the quickblade rapier can treat it as a rapier for the purpose of any of the following feats: Greater Weapon Focus, Greater Weapon Specialization, Improved Critical, Weapon Focus, and Weapon Specialization.

Sword, Short, Broadblade: Broadblade short swords have a wider blade and crossguard than normal swords. This feature makes them more difficult to wield in combat, but the design allows skilled users to defend themselves better when fighting cautiously.

If you are proficient with the broadblade short sword and you fight defensively or employ the total defense combat maneuver, you gain a +2 dodge bonus to AC for the rest of the round in addition to the normal AC bonus from the combat maneuver (+2 for fighting defensively or +4 for total defense). This bonus also applies if you are proficient with the weapon, have the Combat Expertise feat, and shift at least 2 points of your attack bonus to AC for the round. Because of its benefit when fighting defensively, the broadblade short sword is a popular off-hand weapon.

Characters proficient with the broadblade short sword can treat it as a short sword for the purpose of any of the following feats: Greater Weapon Focus, Greater Weapon Specialization, Improved Critical, Weapon Focus, and Weapon Specialization.

EQUIPMENT

In addition to basic gear—a backpack, a rope, a light source, and so forth—various applications of alchemy, superior artisanship, or inventiveness can make an adventurer's job much easier.

ALCHEMICAL ITEMS

For those characters who can't afford magical assistance, or even those looking to gain the tiniest edge, the alchemist's lab offers a wide range of options. Typically a single dose of a cream, gel, balm, or the like is enough to cover a Medium creature. Unless otherwise noted in an item's description, the number of applications needed for creatures of other sizes is doubled (or halved) for each size category larger (or smaller) than Medium.

Blend Cream: This pale gray cream dulls the color of flesh, fur, scales, and hair. It allows those affected to better blend with background and shadow, making it easier to hide.

Applying blend cream is a standard action that provokes attacks of opportunity. Blend cream provides a +1 alchemical bonus on Hide checks. The effects of blend cream last for 1 hour. Blend cream gives no ability to hide in plain sight or without sufficient cover.

Candle, Focusing: This large green taper burns quickly, lasting only 1 hour despite its size. While burning, a focusing candle fills the air with a fresh, crisp odor. The candle is a great boon to those engaged in strenuous mental activity. Characters within 20 feet of a burning candle gain a +1 circumstance bonus on Appraise, Decipher Script, Forgery, and Search checks. When making a skill check that takes more than one action to complete (such as Decipher Script), characters gain the bonus from a focusing candle only if they spend the entire duration of the check within 20 feet of the burning candle.

Catstink: A dose of this alchemical compound sprinkled on your trail temporarily confuses the scent ability of any creature. Any creature using scent to track you must succeed on a DC 15 Survival check or lose your trail. If the trail is lost, the creature can attempt to relocate it using the normal rules for the Track feat, but the check DC increases by 2. The odor of catstink remains in effect for 10 minutes after the substance is used. Sprinkling catstink on one's trail is a standard action that provokes attacks of opportunity.

Fareye Oil: When applied to the eyes, this clear oil sharpens the user's vision for a short time, providing a +1 alchemical bonus on Spot checks for 1 minute.

One dose of fareye oil is enough to affect the eyes of a creature of any size, but the creature must have eyes to gain any benefit from the oil. Applying fareye oil is a standard action that provokes attacks of opportunity.

Flash Pellet: This tiny brittle object is often disguised as a button or other decoration. You can throw a flash pellet as a ranged attack with a range increment of 5 feet. When thrown against a hard surface, it bursts with a bright flash of light. All creatures within a 5-foot-radius burst must succeed on a DC 15 Fortitude save or be blinded for 1 round and dazzled for 1 round after that.

Freeglide: This greenish-gray gel can be applied to a creature's hide, hair, clothing, or armor. The gel makes the affected surface slippery and hard to grab or hold, providing a +1 alchemical bonus on Escape Artist checks for 1 hour.

One dose of freeglide is enough to coat one Medium creature. Applying freeglide is a standard action that provokes attacks of opportunity. If freeglide is applied over clothing or armor, its benefits are lost if the armor or clothing is removed. Likewise, if it is applied to a creature's skin or hide, its benefit is lost if the creature later dons clothing or armor.

Hawk's Ointment: This thick, acidic gel temporarily sharpens the user's vision. Once its beneficial effects wear off, however, the gel burns and stings the eyes for a few minutes. After spreading the gel over her eyes, a character gains a +1 bonus on Search and Spot checks for 2 minutes. After that time, she takes a −2 penalty on Search and Spot checks for 10 minutes. Characters can halve the remaining duration of the penalty by spending a round washing out their eyes with clean water. Applying hawk's ointment or washing out one's eyes is a full-round action that provokes attacks of opportunity.

Healer's Balm: This smooth, sweet-smelling balm allows a healer to better soothe the effects of wounds, disease, and poison. Healer's balm provides a +1 alchemical bonus on Heal checks made to help an affected creature. The effects of healer's balm last for 1 minute.

One dose of healer's balm is enough to coat one Medium creature. Applying healer's balm is a standard action that provokes attacks of opportunity. It can be applied as part of a standard action made to administer first aid, treat a wound, or treat poison.

Keenear Powder: This dry white powder sharpens a creature's hearing when applied to the ear. The powder is effective for only a short time, so it is more often used by those trying to avoid guards or sentries than by those tasked with guarding an area for a longer time. Keenear powder provides a +1 alchemical bonus on Listen checks for 1 minute.

One dose of keenear powder is enough to affect the hearing of a creature of any size, but the creature must have ears to gain any benefit from the powder. Applying keenear powder is a standard action that provokes attacks of opportunity.

Lockslip Grease: Lockslip grease is a thick reddish oil that loosens the mechanical workings of nonmagical locks. The grease is effective for a short time and provides a slight edge to those attempting to pick a lock. Lockslip grease provides a +1 alchemical bonus on Open Lock checks made against the affected lock for 1 minute.

One dose of lockslip grease is enough to affect the mechanism of a lock of any size. Although lockslip grease can affect any kind of mundane mechanical lock, it has no effect on magic locks. Applying lockslip grease to a lock is a standard action that provokes attacks of opportunity.

Nature's Draught: This substance is a murky, pungent liquid. When consumed, nature's draught causes subtle changes in the user's scent. Animals respond well to a character who has consumed nature's draught, finding her less threatening and easier to trust. Drinking a vial of nature's draught provides a +1 alchemical bonus on Handle Animal and wild empathy checks made during the next 12 hours.

Softfoot: Softfoot is a fine gray powder that muffles sound when applied to the bottom of a foot or boot. It provides a +1 alchemical bonus on Move Silently checks for 1 hour.

One dose of softfoot is enough to affect one Medium creature that has one pair of feet; each additional pair of feet (or similar appendages) requires another dose. Applying softfoot is a standard action that provokes attacks of opportunity. If softfoot is applied over a boot or other foot covering, its benefit is lost if the foot covering is removed. Likewise, if it is applied to a creature's skin or hide, its benefit is lost if the creature later dons footwear.

Suregrip: This thick white paste, when applied to hands and feet, strengthens and steadies the user's grip, making it easier for the character to climb. Suregrip provides a +1 alchemical bonus on Climb checks for 1 minute.

One dose of suregrip is enough to cover the hands and feet of one Medium creature. Applying suregrip is a standard action that provokes attacks of opportunity.

ALCHEMICAL CAPSULES

The life of an adventurer demands constant readiness and efficient response to threats. In the heat of combat or the sudden danger of a cave-in, an adventurer rarely has time to apply an alchemical item. Such substances remain useful in those instances where an adventurer knows of a task ahead of time or is lucky enough to spot her foes before they are aware of her presence, but these situations are often the exceptions rather than the rule. To answer the need for a quick-use alchemical item, enterprising adventurers and alchemists have long worked to perfect substances that are easier to apply in the heat of combat, allowing the user to gain the benefit of the item without wasting time that could otherwise be spent attacking the foe or casting a defensive spell.

Alchemy's answer to the adventurer's need is a simple device that allows the wearer to hold a small amount of an alchemical substance in her mouth. The user can quickly break a capsule (as either a standard or swift action, see Delivery Devices, below), allowing her to continue fighting while imbibing the highly concentrated alchemical substance.

Alchemical capsules affect only living creatures with a discernible anatomy. Constructs, elementals, oozes, undead, and other creatures that don't meet this requirement gain no benefit from the use of an alchemical capsule.

TABLE 4–2: ALCHEMICAL ITEMS

Substance	Benefit Applies to . . .	Cost	Weight	Duration	Craft (Alchemy) DC
Blend cream	Hide	50 gp	1 lb.	1 hour	20
Candle, focusing	Appraise, Decipher Script, Forgery, Search	100 gp	1 lb.	1 hour	25
Catstink	n/a	50 gp	—	10 minutes	20
Fareye oil	Spot	25 gp	—	1 minute	20
Flash pellet	n/a	50 gp	—	1 round + 1 round	25
Freeglide	Escape Artist	20 gp	—	1 hour	20
Hawk's ointment	Search, Spot	50 gp	—	2 minutes/10 minutes	25
Healer's balm	Heal	10 gp	—	1 minute	20
Keenear powder	Listen	20 gp	—	1 minute	20
Lockslip grease	Open Lock	50 gp	—	1 minute	20
Nature's draught	Handle Animal, wild empathy	50 gp	—	12 hours	25
Softfoot	Move Silently	50 gp	1 lb.	1 hour	20
Suregrip	Climb	20 gp	—	1 minute	20

Capsule retainer

Alchemical tooth

Triple weapon capsule

Weapon capsule

Illus. by W. England

Delivery Devices

The efficient use of alchemical capsules depends on a delivery device, which may be either a capsule retainer or an alehcmical tooth. Each item is described in detail below.

Only one capsule retainer or alchemical tooth can be worn at any one time, and only one alchemical capsule at a time can be stored in each type of delivery system. Using an alchemical capsule requires only a swift action if it is held in a properly worn capsule retainer or alchemical tooth. In the absence of a capsule retainer or alchemical tooth, using an alchemical capsule is a standard action, just like drinking a potion.

Fitting an alchemical capsule into an empty capsule retainer or alchemical tooth is a full-round action that provokes attacks of opportunity.

Capsule Retainer: A capsule retainer consists of a thin, rubbery strap looped inside the teeth. The strap is fitted with a small, smooth metal ring that can hold one alchemical capsule. The ring can be positioned on either the inside or outside of the user's gums. Some users find that holding the ring inside the gum and keeping the capsule under the tongue is the most comfortable way to wear a capsule retainer, while others find that holding the ring on the outside of the upper gum allows them to tuck the capsule in their cheek comfortably.

Alchemical Tooth: Those relying on secrecy in the use of their alchemical capsules turn instead to the alchemical tooth. As its name suggests, this specially concealed item has been made to look like a tooth. The tooth functions in all respects like a capsule retainer (see above). In addition, it is very hard to find without a thorough search (Search DC 30). The false tooth is most often used as a concealed version of a capsule retainer, but a few extremely dedicated spies and other agents carry a tooth filled with poison as insurance against being captured alive. An alchemical tooth can hold one dose of any contact poison or ingested poison, but such poison can only affect the wearer of the tooth—there's no way to make the tooth an effective delivery mechanism when combined with a bite attack.

Capsule Ingredients

Six of the most popular types of alchemical capsules are described below. Alchemical capsules (including the alchemical weapon capsules described in the next section) can't be used effectively as melee or ranged attacks.

Antitoxin Capsule: This capsule holds a dose of weak antitoxin. When imbibed, it provides a +1 alchemical bonus on Fortitude saving throws made against poison. This bonus lasts for 1 minute.

Ironman Capsule: This capsule holds a thick pale liquid that allows the user to shake off pain and distraction. Anyone using an ironman capsule while staggered can ignore the restrictions on the number of actions taken in a round because of the staggered condition (rather than being limited to one standard action). This benefit applies only to the round in which the capsule is used, and the effect ends immediately after the user has taken his actions for the round.

For example, a staggered character with a capsule retainer can use the capsule at the beginning of his turn (a swift action) and then take a move action and a standard action.

An ironman capsule does not prevent a character from losing a hit point if he is already at or below 0 hit points and does not prevent the user from dying if he reaches –10 hit points.

Leap Capsule: The thick gray liquid in this capsule allows the user to make more powerful jumps for a short time. The user gains a +4 alchemical bonus on Jump checks. The benefit of a leap capsule lasts for only 1 round, ending immediately upon the conclusion of the user's actions for the round.

Stability Capsule: The thick blue liquid in this capsule heightens the user's sense of balance for a short time. While the capsule is in effect, the user gains a +4 alchemical bonus on Balance checks. The benefits of a stability capsule last for only 1 round, ending immediately upon the conclusion of the user's actions for the round.

Strongarm Capsule: This small capsule holds a dose of a thin red liquid. When swallowed, the liquid provides a temporary boost of physical power at the cost of leaving the user fatigued. When used, a strongarm capsule provides the user with a +1 alchemical bonus on Strength checks and melee weapon damage. This benefit lasts for 2 rounds, at the end of which time the user becomes fatigued. If a character who uses a strongarm capsule is already fatigued when the benefit of the capsule ends, she becomes exhausted.

Swiftstride Capsule: This small capsule holds a dose of a thin blue liquid. When swallowed, the liquid quickens the imbiber's stride for a short time, providing a temporary boost of speed at the cost of leaving the user fatigued. A swiftstride capsule increases the user's base land speed by 5 feet. This benefit lasts for 2 rounds, at the end of which time the user becomes fatigued. If a character who uses a swiftstride capsule is already fatigued when the benefit of the capsule ends, he becomes exhausted.

TABLE 4–3: ALCHEMICAL CAPSULES

Item	Cost	Duration	Craft (Alchemy) DC
Capsule retainer	100 gp	n/a	n/a
Alchemical tooth	300 gp	n/a	n/a
Antitoxin capsule	15 gp	1 minute	20
Ironman capsule	15 gp	1 round	20
Leap capsule	15 gp	1 round	25
Stability capsule	15 gp	1 round	20
Strongarm capsule	125 gp	2 rounds	35
Swiftstride capsule	15 gp	2 rounds	35

ALCHEMICAL WEAPON CAPSULES

Just as a capsule retainer provides adventurers with an efficient way to ingest certain alchemical substances without detracting from their other efforts in combat, an alchemical weapon capsule allows the application of a specially prepared substance that affects the properties of a treated weapon.

Using an alchemical weapon capsule requires only a swift action (and does not provoke attacks of opportunity) if it is held in a properly attached weapon capsule retainer (see below). Otherwise, applying an alchemical weapon capsule is the equivalent of applying a magic oil (a standard action that does provoke attacks of opportunity).

Weapon Capsule Retainer: The most common method of delivering the effect of an alchemical weapon capsule is the weapon capsule retainer. This long leather thong, wrapped around a melee weapon or a thrown weapon (but not a projectile weapon) just at the base of the blade or striking surface, holds a thin, fitted ring sized for a single alchemical capsule. A more expensive option is the triple weapon capsule retainer, which stores three capsules rather than one. A character wielding a weapon with a triple retainer can use one, two, or all three capsules it holds as part of the same action.

Only one weapon capsule retainer (or triple retainer) can be attached to any weapon. Attaching a weapon capsule retainer to a weapon or putting a capsule into an empty weapon capsule retainer is a full-round action that provokes attacks of opportunity. Thus, filling an empty triple weapon capsule retainer requires three full-round actions.

An alchemical weapon capsule retainer can be filled with a single dose of an injury poison. Activating the capsule coats the weapon with the poison, allowing the wielder to deliver toxic strikes with the weapon. A character using poison in this way faces all the normal perils of using poison (including accidental exposure when activating the capsule or with a natural 1 on the attack roll).

Ghostblight: A ghostblight alchemical capsule coats a melee weapon or a thrown weapon with a thick gray liquid. This substance allows the weapon to ignore the miss chance that ordinarily applies when the wielder is in combat with incorporeal creatures (as if the weapon had the ghost touch magical property). The capsule's effects last for 3 rounds.

Quickflame: A quickflame alchemical capsule coats a melee weapon or a thrown weapon with a thin sheet of oil that instantly bursts into flame. This substance allows the weapon to deal extra fire damage for a short amount of time without damaging the weapon or its wielder. A weapon treated with quickflame deals 1d6 points of fire damage with each successful strike. The capsule's effects last for 1 round, ending at the beginning of the wielder's next turn. This fire damage doesn't stack with any other fire damage the weapon deals.

Quickfrost: A quickfrost alchemical capsule coats a melee weapon or a thrown weapon with a thin sheet of oil that instantly cools to a dangerously low temperature. This substance allows the weapon to deal extra cold damage for a short amount of time without damaging the weapon or its wielder. A weapon treated with quickfrost deals 1d6 points of cold damage with each successful strike. The capsule's effects last for 1 round, ending at the beginning of the wielder's next turn. This cold damage doesn't stack with any other cold damage the weapon deals.

Quickspark: A quickspark alchemical capsule coats a melee weapon or a thrown weapon with a thin sheet of liquid that crackles and sparks with dangerous electrical energy. This substance allows the weapon to deal extra electricity damage for a short amount of time without damaging the weapon or its wielder. A weapon treated with quickspark deals 1d6 points of electricity damage with each successful strike. The capsule's effects last for 1 round, ending at the beginning of the wielder's next turn. This electricity damage doesn't stack with any other electricity damage the weapon deals.

Quicksilver: A quicksilver alchemical capsule coats a melee weapon or a thrown weapon with a thick silvery liquid. This substance allows the weapon to deal damage as if it were coated with silver (including the normal –1 penalty on damage rolls for silvered weapons). The capsule's effects last for 3 rounds and override any other special material effects of the weapon.

TABLE 4–4: ALCHEMICAL WEAPON CAPSULES

Item	Cost	Duration	Craft (Alchemy) DC
Weapon capsule retainer	100 gp	n/a	n/a
Triple weapon capsule retainer	450 gp	n/a	n/a
Ghostblight	100 gp	3 rounds	35
Quickflame	25 gp	1 round	25
Quickfrost	25 gp	1 round	25
Quickspark	25 gp	1 round	25
Quicksilver	50 gp	3 rounds	30

TOOLS AND SKILL KITS

Some equipment is particularly useful if you have certain skills. In most cases, the items described in this section items expand and specify the masterwork tools that are described in the *Player's Handbook* (pages 129–131). Unless otherwise noted, the items described here are not available in masterwork versions.

Animal Training Kit: This kit includes signal whistles, a short hollow pole with a loop of rope threaded through it, savory treats, and other well-made items suited for the training of animals. This kit grants a +2 circumstance bonus on Handle Animal checks made for teaching animals tricks, training animals for a purpose, or rearing a wild animal. It does not grant a bonus for other uses of the Handle Animal skill.

Balance Pole: This long, flexible pole is the perfect tool for balancing. The pole is 10 feet long, so it cannot be used in any space that allows less than 5 feet of clearance on either side. Provided the user has space to employ the pole properly, it grants a +2 circumstance bonus on Balance checks.

Camouflage Kit: This bag contains face paints, dye, colored cloth, and other accessories appropriate for creating a camouflaged appearance. The kit is the perfect tool for hiding and provides a +2 circumstance bonus on Hide checks. Gaining this bonus requires 1 minute of work. A camouflage kit is exhausted after ten uses.

Forgery Kit: This small case holds a broad selection of paper types, pens, and several colors of ink. In addition, the kit contains samples of prominent family and national crests and the like. This kit is the perfect tool

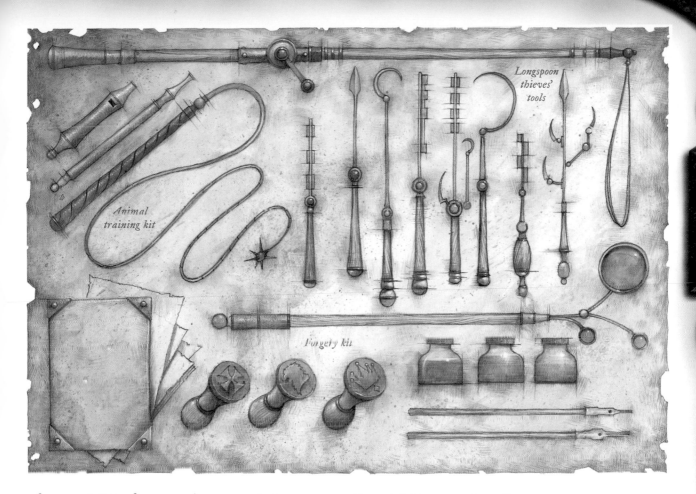

Longspoon
thieves'
tools

Animal
training kit

Forgery kit

Illus. by W. England

for attempting a forgery and grants a +2 circumstance bonus on Forgery checks. A forgery kit is exhausted after ten uses.

Listening Cone: This device is made for listening through doors and other solid surfaces. It provides a +2 circumstance bonus on Listen checks made through a door or some other relatively thin, solid obstacle.

Thieves' Tools, Longspoon: These specially modified thieves' tools are mounted on long, thin handles, enabling the user to manipulate latches, tinker with locks, and probe traps from a position up to 5 feet away and well off to the side of the target device. A 1-inch-diameter mirror mounted on a long handle gives the user a good view of the object being manipulated. Though some traps can inflict harm even at a distance, these tools make it possible for a wary rogue to avoid many common hazards, such as poison needles, spurting acid, and the like.

Using these tools is more time-consuming and less accurate than taking a direct approach; longspoon tools add 2 rounds to the time required to make a Disable Device or Open Lock check and impose a –2 penalty on any Disable Device or Open Lock check for which they are used.

TABLE 4–5: TOOLS AND SKILL KITS

Item	Cost	Weight
Animal training kit	75 gp	15 lb.
Balance pole	5 gp	5 lb.
Camouflage kit	40 gp	5 lb.
Forgery kit	40 gp	5 lb.
Listening cone	20 gp	1 lb.
Thieves' tools, longspoon	80 gp	3 lb.
Thieves' tools, longspoon, masterwork	150 gp	3 lb.
Saddle, masterwork		
Military	210 gp	40 lb.
Riding	180 gp	30 lb.

Longspoon thieves' tools are available in normal or masterwork versions. The masterwork version provides a +2 bonus on Disable Device and Open Lock checks, but the time required to make a check is not reduced.

Saddle, Masterwork: This well-made piece of gear, which can be either a riding saddle or a military saddle, is more comfortable and more responsive than a normal saddle. Because of its excellent craftsmanship, a masterwork saddle grants a +1 circumstance bonus on Ride checks. If a masterwork saddle is also a military saddle, this bonus stacks with the +2 circumstance bonus that a military saddle provides to Ride checks relating to staying in the saddle (see *Player's Handbook*, page 132).

Each masterwork saddle is tailored for a specific kind of creature. As such, it fits best on that kind of creature and thus provides its bonus only when used with that kind of creature. For example, a masterwork saddle made for heavy warhorses would provide its bonus if used on any heavy warhorse, but would not provide a bonus if used on a dragon (assuming the saddle was of an appropriate size for the dragon).

MASTERWORK INSTRUMENTS

This section presents a variety of musical instruments particularly appropriate for adventuring bards. Each entry offers a brief description of an instrument and notes on what races or creatures favor it. This information is not meant as an exhaustive treatment of all such instruments, or even of the wide variations possible within these few. Because each instrument is handcrafted, no two are exactly alike—thus, the size, the number of holes or strings, and other features can vary even between two examples of the same instrument.

Each of these instruments provides a special adjustment to bardic music when a masterwork instrument of that kind is played by a character with a certain bardic music ability. A musician who does not have the bardic music ability, or a bard who plays a nonmasterwork version of one of these instruments, cannot benefit from these bonuses.

TABLE 4–6: INSTRUMENTS BY PERFORM SKILL

Instrument	Perform Skill
Drum	Percussion instruments
Fiddle	String instruments
Flute	Wind instruments
Harp	String instruments
Horn	Wind instruments
Lute	String instruments
Lyre	String instruments
Mandolin	String instruments
Pan pipes	Wind instruments

Drum: A typical drum consists of skin, parchment, or some similar material stretched tightly over the opening of a hollow wooden cylinder or pot. This covered opening is called the drumhead. Striking the drumhead with sticks, mallets, or even hands produces the sound. Some drums have only one drumhead; others have two or more. Drums exist in large varieties (such as kettle drums) as well as smaller varieties (such as bongo drums or the double-ended tabor).

Drums are popular with almost every race and culture for their ability to stir the emotions, establish a background beat for dancing, and provide counterpoint for a melody produced by some other instrument. Dwarves, orcs, and other races that favor underground living particularly enjoy the echoing power of drums. Smaller races, such as goblins and halflings, like bongo drums for their portability. The rare creatures that do not appreciate drum-playing include celestials, who consider drum rhythms primitive, and elves, who find them vaguely disturbing and annoying (a prejudice reinforced, perhaps, by the enthusiasm with which many of their enemies embrace them).

Bardic Music: When a bard uses a drum to inspire courage, the morale bonus on weapon damage rolls increases by 1, but the morale bonus on saves against charm and fear is reduced by 1.

Fiddle: An ancestor of the modern violin, the fiddle is a small, portable stringed instrument with a body shaped rather like an hourglass. Four or five strings made of gut or sinew stretch across the body, anchored by pegs at the end of a long, thin neck. The strings are played with a separate piece called the bow—a long, thin piece of wood strung with fine strands of animal hair. Fiddles vary in length between 2 feet (for Medium fiddlers) and 18 inches (for halfling and kobold fiddlers). To play a fiddle, the musician holds it horizontally, typically with the base tucked under his chin, and draws the bow back and forth across the strings.

The fiddle is popular among bards who prefer lively dance music (reels or jigs) over serene but detached "pure" music. Though welcome almost anywhere, the fiddle is the favorite instrument of kobolds, whose clever hands mastered its fingerings ages ago. (They insist that they invented the fiddle, but other races find that claim dubious.) Kobold minstrels and halfling bards typically caper about while playing, setting their audience an example of the lively dancing their music encourages. Musicians of other races usually sit or stand to play the instrument.

Bardic Music: When used by a bard to inspire courage, a fiddle increases the morale bonus on saves against charm and fear by 1. In the hands of a bard with 5 or more ranks in Perform (dance), the morale bonus instead increases by 2.

A bard who uses a fiddle for bardic music can cast spells while performing, but only if those spells have no somatic, material, or focus components.

Illus. by W. England

Flute: The flute is the highest-pitched of all the woodwinds. This broad category includes instruments ranging from the primitive recorder-flute—a simple, hollow tube that produces music when air is blown straight through it—to the traditional flute, which is held at a right angle to the musician's mouth.

Flutes range in length from 8 inches to about 2 feet. The instrument has six holes (typically), plus a thumbhole that, when covered, lowers each of the other notes by an octave.

Flutes have a reputation for producing gentle, idyllic music, but they can also create more martial effects or distorted wailing sounds. Abyssal flutes always have an odd number of finger holes, and they conform to no scale or key used by humanoid bards. Particularly in the hands of demon pipers, they produce "music" that sounds to mortal ears like a disharmonious combination of sharps, flats, and bizarre, minor-key effects.

Bardic Music: A bard playing a flute gains a +2 bonus on Perform checks made to use the countersong ability.

Harp: A harp typically has seventeen strings but can come with as few as twelve on a smaller instrument or as many as forty-seven on a larger one. Silver wires are the most common choice for strings, but other materials are occasionally used. Harps are usually made of wood, though some artisans carve them from bone or ivory. Whatever their material, most harps are highly polished and elaborately decorated with carvings. The finest rank as works of art in their own right, quite apart from their status as instruments. Though harps can stand up to 6 feet tall, smaller versions (sometimes called lap-harps) are much smaller—about 2 feet high—and more portable.

The harp is especially favored by elf bards for its light, soothing sound and gentle, rippling notes. Harps are often handed down from generation to generation among the elves, and many eventually acquire names and legends of their own. Any character with the bardic knowledge ability who examines an elven harp automatically gains a +5 bonus on his or her bardic knowledge check to identify the instrument and its bearer.

Bardic Music: A bard playing a harp can target one more creature than normal with her *fascinate* and inspire greatness abilities.

A bard who uses a harp for bardic music can cast spells while performing, but only if those spells have no somatic, material, or focus components.

Horn: Originally horns were, as their name indicates, actual horns taken from bulls or more exotic beasts. At its simplest, a horn consists of a narrow tip connected to a wider, circular orifice by a hollow, often curved shaft. A musician plays a horn by simply blowing into the small end. Other forms of horns exist, from the conch shell horn employed by merfolk to the herald's trumpet, but all these instruments function more or less identically.

Horns are popular in primitive societies of all kinds. They come in all sizes; those used by Medium creatures are typically 1 to 2 feet in length. Hobgoblins and orcs in particular enjoy these instruments for their loud, stirring, martial sound. Larger humanoids and giants favor horns made from dire creatures. Legend holds that minotaurs use instruments made from the severed horns of other minotaurs that suffered defeat in one-on-one contests of honor.

A horn makes an excellent signal device—particularly when used underwater, since sound travels much farther in water than in air. Some aquatic races such as merfolk and kuo-toa collect a variety of horn-shaped shells in different sizes and play them in harmony, in sequence, or both. The music of these seashell orchestras can achieve a deep, haunting grandeur.

Bardic Music: When a bard plays a horn to inspire courage, it raises the morale bonus on weapon damage rolls and saves against fear by 1, but the effect lasts for only 1 round after the ally stops hearing the bard perform.

Lute: This ancestor of the guitar has a pear-shaped bowl and a distinctive bent neck with frets for fingering. Between four and eight strings stretch between the base of the bowl and the top of the neck. Lutes vary between 30 and 36 inches in length, with the bowl taking up some two-thirds of that total. The musician either strums or plucks the strings to produce music.

A highly versatile instrument because of its wide range of notes and inflection, the lute is accessible to the beginner but capable of great subtlety in the hands of a master. The deep bowl gives it a rich, full sound unlike that of any other stringed instrument. It is by far the most popular instrument with bards, especially half-elf and human ones.

Bardic Music: A bard playing a lute is treated as one level higher for the purpose of adjudicating the power of his bardic music effects. For example, a 3rd-level bard using a lute could *fascinate* two creatures instead of one, a 6th-level bard using a lute to make a *suggestion* would calculate the save DC as if he were 7th level, and a 7th-level bard using a lute to inspire courage would grant a +2 morale bonus on the appropriate rolls.

A bard who uses a lute for bardic music can cast spells while performing, but only if those spells have no somatic, material, or focus components.

Lyre: A simpler ancestor of the lap-harp, a lyre typically has a body made out of a turtle shell, plus two curved arms and a crossbar to hold its four to six (or, more rarely, eight) gut or sinew strings taut. To play a lyre, the musician holds it in one hand while strumming or plucking the strings with the other.

The very simplicity of a lyre is its charm, since even a novice can strum one to credible effect. Because of this accessibility and the fact that they're easy to make, lyres are popular among the sylvan fey (especially satyrs) and country folk in general. On occasion, however, a true master adopts it as a signature instrument, producing astonishing effects.

Bardic Music: A bard playing a lyre can target one more creature than normal with her *fascinate* ability and inspire heroics abilities.

A bard who uses a lyre for bardic music can cast spells while performing, but only if those spells have no somatic, material, or focus components.

Mandolin: Essentially a smaller version of the lute, a mandolin is usually between 20 inches and 2 feet long. It has a straighter neck than the lute—the end at which the pegs secure the strings tilts back only slightly, if at all. The mandolin is unusual for the number of strings it holds—from four to six pairs (eight to twelve strings total) or even more. A mandolin is typically played with a pick, both to protect the musician's fingers and because the strings are too close together to pluck accurately by hand.

The mandolin has a sweeter sound than the lute and, because of its shorter strings, a higher pitch as well. Its great range of tone and expression have made it a favorite of gnomes and halflings, who champion it as superior even to the lute.

Bardic Music: When a bard uses a mandolin to inspire courage, the morale bonus on attack rolls increases by 1, but the morale bonus on weapon damage rolls and on saves against charm and fear is reduced by 1.

A bard who uses a mandolin for bardic music can cast spells while performing, but only if those spells have no somatic, material, or focus components.

Pan Pipes: In essence, a set of pan pipes is a series of hollow reeds or wooden tubes of varying lengths bound together in a row, from smallest to largest. To play them, the musician blows across the tops of the tubes, producing a sound much like that of several tiny wooden flutes. By moving the pipes from side to side, the piper can play different notes. Switching rapidly among notes creates the sweet, rippling effect for which the instrument is known.

Simple yet evocative, pan pipes are favorites of satyrs and other sylvan fey. Humans and some elves also find their music pleasing.

Bardic Music: A bard using pan pipes gains a +1 bonus on Perform checks made to *fascinate* creatures, and also adds 1 to the save DC against the bard's *suggestion* bardic music ability.

MAGIC ITEMS

The magic items described in this section expand the options available to adventurers of all sorts. They range from objects and devices suited primarily for certain characters (such as bards) to items that have much broader utility.

MAGIC ARMOR AND SHIELDS SPECIAL ABILITY DESCRIPTIONS

The following special abilities are designed to let mobile wearers, particularly rogues and scouts, take full advantage of their abilities.

Beastskin: First created by powerful druids, armor with this special ability is particularly useful to characters of that sort. Whenever you use the wild shape class feature while wearing a suit of armor with the beastskin property, you can expend an additional daily use of your wild shape ability to cause the armor to be transformed with you. When used in this manner, the beastskin armor becomes

a suit of armor fitted for your new form rather than simply merging with your body. The armor continues to grant its armor bonus, applying the appropriate armor check penalty, slowing your movement rate, and otherwise functioning as a suit of armor fitted to the new form. The armor's weight increases or decreases to match your new size (and shape, if you assume a quadrupedal form) and therefore might affect your carrying capacity differently than it does in your natural form.

If in your natural form you are proficient with the type of armor to which the beastskin quality has been applied, then you are proficient with the beastskin armor when you are transformed, regardless of what shape you take.

This special ability can be applied only to armor, not to shields.

Strong transmutation; CL 13th; Craft Magic Arms and Armor, *ironwood*; Price +2 bonus.

Focused: A focused shield helps you anticipate your enemy's moves in battle, helps you see through feints and similar moves, and provides enhanced benefits when you are facing only one creature.

A focused shield grants a +10 circumstance bonus on your Sense Motive check that opposes a Bluff check made to feint. In addition, any time when you are threatened by only one creature, the shield bonus to your AC provided by a focused shield improves by 1.

This special ability can be applied only to shields, not to armor.

Moderate abjuration; CL 11th; Craft Magic Arms and Armor, *shield*; Price +1 bonus.

MAGIC WEAPON SPECIAL ABILITY DESCRIPTIONS

The following weapon special abilities are particularly useful for Small adventurers and for rogues of all sizes.

Sizing: The wielder of a sizing weapon can change the weapon's size category to any other size category as a standard action. Spellcasters who frequently polymorph themselves appreciate weapons with the sizing special ability.

Moderate transmutation; CL 9th; Craft Magic Arms and Armor, *enlarge person, reduce person*; Price +1 bonus.

Deadly Precision: A deadly precision weapon deals an extra 2d6 points of damage when its wielder makes a successful sneak attack. This ability does not bestow the ability to make sneak attacks upon a user who does not already have it.

Moderate transmutation; CL 12th; Craft Magic Arms and Armor, *keen edge*; Price +2 bonus.

*Beastskin armor stays with this druid when
he changes into a bear*

SPECIFIC WEAPONS

The following weapons all have special abilities that make them more versatile (and often more deadly) than a normal weapon of that kind in the right hands.

Blade of Deception: The flat steel blade of this *+3 rapier* is hard to follow in combat. Any time a character uses the Bluff skill to feint in combat while wielding a *blade of deception*, the blade provides a +2 enhancement bonus on the Bluff check. A *blade of deception* provides no bonus on other Bluff checks. In addition, any opponent against whom the wielder successfully feints cannot make attacks of opportunity against the wielder until the beginning of the opponent's next turn. Anyone who was not the target of the feint can make attacks of opportunity against the wielder normally.

Moderate illusion; CL 9th; Craft Magic Arms and Armor, *blur*; Price 19,820 gp; Cost 10,070 gp + 780 XP.

Bow of Songs: Made from fine wood by elf hands, this *+2 shortbow* blends music with every shot to deadly effect. As a move action that does not provoke attacks of opportunity, the wielder can expend one daily use of bardic music to gain a bonus equal to his Charisma bonus on attack rolls and damage rolls with the next single attack made using a *bow of songs*.

Moderate transmutation; CL 8th; Craft Magic Arms and Armor, *sculpt sound*, creator must be an elf, creator must have bardic music ability; Price 32,330 gp; Cost 16,330 gp + 1,280 XP.

Bowstaff: As a move action, the wielder can change this thin, flexible *+2 quarterstaff* into a *+2 longbow* or back again. Both forms perform exactly like a regular magic weapon of their kind.

Strong transmutation; CL 15th; Craft Magic Arms and Armor, *polymorph any object*; Price 10,975 gp; Cost 5,975 gp + 400 XP.

Claws of the Leopard: This pair of *+2 spiked gauntlets* has been shaped to look like the paws of an oversized cat. In addition to their enhancement bonus, the claws provide several feline-like advantages. While wearing *claws of the leopard*, the wielder gains low-light vision and a +10 enhancement bonus on Climb checks. If the wielder charges a foe, she can make a full attack with *claws of the leopard*. This ability functions like the pounce special attack (see page 313 of the *Monster Manual*).

Moderate transmutation; CL 6th; Craft Magic Arms and Armor, *cat's grace*, creator must have 5 ranks in Climb; Price 38,305 gp; Cost 19,305 gp + 1,520 XP.

Dagger of Defense: This *+4 defending dagger* has a long, thin blade and a broad guard, making it an excellent defensive weapon for fending off attacks. In addition, as long as a character holds a *dagger of defense* in his off hand, he cannot be flanked.

Moderate abjuration; CL 12th; Craft Magic Arms and Armor, *shield*; Price 58,302 gp; Cost 29,302 gp + 2,320 XP.

Guerrilla Spear: This *+2 shortspear* is extremely effective when used in ambush. Whenever the wielder makes a successful attack against an opponent who is denied his Dexterity bonus to Armor Class, a *guerrilla spear* deals an extra 2d6 points of damage.

Moderate illusion; CL 7th; Craft Magic Arms and Armor, *invisibility*; Price 32,301 gp; Cost 16,302 gp + 1,280 XP.

Claws of the leopard

Dagger of defense

Illus. by E. Cox and R. Spencer.

Songblade: Every move made with this *+1 rapier* fills the air with sweet sounds. While holding a *songblade* unsheathed, the sword's wielder gains a +2 enhancement bonus on Perform checks. A bard wielding a *songblade* can use her bardic music abilities one additional time per day. The blade is scored in a beautiful, intricate pattern, and air moving across this magical etching generates the music of a *songblade*. The blade's musical qualities do not function underwater, in a vacuum, or in other environments where air cannot freely pass over the blade.

Moderate transmutation; CL 8th; Craft Magic Arms and Armor, *sculpt sound*, creator must have bardic music class feature; Price 6,400 gp; Cost 3,360 gp + 243 XP.

Illus. by R. Spencer

Songblade

POTIONS

The following table includes spells introduced in this book that are appropriate for making into potions. See page 229 of the *Dungeon Master's Guide* for more information on potions.

TABLE 4–7: POTIONS AND OILS

Potion or Oil	Market Price
Healthful rest (potion)	50 gp
Exacting shot (oil)	100 gp
Iron silence (oil)	300 gp
Nature's favor (potion)	300 gp
Sonic weapon (oil)	300 gp
Train animal (potion)	300 gp
Absorb weapon (oil)	750 gp
Entangling staff (oil)	750 gp

RINGS

A character can effectively wear only two magic rings. A third magic ring doesn't work if the owner already wears two.

Ring	Market Price
Filcher's friend	2,500 gp
Lockpicking	4,500 gp

Filcher's Friend: When activated, this plain steel ring draws toward it any loose metal object within 1 foot and weighing no more than 1 ounce (usually coins, jewelry, or small keys). The objects do not have to be ferrous, simply metal in some way. A *filcher's friend* also grants a +5 bonus on Sleight of Hand checks involving metal objects.

Faint transmutation; CL 12th; Forge Ring, *mage hand*; Price 2,500 gp.

Lockpicking: This ring is made up of tiny prongs, wires, and other small devices that spring to life on command. A *lockpicking ring* grants the wearer a +5 competence bonus on Open Lock checks and the ability to use *knock* once per day if the wearer touches a portal she wishes to open.

Faint transmutation; CL 3rd; Forge Ring, *knock*; Price 4,500 gp.

SCROLLS

The following tables include scrolls of all spells introduced in this book. See page 237 of the *Dungeon Master's Guide* for more information on scrolls.

Lockpicking ring

TABLE 4–8: ARCANE SPELL SCROLLS

1st-Level Arcane Spells	Market Price
Accelerated movement	25 gp
Arrow mind	25 gp
Critical strike	25 gp
Distort speech	50 gp
Distract assailant	25 gp
Expeditious retreat, swift	25 gp
Focusing chant	50 gp
Golem strike	25 gp
Guided shot	25 gp
Healthful rest	50 gp
Herald's call	50 gp
Insightful feint	25 gp
Inspirational boost	50 gp
Instant locksmith	25 gp
Instant search	25 gp
Joyful noise	50 gp
Master's touch	25 gp
Sniper's shot	25 gp

2nd-Level Arcane Spells	Market Price
Balancing lorecall	150 gp
Bladeweave	150 gp
Daggerspell stance	150 gp
Fly, swift	150 gp
Insidious rhythm	200 gp
Invisibility, swift	150 gp
Iron silence	200 gp
Listening lorecall	150 gp
Mindless rage	150 gp
Sonic weapon	150 gp
Tactical precision	200 gp
Wracking touch	150 gp
Wraithstrike	150 gp

3rd-Level Arcane Spells	Market Price
Absorb weapon	375 gp
Allegro	525 gp
Dirge of discord	525 gp
Dissonant chord	525 gp
Harmonic chorus	525 gp
Hymn of praise	525 gp
Infernal threnody	525 gp
Spectral weapon	375 gp
Speechlink	525 gp

4th-Level Arcane Spells	Market Price
Entangling staff	700 gp
Listening coin	1,000 gp
Sniper's eye	700 gp
War cry	1,000 gp

5th-Level Arcane Spells	Market Price
Improvisation	1,625 gp
Nightstalker's transformation	1,125 gp
Shadow form	1,125 gp
Wail of doom	1,625 gp

6th-Level Arcane Spells	Market Price
Cloak of the sea	1,650 gp
Protégé	2,400 gp

7th-Level Arcane Spell	Market Price
Cacophonic shield	2,275 gp

9th-Level Arcane Spell	Market Price
Hindsight	3,825 gp

TABLE 4–9: DIVINE SPELL SCROLLS

1st-Level Divine Spells	Market Price
Accelerated movement	50 gp
Arrow mind	50 gp
Bloodhound	50 gp
Exacting shot	50 gp
Grave strike	25 gp
Guided shot	50 gp
Hawkeye	25 gp
Healthful rest	25 gp
Instant search	50 gp
Sniper's shot	50 gp
Vine strike	25 gp

2nd-Level Divine Spells	Market Price
Balancing lorecall	150 gp
Branch to branch	150 gp
Daggerspell stance	150 gp
Divine insight	150 gp
Easy climb	200 gp
Easy trail	150 gp
Embrace the wild	150 gp
Haste, swift	200 gp
Healing lorecall	150 gp
Iron silence	150 gp
Listening lorecall	150 gp
Nature's favor	150 gp
Train animal	150 gp
Wracking touch	150 gp

3rd-Level Divine Spells	Market Price
Blade storm	375 gp
Entangling staff	375 gp
Fly, swift	375 gp

4th-Level Divine Spells	Market Price
Arrow storm	700 gp
Foebane	700 gp
Forestfold	700 gp

5th-Level Divine Spell	Market Price
Cloak of the sea	1,125 gp

WANDS

The following table includes a selection of new spells introduced in this book. See page 245 of the *Dungeon Master's Guide* for more information on wands.

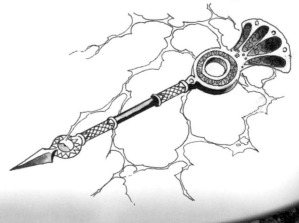

TABLE 4–10: WANDS

Wand	Market Price
Golem strike	750 gp
Grave strike	750 gp
Hawkeye	750 gp
Healthful rest	750 gp
Vine strike	750 gp
Divine insight	4,500 gp
Iron silence	4,500 gp
Mindless rage	4,500 gp
Nature's favor	4,500 gp
Sonic weapon	4,500 gp
Train animal	4,500 gp
Wracking touch	4,500 gp
Wraithstrike	4,500 gp

WONDROUS ITEMS

The following items were all created to allow adventurers to take more advantage of skills they already possess. Although some of the items described below involve the use of skills, the user need not have any ranks in a specified skill to use the item unless otherwise noted in an item's description.

Spells referred to in this section and marked with a dagger (†) are new spells detailed in Chapter 5 of this book.

Amulet of Aberrant Empathy: This strange, twisted amulet allows the wearer to use the Handle Animal skill in place of the Diplomacy skill when dealing with some aberrations.

While wearing an *amulet of aberrant empathy,* a character can make Handle Animal checks rather than Diplomacy checks to influence the attitude of aberrations with an Intelligence of 9 or lower.

Moderate enchantment; CL 11th; Craft Wondrous Item, *charm monster;* Price 1,400 gp.

Armbands of Might: These bronze armbands grant their wearer a +2 bonus on Strength checks and Strength-based skill checks. If the wearer has the Power Attack feat, he gains a +2 bonus on melee damage rolls on any attack on which he uses the Power Attack feat and takes a penalty of at least –2 on his attack roll.

Armbands occupy the same space on the body as a pair of bracers or bracelets.

Faint transmutation; CL 3rd; Craft Wondrous Item, *bull's strength;* Price 4,100 gp.

Badge of Valor: This golden brooch provides its wearer with a +2 morale bonus on saves against fear effects. This bonus improves to +4 on level checks made to avoid being intimidated.

The morale bonus of this badge stacks with the morale bonus granted by the paladin's aura of courage ability and the bard's inspire courage ability.

Faint enchantment; CL 4th; Craft Wondrous Item; *heroism;* Price 1,000 gp.

Choker of Eloquence: Coveted by bards, singers, and public speakers, this beautiful necklace is carved from ivory and jade. There are two versions of these chokers. A *lesser choker of eloquence* grants a +5 competence bonus on Diplomacy, Bluff, and Perform (sing) checks. A *greater choker of eloquence* increases the bonus to +10.

Moderate transmutaion; CL 6th; Craft Wondrous Item, creator must be a spellcaster of at least 6th level; Price 6,000 gp (*lesser*), 24,000 gp (*greater*).

Collar of Obedience: Any animal or magical beast wearing this collar becomes easier to handle. The DC of any Handle Animal check to handle, push, teach, train, or rear the wearer is decreased by 5.

A collar occupies the same space on the body as an amulet, brooch, or other item meant to be worn around the neck..

Faint enchantment; CL 3rd; Craft Wondrous Item, *charm animal;* Price 1,500 gp.

Crown of Steady Rulership: This ornate golden crown is a useful tool for princes and potentates, for it allows them to see through the falsehoods that parade before them. The wearer gains a +5 competence bonus on Sense Motive checks and on Spot checks made to see through disguises.

Faint divination; CL 3rd; Craft Wondrous Item, *see invisibility;* Price 4,500 gp.

Flute of the Snake: The music of this flute has the power to charm snakes of all kinds. By playing this flute and making a DC 15 Perform (wind instruments) check, the musician can produce a *charm animal* effect that affects only snakes. This power can be used three times per day.

Once per day, by playing a droning sequence of notes for 1 full round and succeeding on a DC 20 Perform (wind instruments) check, a musician can summon 1d4+1 Medium vipers. These snakes appear wherever the flutist designates within 30 feet of her location. They fight on the musician's behalf, attacking on her turn, and remain for 7 rounds or until killed.

Moderate conjuration and enchantment; CL 7th; Craft Wondrous Item, *charm animal, summon nature's ally IV;* Price 15,400 gp.

Harp of the Immortal Maestro: This pinnacle of instrument design functions as a masterwork harp with minor magical effects in the hands of someone with 1 or more ranks in Perform (string instruments). By speaking the correct command words, such a musician can use *levitate* and *magic circle against evil* once per day each.

A *harp of the immortal maestro* functions best in the hands of a musician with at least 15 ranks in Perform (string instruments). Such a user can, simply by strumming the harp, generate the following effects once per day each: *cure critical wounds*, *displacement*, and *summon monster V*.

Moderate abjuration, conjuration, illusion, and transmutation; CL 9th; Craft Wondrous Item, *cure critical wounds*, *displacement*, *levitate*, *magic circle against evil*, *summon monster V*, creator must have 15 ranks in Perform (string instruments); Price 51,000 gp; Weight 3 lb.

Headband of Conscious Effort: Anyone wearing a *headband of conscious effort* can make a Concentration check in place of a required Fortitude saving throw. This ability can be activated once per day. Activating the headband is an immediate action that does not provoke attacks of opportunity.

Moderate transmutation; CL 6th; Craft Wondrous Item, Combat Casting, *bear's endurance*; Price 4,000 gp.

Jumping Caltrops: These unusual items are actually Diminutive animated objects. When released from their bag, they begin hopping around the 5-foot square in which they land. When someone tries to move into, through, or within that square on foot, the *jumping caltrops* immediately try to scurry under the interloper's feet. *Jumping caltrops* can't move from the square in which they land.

The number of caltrop attacks a creature is subject to while within the affected area depends on its current speed: four if it moved into the square at normal speed, two if it moved into the square at half speed, and none if it moved into the square at one-quarter speed or less. (One-quarter speed assumes that the creature is shuffling forward without picking up its feet.) The target's shield, armor, and deflection bonuses don't count against these attacks. A target that is wearing shoes or other footwear, however, gets a +2 bonus to AC. The speed of any target that takes damage from the caltrop attack is reduced to one-half normal because of the foot injury.

Once they are released, *jumping caltrops* continue to move for 11 rounds, though the owner can order them back into the bag before the duration expires if desired. However, they can move (and thus attack on their own) only upon their first use; thereafter, they become normal caltrops.

Jumping Caltrop: CR 1/4; Diminutive construct; HD 1/4 d10; hp 1; Init +3; Spd n/a; AC 17, touch 17, flat-footed 14; Base Atk +0; Grp –14; Atk or Full Atk +7 melee (1, impale); Space/Reach 1/2 ft. by 1/2 ft./0 ft.; SQ construct traits,

Table 4–11: Wondrous Items

Minor Wondrous Items	Market Price
Jumping caltrops	150 gp
Scarf of warmth	250 gp
Badge of valor	1,000 gp
Medal of gallantry	1,100 gp
Amulet of aberrant empathy	1,400 gp
Collar of obedience	1,500 gp
Possum pouch	1,800 gp
Papyrus of deception	2,000 gp
Spool of endless rope	2,000 gp
Vial of the last gasp	2,200 gp
Spellsight spectacles	2,500 gp
Tunic of steady spellcasting	2,500 gp
Rope of stone	2,800 gp
Stylus of the masterful hand	3,000 gp
Pendant of draconic empathy	3,300 gp
Shawl of bewitching	3,500 gp
Headband of conscious effort	4,000 gp
Armbands of might	4,100 gp
Crown of steady rulership	4,500 gp
Choker of eloquence, lesser	6,000 gp
Monocle of perusal	6,500 gp

Medium Wondrous Items	Market Price
Trumpeter's gift	12,700 gp
Sandals of harmonious balance	14,000 gp
Flute of the snake	15,400 gp
Mask of lies	17,000 gp
Choker of eloquence, greater	24,000 gp

Major Wondrous Items	Market Price
Lute of the wandering minstrel	29,500 gp
Mandolin of the inspiring muse	42,000 gp
Strings of spell storing	45,000 gp
Harp of the immortal maestro	51,000 gp

use Dexterity instead of Strength for melee attacks; AL N; SV Fort +0, Ref +3, Will –5; Str 6, Dex 10, Con —, Int —, Wis 1, Cha 1

Moderate transmutation; CL 11th; Craft Wondrous Item, *animate objects*; Price 150 gp; Weight 2 lb.

Lute of the Wandering Minstrel: This finely wrought instrument functions as a masterwork lute with minor magical effects in the hands of someone with 1 or more ranks in Perform (string instruments). By speaking the correct command words, such a musician can use *levitate* and *magic circle against evil* once per day each.

A musician with 5 or more ranks in Perform (string instruments) can coax additional magical effects from this instrument. By playing a single chord on the lute, such a performer can generate an *expeditious retreat*, *haste*, or *phantom steed* effect. Each of these abilities is usable once per day.

Faint abjuration, conjuration, and transmutation; CL 5th; Craft Wondrous Item, *expeditious retreat*, *haste*, *levitate*, *magic circle against evil*, *phantom steed*, creator must have 5 ranks in Perform (string instruments); Price 29,500 gp; Weight 3 lb.

Mandolin of the Inspiring Muse: Bards and other musicians prize this carefully crafted mandolin, which functions as a masterwork mandolin with minor magical effects in the hands of someone with 1 or more ranks in Perform (string instruments). By speaking the correct command words, such a musician can utilize *levitate* and *magic circle against evil* once per day each.

In addition, an owner with at least 15 ranks in Perform (string instruments) can use the mandolin to generate the effects of *crushing despair*, *dominate person*, and *good hope* each once per day each by playing the correct notes.

Moderate abjuration, enchantment, and transmutation; CL 9th; Craft Wondrous Item, *crushing despair*, *dominate person*, *good hope*, *levitate*, *magic circle against evil*, creator must have 10 ranks in Perform (string instruments); Price 42,000 gp; Weight 3 lb.

Illus. by R. Spencer

Mask of lies

Mask of Lies: This black, featureless mask has only slits for eyes and mouth. The wearer can use *disguise self* on herself at will and is continually under the effect of *undetectable alignment*. In addition, she gains a +5 competence bonus on Bluff checks.

A mask occupies the same space on the body as eye lenses or goggles.

Faint abjuration and illusion; CL 5th; Craft Wondrous Item, *disguise self*, *undetectable alignment*; Price 17,000 gp.

Medal of Gallantry: This silver sun-shaped brooch grants its wearer a +2 bonus on Diplomacy checks but imposes a −2 penalty on Bluff checks. This penalty remains for 24 hours after the medal is removed.

Three times per day the wearer can use *sanctuary* on himself as a swift action. If the wearer attacks while protected by this effect, he takes a −1 morale penalty on that attack and all subsequent attacks for 1 hour afterward.

Faint abjuration; CL 3rd; Craft Wondrous Item, *sanctuary*; Price 1,100 gp.

Monocle of Perusal: This crystal lens provides the user with a +5 competence bonus on Appraise checks. Once per day the user can use *identify*.

A monocle occupies the same space on the body as a pair of eye lenses or goggles.

Faint divination; CL 3rd; Craft Wondrous Item, *identify*; Price 6,500 gp.

Papyrus of Deception: This enchanted sheet of paper usually looks thick and yellowed with age. However, when used as the basis for a forged document, the papyrus is extremely useful, since it changes its size, consistency, and appearance to match the mental description of the forger. When used as part of a forgery, *papyrus of deception* adds a +5 enhancement bonus to the Forgery check. The papyrus can never duplicate a sheet of paper larger than 12 inches on a side or smaller than 3 inches on a side. *Papyrus of deception* can be reused.

Faint divination; CL 5th; Craft Wondrous Item, *read magic*; Price 2,000 gp.

Pendant of Draconic Empathy: This enchanted amulet allows the wearer to use the Handle Animal skill in place of the Diplomacy skill when dealing with dragons whose Intelligence is 11 or lower.

Moderate enchantment; CL 11th; Craft Wondrous Item, *charm monster*; Price 3,300 gp.

Possum Pouch: Also known as a false stomach, a *possum pouch* is a small, flat, circular bag about 10 to 12 inches in diameter and up to 2 inches thick. When placed against a humanoid's abdomen and sealed there with a command word, it blends in unobtrusively with the surrounding skin, requiring a DC 30 Search check to detect. Spies and couriers find these items useful as diplomatic pouches, while nobles and wealthy merchants sometimes use them as money belts. Assassins, ninjas, and sneak-thieves love *possum pouches* because they make it easy to smuggle poison, daggers, and small valuables into or out of well-guarded houses.

Faint illusion; CL 3rd; Craft Wondrous Item, *disguise self*; Price 1,800 gp; Weight 1 lb.

Rope of Stone: This normal-looking, 50-foot coil of silk rope becomes as hard as stone (hardness 8, 15 hp) when a command word is spoken. A second command word returns the rope to its normal composition. The rope retains its exact shape when hardened (which adds 5 to the DC of Escape Artist checks made to slip free of it). If it is ever broken in either form, the rope is destroyed.

Faint transmutation; CL 5th; Craft Wondrous Item, *stone shape*; Price 2,800 gp; Weight 5 lb.

Sandals of Harmonious Balance: These plain-looking wood and leather sandals make it possible to undertake incredible feats of balance. While wearing *sandals of harmonious balance*, a character gains a +10 insight bonus on Balance checks and can balance on vertical surfaces. The normal DC modifiers (such as for a slippery surface) apply, except for the modifier for a sloped or angled surface. If balanced on a vertical surface, the wearer can move up or down as if she were climbing. However, she is not actually climbing, so she can make attacks normally, retains her Dexterity bonus to Armor Class, and generally follows the rules of the Balance skill rather than the Climb skill.

If the wearer has 10 or more ranks in Balance, she can balance on liquids, semisolid surfaces such as mud or snow, or similar surfaces that normally couldn't support her weight. For each consecutive round that she begins balanced on a particular surface of this sort, the DC of her Balance check increases by 5. As with all uses of the Balance skill, the wearer moves at half speed unless she decides to use the accelerated movement option (thereby increasing the DC of the Balance check by 5). For more information on the Balance skill, see page 67 of the *Player's Handbook*.

Moderate transmutation; CL 8th; Craft Wondrous Item, *balancing lorecall†*; Price 14,000 gp.

Medal of gallantry

Scarf of Warmth: This woolen scarf provides the wearer with a +4 bonus on Fortitude saves made to resist the effects of cold weather (see Cold Dangers, page 302 of the *Dungeon Master's Guide*).

A scarf occupies the same space on the body as an amulet, necklace, or other item worn around the neck.

Faint abjuration; CL 3rd; Craft Wondrous Item, *endure elements*; Price 250 gp.

Shawl of Bewitching: A character wearing this simple-looking shawl gains a +5 competence bonus on Bluff checks made to conceal the truth (but not on any other use of the Bluff skill, including feinting in combat, creating a diversion to hide, or delivering a secret message). It also adds 1 to the wearer's caster level when he casts any enchantment (charm) spell.

A shawl occupies the same space on the body as a cloak, cape, or mantle.

Faint enchantment; CL 3rd; Craft Wondrous Item, *charm person*; Price 3,500 gp.

Spellsight Spectacles: These spectacles grant the wearer a +5 competence bonus on Spellcraft checks made to decipher scrolls, and a +5 competence bonus on Use Magic Device checks made to use scrolls.

Spectacles occupy the same space on the body as a pair of eye lenses or goggles.

Faint divination; CL 3rd; Craft Wondrous Item, *read magic*; Price 2,500 gp.

Spool of Endless Rope: Some adventurers never seem to have enough rope. A *spool of endless rope* contains an unlimited amount of the finest silk rope, yet the whole spool weighs only a single pound. The spool comes with a belt loop so that it can be hung conveniently at an adventurer's side.

To use a *spool of endless rope*, the owner feeds out as little or as much rope as desired, up to a maximum of 500 feet at any one time. When finished with the rope, the owner can simply wind it back onto the spool. (Feeding out or rewinding requires 1 round per 50 feet of rope.)

The rope can't be entirely separated from the spool, though it can be cut or broken as a normal silk rope can be. Any portion of rope cut away from the spool disappears instantly, but the spool immediately replenishes the missing rope.

Illus. by R. Spence

Illus. by D. Kovacs

The rope from a *spool of endless rope* can be spliced or knotted together with another rope (including a rope from a second *spool of endless rope*), but the rope can't be wound back into the spool while so attached.

Moderate conjuration; CL 9th; Craft Wondrous Item, *Leomund's secret chest*; Price 2,000 gp; Weight 1 lb.

Strings of Spell Storing: This set of catgut strings for a lute, mandolin, or other string instrument can store up to five levels of spells. By making a DC 15 Perform (string instruments) check while employing a masterwork instrument equipped with these strings, a musician can unleash the desired spell. Each spell has a caster level equal to the minimum level needed to cast the spell. The user need not provide any material components or focus, or pay an XP cost to cast the spell, and there is no arcane spell failure chance for any armor the user is wearing. The activation time for the strings is the same as the casting time for the relevant spell, with a minimum of 1 standard action.

Treat a randomly generated set of *strings of spell storing* as a scroll for determining what spells are stored within it (see pages 238–243 of the *Dungeon Master's Guide*). If you roll a spell that would put the set over its five-level limit, ignore that roll; those strings have no more spells in them. (Not every newly discovered set of strings is fully charged.) The strings magically impart to the user the names of all spells currently stored within them.

Casting spells into the strings functions identically to casting spells into a *ring of spell storing* (see page 233 of the *Dungeon Master's Guide*), except that the caster must have at least 1 rank of Perform (string instruments) and must make a successful Perform (string instruments) check (DC 10 + spell level). Failure causes the spell to be lost to no effect.

Moderate evocation; CL 9th; Craft Wondrous Item, *imbue with spell ability*, creator must have 5 ranks in Perform (string instruments); Price 45,000 gp.

Stylus of the Masterful Hand: This elegant but sturdy metal stylus grants a +5 competence bonus on Forgery checks. On command, a *stylus of the masterful hand* can also remember up to three different types of handwriting, which allows a later attempt to create a forgery of a document without requiring the forger to have a sample of the handwriting (see Forgery, page 74 of the *Player's Handbook*). The DC to reproduce that handwriting is fixed at whatever check result was achieved during the attempt in which the sample was collected. A second command word allows the user to erase a sample of handwriting stored in a stylus.

Faint divination; CL 3rd; Craft Wondrous Item, *read magic*; Price 3,000 gp.

Trumpeter's Gift: This shiny mouthpiece fits any wind instrument, such as a trumpet or other horn. It grants a +5 competence bonus on Perform (wind instruments) checks using the instrument. Once per day, the trumpeter can use the horn to produce a *shout* effect. If the horn is not of masterwork quality, however, it is destroyed once this effect is produced.

Moderate evocation; CL 7th; Craft Wondrous Item, *shout*; Price 12,700 gp.

Tunic of Steady Spellcasting: The wearer of this tunic gains a +5 competence bonus on Concentration checks. Despite the item's name, its bonus applies on all Concentration checks, not just those made to cast spells.

Faint transmutation; CL 3rd; Craft Wondrous Item, *bear's endurance*; Price 2,500 gp.

Vial of the Last Gasp: This is actually the necromantically preserved last breath of some famous figure, trapped in a vial. A *vial of the last gasp* allow the user to draw strength and knowledge from the dead creature. Anyone who unstoppers the vial and inhales its vapors (the equivalent of drinking a potion) gains 1d8 temporary hit points, a +2 enhancement bonus to Strength, and a +4 insight bonus on checks using one Craft, Knowledge, or Profession skill possessed by the deceased. (However, the vapors in a *vial of the last gasp* do not allow an untrained user to make use of a trained-only skill.) The creator specifies the skill to which the bonus applies upon creating the item; it is usually the skill in which the deceased has the greatest number of ranks. In addition, the fumes increase the user's effective caster level by 1. These effects last for 10 minutes.

Faint necromancy; CL 4th; Craft Wondrous Item, *death knell*; Price 2,200 gp.

Illus. by D. Kovacs

From the assassin lurking in the corner, his dagger dripping with magically enhanced poison, to the ranger who fills the forest with a hail of magically propelled arrows, skilled adventurers of all kinds rely on spells to enhance their skills, avoid an enemy's blows, and strike with deadly accuracy. In keeping with the theme of *Complete Adventurer*, the spells described in this chapter emphasize skill use—providing bonuses on skill checks, offering new uses for skills, and making skill use in combat more rewarding. These spells also often feature enhanced benefits or effects for characters who have mastered unusual combinations of skills and abilities. These spells emphasize the versatility of the successful adventurer and should be of particular interest to multiclass characters.

An ᴹ appearing at the end of a spell's name in the spell lists denotes a spell with a material component that is not normally included in a spell component pouch.

SWIFT ACTIONS AND IMMEDIATE ACTIONS

Some of the spells in this chapter refer to swift or immediate actions. These are types of actions, like a move action or standard action.

Swift Action: A swift action consumes a very small amount of time but represents a larger expenditure of effort and energy than a free action. You can perform one swift action per turn, without affecting your ability to perform other actions. In that regard, a swift action is like a free action. However, you can perform only a single swift action per turn, regardless of what other actions you take. You can take a swift action at any time you would normally be allowed to take a free action. Swift actions usually involve spellcasting or the activation of magic items; many characters (especially those who don't cast spells) never have an opportunity to take a swift action.

Casting a quickened spell is a swift action (instead of a free action, as stated in the Quicken Spell feat description in the *Player's Handbook*). In addition, casting any spell with a casting time of 1 swift action (such as *critical strike*) is a swift action.

Casting a spell with a casting time of 1 swift action does not provoke attacks of opportunity.

Immediate Action: Much like a swift action, an immediate action consumes a very small amount of time but represents a larger expenditure of effort and energy than a free action. However, unlike a swift action, an immediate action can be performed at any time—even when it's not your turn. Casting *feather fall* is an immediate action (instead of a free action, as stated in the spell description in the *Player's Handbook*), since the spell can be cast at any time.

Using an immediate action on your turn is the same as using a swift action, and counts as your swift action for that turn. You cannot use another immediate action or a swift action until after your next turn if you have used an immediate action when it is not currently your turn (effectively, using an immediate action before your turn is equivalent to using your swift action for the coming turn). You also cannot use an immediate action if you are currently flat-footed.

NEW ASSASSIN SPELLS

1ST-LEVEL ASSASSIN SPELLS

Critical Strike: Swift. For 1 round you gain +1d6 damage, doubled threat range, and +4 on attack rolls to confirm critical hits.

Distract Assailant: Swift. One creature is flat-footed for 1 round.

Insightful Feint: Swift. Gain +10 on your next Bluff check to feint in combat.

Instant Locksmith: Swift. Make Disable Device or Open Lock check at +2 as free action.

Instant Search: Swift. Make Search check at +2 as free action.

Sniper's Shot: Swift. No range limit on next ranged sneak attack.

2ND-LEVEL ASSASSIN SPELLS

Invisibility, Swift: Swift. You are invisible for 1 round or until you attack.

Iron Silence: Armor touched has no armor check penalty on Hide and Move Silently for 1 hour/level.

Wraithstrike: Swift. Your melee attacks strike as touch attacks for 1 round.

3RD-LEVEL ASSASSIN SPELLS

Absorb Weapon: Hide a weapon, gain a Bluff check with a +4 bonus to feint when you draw it.

Spectral Weapon: Swift. Use quasi-real weapon to make touch attacks.

4TH-LEVEL ASSASSIN SPELLS

Shadow Form: Gain +4 on Hide, Move Silently, and Escape Artist checks, and concealment; you can move through obstacles if you have ranks in Escape Artist.

Sniper's Eye: Gain +10 Spot, darkvision, 60-ft. range for sneak attacks, and death attacks with ranged weapons.

NEW BARD SPELLS

1ST-LEVEL BARD SPELLS

Accelerated Movement: Swift. Balance, Climb, or Move Silently at normal speed with no penalty on skill check.

Distort Speech: Subject's speech is 50% unintelligible; subject may miscast spells.

Expeditious Retreat, Swift: Swift. Your speed increases by 30 ft. for 1 round.

Focusing Chant: Gain +1 on attack rolls, skill checks, and ability checks, so long as you don't speak or cast other spells.

Healthful Rest: Subjects heal at twice the normal rate.

Herald's Call: Swift. Creatures of 5 HD or less within 20 ft. *slowed* for 1 round.

Inspirational Boost: Swift. The bonuses granted by your inspire courage ability increase by 1.

Joyful Noise: You negate *silence* in a 10-ft.-radius emanation for as long as you concentrate.

Master's Touch: Swift. You gain proficiency in a weapon or shield touched for 1 min./level.

2ND-LEVEL BARD SPELLS

Bladeweave: Swift. Your melee attack dazes your opponent.

Fly, Swift: Swift. Gain fly speed of 60 ft. for 1 round.

Insidious Rhythm: Subject has −4 penalty on Intelligence-based skill checks and Concentration checks, and must make Concentration check to cast spells.

Invisibility, Swift: Swift. You are invisible for 1 round or until you attack.

Iron Silence: Armor touched has no armor check penalty on Hide and Move Silently for 1 hour/level.

Mindless Rage: Target compelled to attack you physically for 1 round/level.

Sonic Weapon: Weapon touched deals +1d6 sonic damage with each hit.

Tactical Precision: Allies gain additional +2 bonus on attack rolls and +1d6 additional damage against flanked foes.

3RD-LEVEL BARD SPELLS

Allegro: You and your allies gain +30 ft. speed for 1 min./level.

Dirge of Discord: All within 20 ft. take −4 on attack rolls, Concentration checks, and Dexterity, and reduce speed by 50%.

Dissonant Chord: Deal 1d8/2 levels sonic damage in 10-ft. burst.

Harmonic Chorus: Give another caster +2 caster levels and +2 on save DCs as long as you concentrate.

Hymn of Praise: Add +2 caster levels to all good divine casters within range.

Infernal Threnody: Add +2 caster levels to all evil divine casters within range.

Speechlink: You and one other creature can talk, no matter how far apart.

4TH-LEVEL BARD SPELLS

Listening Coin: You can eavesdrop through a magic coin.

Spectral Weapon: Swift. Use quasi-real weapon to make touch attacks.

War Cry: Swift. Gain +2 morale bonus on attack and damage rolls, or +4 if you charge, for 1 round/level. Any opponent you damage must save or become panicked for 1 round.

5TH-LEVEL BARD SPELLS

Improvisation: You gain a pool of luck bonus points equal to twice your caster level and can spend them to improve attack rolls, skill checks, and ability checks.

Wail of Doom: Deal 1d4 damage/level in 30-ft. cone, plus targets panicked or shaken.

6TH-LEVEL BARD SPELLS

Cacophonic Shield: Shield 10 ft. from you blocks sounds, deals 1d6+1/level sonic damage, and deafens creatures passing through.

Hindsight[M]**:** You see into the past.

Protégé: Subject can use bardic music and bardic knowledge as bard of half your level.

NEW CLERIC SPELLS

1ST-LEVEL CLERIC SPELL

Grave Strike: Swift. You can sneak attack undead for 1 round.

2ND-LEVEL CLERIC SPELLS

Divine Insight: You gain insight bonus of 5 + caster level on one single skill check.

Healing Lorecall: If you have 5 or more ranks in Heal, you can remove harmful conditions with conjuration (healing) spells.

Iron Silence: Armor touched has no armor check penalty on Hide and Move Silently checks for 1 hour/level.

USING THE HEXBLADE WITH COMPLETE ADVENTURER

The hexblade (a new standard class introduced in *Complete Warrior*) has its own class spell list, which focuses on enchantment, necromancy, and transmutation spells but also includes some abjurations, illusions, and other effects. If you use this class, add the following new spells that appear in this book to the hexblade's class spell list.

1st-Level Hexblade Spells
Distract Assailant: Swift. One creature is flat-footed for 1 round.

2nd-Level Hexblade Spells
Critical Strike: Swift. For 1 round you gain +1d6 damage, doubled threat range, and +4 on attack rolls to confirm critical hits.

Invisibility, Swift: Swift. You are invisible for 1 round or until you attack.

3rd-Level Hexblade Spells
Spectral Weapon: Swift. Use quasi-real weapon to make touch attacks.

4th-Level Hexblade Spells
Shadow Form: Gain +4 on Hide, Move Silently, and Escape Artist checks, and concealment; you can move through obstacles if you have ranks in Escape Artist.

NEW DRUID SPELLS

1ST-LEVEL DRUID SPELLS

Hawkeye: Increase range increments by 50%, +5 on Spot checks.

Healthful Rest: Subjects heal at twice the normal rate.

Vine Strike: Swift. You can sneak attack plant creatures for 1 round.

2ND-LEVEL DRUID SPELLS

Balancing Lorecall: You gain a +4 bonus on Balance checks and can balance on impossible surfaces if you have 5 or more ranks in Balance.

Branch to Branch: You gain +10 competence bonus on Climb checks in trees and can brachiate through forest.

Daggerspell Stance: Swift. You gain +2 insight bonus on attack and damage if you make a full attack, SR 5 + caster level if you fight defensively, and DR 5/magic if you use the total defense action.

Easy Trail: You make a temporary trail through any kind of undergrowth.

Embrace the Wild: You gain an animal's senses for 10 min./level.

Healing Lorecall: If you have 5 or more ranks in Heal, you can remove harmful conditions with conjuration (healing) spells.

Listening Lorecall: You gain +4 on Listen checks, plus blindsense or blindsight if you have 5 or more ranks in Listen.

Nature's Favor: Animal touched gains luck bonus on attack and damage rolls of +1/3 levels.

Train Animal: Affected animal gains additional tricks equal to 1/2 caster level for 1 hour/level.

Wracking Touch: Deal 1d6 damage +1/level; you also deal sneak attack damage if you have any.

3RD-LEVEL DRUID SPELLS

Entangling Staff: Swift. Quarterstaff gains improved grab and can constrict grappled foes.

Fly, Swift: Swift. Gain fly speed of 60 ft. for 1 round.

4TH-LEVEL DRUID SPELL

Forestfold: Gain +20 competence bonus on Hide and Move Silently checks in one type of terrain.

5TH-LEVEL DRUID SPELL

Cloak of the Sea: Gain *blur, freedom of movement,* and *water breathing* while in water.

NEW PALADIN SPELLS

1ST-LEVEL PALADIN SPELL

Grave Strike: Swift. You can sneak attack undead for 1 round.

2ND-LEVEL PALADIN SPELL

Divine Insight: You gain insight bonus of 5 + caster level on one single skill check.

NEW RANGER SPELLS

1ST-LEVEL RANGER SPELLS

Accelerated Movement: Swift. Balance, Climb, or Move Silently at normal speed with no penalty on skill check.

Arrow Mind: Immediate. You threaten nearby squares with your bow and fire without provoking attacks of opportunity.

Bloodhound: You gain an immediate retry if you fail a Survival check while tracking.

Branch to Branch: You gain +10 competence bonus on Climb checks in trees and can brachiate through forest.

Easy Trail: You make a temporary trail through any kind of undergrowth.

Embrace the Wild: You gain an animal's senses for 10 min./level.

Exacting Shot: Your ranged weapon automatically confirms critical hits against favored enemies.

Guided Shot: Swift. You ignore distance penalties with your ranged attacks for 1 round.

Hawkeye: Increase range increments by 50%, +5 on Spot checks.

Healing Lorecall: If you have 5 or more ranks in Heal, you can remove harmful conditions with conjuration (healing) spells.

Instant Search: Swift. Make Search check at +2 as free action.

Sniper's Shot: Swift. No range limit on next ranged sneak attack.

Vine Strike: Swift. You can sneak attack plant creatures for 1 round.

2ND-LEVEL RANGER SPELLS

Balancing Lorecall: You gain a +4 bonus on Balance checks and can balance on impossible surfaces if you have 5 or more ranks in Balance.

Easy Climb: You make a vertical surface easy to Climb (DC 10).

Haste, Swift: Swift. Move faster, +1 on attacks, AC, Reflex saves.

Listening Lorecall: You gain +4 on Listen checks, plus blindsense or blindsight if you have 5 or more ranks in Listen.

Nature's Favor: Animal touched gains luck bonus on attack and damage rolls of +1/3 levels.

Train Animal: Affected animal gains additional tricks equal to 1/2 caster level for 1 hour/level.

3RD-LEVEL RANGER SPELLS

Blade Storm: Swift. You make melee attacks against every foe you threaten.

Forestfold: You gain +20 competence bonus on Hide and Move Silently checks in one type of terrain.

4TH-LEVEL RANGER SPELLS

Arrow Storm: Swift. You make one ranged attack against each foe within one range increment.

Foebane: Your weapon becomes +5 and deals +2d6 damage against a favored enemy.

NEW SORCERER/ WIZARD SPELLS

1ST-LEVEL SORCERER/ WIZARD SPELLS

Div   **Arrow Mind:** Immediate. You threaten nearby squares with your bow and fire without provoking attacks of opportunity.

Critical Strike: Swift. For 1 round you gain +1d6 damage, doubled threat range, and +4 on attack rolls to confirm critical hits.

Golem Strike: Swift. You can sneak attack constructs for 1 round.

Guided Shot: Swift. You ignore distance penalties with your ranged attacks for 1 round.

Insightful Feint: Swift. Gain +10 on your next Bluff check to feint in combat.

Instant Locksmith: Swift. Make Disable Device or Open Lock check at +2 as free action.

Instant Search: Swift. Make Search check at +2 as free action.

Master's Touch: Swift. You gain proficiency in a weapon or shield touched for 1 min./level.

Sniper's Shot: Swift. No range limit on next ranged sneak attack.

Ench   **Distract Assailant:** Swift. One creature is flat-footed for 1 round.

Trans   **Accelerated Movement:** Swift. Balance, Climb, or Move Silently at normal speed with no penalty on skill check.

Trans   **Expeditious Retreat, Swift:** Swift. Your speed increases by 30 ft. for 1 round.

2ND-LEVEL SORCERER/ WIZARD SPELLS

Abjur   **Daggerspell Stance:** Swift. You gain +2 insight bonus on attack and damage if you make a full attack, SR 5 + caster level if you fight defensively, and DR 5/magic if you use the total defense action.

Div   **Balancing Lorecall:** You gain a +4 bonus on Balance checks and can balance on impossible surfaces if you have 5 or more ranks in Balance.

Listening Lorecall: Gain +4 on Listen checks, plus blindsense or blindsight if you have 5 or more ranks in Listen.

Ench   **Mindless Rage:** Target compelled to attack you physically for 1 round/level.

Illus   **Bladeweave:** Swift. Your melee attack dazes your opponent.

Necro   **Wracking Touch:** Deal 1d6 damage +1/level; you also deal sneak attack damage if you have any.

Trans   **Fly, Swift:** Swift. Gain fly speed of 60 ft. for 1 round.

Sonic Weapon: Weapon touched deals +1d6 sonic damage with each hit.

Wraithstrike: Swift. Your melee attacks strike as touch attacks for 1 round.

Illus. by D. Kovacs

3RD-LEVEL SORCERER/ WIZARD SPELL

Illus **Spectral Weapon:** Swift. Use quasi-real weapon to make touch attacks.

4TH-LEVEL SORCERER/ WIZARD SPELL

Trans **Entangling Staff:** Swift. Quarterstaff gains improved grab and can constrict grappled foes.

5TH-LEVEL SORCERER/ WIZARD SPELLS

Trans **Nightstalker's Transformation**^M: Gain +4 Dex, +3 luck bonus to AC, +5 luck bonus on Ref saves, +3d6 sneak attack, and evasion.

Illus **Shadow Form:** Gain +4 on Hide, Move Silently, and Escape Artist checks, and concealment; you can move through obstacles if you have ranks in Escape Artist.

6TH-LEVEL SORCERER/ WIZARD SPELL

Trans **Cloak of the Sea:** Gain *blur, freedom of movement,* and *water breathing* while in water.

7TH-LEVEL SORCERER/ WIZARD SPELL

Evoc **Cacophonic Shield:** Immobile shield 10 ft. from you blocks sounds, deals 1d6+1/level sonic damage, and deafens creatures passing through.

9TH-LEVEL SORCERER/ WIZARD SPELL

Div **Hindsight**^M: You see into the past.

NEW SPELLS

The following spells supplement those found in Chapter 11 of the *Player's Handbook.*

ABSORB WEAPON

Transmutation
Level: Assassin 3
Components: V, S
Casting Time: 1 standard action
Range: Touch
Effect: One touched weapon not in another creature's possession
Duration: 1 hour/level (D)
Saving Throw: Will negates (object); see text
Spell Resistance: Yes (object)

You can harmlessly absorb a weapon you are touching (even a poisoned one) into your arm, so long as it is not in another creature's possession. The weapon must be a light weapon for you at the time you cast the spell. The absorbed weapon cannot be felt under the skin and doesn't restrict your range of motion in any way. An absorbed weapon cannot be detected with even a careful search, although a *detect magic* spell reveals the presence of a magical aura. The only evidence of its presence is a faint blotch on your skin shaped vaguely like the weapon.

When you touch the spot (an action equivalent to drawing a weapon), or when the spell duration expires, the weapon appears in your hand and the spell ends. If you attack with the weapon in the same round that you retrieve it from its hiding place, you can attempt a Bluff check to feint in combat as a free action, and you gain a +4 bonus on the Bluff check. An intelligent magic weapon gets a saving throw against this spell, but other weapons do not.

ACCELERATED MOVEMENT

Transmutation
Level: Bard 1, ranger 1, sorcerer/ wizard 1
Components: V, S, M
Casting Time: 1 swift action
Range: Personal
Target: You
Duration: 1 round/level (D)

While this spell is in effect, you can move at your normal speed when using Balance, Climb, or Move Silently without taking any penalty on your check. This spell does not affect the penalty for using these skills while running or charging.

Material Component: A dead cockroach.

ALLEGRO

Transmutation
Level: Bard 3
Components: V, S, M
Casting Time: 1 standard action
Range: 10 ft.
Area: 10-ft.-radius burst, centered on you
Duration: 1 minute/level (D)
Saving Throw: Fortitude negates (harmless)
Spell Resistance: Yes (harmless)

This spell makes you and your companions extraordinarily fleet of foot. Each creature within the spell's area gains a 30-foot enhancement bonus to its land speed, up to a maximum of double the creature's land speed. Affected creatures retain these effects for the duration of the spell, even if they leave the original area.

Material Component: A tailfeather from a bird of prey.

ARROW MIND

Divination
Level: Ranger 1, sorcerer/wizard 1
Components: V, S, M
Casting Time: 1 immediate action
Range: Personal
Target: You
Duration: 1 minute/level (D)

You sharpen your senses and focus your mind on the use of a bow. While this spell is in effect and you are wielding a longbow, shortbow, greatbow*, composite great-bow*, composite shortbow, or composite longbow, you threaten all squares within your normal melee reach (5 feet if Small or Medium, 10 feet if Large) with your bow, allowing you to make attacks of opportunity with arrows shot from the bow. In addition, you do not provoke attacks of opportunity when you shoot a bow while you are in another creature's threatened square.

Material Component: A flint arrowhead.

**See Complete Warrior.*

ARROW STORM

Transmutation
Level: Ranger 4
Components: V
Casting Time: 1 swift action
Range: Personal
Target: You
Duration: 1 round

You can cast this spell only at the beginning of your turn, before you take any other actions. After casting *arrow storm*, you can use a full-round action to make one ranged attack with a bow with which you are proficient against every foe within a distance equal to the weapon's range increment. You can attack a maximum number of individual targets equal to your character level. If you choose not to spend a full-round action in this fashion after casting the spell, the spell has no effect.

Arrow storm

BALANCING LORECALL

Divination
Level: Druid 2, ranger 2, sorcerer/wizard 2
Components: V, S, M/DF
Casting Time: 1 standard action
Range: Personal
Target: You
Duration: 1 minute/level (D)

You intuit the precise spot and stance necessary to stand on areas of even the most unstable footing. You gain a +4 insight bonus on Balance checks. If you have sufficient ranks in the Balance skill, you can even balance on an otherwise impossible surface with a DC 20 Balance check.

If you have 5 or more ranks in Balance, you can balance on vertical surfaces; the normal modifier for a sloped or angled surface no longer applies to you, though other DC modifiers (such as for a slippery surface) do apply. If you balance on a vertical surface, you can move up or down as if you were climbing. However, you are not actually climbing, so you can make attacks normally, retain your Dexterity bonus to Armor Class, and generally follow the rules of the Balance skill rather than the Climb skill.

If you have 10 or more ranks in Balance, you can balance on liquids, semisolid surfaces such as mud or snow, or similar surfaces that normally couldn't support your weight. For each consecutive round that you begin balanced on a particular surface of this sort, the DC of your Balance check increases by 5. As with all uses of the Balance skill, you move at half speed unless you decide to use the accelerated movement option (thereby increasing the DC of the Balance check by 5). For more information on the Balance skill, see page 67 of the *Player's Handbook*.

Arcane Material Component: A thin, three-inch-long wooden dowel.

Illus. by S. Ellis

BLADE STORM

Transmutation
Level: Ranger 3
Components: V
Casting Time: 1 swift action
Range: Personal
Target: You
Duration: 1 round

You can cast this spell only at the beginning of your turn, before you take any other actions. After casting *blade storm,* you can take a full-round action to make one attack with each melee weapon you are currently wielding against every foe within reach. If you wield two weapons, or a double weapon, you can attack each foe once with each weapon or end, using the normal rules for two-weapon fighting. So, a ranger wielding a longsword and a short sword could attack each opponent he can reach with both weapons. You can attack a maximum number of individual targets equal to your character level. If you choose not to spend a full-round action in this fashion after casting the spell, the spell has no effect.

BLADEWEAVE

Illusion [Pattern]
Level: Bard 2, sorcerer/wizard 2
Components: V
Casting Time: 1 swift action
Range: Personal
Target: You
Duration: 1 round/level (D)
Saving Throw: See text
Spell Resistance: See text

A *bladeweave* spell imbues your melee attacks with a fascinating pattern or rhythm that entrances your opponent. Any round that you attack with a melee weapon, you can make a single additional touch attack with that weapon at your normal attack bonus as a free action. This attack

deals no damage. Instead, anyone successfully touched by the weapon must succeed on a Will save or be dazed for 1 round. Spell resistance applies to this effect.

BLOODHOUND

Divination
Level: Ranger 1
Components: V, S
Casting Time: 1 standard action
Range: Personal
Target: You
Duration: 24 hours (D)

If you fail a Survival check to track a creature while this spell functions, you can immediately attempt another roll against the same DC to reestablish the trail. If the reroll fails, you must search for the trail for 30 minutes (if outdoors) or 5 minutes (if indoors) before trying again.

BRANCH TO BRANCH

Transmutation
Level: Druid 2, ranger 1
Components: V, S
Casting Time: 1 standard action
Range: Personal
Target: You
Duration: 10 minutes/level (D)

You gain a +10 competence bonus on Climb checks made in trees. As long as you remain at least 10 feet above the ground, you can brachiate (swing via branches and vines) in medium or dense forest, but not in sparse forest. When you brachiate, you gain a 10-foot enhancement bonus to your land speed and ignore the hampered movement penalties for undergrowth and other terrain features. You can charge while brachiating, but you can't run. Naturally, some local conditions such as areas of sparse forest, clearings, wide rivers, or other breaks in the forest

canopy might force you to return to the ground.

CACOPHONIC SHIELD

Evocation [Sonic]
Level: Bard 6, sorcerer/wizard 7
Components: V, S
Casting Time: 1 standard action
Range: 10 ft.
Area: 10-ft.-radius emanation, centered on you
Duration: 1 minute/level (D)
Saving Throw: Fortitude partial
Spell Resistance: Yes

You create a barrier of sonic energy at a distance of 10 feet from yourself. Creatures on either side of the barrier hear it as a loud but harmless buzzing. Nonmagical sound (including sound produced by a thunderstone) does not cross the barrier. Supernatural or spell-based sounds or sonic effects penetrate the barrier only if the caster or originator of the effect succeeds on a caster level check (DC 11 + your caster level).

A creature that crosses the barrier takes 1d6 points of sonic damage +1 point per caster level (maximum +20) and must make a Fortitude save or be deafened for 1 minute. The sonic vibrations create a 20% miss chance for any missiles crossing the barrier in either direction. The barrier moves with you, but you cannot force another creature to pass through it (for example, by moving adjacent to an enemy). If you force a creature to pass through, the barrier has no effect on that creature.

CLOAK OF THE SEA

Transmutation
Level: Druid 5, sorcerer/wizard 6
Components: V, S, DF
Casting Time: 1 standard action
Range: Touch
Target: Creature touched
Duration: 1 hour/level (D)

Saving Throw: Will negates (harmless)
Spell Resistance: Yes (harmless)

The subject retains his or her form but takes on a blue-green watery appearance. While underwater, the subject functions as if affected by *blur, freedom of movement,* and *water breathing* and doesn't take nonlethal damage from water pressure or hypothermia for the duration of the spell. When out of the water (or even partially out), the subject gains none of these advantages except *water breathing*. The subject can leave and reenter water without ending the spell.

CRITICAL STRIKE

Divination
Level: Assassin 1, sorcerer/wizard 1
Components: V
Casting Time: 1 swift action
Range: Personal
Target: You
Duration: 1 round

While this spell is in effect, your melee attacks are more likely to strike a foe's vital areas. Whenever you make a melee attack against a flanked foe or against a foe denied its Dexterity bonus, you deal an extra 1d6 points of damage, your weapon's threat range is doubled (as if under the effect of *keen edge*), and you gain a +4 insight bonus on rolls made to confirm critical hits. The increased threat range granted by this spell doesn't stack with any other effect that increases your weapon's threat range. Creatures immune to sneak attacks are immune to the extra damage dealt by your attacks.

DAGGERSPELL STANCE

Abjuration
Level: Druid 2, sorcerer/wizard 2
Components: V, F
Casting Time: 1 swift action
Range: Personal
Target: You
Duration: 1 round/level (D)

This spell, favored by the Daggerspell Guardians (see page 167), improves your ability to defend yourself when wielding a pair of daggers. The spell, like many of the daggerspell techniques, depends on the use of daggers to bring down a foe. The spell's effect cannot be realized unless you are wielding two daggers, but the spell does not end if you drop, throw, or otherwise lose a hold on one or both of your daggers.

While this spell is in effect, if you make a full attack while holding a dagger in each hand, you gain a +2 insight bonus on attack rolls and damage rolls made with daggers in that round.

The magical energy that permeates your daggers while this spell is active allows you to deflect the magical energy of many spells. When wielding two daggers and fighting defensively, you gain spell resistance equal to 5 + your caster level.

The spell focuses your concentration so that when you devote all of your attention to defense, you can turn the force of most blows away from your body with your daggers. When wielding two daggers and using the total defense action, you gain both the spell resistance benefit described above and damage reduction 5/magic.

Focus: A pair of daggers.

DIRGE OF DISCORD

Enchantment (Compulsion) [Evil, Mind-Affecting]
Level: Bard 3
Components: V, S, M
Casting Time: 1 standard action
Range: Close (25 ft. + 5 ft./2 levels)
Area: 20-ft.-radius spread
Duration: Concentration + 1 round/level
Saving Throw: Will negates
Spell Resistance: Yes

You create an unholy, cacophonous dirge that fills the subjects' minds with the screams of the dying, the wailing of the damned, and the howling of the mad. Affected creatures take a –4 penalty on attack rolls and Concentration checks, a –4 penalty to Dexterity, and a 50% reduction in their speed (to a minimum of 5 feet).

Material Component: A pinch of ashes from a destrachan.

DISSONANT CHORD

Evocation [Sonic]
Level: Bard 3
Components: V, S
Casting Time: 1 standard action
Range: 10 ft.
Area: 10-ft.-radius burst centered on you
Duration: Instantaneous
Saving Throw: Fortitude half
Spell Resistance: Yes

You emit a terrible, piercing note. Creatures (other than you) in the affected area take 1d8 points of sonic damage per two caster levels (maximum 5d8).

DISTORT SPEECH

Transmutation [Sonic]
Level: Bard 1
Components: V, S
Casting Time: 1 standard action
Range: Close (25 ft. + 5 ft./2 levels)
Target: One creature
Duration: 1 round/level
Saving Throw: Fortitude negates
Spell Resistance: Yes

You distort a creature's vocalizations. The voice of the subject becomes warped and nearly incomprehensible. For the duration of this spell, the subject has a 50% chance to miscast spells that have verbal components, and any time the subject speaks (including the use of magic items activated by command words), there is a 50% chance that the utterance is completely incomprehensible and therefore ineffective.

DISTRACT ASSAILANT
Enchantment (Compulsion) [Mind-Affecting]
Level: Assassin 1, sorcerer/ wizard 1
Components: V, S, M
Casting Time: 1 swift action
Range: Close (25 ft. + 5 ft./2 levels)
Target: One creature
Duration: 1 round
Saving Throw: Will negates
Spell Resistance: Yes

The subject of this spell is distracted, flinching at blows that seem to come from the shadows. A creature affected by this spell is flat-footed until the beginning of its next turn.
Material Component: The dried wing of a fly.

A distract assailant spell fools an ogre long enough to give an assassin the upper hand

DIVINE INSIGHT

Divination
Level: Cleric 2, paladin 2
Components: V, S, DF
Casting Time: 1 standard action
Range: Personal
Target: You
Duration: 1 hour/level or until discharged (D)

When you cast this spell, you invoke the power of your deity to guide your actions. Once during the spell's duration, you can choose to use its effect. This spell grants you an insight bonus equal to 5 + your caster level (maximum bonus of +15) on any single skill check. Activating the effect requires an immediate action. You must choose to use *divine insight* before you make the check you want to modify. Once used, the spell ends.

You can't have more than one *divine insight* effect active on you at the same time.

EASY CLIMB

Transmutation
Level: Ranger 2
Components: V, S
Casting Time: 1 standard action
Range: Medium (100 ft. +10 ft./level)
Area: Vertical path 10 ft. wide and 20 ft. tall/level
Duration: 10 minutes/level (D)
Saving Throw: None (object)
Spell Resistance: Yes (object)

You create a path of handholds and footholds up the surface of a cliff face, tree trunk, wall, or other vertical obstacle. This effect changes the surface to the equivalent of a very rough wall (DC 10 to climb).

EASY TRAIL

Abjuration
Level: Druid 2, ranger 1

Components: V, S
Casting Time: 1 standard action
Range: 40 ft.
Area: 40-ft. radius emanation
Duration: 1 hour/level (D)
Saving Throw: None
Spell Resistance: Yes

You radiate an energy that gently pushes plants aside, allowing easy passage and hiding your trail after you pass.

Anyone in the area of the spell (including you) finds the undergrowth held aside while she passes. This effect essentially provides a trail through any kind of undergrowth, reducing any movement penalties from terrain caused by dense vegetation (see Table 9–5: Terrain and Overland Movement, page 164 of the *Player's Handbook*). Once the effect of the spell passes, the plants return to their normal shape. The DC to track anyone who traveled within the area of this spell increases by 5 (the equivalent of hiding the trail).

This spell has no effect on plant creatures (that is, they aren't pushed or held aside by its effect).

EMBRACE THE WILD

Transmutation
Level: Druid 2, ranger 1
Components: V
Casting Time: 1 standard action
Range: Personal
Target: You
Duration: 10 minutes/level (D)

This spell allows you to adopt the nature and some of the abilities of a particular animal. Upon casting the spell, you can choose any animal whose Hit Dice are equal to or less than your caster level. You retain your own form, but you gain the natural and extraordinary senses of the creature you choose, including blindsense, blindsight, darkvision,

low-light vision, and scent, as applicable. You can also choose to replace either or both of your Listen and Spot check modifiers with those of the animal chosen.

For example, a 3rd-level druid casting this spell might choose to adopt the nature of a wolverine to gain low-light vision, scent, and Listen and Spot check modifiers of +6. Alternatively, she could select the eagle and gain low-light vision, Listen +2, and Spot +14. If the druid's Listen check modifier were better than +2, she could retain her own Listen check modifier while gaining the eagle's Spot check modifier.

ENTANGLING STAFF

Transmutation
Level: Druid 3, sorcerer/wizard 4
Components: V, F
Casting Time: 1 swift action
Range: Touch
Target: Quarterstaff touched
Duration: 1 round/level (D)
Saving Throw: Yes (harmless, object)
Spell Resistance: Yes (harmless)

You cause your quarterstaff to extrude writhing vines that allow you to easily grab and entrap foes. Each time you successfully strike a foe with the staff (a normal melee attack), you deal normal damage and can attempt to start a grapple as a free action without provoking attacks of opportunity (see Starting a Grapple, page 156 of the *Player's Handbook*). This grapple attempt does not require a separate touch attack. You gain a +8 bonus on grapple checks you cause by striking a foe with the *entangling staff*. You can attempt to grapple creatures up to one size category larger than you.

If your grapple check succeeds, your quarterstaff's vines constrict your foe, dealing 2d6 points of damage (you can choose to deal nonlethal damage instead of normal damage if you wish). You then have two choices:

Release: You release your opponent from the grapple. Some vines remain clinging to your foe, leaving it entangled for the duration of the spell. You can attack different enemies in later rounds with the *entan-* *gling staff,* potentially grappling and constricting or entangling them.

Maintain: You maintain your hold. In subsequent rounds, you deal constriction damage with a successful grapple check. You can then choose to release or maintain the hold again.

Focus: A quarterstaff.

EXACTING SHOT

Transmutation
Level: Ranger 1
Components: V, S
Casting Time: 1 standard action
Range: Touch
Target: Ranged weapon touched
Duration: 1 minute/level
Saving Throw: Will negates (harmless, object)
Spell Resistance: Yes (harmless, object)

This transmutation makes a ranged weapon strike true against your favored enemies. All rolls made to confirm critical hits by the weapon against favored enemies automatically succeed, so every threat is a critical hit. The affected weapon also ignores any miss chance due to concealment whenever you fire at a favored enemy (unless the target has total concealment, in which case the normal miss chance applies). If the ranged weapon or the pro-

Illus. by J. Jarvis

Entangling staff

jectile fired has any magical effect or property related to critical hits, this spell has no effect on it.

EXPEDITIOUS RETREAT, SWIFT

Transmutation
Level: Bard 1, sorcerer/wizard 1
Components: V
Casting Time: 1 swift action
Range: Personal
Target: You
Duration: 1 round

This spell functions like *expeditious retreat* (see page 228 of the *Player's Handbook*), except as noted above.

FLY, SWIFT

Transmutation
Level: Bard 2, druid 3, sorcerer/ wizard 2
Components: V
Casting Time: 1 swift action
Range: Personal
Target: You
Duration: 1 round

This spell functions like *fly* (see page 232 of the *Player's Handbook*), except as noted above.

FOCUSING CHANT

Enchantment (Compulsion) [Mind-Affecting]
Level: Bard 1
Components: V
Casting Time: 1 standard action
Range: Personal
Target: You
Duration: 1 minute (D)

You can use *focusing chant* to block out distractions and hone your attention. You gain a +1 circumstance bonus on attack rolls, skill checks, and ability checks for the duration of the spell. You need not concentrate on

focusing chant, but you must continue to mutter the syllables of the chant to maintain the spell. Therefore, you cannot speak, use bardic music effects, or cast spells with verbal components while a *focusing chant* spell is in effect.

Dismissing *focusing chant* is an immediate action.

FOEBANE

Evocation
Level: Ranger 4
Components: V, S
Casting Time: 1 standard action
Range: Touch
Target: Weapon touched
Duration: 1 round/level (D)
Saving Throw: Will negates (harmless, object)
Spell Resistance: Yes (harmless, object)

This spell imbues one of your weapons with great killing power against a single favored enemy type. Against creatures of that type, the weapon acts as a +5 magic weapon and deals an extra 2d6 points of damage. Furthermore, while you wield the weapon, you gain a +4 resistance bonus on saving throws against effects created by creatures of that type.

The spell is automatically canceled 1 round after the weapon leaves your hand for any reason. You cannot have more than one *foebane weapon* active at a time.

If this spell is cast on a magic weapon, the powers of the spell supersede any that the weapon normally has, rendering the normal enhancement bonus and powers of the weapon inoperative for the duration of the spell. This spell is not cumulative with any other spell that might modify the weapon in any way. This spell does not work on artifacts.

FORESTFOLD

Transmutation
Level: Druid 4, ranger 3
Components: V, S
Casting Time: 1 standard action
Range: Personal
Target: You
Duration: 10 minutes/level (D)

You change your coloring and attune your footfalls to one specific kind of terrain (aquatic, desert, plains, forest, hills, mountains, marsh, or underground). While you are in terrain of that kind, you gain a +20 competence bonus on Hide and Move Silently checks. You retain these bonuses even if you leave the designated terrain and return within the duration of the spell.

GOLEM STRIKE

Divination
Level: Sorcerer/wizard 1
Components: V
Casting Time: 1 swift action
Range: Personal
Target: You
Duration: 1 round

Illus. by D. Kovacs

While this spell is in effect, you have a special connection to the arcane forces that animate constructs. For 1 round, you can deliver sneak attacks against constructs as if they were not immune to sneak attacks. To attack a construct in this manner, you must still meet the other requirements for making a sneak attack.

This spell applies only to sneak attack damage. It gives you no ability to affect constructs with critical hits, nor does it confer any special ability to overcome the damage reduction or other defenses of constructs.

GRAVE STRIKE

Divination [Good]
Level: Cleric 1, paladin 1
Components: V, DF
Casting Time: 1 swift action
Range: Personal
Target: You
Duration: 1 round

While this spell is in effect, you have a special connection to the forces of light and positive energy. For 1 round, you can deliver sneak attacks against undead as if they were not immune to sneak attacks. To attack an undead creature in this manner, you must still meet the other requirements for making a sneak attack.

This spell applies only to sneak attack damage. It gives you no ability to affect undead with critical hits, nor does it confer any special ability to overcome the damage reduction or other defenses of undead creatures.

GUIDED SHOT

Divination
Level: Ranger 1, sorcerer/wizard 1
Components: V
Casting Time: 1 swift action
Range: Personal
Target: You
Duration: 1 round

Golem strike

You use magical energy to briefly focus your mind and body on making a perfect shot. While this spell is in effect, your ranged attacks do not take a penalty due to distance.

In addition, while this spell is in effect, your ranged attacks ignore the AC bonus granted to targets by anything less than total cover.

This spell does not provide any ability to exceed the maximum range of the weapon with which you are attacking, nor does it confer any ability to attack targets protected by total cover.

HARMONIC CHORUS

Enchantment (Compulsion) [Mind-Affecting]
Level: Bard 3
Components: V, S, F
Casting Time: 1 standard action
Range: Close (25 ft. + 5 ft./2 levels)
Target: One living creature
Duration: Concentration, up to 1 round/level (D)
Saving Throw: Will negates (harmless)
Spell Resistance: Yes

Harmonic chorus lets you improve the spellcasting ability of another spellcaster. For the duration of the spell, the subject gains a +2 morale bonus to caster level and a +2 morale bonus on save DCs for all spells she casts.

Focus: A tuning fork.

HASTE, SWIFT

Transmutation
Level: Ranger 2
Components: V
Casting Time: 1 swift action
Range: Personal
Target: You
Duration: 1 round

This spell functions as *haste* (see page 239 of the *Player's Handbook*), except as noted above.

HAWKEYE

Transmutation
Level: Druid 1, ranger 1
Components: V
Casting Time: 1 standard action
Range: Personal
Target: You
Duration: 10 minutes/level (D)

This spell gives you the ability to see accurately at long distances. Your range increment for ranged weapons increases by 50%, and you gain a +5 competence bonus on Spot checks.

HEALING LORECALL

Divination
Level: Cleric 2, druid 2, ranger 1
Components: V, S, M
Casting Time: 1 standard action
Range: Personal
Target: You
Duration: 1 minute/level

You tap into your healing acumen to make your curative spells more potent. A caster with 5 or more ranks in Heal can, when casting a conjuration (healing) spell, choose to remove any one of the following conditions affecting the target of the spell, in addition to the spell's normal effects: dazed, dazzled, or fatigued. A caster with 10 or more ranks in Heal can choose from the following conditions in addition to

those above: exhausted, nauseated, or sickened.

Also, when determining the amount of damage healed by your conjuration (healing) spells, you can substitute your total ranks in Heal for your caster level. The normal caster level limit for individual spells still applies; thus, a 3rd-level cleric with 6 ranks in Heal when under the effect of *healing lorecall* cures 1d8+5 points of damage with a *cure light wounds* spell.

Material Component: A small mint leaf.

HEALTHFUL REST

Conjuration (Healing)
Level: Bard 1, druid 1
Components: V, S
Casting Time: 10 minutes
Range: Close (25 ft. + 5 ft./2 levels)
Targets: One creature/level, no two of which can be more than 30 feet apart
Duration: 24 hours
Saving Throw: Will negates (harmless)
Spell Resistance: Yes (harmless)

Healthful rest doubles the subjects' natural healing rate. Each affected creature regains twice the hit points it otherwise would have regained during that day, depending on its activity level (see page 76 of the *Player's Handbook*).

HERALD'S CALL

Enchantment (Compulsion)
[Mind-Affecting, Sonic]
Level: Bard 1
Components: V, S
Casting Time: 1 swift action
Range: 20 ft.
Area: 20-ft.-radius burst centered on you
Duration: 1 round
Saving Throw: Will negates
Spell Resistance: Yes

You produce a crowd-stopping shout that holds an air of authority others find difficult to ignore. Any creature with 5 Hit Dice or less is *slowed* for 1 round.

Creatures beyond the radius of the burst might hear the shout, but they are not *slowed*.

HINDSIGHT

Divination
Level: Bard 6, sorcerer/wizard 9
Components: V, S, M
Casting Time: 1 hour
Range: Personal
Area: 60-ft. radius, centered on you
Duration: Instantaneous
Saving Throw: None
Spell Resistance: No

You can see and hear into the past, getting a look at events that happened previously at your current location. The level of detail you see and hear by means of this spell depends on the span of time you wish to observe; concentrating on a span of days renders a more detailed perspective than, say, a span of centuries. You can view only one span of time per casting, chosen from the following options.

Days: You sense the events of the past, stretching back one day per caster level. You gain detailed knowledge of the people, conversations, and events that transpired.

Weeks: You gain a summary of the events of the past, stretching back one week per caster level. Exact wording and details are lost, but you know all the participants and the highlights of the conversations and events that took place.

Years: You gain a general idea of the events of the past, stretching back one year per caster level. You notice only noteworthy events such as deaths, battles, scenes of great emotion, important discoveries, and significant happenings.

Centuries: You gain a general idea of the events of the past, stretching back one century plus an additional century for every four caster levels beyond 1st. For instance, a 16th-level caster would gain insight into the events of four centuries in the past, and a 17th-level caster would see back across five centuries. You notice only the most remarkable of events: coronations, deaths of important personages, major battles, and other truly historic happenings.

Material Component: An hourglass-shaped diamond worth at least 1,000 gp.

HYMN OF PRAISE
Evocation [Good, Sonic]
Level: Bard 3
Components: V, S
Casting Time: 1 standard action
Range: Medium (100 ft. + 10 ft./ level)
Area: A sphere-shaped emanation with a radius equal to the range, centered on you
Duration: 1 round/level (D)
Saving Throw: Will negates
Spell Resistance: Yes

You can strike up a rousing, inspirational song that temporarily boosts by 2 the effective caster level of each good-aligned divine spellcaster within range. This increase does not grant access to additional spells, but it does improve all spell effects that are dependent on caster level. In addition, *hymn of praise* mimics the effect of a *hallow* spell with respect to turning or rebuking undead. Within the spell's area, each good-aligned divine spellcaster gains a +4 sacred bonus on Charisma checks to turn undead, and each evil-aligned divine spellcaster takes a –4 sacred penalty on Charisma checks to rebuke undead.

IMPROVISATION
Transmutation
Level: Bard 5
Components: V, S, M
Casting Time: 1 standard action
Range: Personal
Target: You
Duration: 1 round/level (D)

You gain access to a floating "pool" of luck, which manifests as bonus points you can use as desired to improve your odds of success at various tasks. This bonus pool consists of 2 points per caster level, which you can spend as you like to improve attack rolls, skill checks, and ability checks, although no single check can receive a bonus greater than one-half your caster level. You must declare any bonus point usage before the appropriate roll is made. Used points disappear from the pool, and any points remaining when the spell ends are wasted. These points count as luck bonuses for purposes of stacking.

For example, a 14th-level bard pauses while chasing a pickpocket to cast *improvisation*. At any time during the next 14 rounds, he could use the points to provide him a +7 luck bonus on a Spot check, a +7 luck bonus on a Climb check, and a +7 luck bonus on two of his attacks.

Material Component: A pair of dice.

INFERNAL THRENODY
Evocation [Evil, Sonic]
Level: Bard 3
Components: V, S
Casting Time: 1 round
Range: Medium (100 ft. + 10 ft./ level)
Area: A sphere-shaped emanation with a radius equal to the range, centered on you
Duration: 1 round/level (D)
Saving Throw: Will negates
Spell Resistance: Yes

You can strike up a pulsing, powerful rhythm that temporarily boosts by 2 the effective caster level of each evil-aligned divine spellcaster within range. This increase does not grant access to addition al spells, but it does improve all spell effects that are dependent on caster level. In addition, *infernal threnody* mimics the effect of an *unhallow* spell with respect to turning or rebuking undead. Within the spell's area, each evil-aligned divine spellcaster gains a +4 profane bonus on Charisma checks to rebuke undead, and each good-aligned divine spellcaster takes a –4 profane penalty on Charisma checks to turn undead.

INSIDIOUS RHYTHM
Enchantment (Compulsion) [Mind-Affecting]
Level: Bard 2
Components: V, S
Casting Time: 1 standard action
Range: Medium (100 ft. + 10 ft./ level)
Target: One creature
Duration: 1 minute/level
Saving Throw: Will negates
Spell Resistance: Yes

You play a catchy, silly little tune that gets stuck in the mind of the subject unless she succeeds on a Will save. The endlessly recycling melody makes it difficult for the subject to cast spells or perform any other action that requires mental focus. The subject takes a –4 penalty on all Intelligence-based skill checks and Concentration checks. Whenever the target attempts to cast, concentrate on, or direct a spell, she must succeed on a Concentration check (DC equal to *insidious rhythm*'s save DC + spell's level) or fail at the attempt.

INSIGHTFUL FEINT

Divination
Level: Assassin 1, sorcerer/
wizard 1
Components: V
Casting Time: 1 swift action
Range: Personal
Target: You
Duration: 1 round

You gain temporary insight into the way your opponent moves and reacts.

You gain a +10 insight bonus on the next single Bluff check (if it is made before the start of your next turn) that you make to feint in combat (see Bluff, page 68 of the *Player's Handbook*).

INSPIRATIONAL BOOST

Enchantment (Compulsion)
[Mind-Affecting, Sonic]
Level: Bard 1
Components: V, S
Casting Time: 1 swift action
Range: Personal
Targets: You
Duration: 1 round or special; see text

When you play your instrument, sing your song, recite your epic poem, or speak your words of encouragement, you fill your allies with greater confidence than normal. While this spell is in effect, the morale bonus granted by your inspire courage bardic music increases by 1.

The effect lasts until your inspire courage effect ends. If you don't begin to use your inspire courage

Insidious rhythm

ability before the beginning of your next turn, the spell's effect ends.

INSTANT LOCKSMITH

Divination
Level: Assassin 1, sorcerer/
wizard 1
Components: V, S
Casting Time: 1 swift action
Range: Personal
Target: You
Duration: 1 round

You can make one Disable Device check or one Open Lock check in this round as a free action. You gain a +2 insight bonus on the check.

INSTANT SEARCH

Divination
Level: Assassin 1, ranger 1,
sorcerer/wizard 1
Components: V, S
Casting Time: 1 swift action
Range: Personal
Target: You
Duration: 1 round

You can make one Search check in this round as a free action. You gain a +2 insight bonus on the check.

INVISIBILITY, SWIFT

Illusion (Glamer)
Level: Assassin 2, bard 2
Components: V
Casting Time: 1 swift action
Range: Personal
Target: You
Duration: 1 round

This spell functions like *invisibility* (see page 245 of the *Player's Handbook*), except as noted above.

IRON SILENCE

Transmutation
Level: Assassin 2, bard 2, cleric 2
Components: V, S, DF
Casting Time: 1 standard action
Range: Touch
Target: One suit of armor touched per three levels
Duration: 1 hour/level (D)
Saving Throw: Will negates (harmless, object)
Spell Resistance: Yes (harmless, object)

While this spell is in effect, the armor check penalty from the affected suit or suits of armor does not apply on Hide and Move Silently

153

checks. Only wearers proficient in the armor's use get this benefit when wearing the affected armor. The armor check penalty still applies to other skill checks as normal.

JOYFUL NOISE

Abjuration
Level: Bard 1
Components: S
Casting Time: 1 standard action
Range: 10 ft.
Area: 10-ft.-radius emanation, centered on you
Duration: Concentration; see text
Saving Throw: None
Spell Resistance: No

You create sonic vibrations that negate any magical *silence* effect in the area. This zone of negation moves with you and lasts as long as you continue to concentrate.

The *silence* is not dispelled but simply held in abeyance; it remains in effect outside the area of the *joyful noise* effect. Thus, this spell is usually used to move a group out of range of a *silence* effect.

LISTENING COIN

Divination (Scrying)
Level: Bard 4
Components: V, S, F
Casting Time: 1 standard action
Range: Touch
Effect: Magical sensor
Duration: 1 hour/level (D)
Saving Throw: None
Spell Resistance: No

You can turn two ordinary coins into magic listening devices—one a sensor and the other a receiver. After casting the spell, you simply give the sensor coin away, either surreptitiously or overtly. By holding the receiver coin up to your ear,

you can hear whatever transpires near the sensor as if you were there (much like a *clairaudience* effect). If the sensor coin is in a pocket, pouch, or sack, the DC of the Listen check increases by 5.

The coins continue to function no matter how far apart they are, although they fall silent if they're on different planes.

Focus: The pair of coins.

LISTENING LORECALL

Divination
Level: Druid 2, ranger 2, sorcerer/wizard 2
Components: V, S, DF
Casting Time: 1 standard action
Range: Personal
Target: You
Duration: 10 minutes/level

You gain the ability to precisely and instantaneously identify and locate the origins of even the most minute sounds you detect. You gain a +4 insight bonus on Listen checks.

In addition, if you have 5 or more ranks in Listen, you gain blindsense out to 30 feet. If you have 10 or more ranks in Listen, you gain blindsight out to 30 feet instead.

A *silence* spell or effect negates blindsense or blindsight granted by a *listening lorecall* spell.

MASTER'S TOUCH

Divination
Level: Bard 1, sorcerer/wizard 1
Components: V, F
Casting Time: 1 swift action
Range: Personal
Target: You
Duration: 1 minute/level (D)

Master's touch is a spell often found in the repertoire of adventurers who specialize in casting arcane spells. You gain proficiency with a single weapon or shield you hold in your hands when the spell is cast. The lack of a somatic component means the spell can be cast in the middle of a fight while you keep ready whatever items stand between you and danger.

Proficiency is granted for only a single, specific item, although multiple castings allow for multiple proficiencies. For example, if you hold a short sword and a rapier, with a buckler strapped to your off hand, you could cast the spell three times, once for each weapon and once for the shield.

This spell does not grant proficiency for a kind or category of item (such as short swords) but only for the one specific item held in your hand at the time the spell is cast (*this* short sword). Should you set that item down or otherwise lose your grip on it, the proficiency does not transfer to a different item of the same kind you might pick up. However, if you recover the original item before the spell's effect runs out, you are still proficient with that specific weapon or shield for the duration.

Focus: The item in whose use you wish to be proficient.

Illus. by D. Kovacs

MINDLESS RAGE

Enchantment (Compulsion)
 [Mind-Affecting]
Level: Bard 2, sorcerer/wizard 2
Components: V, S, F
Casting Time: 1 standard action
Range: Close (25 ft. + 5 ft./2 levels)
Target: One creature
Duration: 1 round/level
Saving Throw: Will negates
Spell Resistance: Yes

You fill the subject with so great a rage that it can do nothing but focus on engaging you in personal physical combat. The target must be able to see you when you cast this spell. If the subject later loses line of sight to you, the spell immediately ends. (A subject can't voluntarily break line of sight with you, such as by closing its eyes, to end this spell prematurely.)

If the subject threatens you, it must make a full attack against you using its melee weapons or natural melee attacks. If the subject doesn't threaten you, it must move at up to twice its speed, ending its movement as close to you as possible. If it moves close enough with a single move to threaten you, it may stop and make a melee attack against you as normal.

While under the effect of a *mindless rage* spell, the subject can make use of all normal melee combat skills, abilities, and feats—either offensive or defensive. However, the subject can't make ranged attacks, cast spells, or activate magic items that require a command word, a spell trigger, or spell completion to function. The subject can't make any attack against a creature other than you.

The subject of this spell, though overcome with rage, is by no means rendered idiotic or suicidal. For example, an affected creature will not charge off a cliff in an attempt to reach you.

An interesting side effect of *mindless rage* occurs when the spell affects any character or creature with the rage ability (such as a barbarian). In these cases, the *mindless rage* spell automatically activates the character's rage ability (and counts as one of the character's uses of rage for that day).

Focus: A scarlet handkerchief or similar piece of cloth, waved in the target's direction while you vocalize the verbal component.

NATURE'S FAVOR

Evocation
Level: Druid 2, ranger 2
Components: V, S, DF
Casting Time: 1 standard action
Range: Touch
Target: Animal touched
Duration: 1 minute
Saving Throw: Will negates
 (harmless)
Spell Resistance: Yes (harmless)

By calling on the power of nature, you grant the subject animal a +1 luck bonus on attack and damage rolls for every three caster levels you possess, to a maximum bonus of +5 at 15th level.

NIGHTSTALKER'S TRANSFORMATION

Transmutation
Level: Sorcerer/wizard 5
Components: V, S, M
Casting Time: 1 standard action
Range: Personal
Target: You
Duration: 1 round/level (D)

You become a stealthy and dangerous combatant. Your mind-set changes so that you relish stealth, deception, and surprise attacks over magical assaults.

You gain a +4 enhancement bonus to Dexterity, a +3 luck bonus to Armor Class, a +5 luck bonus on Reflex saving throws, a +5 competence bonus on Spot, Listen, Hide, and Move Silently checks, and proficiency with all simple weapons plus the hand crossbow, rapier, sap, shortbow, and short sword. You also gain the Weapon Finesse feat and the evasion ability (see page 50 of the *Player's Handbook*). You deal an extra 3d6 points of damage whenever you attack an opponent that you flank or an opponent denied its Dexterity bonus to Armor Class. This extra damage works like the rogue's sneak attack ability.

You lose your spellcasting ability for the duration of the spell, including your ability to use spell activation or spell completion magic items, just as if the spells were no longer on your class list.

Material Component: A *potion of cat's grace*, which you drink (and whose effects are subsumed by the spell effects).

PROTÉGÉ

Transmutation
Level: Bard 6
Components: V, S
Casting Time: 1 round
Range: Touch
Target: Creature touched
Duration: 1 minute/level (D)
Saving Throw: Will negates
 (harmless)
Spell Resistance: Yes (harmless)

You briefly grant bardic abilities to a creature of your choice. The subject of the spell can then function as a bard of one-half your current bard level with respect to bardic music and bardic knowledge. However, *protégé* imparts no spellcasting ability and does not grant access to spells not normally available to the subject. For Perform checks and bardic music prerequisites, the creature uses its own ranks in Perform or one-half of your ranks (modified by its own Charisma modifier), whichever is better.

SHADOW FORM

Illusion (Shadow)
Level: Assassin 4, sorcerer/wizard 5
Components: V, S, M

Shadow form

Casting Time: 1 standard action
Range: Personal
Target: You
Duration: 1 minute/level (D)

You call forth the power of shadow, enveloping yourself in a clinging, concealing shroud of darkness. While this spell is in effect, you gain

a number of benefits. The shadows wrapping your form grant you a +4 competence bonus on Escape Artist, Hide, and Move Silently checks. Your shadowy form also provides you with concealment. This shadowy concealment is not negated by a *see invisibility* spell, but a *true seeing* spell counteracts the effect. Standing within the radius of a *daylight* spell or in bright natural sunlight temporarily suppresses the concealment effect.

In addition, if you have 5 ranks in Escape Artist, you can attempt to slip through a solid object or barrier up to 5 feet thick with a DC 20 Escape Artist check, though doing this ends the spell as soon as the attempt is completed (regardless of success). If you have 10 ranks in Escape Artist, you can attempt to

pass through an object or barrier up to 10 feet thick. If you have 15 ranks in Escape Artist, you can attempt to pass through a barrier composed of magical force (or similar magical obstacles).

Material Component: A small piece of black cloth taken from a funeral shroud.

SNIPER'S EYE

Transmutation
Level: Assassin 4
Components: V, S, F
Casting Time: 1 standard action
Range: Personal
Target: You
Duration: 1 round/level (D)

This spell magically enhances your senses, making you deadly with ranged weapons. When you cast *sniper's eye*, you gain the following benefits.

- +10 competence bonus on Spot checks.
- Darkvision out to 60 feet.
- The ability to make a ranged sneak attack at a range of up to 60 feet, rather than 30 feet.
- The ability to make a death attack with a ranged weapon rather than just with a melee weapon. The target must be within 60 feet.

This spell doesn't grant you the ability to make a sneak attack or death attack if you don't already have that ability.

Sniper's eye attunes you completely to the vantage point you had when you cast the spell. You understand the nuances of the breeze and every angle and shadow—from that spot. If you move even 5 feet from the place where you cast the spell, you lose the benefits of *sniper's eye* until you return to that spot.

Focus: A magnifying glass lens.

SNIPER'S SHOT

Divination
Level: Assassin 1, ranger 1, sorcerer/wizard 1
Components: V, S
Casting Time: 1 swift action
Range: Personal
Target: You
Duration: 1 round

When you cast this spell, you extend and sharpen your perceptions for one devastating ranged attack. Your next single ranged attack (if it is made before the start of your next turn) can be a sneak attack regardless of the distance between you and your target.

This spell doesn't grant you the ability to make a sneak attack if you don't already have that ability.

SONIC WEAPON

Transmutation [Sonic]
Level: Bard 2, sorcerer/wizard 2
Components: V
Casting Time: 1 standard action
Range: Touch
Target: Weapon touched
Duration: 1 minute/level (D)

This spell temporarily sheathes a weapon in sonic energy. While the spell is in effect, the affected weapon deals an extra 1d6 points of sonic damage with each successful attack. The sonic energy does not harm the weapon's wielder. Bows, crossbows, and slings that are affected by this spell bestow the sonic energy upon their ammunition.

SPECTRAL WEAPON

Illusion (Shadow)
Level: Assassin 3, bard 4, sorcerer/wizard 3
Components: V, S
Casting Time: 1 swift action
Range: Personal
Target: You

Duration: 1 round/level (D)
Saving Throw: Will partial; see text
Spell Resistance: Yes; see text

Using material from the Plane of Shadow, you can fashion a quasi-real weapon of any type with which you are proficient. This *spectral weapon* appears in your hand and behaves as a normal weapon of its type, with two exceptions. First, you resolve attacks with your *spectral weapon* as melee touch attacks instead of melee attacks. Second, any foe you hit is entitled to a Will save to recognize the weapon's shadowy nature. If the save is successful, that opponent takes only one-fifth normal damage from the weapon on that attack and all subsequent attacks, and is only 20% likely to suffer any special effects of your attacks (such as a death attack delivered with the weapon).

You can maintain only one *spectral weapon* at a time, and only you can wield it. The weapon dissipates when you let go of it or when the spell's duration expires, whichever comes first.

SPEECHLINK

Divination
Level: Bard 3
Components: V, S
Casting Time: 1 standard action
Range: Touch
Targets: You and one creature touched
Duration: 10 minutes/level (D)
Saving Throw: None
Spell Resistance: No

You and a willing target can communicate verbally no matter how much distance you put between yourselves on the same plane. Either participant can end the spell at any time. *Speechlink* allows each

to hear the other's vocalizations, whatever their volume. It does not transfer other sounds from either participant's location. This spell works on any creatures, including animals, but does not convey any special language comprehension abilities.

TACTICAL PRECISION

Divination [Mind-Affecting]
Level: Bard 2
Components: V, S, M
Casting Time: 1 standard action
Range: Close (25 ft. + 5 ft./2 levels)
Targets: One creature/level, no two of which can be more than 30 ft. apart
Duration: 1 round/level
Saving Throw: Will negates (harmless)
Spell Resistance: Yes (harmless)

When you cast this spell, you grant your allies greater insight into one another's actions, allowing them to better coordinate their attacks. If two affected allies flank the same creature, each gains a +2 insight bonus on attack rolls made against the flanked creature. This bonus is in addition to the normal +2 bonus on attack rolls granted to flanking creatures.

In addition, if an affected ally successfully deals damage against an opponent that is flanked by another affected ally, she deals an extra 1d6 points of damage. Creatures immune to sneak attacks are immune to this extra damage.

Material Component: A toy soldier.

TRAIN ANIMAL

Enchantment (Charm) [Mind-Affecting]
Level: Druid 2, ranger 2
Components: V, S, DF
Casting Time: 10 minutes

Range: Touch
Target: Animal touched
Duration: 1 hour/level
Saving Throw: Will negates (harmless)
Spell Resistance: Yes (harmless)

You temporarily boost the number of tricks that an animal knows. While this spell is in effect, the affected animal gains a number of additional tricks equal to half your caster level (maximum five). For more information on tricks and trained animals, see the descriptions of the Handle Animal skill, page 100 of this book, and pages 74–75 of the *Player's Handbook*.

This spell does not modify an animal's attitude toward you, nor does it guarantee that an animal will cooperate when instructed to perform the newly learned tricks.

VINE STRIKE

Divination
Level: Druid 1, ranger 1
Components: V, DF
Casting Time: 1 swift action
Range: Personal
Target: You
Duration: 1 round

While this spell is in effect, you have a special connection to the forces of nature that allows you to deliver sneak attacks on plant creatures as if they were not immune to sneak attacks. To attack a plant creature in this manner, you must still meet the other requirements for making a sneak attack.

This spell applies only to sneak attack damage. It gives you no ability to affect plant creatures with critical hits, nor does it confer any special ability to overcome the damage reduction or other defenses of plant creatures.

WAIL OF DOOM

Necromancy [Fear, Mind-Affecting, Sonic]
Level: Bard 5
Components: V
Casting Time: 1 standard action
Range: 30 ft.
Area: Cone-shaped burst
Duration: Instantaneous and 1 round/level or 1 round; see text
Saving Throw: Will partial; see text
Spell Resistance: Yes

Anyone caught in the area of this spell suffers excruciating pain and becomes demoralized. Each creature takes 1d4 points of damage per caster level (up to a maximum of 15d4) and becomes panicked for 1 round per caster level. A successful Will save halves the damage, reduces the panicked effect to shaken, and reduces the duration of the shaken effect to 1 round.

WAR CRY

Enchantment (Compulsion) [Mind-Affecting, Sonic]
Level: Bard 4
Components: V, S
Casting Time: 1 swift action
Range: Personal
Target: You
Duration: 1 round/level (D)
Saving Throw: See text
Spell Resistance: See text

You attack with a cry that bolsters your own courage as well as intimidating your enemies. As a result of this spell, you gain a +2 morale bonus on attack rolls and damage rolls, or a +4 morale bonus on attack rolls and damage rolls made as part of a charge.

If you deal damage with a melee attack, your foe must succeed on a Will save or become panicked for 1 round (spell resistance applies to this effect). An opponent who makes a successful saving throw against this effect cannot be affected again by the same casting of *war cry*.

WRACKING TOUCH

Necromancy
Level: Druid 2, sorcerer/wizard 2
Components: V, S
Casting Time: 1 standard action
Range: Touch
Target: Creature touched
Duration: Instantaneous
Saving Throw: Fortitude half
Spell Resistance: Yes

Your touch causes horrible agony in a creature's vital area. You lay your hand upon a creature and deal 1d6 points of damage +1 point per caster level (maximum +10). In addition, if you have the sneak attack ability, you also deal sneak attack damage to the affected creature unless the creature is immune to extra damage from critical hits. The creature still takes the spell damage even if it does not take the sneak attack damage. Unlike a normal use of sneak attack, your target need not be flanked or denied its Dexterity bonus to take sneak attack damage from this spell.

WRAITHSTRIKE

Transmutation
Level: Assassin 2, sorcerer/wizard 2
Components: V, S
Casting Time: 1 swift action
Range: Personal
Target: You
Duration: 1 round

When you cast this spell, your melee weapons or natural weapons become ghostly and nearly transparent for a brief time. While this spell is in effect, your melee attacks are resolved as melee touch attacks rather than normal melee attacks.

Clans, guilds, and other organizations provide many interesting opportunities for characters of any class. Defining a bard's preferred performance styles by the precepts of his bardic college, choosing wizard spells based on the preferences of a magic academy, or taking jobs based on the directives of a thieves guild: All these add flavor to a campaign world. Their breadth hints at the presence of organizations for nearly every class. The organizations described here, however, focus on groups whose members use a large variety of skills or who achieve unusually great expertise in a particular group of skills. Often, this expertise is associated with a criminal organization or its law-enforcement counterpart, but it also allows for many other types of organizations and the characters who belong to them.

Being part of an organization must come with responsibilities and benefits, or a character won't feel connected to this important choice of allegiance. The descriptions of the organizations in this chapter describe the membership in general terms, allowing players and DMs to shape specific details to fit their campaign world. Whenever a player chooses to affiliate a character with an organization, players and DMs should discuss the role of the group in the campaign world. The discussion should cover what the character seeks to gain from belonging, what responsibilities the character will have, how often the organization will be featured in a gaming session, and anything else that either the player or DM deems relevant.

The organizations in this chapter are described using the following format.

ORGANIZATION NAME

The first few paragraphs offer a general description of the organization, its purpose, its motives, and its main activities.

Joining the Organization: How a character becomes a trusted member of the group.

Character Benefits: The benefits that an individual gains from membership. Although this section is geared toward players, the DM is free to change the benefits or impose restrictions on these benefits as he or she sees fit.

Roleplaying Suggestions: Guidelines (not rules) on roleplaying a character affiliated with the organization. These suggestions should never usurp a sense of character choice, but remember that a character is much more likely to feel at home as part of an organization if her personality matches the majority of the organization's members.

Typical Member: A short description of a typical member of the organization.

Prestige Classes: The prestige classes held by members, their relative frequency and importance to the guild, and guidelines on how important it is for a member of the organization to eventually join a particular prestige class.

Lore of the Guild: An unusual aspect of the guild, such as a legend or story about the group, a famous (or infamous) member, the origin of the guild, or a commonly held misconception about the organization.

A Guild Campaign: A brief description of how a campaign might work if the majority of the player characters were members of the guild in question. When appropriate, it discusses ways for an adventuring group to act as an official part of the organization and the requirements and benefits of such an arrangement.

Sample Organization Member

Each description ends with a statistics block for a representative member of the organization.

BLACKLOCK LORESEEKERS

Formerly a small collection of rogues and wizards dedicated to unearthing lost scraps of knowledge, the Blacklock Loreseekers have become a large and powerful organization of adventurers. The guild has chapterhouses in nearly every major city and many large towns, as well as in smaller outposts in outlying communities. As it has grown, the guild has become more focused on the mercantile aspects of adventuring, finding lost tombs and ancient artifacts with an eye toward profit rather than knowledge.

The Blacklock Loreseekers take their name from the guild's founder, a dwarf adventurer by the name of Kurgarn Blacklock. Kurgarn long sought leads to the whereabouts of an artifact held sacred by his clan, and after he grew too old to continue adventuring himself, he formed the loreseekers to guide the efforts of younger mercenaries. Although Kurgan always saw the organiza-

---

EMPHASIZING AN ORGANIZATION WITHIN A CAMPAIGN

Creating interesting and consistent organizations adds a great deal to a campaign world, but a DM must choose when and how to introduce such organizations very carefully. If they are mentioned too often, these organizations might become more important in the player's eyes than the DM intends, but if they are relegated to the background and not mentioned enough, players forget them quickly and the DM's work in incorporating them into the world becomes wasted effort. Here are a few ways to gracefully include reminders of an organization's importance and flavor in a campaign.

Rumors: Entirely under the DM's control, rumors of a guild's activity can remind players of a guild's importance, provide adventure opportunities, and remind characters who belong to the organization that they have concerns beyond the needs of their own adventuring group.

Leadership Feat: Any character who belongs to an organization should gain cohorts and followers who also belong to the organization.

Architecture and Geography: Merely mentioning that the characters are passing the compound of the Order of Illumination as they travel through a town reminds them that the organization has an important role in the community and the campaign. Taking time to describe its size or its architecture gives the players further clues about the group, and such details make them more likely to remember the organization when they encounter it in a later adventure.

NPCs: Nonplayer characters are the most useful tool to convey the importance of an organization, and they can help a DM describe or emphasize a group in several ways.

Small Favors: Because NPCs are the most noticeable representatives of an organization, players will come to trust a group of NPC members to do them small favors because of that affiliation. For example, an innkeeper who is clearly affiliated with the Daggerspell Guardians might allow the player characters to stay at a 5% discount—even if they're not members themselves—if they have helped the organization or have done notable good deeds in the past.

Small Hindrances: Like those who do small favors for the party, NPCs who pose small (noncombat) hindrances because of their affiliations build the feel and flavor of the organization quickly.

Aspiring Members: One of the best ways to emphasize an organization in a campaign is to present a visible example of the kind of person who would want to join the group. The eager young paladin who wants to join the Order of Illumination might emphasize the organization's extreme approach to law and righteousness and the somewhat naïve outlook that accompanies their approach.

Former Members: Another great way to highlight an organization is to present one of its castoffs. Whether this means introducing an exile who returns to take revenge or a more complex figure whose departure was more amicable, an NPC who is a former member of an organization provides an excellent way to clarify the group's stance on subtle points or emphasize how the group punishes those who violate its ideals or laws.

Buyers of Extra Loot: A subtle way to make an organization's presence felt is to have its members buy the PCs' extra loot. If the Nightsong Guild buys all fifteen of the masterwork rapiers that the adventurers hauled out of the last dungeon, it reminds the party of the guild's presence without overemphasizing their importance.

tion as primarily focused on amassing knowledge, in the long years since his death, the guild has become far more concerned with the acquisition and resale of valuable treasures and magic items.

Although the Loreseekers' focus on profit makes some suspicious of their motives, the group remains an adventuring-oriented organization and does not engage in thievery or other criminal activities. The guild offers its members ready access to adventuring leads of all kinds, and its minimal entrance requirements make it an excellent way for young explorers to find like-minded souls and learn of challenges suited to their limited experience.

Joining the Blacklock Loreseekers: The Blacklock Loreseekers require that members pay a 10 gp annual fee and register the name of their adventuring group. All members of a party must be members of the guild for any of the characters to gain the benefits described below.

Character Benefits: Loreseeker-affiliated adventuring groups gain a 5% discount on lodging in any city with a Loreseekers chapterhouse, access to the many small libraries maintained in these chapterhouses, a ready source of adventuring leads and, perhaps most importantly, maps. The Loreseekers actively collect maps, and members are free to copy (but not remove) maps stored in the chapterhouse libraries. Members also can treat any community with a chapterhouse as one size larger for purposes of determining the community's gold piece limit. (See page 137 of the *Dungeon Master's Guide* for more information on community size and gold piece spending limits.) This benefit allows members to sell more valuable items in smaller communities, and often presents them with more purchasing options as well.

The guild is particularly good at making the heroic work of its members known to the common folk, and the DM should award small circumstance bonuses on the Diplomacy and Intimidate checks made by guild members against those who have heard of their exploits.

In general, these bonuses should never be more than +2 and shouldn't be awarded until the member has advanced to 6th level or higher.

Roleplaying Suggestions: Most members of the Blacklock Loreseekers adventure because they hope to grow rich from the treasure they find, and the guild heavily stresses the mercantile aspects of adventuring. Most guild members prefer to have some guaranteed pay for their efforts, and often seek rich or noble patrons. In roleplaying situations, a guild member is likely to look for ways to profit from an adventuring group's efforts and emphasize that the danger of adventuring must come with reward.

A small portion of the guild, mostly comprising low-level wizards and bards, still focuses its efforts on amassing knowledge. These members are typically quieter, bookish sorts who travel with other guild members for physical protection during adventures and for the benefits that the guild provides.

Typical Member: The typical Blacklock Loreseeker is a low-level rogue, fighter, or warrior who has completed one or two small adventuring goals and decided to join the guild. The membership includes several powerful adventurers and adventuring groups, many of whom are now more focused on individual goals and interests than on the guild's. Although most members have a level or two in the three classes mentioned, the guild includes a broad range of individuals with levels in nearly every character class. Many rangers join to act as overland guides and to gain access to the guild's excellent maps, but virtually no druids are members.

Although the group takes its name from an individual, many chapterhouses have started to feature black locks on their doors as a sign of their allegiance to the guild. This recent trend started well after the death of Kurgarn Blacklock, and it is not yet a reliable way to identify a chapterhouse.

Blacklock Loreseekers symbol

Illus. by C. Lukacs

Prestige Classes: Although no specific prestige class is associated with the Blacklock Loreseekers, members do tend toward certain choices. Perhaps unsurprisingly, the loremaster prestige class is popular among the high-level wizards and clerics affiliated with the guild. Likewise, the many members with levels in rogue aspire to the dungeon delver prestige class.

Lore of the Guild: The *key of night*, an artifact that was long sought by founder Kurgarn Blacklock, was once the focus of the guild's efforts, and new members still dream of unlocking its great power. The guild has pursued many rumors of the key's whereabouts since its founding, and has met with many frustrating failures. The best information that the guild has on the key now points to one of two locations: the hoard of the black dragon Iyriddelmirev (described in *Draconomicon*) or the ruins of the ancient drow city Neggazzoth. Both the dragon and the ruined drow city are formidable enough challenges that no Loreseeker-affiliated adventurers have tried to verify these theories.

A Blacklock Loreseeker Campaign: The Blacklock Loreseekers accept members of all classes and levels, making the organization an easy way to find and form an adventuring group. For this reason, the Loreseekers provide an excellent way to begin a campaign and to unite the characters. Although the guild has a relatively simple agenda (buying and selling the proceeds of its members' adventures), it can provide an interesting backdrop for a campaign of any level. Its ability to provide adventure leads is limitless, and the characters' differing motivations for adventuring should provide an interesting contrast to the guild's interests throughout the campaign

Sample Blacklock Loreseeker

Fidran: Human male rogue 3; CR 3; Medium humanoid; HD 3d6+3; hp 16; Init +2; Spd 30 ft.; AC 17, touch 12, flat-footed 15; Base Atk +2; Grp +3; Atk or Full Atk +5 melee (1d6+1/19–20, masterwork short sword) or +5 ranged (1d6+1/×3, masterwork composite shortbow); SA sneak attack +2d6; SQ evasion, trap sense +1, trapfinding; AL N; SV Fort +2, Ref +5, Will +3; Str 13, Dex 15, Con 12, Int 10, Wis 14, Cha 8.

Skills and Feats: Climb +6, Craft (stonemasonry) +6, Disable Device +6, Hide +7, Knowledge (dungeoneering) +3, Spot +4, Move Silently +7, Open Lock +8, Search +6, Spot +10; Alertness, Blind-Fight, Weapon Finesse.

Language: Common.

Sneak Attack (Ex): Fidran deals an extra 2d6 points of damage on any successful attack against flat-footed or flanked targets, or against a target that has been denied its Dexterity bonus for any reason. This damage also applies to ranged attacks against targets up to 30 feet away. Creatures with concealment, creatures without discernible anatomies, and creatures immune to extra damage from critical hits are all immune to sneak attacks. Fidran can choose to deliver nonlethal damage with his sneak attack, but only when using a weapon designed for that purpose, such as a sap (blackjack).

Evasion (Ex): If Fidran is exposed to any effect that normally allows him to attempt a Reflex saving throw for half damage, he takes no damage with a successful saving throw.

Trapfinding: Fidran can find, disarm, or bypass traps with a DC of 20 or higher. He can use the Search skill to find, and the Disable Device skill to disarm, magic traps (DC 25 + the level of the spell used to create it). If his Disable Device result exceeds the trap's DC by 10 or more, he discovers how to bypass the trap without triggering or disarming it.

Possessions: +1 *chain shirt*, masterwork short sword, masterwork composite shortbow (+1 Str bonus) with 20 arrows, *potion of cure moderate wounds*, 35 gp.

THE BLOODHOUNDS

The organization known as the Bloodhounds is dedicated to finding people and bringing them to justice (or whatever fate awaits them). Some members limit themselves to tracking down criminals; others

Illus. by D. Kovacs

are willing to hunt anyone for a client who can pay the price. The group's leaders don't concern themselves with such issues, only with maintaining the organization's reputation as the place to go to find someone.

Bloodhounds can take any assignments they choose. Some jobs come directly from clients who contact individual members. Others come through the grapevine, since members pass word to each other. Individuals are fiercely competitive, and if one succeeds where another has failed, the winner gloats over the victory. In fact, members often tell each other about the assignments they've taken, in effect challenging to beat them to the mark (their quarry). Members may work together, but most work alone or with nonmembers so that word spreads of their personal fame. Thus, whenever several Bloodhounds form a posse to catch a particularly elusive foe, word spreads far and wide.

Despite this rivalry, when a mark is too important to go free, a member can spread the word of a "free" bounty among the Bloodhounds. This means that any member who brings in the mark can claim the prize. Members who spread free bounties lose no face in the organization for doing so.

Bloodhounds resent the concept of giving their earnings to anyone. Thus, the organization does not demand a portion of its members' income. No official guildhalls or strongholds exist because no self-respecting member would limit herself to one base of operations.

Since so many of the group's marks are human, rangers who have taken humans as favored enemies have an advantage in assignments. As a result, a large percentage of the membership is nonhuman, and differing alignments are rarely an impediment to teaming up. In fact, rumor has it that a good-aligned female elf and an evil-aligned male gnoll regularly work together, since between them they can function in any society. The gulf between their alignments is spanned by the bridge of their common goals.

Joining the Bloodhounds: Membership in the Bloodhounds is by invitation only. Members report on capable trackers they encounter in their travels, and from these reports, the organization's leaders select candidates for membership. A member of the group tracks each candidate surreptitiously for a while. If the agent reports that the candidate has the necessary fervor and talents, the leaders offer her a chance to try out for membership. A candidate who actually notices an agent following her is almost guaranteed an offer.

To be accepted for membership, the candidate must track a member considerably more experienced than herself. The quarry makes the job difficult by leaving false trails, telling locals deceitful stories, and even hiring brigands to ambush the candidate along the way. The member must not assist the candidate in this task; otherwise, the test is void. A candidate who succeeds in finding the target passes the test and may join the organization.

Character Benefits: Player characters who belong to the Bloodhounds gain access to many adventure leads, potentially lucrative commissions, and a loose network of allied trackers. Although the Bloodhounds organization as a whole does not take a stand in moral or political matters, the group still serves as a useful meeting place for like-minded adventurers.

Roleplaying Suggestions: Bloodhounds are direct but cautious in their personal interactions. They make a habit of sizing up every creature they meet, because

Bloodhounds symbol

Illus. by C. Lukacs

anyone might someday be a mark. This attitude can make them seem distant, and the solitary lives that most lead reinforce this impression.

Typical Member: Almost all Bloodhounds have at least one level of ranger, and most are single-class rangers of 5th to 8th level. The organization has a small membership, but each individual is a capable survivalist and tracker.

Prestige Classes: The bloodhound prestige class is greatly favored by members of the organization. The few who attain high levels in that class serve as the standard by which other trackers are judged. Members who work in exclusively urban areas sometimes prefer the vigilante prestige class, which offers excellent information-gathering abilities that often are more useful in a setting where physical tracks and the like are easily obscured.

Lore of the Guild: The Bloodhounds have a nearly unblemished record, having successfully caught every mark they've pursued except for a half-dragon sorcerer named Zerin the Flayed. Zerin has used a combination of powerful spells and physical might to elude three high-level Bloodhounds, two of which he managed to slay over the course of prolonged and exhausting battles. Unwilling to throw lives away, the guild leadership continues to ponder ways to complete the dangerous commission without asking for outside assistance and thereby weakening the guild's reputation.

A Bloodhound Campaign: An organization as results-oriented as the Bloodhounds lends itself to a campaign in many ways. In a campaign with one or more guildmember PCs, several adventures should involve pursuing marks on behalf of the guild, but deviating from this formula is also important. Because they never give up on a mark, the Bloodhounds also make excellent antagonists for mid- to high-level adventurers. Constant pursuit by experienced trackers can make even the most powerful party feel harried and troubled. However, the Bloodhounds are best used as a recurring minor threat rather than as the major antagonist of a campaign.

Sample Bloodhound

Sharla Redbow: Female half-elf ranger 5; CR 5; Medium humanoid (elf); HD 5d8+5; hp 31; Init +3; Spd 30 ft.; AC 17, touch 13, flat-footed 14; Base Atk +5; Grp +6; Atk +7 melee (2d6+1/19–20, masterwork greatsword) or +9 ranged (1d8+1/×3, +1 composite longbow); Full Atk +7 melee (2d6+1/19–20, masterwork greatsword) or +7/+7 ranged (1d8+1/×3, +1 composite longbow); SA favored enemy humans +4, favored enemy orcs +2; SQ animal companion (riding dog), animal companion benefits, half-

elf traits, low-light vision, wild empathy +4 (+0 magical beasts); AL NG; SV Fort +5, Ref +7, Will +3; Str 12, Dex 16, Con 13, Int 10, Wis 14, Cha 8.

Skills and Feats: Diplomacy +1, Gather Information +7, Hide +11, Listen +6, Move Silently +11, Search +8, Spot +11, Survival +10 (+12 following tracks); Endurance[B], Investigator, Point Blank Shot, Rapid Shot[B], Track[B].

Languages: Common, Elven.

Favored Enemy (Ex): Sharla gains a +4 bonus on her Bluff, Listen, Sense Motive, Spot, and Survival checks when using these skills against humans. She gains the same bonus on weapon damage.

Against orcs, she gains a +2 bonus on these skill checks and on weapon damage rolls.

Animal Companion (Ex): Sharla has a war-trained riding dog named Dauntless as an animal companion. Dauntless's abilities and characteristics are summarized below.

Animal Companion Benefits: Sharla and Dauntless enjoy the link and share spells special qualities.

Link (Ex): Sharla can handle Dauntless as a free action. She also gains a +4 circumstance bonus on all wild empathy checks and Handle Animal checks made regarding her riding dog.

Share Spells (Ex): Sharla can have any spell she casts on herself also affect Dauntless if the latter is within 5 feet at the time. She can also cast a spell with a target of "You" on her animal companion.

Half-Elf Traits: Half-elves have immunity to magic sleep effects. For all effects related to race, a half-elf is considered an elf.

Ranger Spell Prepared (caster level 2nd): 1st—*longstrider*.

Possessions: Mithral shirt, masterwork greatsword, +1 composite longbow (+1 Str bonus), 10 cold iron arrows, 9 silver arrows, 1 +1 holy arrow, 17 gp.

Dauntless, Riding Dog Companion: CR —; Medium animal; HD 2d8+4; hp 13; Init +2; Spd 40 ft.; AC 16, touch 12, flat-footed 14; Base Atk +1; Grp +3; Atk +3 melee (1d6+3, bite); Full Atk +3 melee (1d6+3, bite); SA trip; SQ bonus trick, low-light vision, scent; AL N; SV Fort +5, Ref +5, Will +1; Str 15, Dex 15, Con 15, Int 2, Wis 12, Cha 6.

Skills and Feats: Jump +8, Listen +5, Spot +5, Survival +1 (+5 when tracking by scent), Swim +3; Alertness, Track[B].

Trip (Ex): A war-trained riding dog that hits with a bite attack can attempt to trip the opponent (+1 check modifier) as a free action without making a touch attack or provoking attacks of opportunity. If the attempt fails, the opponent cannot react to trip the dog.

Tricks: Dauntless knows the following tricks (including his bonus trick): assist attack†, assist track†, attack, down, heel, stay, track.

† New trick described on page 100.

Scent (Ex): Can detect approaching enemies, sniff out hidden foes, and track by sense of smell. See page 314 of the *Monster Manual*.

COLLEGE OF CONCRESCENT LORE

This bardic college, one of the largest in existence, focuses on the acquisition of hidden lore, particularly of the historical or magical variety. Its members eagerly page through dusty tomes, seeking to uncover secrets about long-dead societies, strange magical rituals, and other unusual topics. A council of three administrators runs the college. Each has been a member for ten years or more and embraced at least three fields of study during that time. These three no longer conduct active research and instead review others' findings, distribute reports, and maintain the membership list.

History and magical lore are the bread and butter of this college. Many of the world's greatest historians are at least adjunct members, and several powerful wizards have joined the college to gain access to its magic texts. The study of history here has an archeological bent, and members focus on understanding the languages, architecture, rituals, and leaders of lost civilizations.

All significant member findings, from new discoveries to the results of long-term studies, are circulated to colleagues with relevant specialties. Thus, a member who specializes in Kreidikan history might receive field notes from an expedition to a newly discovered Kreidikan ruin, a translation of a poem that mentions a Kreidikan

College of Concrescent Lore symbol

sorcerer-king, and a fragment of the *fountain of blood* spell that Kreidikan mages favor, all in the same month. Exactly who receives the results of particularly important research is currently the subject of bitter debate—some researchers are livid because they did not receive copies of studies they thought were vital to their own research. The college also has a strict policy that prohibits sharing research results with anyone outside the college. Centuries ago, this "no eyes but the learned" policy caused a split in the organization that led to the formation of the Talespinners League (see page 182).

"Until we accumulate infinity" is the college's motto. Collegians wear dark robes with red stripes encircling the upper sleeves.

The College of Concrescent Lore maintains a friendly rivalry with a similar group, the College of Arcanobiological Studies, and a not-so-friendly rivalry with the Talespinners League. However, members give the cold shoulder to wizards "who just want to copy our books for the spells, not because they want to *learn* anything."

Joining the College of Concrescent Lore: Candidates for membership must pass a series of examinations to gain admission. Each test is unique, composed of questions posed by collegians with specialties similar to the one the candidate has requested. Because those who contribute to the test tend to be widely scattered, it can take months for the college to prepare an exam and even longer for the contributors to grade it. Those who contributed test questions have the sole authority to admit the candidate, and particularly petty collegians have been known to create unthinkably difficult questions just to keep new blood out of their favorite disciplines.

Passing a typical examination requires the following successful skill checks: DC 25 Knowledge (arcana), DC

25 Knowledge (history), and either DC 15 Knowledge (architecture and engineering) or DC 15 Knowledge (geography). In addition, the candidate must be able to read and write at least one obscure language. Depending on the desired specialty, the DCs may be higher or lower. Retries are allowed, but only to apply for a different specialty.

The initial membership fee is 500 gp, which goes to pay for the creation and grading of the test. Annual dues are 250 gp; active collegians spend much more than this on their research, correspondence with other members, and occasional regional meetings.

Character Benefits: The greatest advantage to membership in this college is access to the volumes of research its members produce each year. Unless they've somehow made enemies among their colleagues, members can count on receiving advance word of every discovery made in their fields.

Members with specific questions also have the right to query members outside their own specialties for information. Answering such a query is rarely a high priority, however, especially if no reason is given for the request.

Roleplaying Suggestions: Members of the college tend to be intelligent, focused on their academic pursuits, and strangely secretive. They prefer to ask questions rather than provide answers. Some nonmembers find this off-putting. Few resent the pursuit of knowledge, but the college's secretive nature sometimes angers those who enjoy a more free-flowing exchange of information. In particular, members of the Talespinners League resent the collegians.

Typical Member: Most of the college's members are mid-level bards, wizards, and experts with maximum ranks in several Knowledge skills. Each member chooses an area of knowledge (such as "The Second Empire of Qirtaia" or "Vordhavian Death Magic") as a specialty upon entering the college, but this choice can be changed as often as once a year. The administrators update the list of members and specialties annually and circulate that document, called a "yearbook," to the current membership.

Prestige Classes: Wizards and clerics who become members of the college typically aspire to take levels in the loremaster prestige class. Bards occasionally pursue the loremaster class, but more aspire to the virtuoso prestige class, hoping to continue the development of their musical abilities while focusing on their knowledge and magical talents.

Lore of the Guild: The college focuses on acquiring knowledge developed by others rather than performing specific deeds or accomplishing heroic missions. Although a few of the organization's younger members remain active adventurers in order to seek out and recover lost tomes, scrolls, and other repositories of knowledge, the bulk of the guild's membership spends most of its time in quiet study. Nonetheless, the famous split between the Talespinners League and the college is occasionally the subject of debate in all levels of society, especially by those concerned with the distribution of magical knowledge or ancient relics.

A College of Concrescent Lore Campaign: A campaign centering on the acquisition of hidden and magical lore offers great potential for parties of any level and class composition, especially if the party must deal with internal and external conflicts around whether or not to share that knowledge. In most cases, a campaign that includes the college should also include the rivalry between the college and the Talespinners League. These two organizations might even be represented in the same party, with the members of the college struggling to safeguard any lore the party finds and the talespinners pushing the group to share the knowledge with any who express an interest.

Sample Concrescent Lorist

Pyrus: Male elf diviner 5; CR 5; Medium humanoid; HD 5d4; hp 14; Init +1; Spd 30 ft.; AC 11, touch 11, flat-footed 10; Base Atk +2; Grp +1; Atk or Full Atk +1 melee (1d6–1, quarterstaff); SA spells; SQ elf traits, familiar (cat), familiar benefits, low-light vision; AL N; SV Fort +1, Ref +2, Will +6 (+8 against enchantments); Str 8, Dex 12, Con 10, Int 16, Wis 14, Cha 13.

Skills and Feats: Decipher Script +10, Knowledge (arcana) +11, Knowledge (geography) +8, Knowledge (history) +11, Knowledge (the planes) +11, Listen +6, Move Silently +4, Search +5, Spellcraft +13, Spot +6; Alertness, Craft Wondrous Item[B], Open Minded† (2), Scribe Scroll[B].

† New feat described on page 111.

Languages: Common, Elven; Draconic, Giant, Sylvan.

Familiar: Pyrus's familiar is a cat named Quill. The familiar uses the better of its own and Pyrus's base save bonuses. The creature's abilities and characteristics are summarized below.

Familiar Benefits: Pyrus gains special benefits from having a familiar. This creature grants Pyrus a +3 bonus on Move Silently checks (included in the above statistics). Pyrus and Quill enjoy the empathic link and share spells special qualities.

Alertness (Ex): Quill grants its master Alertness as long as it is within 5 feet.

Empathic Link (Su): Pyrus can communicate telepathically with his familiar at a distance of up to 1 mile. The master has the same connection to an item or a place that the familiar does.

Share Spells (Su): Pyrus can have any spell he casts on himself also affect his familiar if the latter is within 5 feet at the time. He can also cast a spell with a target of "You" on his familiar.

Diviner Spells Prepared (caster level 5th; prohibited school evocation): 0—*arcane mark, detect magic, detect poison, mage hand, read magic;* 1st—*alarm, color spray* (DC 14), *comprehend languages, identify, unseen servant;* 2nd—*detect thoughts, fox's cunning, glitterdust* (DC 15), *locate object;* 3rd—*arcane sight, deep slumber* (DC 16), *tongues.*

Spellbook: as above plus 0—all except evocation; 1st—*erase, mage armor, mount, obscuring mist;* 2nd—*arcane lock, mirror image;* 3rd— *dispel magic, gaseous form.*

Possessions: ring of protection +1, quarterstaff, arcane scroll of *greater magic weapon,* arcane scroll of *dispel magic,* spellbook, spell component pouch, 4 pearls (100 gp each), 60 pp.

Quill, Cat Familiar: CR —; Tiny animal; HD 6; hp 23; Init +2; Spd 30 ft.; AC 17, touch 14, flat-footed 15; Base Atk +5; Grp –7; Atk +9 melee (1d2–4, claw) Full Atk +9 melee (1d2–4, 2 claws); SA deliver touch spells; SQ improved evasion, low-light vision, scent, speak with master; AL NG; SV Fort +3, Ref +5, Will +9; Str 3, Dex 15, Con 10, Int 8; Wis 12, Cha 7.

Skills and Feats: Balance +10, Climb +6, Hide +16*, Jump +10, Listen +3, Move Silently +8, Spot +6; Stealthy, Weapon Finesse[B].

Deliver Touch Spells (Su): Quill can deliver touch spells for Pyrus (see Familiars, page 52 of the *Player's Handbook*).

Improved Evasion (Ex): If Quill is exposed to any effect that normally allows it to attempt a Reflex saving throw for half damage, it takes no damage with a successful saving throw and half damage if the saving throw fails.

Speak with Master (Ex): Quill can communicate verbally with Pyrus. Other creatures do not understand the communication without magical help.

Skills: Cats have a +4 racial bonus on Climb, Hide, and Move Silently checks and a +8 racial bonus on Jump checks. Cats have a +8 racial bonus on Balance checks. They use their Dexterity modifier instead of their Strength modifier for Climb and Jump checks. *In areas of tall grass or heavy undergrowth, the Hide bonus rises to +8.

DAGGERSPELL GUARDIANS

Exotic spellcasters who wield matched pairs of daggers and deadly magical powers, the Daggerspell Guardians use their varied abilities to promote their own fair-minded sense of justice. Individual members lead adventuring parties, root out evil hiding in civilized communities, and act as self-appointed investigators and law enforcers when necessary. Groups rarely act together and instead concentrate on training new members, researching new spells, or perfecting new aspects of their unusual fighting style.

Daggerspell Guardians symbol

One of the most interesting aspects of the Daggerspell Guardians is their emphasis on both martial and magical power. Although they still focus on spellcasting as their primary means of dealing with foes, they all wield their twin daggers with surprising skill. Some use their spells to enhance their physical abilities and then enter melee, casting amid a whirlwind of flashing knives. Others use their spells to bring down foes and reveal their deadly sets of knives only when an enemy seeks to target a spellcaster who might look physically weak.

Two spellcasting prestige classes are associated with the guild. The daggerspell shapers (see page 36) appeal to druids and other divine spellcasters, and the daggerspell mages (see page 31) appeal to wizards and other arcane spellcasters. These two groups within the organization are separate only in the type of spells they cast and the

Illus. by C. Lukacs

training they undergo. In all other aspects, the two hold equal sway and numbers within the organization.

Joining the Daggerspell Guardians: The Daggerspell Guardians have never been large in number, and although they always look for new members, they take only a small percentage of those who wish to join. Although candidates need not be of a high enough level to join one of the daggerspell prestige classes, they usually need some spellcasting ability, a Dexterity score high enough to eventually train in using two weapons at once, and most important, a sincere and compassionate drive to do good. Those hoping to join the guild must find a sponsor—usually an existing member of the guild, but other noted good-aligned adventurers or community leaders occasionally sponsor members as well—and petition the guild leadership for membership. The leadership usually sends a representative to talk with the candidate and measure her abilities. Once accepted, a candidate usually receives training from another member of the Daggerspell Guardians.

Character Benefits: Characters who belong to the Daggerspell Guardians find that opinions vary greatly about their activities and the organization to which they belong. In many places, a member receives a small (typically 5%) discount on mundane services such as lodging and food, as long as she makes it known that she belongs to the guild. On the other hand, some local rulers don't enjoy the idea of a group of powerful warrior-spellcasters roaming through the realm and following their own moral code, however noble their purpose. These rulers, and those who serve them, have been known to turn a cold shoulder to a Guardian's requests and to devise other subtle means of encouraging her to continue her travels in another realm.

Many communities welcome the arrival of a Guardian, but they are also likely to approach her with requests for assistance. Whether the area is beset by a powerful bugbear tribe or one farmer claims that another has infringed on his fields, a guardian is someone outside the immediate community who can provide help and judgment.

Roleplaying Suggestions: Most Daggerspell Guardians are calm and reserved. While they are confident in their ability to decide between right and wrong, they hold their judgment, in part to gauge the reactions of others and to better learn about their adventuring companions. They also do it to ensure that they make a correct assessment of the situation. In most roleplaying situations, a member should ask more questions than she answers and keep her opinions to herself until asked. Another good approach to roleplaying a Guardian is to emphasize her caution when dealing with other people without letting this devolve into outright suspicion.

Typical Member: The typical Daggerspell Guardian is a low-level druid or wizard who has made the unorthodox choice of learning to fight with two weapons—specifically, two daggers. After she has finished her apprenticeship, a member often joins a group of adventurers. The guild encourages members to fight against evil actively, discover lost treasures or wells of power, and work diligently to oppose monstrous creatures that threaten civilized areas. When not adventuring, a typical member lives off the proceeds of past adventures, although a few find work in law enforcement or as special investigators in communities where crime is a problem. Because they are so focused on spellcasting, Guardians often spend time with other guild members, learning more advanced spells or practicing their fighting techniques.

Prestige Classes: Most members of the Daggerspell Guardians aspire to become either daggerspell shapers or daggerspell mages, depending on whether they have an affinity for divine or arcane magic. Members of the daggerspell prestige classes are afforded special respect in the guild, and even those with little spellcasting ability see themselves on the path to entering one of the prestige classes. The highest-ranking members have levels in one of the two daggerspell classes, but powerful and influential members of other classes have forged lasting alliances with the Guardians without taking levels in either prestige class or formally becoming members of the organization.

Lore of the Guild: Many of the greatest treasures of the Daggerspell Guardians are, not surprisingly, pairs of matched magic daggers of great power. Two of the most treasured of these daggersw, the *emerald knives of seven truths*, were lost years ago by a daggerspell shaper who fell in battle against a powerful vampire named Malkan Ry-Ul. Both the knives and the vampire have been missing for many years, but recently travelers from the east have reported that a great city there is haunted by a killer who leaves strange green cuts on the bodies of his victims—a signature side effect of the magic of the emerald knives.

A Daggerspell Campaign: A campaign centering on the Daggerspell Guardians need include only one or two PCs who belong to the guild. Members often adventure with nonmembers, and the group's activities provide an excellent set of hooks for good characters of any class. Because the guild believes in very lofty and open versions of good and justice, a campaign focused on the Daggerspell Guardians should include adventures that deal with subtle moral problems and emphasize that the characters form their own definition of the word "good." A mix of dungeon adventuring and political intrigue is the perfect blend for a group affiliated with the guild.

Sample Daggerspell Guardian

Seraphina Thorngage: Female halfling druid 3; CR 3; Small humanoid; HD 3d8; hp 17; Init +3; Spd 20 ft.; AC 17, touch 14, flat-footed 14; Base Atk +2; Grp –2; Atk +6 melee (1d3, masterwork dagger); Full Atk +4 melee (1d3, 2 masterwork daggers); SA spells; SQ animal companion (eagle), animal companion benefits, trackless step, wild empathy +4 (+0 magical beasts), woodland stride; AL NG; SV Fort +4, Ref +5, Will +6 (+8 against fear); Str 10, Dex 16, Con 10, Int 8, Wis 15, Cha 13.

Skills and Feats: Climb +2, Concentration +6, Handle Animal +6, Hide +6, Jump –2, Knowledge (nature) +2, Listen +4, Move Silently +5, Survival +4; Two-Weapon Fighting, Weapon Finesse.

Languages: Common, Druidic, Halfling.

Animal Companion (Ex): Seraphina has an eagle named Keeneye as an animal companion. Keeneye's abilities and characteristics are summarized below.

Animal Companion Benefits: Seraphina and Keeneye enjoy the link and share spells special qualities.

Link (Ex): Seraphina can handle Keeneye as a free action. She also gains a +4 circumstance bonus on all wild empathy checks and Handle Animal checks made regarding her eagle.

Share Spells (Ex): Seraphina can have any spell she casts on herself also affect her animal companion if the latter is within 5 feet at the time. She can also cast a spell with a target of "You" on her animal companion.

Trackless Step (Ex): Seraphina leaves no trail in natural surroundings and cannot be tracked.

Woodland Stride (Ex): Seraphina can move through natural thorns, briars, overgrown areas, and similar terrain at her normal speed and without damage or other impairment. However, thorns, briars, and overgrown areas that are magically manipulated to impede motion still affect her.

Druid Spells Prepared (caster level 3rd): 0—*create water, detect magic, light, purify food and drink;* 1st—*cure light wounds, longstrider, magic fang;* 2nd—*cat's grace, daggerspell stance†.*

† New spell described on page 145.

Possessions: +1 *leather armor,* two masterwork daggers, 2 *potions of cure moderate wounds,* spell component pouch, 75 gp.

Keeneye, Eagle Companion: CR —; Small animal; HD 3d8+3; hp 16; Init +3; Spd 10 ft., fly 80 ft. (average); AC 17, touch 14, flat-footed 14; Base Atk +2; Grp –2; Atk +7 melee (1d4, talon); Full Atk +7 melee (1d4, 2 talons) and +1 melee (1d4, bite); SA —; SQ bonus tricks (2), evasion, low-light vision; AL N; SV Fort +4, Ref +6, Will +3; Str 11, Dex 16, Con 12, Int 2, Wis 14, Cha 6.

Skills and Feats: Listen +2, Spot +16; Weapon Finesse, Weapon Focus (talons).

Evasion (Ex): If Keeneye is exposed to any effect that normally allows it to attempt a Reflex saving throw for half damage, it takes no damage with a successful saving throw.

Tricks: Keeneye knows the following tricks (including his bonus tricks): assist attack†, assist defend†, attack, defend, down, heel, hunt†, seek.

† New tricks described on page 100.

DRAGONBLADE NINJA CLAN

Long ago, a powerful family suffered a great betrayal at the hands of an ambitious prince. After the treachery, few of the family members or their most trusted retainers were left standing, and those who were still alive faced a hard choice: sacrifice their honor by fleeing, or perish against the overwhelming forces of their united enemies. While the bulk of the family stood and fought, a few of the remaining warriors were entrusted with escorting some of the family's youngest members to a secret estate far to the north.

This ancient holding was kept hidden from all but a few of the family's highest-ranking members because it concealed a secret greater than even the family's honor. A dying silver dragon of great power had charged the family with guarding its last clutch of eggs, but due to a terrible curse put upon them by a rival dragon, the eggs took centuries to hatch. When the remaining family members arrived at the estate, they realized that they could not fail such a trust despite the setbacks they had encountered, and so they resigned themselves to fading into obscurity rather than appealing to other rivals of the traitorous prince for aid.

Because the premier warriors of the family had fallen in the betrayal, the clan was left without martial teachings of its own. After a few quiet centuries, the family name had been forgotten by all but a few jaded historians who toiled deep in the vast imperial libraries. Eventually the silver dragon's eggs hatched, and as the dragons matured they learned of their great debt to the family. The young dragons left, and many human generations passed before one returned with a gift. Now grown to great power, the dragon Silverwing offered knowledge of the fighting techniques of a long-lost group of warriors who had mastered subtle skills.

After long periods of training under Silverwing's tutelage, the new family warriors began to exact their vengeance for crimes long forgotten by the rest of the empire. They earned the name dragonblade ninjas from those few bystanders who saw them fight and lived to speak of it afterward. Within a few years, every last descendant of the traitorous prince had been killed, and the family's vengeance was complete.

His debt repaid, Silverwing left the family to make his own choices about his role in the world. Generations later, the family still remains in hiding, although it now recruits a few trusted individuals into its ranks every few years. Without the dragon's guidance or the burning quest of vengeance to drive it, however, the family's will has fragmented, and its warriors pursue diverse and sometimes conflicting goals. Some wish to reveal themselves and claim their right as a prominent family. Others wish to remain in hiding and use their skills for profit and adventure. Still others take an even more sinister path, selling their lethal skills as assassins to anyone who can pay their high fees.

Joining the Dragonblade Ninja Clan:
The vast majority of Dragonblade Ninja Clan members are born into the organization, but the group is not closed to outsiders. The clan remains very protective of its secrets and the identities of its most powerful leaders, but it still extends membership invitations to those who prove to be worthy allies and loyal companions. These rare instances of acceptance into the clan often involve a wandering dragonblade warrior who adventures with trusted companions and, after his comrades have proven their worth time and time again, invites them into the clan. Membership in the Dragonblade Ninja Clan is a

Dragonblade Ninja Clan symbol

lifelong commitment, and it is never to be undertaken lightly.

Character Benefits: The Dragonblade Ninja Clan offers access to many strange items and fighting techniques not available to other characters. Consider allowing members access to a small selection of prestige classes and items from the *Oriental Adventures* supplement even if they are not normally available in your campaign world. This access might include the ninja class described in Chapter 1 of this book, if you don't choose to make it available to all characters in the campaign.

Roleplaying Suggestions: Most dragonblade ninjas remain honest and honorable, despite the setbacks that their clan has suffered and despite the fact that their training favors stealth and assassination rather than open warfare.

Typical Member: Many members of the Dragonblade Ninja Clan have at least one level in ninja, although a fair portion are rogues, experts, or warriors. They spend the majority of their time tending to the quieter pursuits of the clan, such as guarding its hidden fortresses and performing basic acts of espionage that allow the clan to maintain its secrecy while remaining informed about the world.

Prestige Classes: The highest-level members of the Dragonblade Ninja Clan often take levels in the ghost-faced killer, assassin, or shadowdancer prestige classes. These classes represent three very different approaches to missions, adventuring, and killing that members of the clan espouse. Those who follow the path of the ghost-faced killer see their abilities as a powerful tool to use with deliberate purpose. Those who pursue the path of the assassin see their skills as the perfect commodity to sell to the highest bidder, caring less about issues of morality. Those who seek to attain levels in the shadowdancer prestige class have a much looser approach to the clan and its honor (although they still carefully maintain their oaths of secrecy) and prefer lives of adventure to lives of intrigue.

Lore of the Guild: The founding of the Dragonblade Ninja Clan is the stuff of legend, but many recent deeds attributed to the clan are worthy of discussion. In fact, tales of the clan's activities are so popular with portions of the common populace that bards now recount these tales in song and story, and every village has at least one local tough who intimates that he has special knowledge of the clan and its activities. Many of the recent tales involve the death of a young half-elf named Krialla and the disappearance of her magic sword *Nightbloom*. Krialla, an adventurer who had enjoyed a few minor successes, apparently came upon the powerful sword in the hands of a gravely wounded warrior as she was returning from an adventure. Rather than render aid, the half-elf took advantage of the warrior's wounded state and seized the sword for her own. Although the warrior was too weak to resist, he promised that within a year ghosts would come to claim the sword and take his revenge. With Krialla now dead and the weapon missing, many of the common folk have concluded that the warrior was a dragonblade ninja, and that whoever now wields *Nightbloom* also must be a member of the vaunted clan.

A Dragonblade Ninja Clan Campaign: Because of its varied and sometimes conflicting interests, the Dragonblade Ninja Clan offers a fascinating center for a campaign. Characters can attempt to guide the family's interests, flee from the family to pursue their own goals and adventures, or even join the organization later in their careers and filter the tensions within the clan through their own experiences.

Sample Dragonblade Ninja

Li Fan: Male human ninja 3; CR 3; Medium humanoid; HD 3d6+3; hp 16; Init +6; Spd 30 ft.; AC 14, touch 14, flat-footed 12; Base Atk +2; Grp +3; Atk or Full Atk +4 melee (1d6+2/19–20, short sword) or +4 melee (1d6/×3, masterwork shortbow); SA *ki* power 3/day, sudden strike +2d6, SQ ghost step, poison use, trapfinding; AL N; SV Fort +2, Ref +5, Will +3; Str 12, Dex 15, Con 13, Int 10, Wis 14, Cha 8.

Skills and Feats: Balance +7, Climb +5, Disable Device +10, Hide +8, Jump +3, Move Silently +8, Open Lock +7, Search +4, Spot +8, Tumble +8; Dodge, Improved Initiative, Tactile Trapsmith†.

† New feat described on page 112.

Language: Common.

Ghost Step (Su): Li can spend one daily use of his *ki* power to become invisible for 1 round. Using this ability is a swift action (see page 137) that does not provoke attacks of opportunity.

Ki Power (Su): Li can use his *ki* power three times per day, and only if he is wearing no armor and is unencum-

bered. Because he is a 3rd-level ninja, his only *ki* power is ghost step.

As long as Li's *ki* pool isn't empty (that is, as long as he has at least one daily use remaining), he gains a +2 bonus on his Will saves.

Poison Use (Ex): Li never risks accidentally poisoning himself when applying poison to a weapon.

Sudden Strike (Ex): Li deals an extra 2d6 points of damage on any successful attack against flat-footed or flanked targets, or against a target that has been denied its Dexterity bonus for any reason. This damage also applies to ranged attacks against targets up to 30 feet away. Creatures with concealment, creatures without discernible anatomies, and creatures immune to extra damage from critical hits are all immune to sudden strikes.

Trapfinding (Ex): Li can find, disarm, or bypass traps with a DC of 20 or higher. He can use the Search skill to find, and the Disable Device skill to disarm, magic traps (DC 25 + the level of the spell used to create it). If his Disable Device result exceeds the trap's DC by 10 or more, he discovers how to bypass the trap without triggering or disarming it.

Possessions: +1 *short sword*, masterwork shortbow with 20 arrows, masterwork thieves' tools, 1 dose of greenblood oil.

EYES OF THE OVERKING

As one of the premier information-gathering and espionage groups in the world, the Eyes of the Overking are respected and even feared by the few who know they exist. Born in service to a legend, the guild devotes itself to preparing the world for the return of the Overking, a near-mythical figure who supposedly once held the human, elf, and dwarf people united as one nation for hundreds of years. The Eyes focus on espionage and information-gathering because their teachings hold that they will be responsible for helping the newly risen Overking see the world as it really is and for keeping him apprised of the most important matters while he builds and protects a new united realm.

In practical terms, the Eyes of the Overking stray far from these roots and remain the most effective intelligence organization for several neighboring kingdoms. The guild holds that these kingdoms are the lost fragments of the Overking's great kingdom, but that fact (if it's true) has little meaning to the rulers of the realms. These rulers cautiously pay the organization for its excellent intelligence work and its apparently loyal stance on national issues. Although the kingdoms that the Eyes serve occasionally have conflicts between them, the organization never betrays confidences between one kingdom and another and often works to keep nations on friendly terms (the better to prepare for their eventual reunification).

This approach makes the Eyes a subtle but powerful force for order in much of the world. They often put their influence and contacts to work directly against evil cults, kingdoms, and even powerful evil individuals. While the organization remains focused on peace and unity, it is far from wholly good, and its agents do not hesitate to use blackmail, extortion, or even assassination to maintain peaceful relations between the diverse rulers that they support.

Although many individual members join and serve the organization for much more practical reasons, the core of the organization remains focused on the Overking's return.

Joining the Eyes of the Overking: The Eyes of the Overking constantly work to build new contacts, especially among fledgling adventurers. These contacts include those with the potential to join the guild, those most likely to obtain rare or valuable information in the future, and those worthy of notice should they turn to crime. The Eyes prefer to approach potential members through intermediaries first, measuring a potential recruit's skill and resourcefulness while ensuring that she is likely to remain trustworthy. Whenever possible, they attempt to recruit entire adventuring groups, knowing that each individual in the group is more likely to remain loyal to the organization if she knows that her friends have also pledged themselves to the guild.

Character Benefits: Characters who belong to the Eyes of the Overking have access to missions and secret information beyond the reach of most other characters. The guild works tirelessly to track criminals, spy on the nobility, and defend the kingdom through all manner of espionage acts. These activities benefit PCs associated with the guild by providing endless adventure opportunities, but even more important, they provide connections and contacts among the highest ranks of the kingdom's nobility. Depending on a member's character level and past successes, the organization should be able to provide an avenue through which she can have access to those in power within a community.

Roleplaying Suggestions: The Eyes of the Overking maintain a veil of secrecy even though knowledge of their existence has generally spread throughout the populace. This policy prevents characters from revealing their affiliation with the organization in all but the most trying or important circumstances. Therefore, membership has little direct effect on most roleplaying encounters except to emphasize the need for discretion. In general, members are observant, efficient, and personable. One trait that the Eyes stress is the ability to act swiftly and decisively when needed. For this reason, members of the organization remain deceptively calm for long periods of time and then burst into short periods of activity. Once an agent decides to commit to a course of action, there is no holding back, and her swiftness often catches opponents by surprise.

Typical Member: The typical member of the Eyes of the Overking is a low-level rogue, bard, or scout. Because such individuals are often skilled in both disguise and melee combat, they work in subtle ways to keep the organization's leadership apprised of criminal and political events within the kingdom. They occasionally add numbers to an important raid led by a higher-level member of the organization, and they often serve as guards in the organization's safe houses and headquarters.

Prestige Classes: High-level members of the Eyes of the Overking are spies of consummate skill, but few use

Eyes of the Overking symbol

Illus. by C. Lukacs

exactly the same techniques. Most of the mid- and high-level members are rogues or ninjas, but many have levels in a prestige class as well. Members prefer training as spymasters, shadowminds, vigilantes, and bloodhounds, but they also take levels in prestige classes less obviously associated with espionage, such as loremaster.

Lore of the Guild: Although the Eyes of the Overking serve many good-aligned rulers well, their existence rests on the belief that the rightful Overking will rise again. Members renew a vow each year to devote their efforts to readying the world for the Overking's return. Most of the legends of the guild's exploits, therefore, involve daring acts in search of the final resting place of the Overking or steps to make the world ready for his return.

An Eyes of the Overking Campaign: As one of the premier intelligence-gathering and espionage agencies in the world, the Eyes of the Overking offers great potential for use as the center of a campaign, as one aspect of a complex setting, or even as a major antagonist capable of challenging a party of any level. Campaigns in which the PCs are affiliated with the Eyes usually stress themes of nationalism and potentially deal with the return of the Overking himself. Campaigns that include the organization as a major antagonist feature foes who know more about the political and criminal powers in the world than the PCs do, and should constantly present the players with surprising twists and plots by members of the organization.

If a suitable figure does not exist in the history of your campaign world, the Eyes of the Overking need not be tied to a long-dead ruler. Simply substitute a powerful living figure, and change the name of the organization to match.

Sample Eyes of the Overking Member

Shauna Edwit: Female half-elf rogue 4; CR 4; Medium humanoid (elf), HD 4d6+4, hp 20, Init +3; Spd 30 ft.; AC 16, touch 13, flat-footed 16; Base Atk +3; Grp +2; Atk or Full Atk +7 melee (1d6/18–20, +1 rapier); SA sneak attack +2d6; SQ evasion, low-light vision, half-elf traits, trap sense +1, trapfinding, uncanny dodge; AL LN; SV Fort +2; Ref +7, Will +1; Str 8, Dex 16, Con 12, Int 13, Wis 10, Cha 14.

Languages: Common, Elven; Dwarven.

Skills and Feats: Bluff +9, Diplomacy +14, Disguise +11 (+13 acting in character), Gather Information +4, Intimidate +4, Knowledge (nobility and royalty) +6, Listen +8, Search +2, Sense Motive +9, Sleight of Hand +12, Spot +1, Tumble +10; Negotiator, Weapon Finesse.

Sneak Attack (Ex): Shauna deals an extra 2d6 points of damage on any successful attack against flat-footed or flanked targets, or against a target that has been denied its Dexterity bonus for any reason. This damage also applies to ranged attacks against targets up to 30 feet away. Creatures with concealment, creatures without discernible anatomies, and creatures immune to extra damage from critical hits are all immune to sneak attacks. Shauna can choose to deliver nonlethal damage with her sneak attack, but only when using a weapon designed for that purpose, such as a sap (blackjack).

Evasion (Ex): If Shauna is exposed to any effect that normally allows her to attempt a Reflex saving throw for half damage, she takes no damage with a successful saving throw.

Half-Elf Traits: Half-elves have immunity to magic sleep effects. For all effects related to race, a half-elf is considered an elf.

Trapfinding (Ex): Shauna can find, disarm, or bypass traps with a DC of 20 or higher. She can use the Search skill to find, and the Disable Device skill to disarm, magic traps (DC 25 + the level of the spell used to create it). If her Disable Device result exceeds the trap's DC by 10 or more, she discovers how to bypass the trap without triggering or disarming it.

Uncanny Dodge (Ex): Shauna retains her Dexterity bonus to AC even when flat-footed or targeted by an unseen foe (she still loses her Dexterity bonus if paralyzed or otherwise immobile).

Possessions: Masterwork studded leather armor, +1 rapier, 2 potions of eagle's splendor, disguise kit, 80 gp.

GRAYHAUNT INVESTIGATORS

A few years ago, a group of moderately successful adventurers turned their skills to investigation and private crime solving. After a few quick successes, they started receiving more investigative work than they could ever handle themselves, and they saw the potential to profitably expand to new communities. The group immediately focused its efforts on the business and organizational aspects of recruiting low- and mid-level adventurers with analytical minds and the right mix of skills.

In the short years since its founding, the Grayhaunt Investigators guild has spread to five major cities spanning several nations and now coordinates hundreds of functioning investigative teams. These teams resemble adventuring groups, but they emphasize careful observation and good detective work (including the use of divination magic) rather than sheer combat power.

The guild takes its unusual name from its willingness to handle murder cases and its high level of expertise in discovering and countering the machinations of powerful undead creatures.

Joining the Grayhaunt Investigators: The Grayhaunt Investigators accept applications for membership throughout the year. Candidates must prove their investigative skills by solving a series of puzzles and traps prepared by the guild. Applicants are allowed to participate in this test as a team, because the guild encourages its investigators to work in teams at all times. Each team passes or fails the entrance test as a group, but in rare cases when one applicant is clearly superior to the rest of the team, the guild has been known to make exceptions. Joining the guild costs nothing, but members are expected to accept at least two guild-endorsed investigations each year and pay 5% of the commissions earned on such investigations.

Character Benefits: Characters who belong to the Grayhaunt Investigators have ready access to commissions and adventure leads, as well as the ability to quickly find experts on a wide range of academic topics. The guild maintains robust relationships with experts and sages in nearly every field, and guild members often consult these knowledgeable individuals free of the usual charges. For extreme cases or long research projects, investigators must still pay their own fees, but the guild picks up 10% of such costs as long as the character is a member in good standing and has successfully completed at least one investigation in the last year.

Roleplaying Suggestions: Investigators employed by the guild must have sharp, analytical minds, and their speech and mannerisms reflect this. They speak in precise sentences, observe before they interact in most situations, and spend a great deal of time questioning conclusions that might seem certain to others.

Illus. by C. Lukacs

Grayhaunt Investigators symbol

Typical Member: Most investigators have levels in rogue, wizard, or ranger, although the guild also allows members of other classes to join if they work well with an investigative team. Members often devote their skill points to improving their Search, Spot, Listen, and Sense Motive skills before allocating points to other skills. Rogues in the guild often focus on improving their Open Lock and Disable Device skills.

Prestige Classes: While no single prestige class is associated with the guild, many provide special abilities that aid investigators in their missions. Spellcasters aspire to classes that provide them with an excellent base of Knowledge skills or divination powers. Some rogues and rangers aim for classes such as the bloodhound or spymaster instead.

Lore of the Guild: As a relatively new guild, the Grayhaunt Investigators boast few of the tales that similar-sized guilds celebrate. The guild has proven to be quite effective at its chosen missions, however, and stories of its expertise continue to grow.

A Grayhaunt Investigator Campaign: Because the guild encourages its members to work in teams, the Grayhaunt Investigators make an excellent uniting and driving force for a campaign that features a fair amount of investigation or puzzle solving.

Sample Grayhaunt Investigator

Diesa Ungart: Female dwarf rogue 5; CR 5; Medium humanoid; HD 5d6; hp 20; Init +2; Spd 20 ft.; AC 17, touch 12, flat-footed 17; Base Atk +3; Grp +3; Atk or Full Atk +4 melee (1d6 nonlethal, masterwork sap) or +4 melee (1d3 nonlethal, masterwork whip); Space/Reach 5 ft./5 ft. (15 ft. with whip); SA sneak attack +3d6; SQ darkvision 60 ft., dwarf traits, evasion, trap sense +1, trapfinding, uncanny dodge; AL LN; SV Fort +1* (+3 against poison), Ref +6*, Will +3*; Str 10, Dex 14, Con 10, Int 13, Wis 14, Cha 12.

Skills and Feats: Decipher Script +9, Diplomacy +3, Disable Device +11, Gather Information +11, Knowledge (local) +9, Listen +10, Open Lock +12, Search +9 (+14 to find secret doors, traps, and similar concealed objects), Sense Motive +10, Spot +10; Combat Expertise, Exotic Weapon Proficiency (whip).

Languages: Common, Dwarven; Gnome.

Sneak Attack (Ex): Diesa deals an extra 3d6 points of damage on any successful attack against flat-footed or flanked targets, or against a target that has been denied its Dexterity bonus for any reason. This damage also applies to ranged attacks against targets up to 30 feet away. Creatures with concealment, creatures without discernible anatomies, and creatures immune to extra damage from critical hits are all immune to sneak attacks. Diesa can choose to deliver nonlethal damage with her sneak attack, but only when using a weapon designed for that purpose, such as a sap (blackjack).

Dwarf Traits: Dwarves have stonecunning, which grants them a +2 racial bonus on Search checks to notice unusual stonework. A dwarf who merely comes within 10 feet of it can make a Search check as if actively searching.

When standing on the ground, dwarves are exceptionally stable and have a +4 bonus on ability checks made to resist being bull rushed or tripped. They have a +1 racial bonus on attack rolls against orcs and goblinoids. Dwarves have a +4 racial bonus to Armor Class against giants. Their race also gives them a +2 bonus on Appraise or Craft checks that are related to stone or metal items.

*Dwarves have a +2 racial bonus on saving throws against spells and spell-like effects.

Evasion (Ex): If Diesa is exposed to any effect that normally allows her to attempt a Reflex saving throw for half damage, she takes no damage with a successful saving throw.

Trapfinding (Ex): Diesa can find, disarm, or bypass traps with a DC of 20 or higher. She can use the Search skill to find, and the Disable Device skill to disarm, magic traps (DC 25 + the level of the spell used to create it). If her Disable Device result exceeds the trap's DC by 10 or more, she discovers how to bypass the trap without triggering or disarming it.

Uncanny Dodge (Ex): Diesa retains her Dexterity bonus to AC even when flat-footed or targeted by an unseen foe (she still loses her Dexterity bonus if paralyzed or otherwise immobile).

Possessions: +1 chain shirt, masterwork whip, masterwork sap, *goggles of minute seeing*, 2 *potions of cat's grace*, masterwork thieves' tools, 2 *potions of hide from animals*, 400 gp.

LEAGUE OF BOOT AND TRAIL

Members of this unusual organization regard every road as a classroom and every inn as a laboratory. Devoted to travel for its own sake, they accumulate little lore but see much of the world—and worlds beyond as well. Anything of interest to travelers is of interest to the League of Boot and Trail. Although it is organized much like a college, the guild offers no formal academic studies; instead, its members are renowned guides and scouts. They know, for example, the last known location of a floating isle, the best way to cross the Midnight Desert, and which church now rules the province of Aramador.

Because its members are rarely in the same place for long, the League of Boot and Trail has little formal organization and no central leadership. Nearly every city of any size has a league station, where members can file reports on their travels, conduct research for future journeys, and share drinks and tales of the road. A senior member serves as station head at each location. If a crisis affects the guild as a whole, as many station heads as possible meet somewhere and reach a solution by consensus.

Each league member must help to run a league station for one month out of every year. The most senior league member of a given month's working group serves as station head.

Each member who stops at a league station must file a report describing his or her travels since the last station stop. The report should include hazards, weather conditions, encounters, and any other information that might prove useful to other travelers.

Each of the guild's stations bears a red boot symbol. This same symbol also appears as a tattoo on each league member's left forearm. Though wearing actual red boots is not required, most members do put red trim on their boots. In addition, every member carves two small notches in each boot heel so as to leave distinctive tracks.

Occasionally, league members band together to bring to justice to anyone who displays a league tattoo but isn't actually a member. The league pays handsomely for such services out of its own coffers, but most members would take on such tasks even without pay to protect the league's reputation.

For the most part, the League of Boot and Trail has few dealings with other organizations. However, its members gladly swap stories with any members of the Talespinners League they happen to encounter. Those who make their living catering to travelers treat Boot and Trail members well in the hope that more red-booted business will come their way.

Joining the League of Boot and Trail: To join the League of Boot and Trail, a prospective member must present a station head with three gifts, all originating from at least 300 miles away. One of these gifts must be a case of liquor worth at least 250 gp, one must be an object of art worth at least 300 gp, and the last must be a riding horse or warhorse. If the gifts meet all the requirements, the candidate is tattooed with the red boot and accepted as a member after a riotous party.

Dues are 500 gp per year, payable at the time of the member's one-month service at a station.

Character Benefits: The most significant benefit of membership in the League of Boot and Trail is access to the reports of previous travelers. A league station's information about travel hazards, monsters, and current events isn't fully up to date, of course, but it's highly reliable.

Any member can use the accommodations at a league station free of charge. Many league stations operate general stores that sell adventuring gear for 20% less than the going rate to those bearing the red tattoo, as well as horses for half price. In addition, merchants and innkeepers along important trade routes often offer discounts to travelers with red boot tattoos, hoping for good reviews on the next set of league reports.

Roleplaying Suggestions: Members of the League of Boot and Trail fall into two distinct social groups: solitary wanderers who prefer life on the road because it gives them the sense of anonymity they find comfortable, and more outgoing personalities who enjoy travel because it provides a wealth of new experiences and new chances for social interaction.

The first group remains reserved in most conversations, content to learn about others by watching rather than through direct interaction. These members aren't recluses and are not deficient in social skills—they simply prefer life on the road over the deeper roots that come with settling in one place. The one month per year that they must work at a league station and the sense of belonging that the league provides are often the only sense of home and family that these individuals need.

Most members of the league are much more outgoing, using their many travels to meet interesting individuals, exchange stories with new friends, and learn of distant places from other experienced travelers. These individuals often start conversations with complete strangers, and their broad range of personal experience makes them excellent diplomats.

Typical Member: Most members of the League of Boot and Trail are low-level bards, although a fair number of scouts and rangers also become members. The rest of the membership is made up of small numbers of each of the other PC and NPC classes. Most members prefer to spend much of the spring and summer traveling, although those required to serve at league stations during these prime traveling months do so willingly.

Prestige Classes: Many of the league's members do not prefer a specific prestige class, instead viewing their love for travel and their involvement in the league as something separate from the development of their combat, magical, or professional skills. The most common prestige class among league members is the horizon walker (see page 189 of the *Dungeon Master's Guide*). Members who develop an affinity for mounted travel sometimes pursue the wild plains outrider prestige class (see page 92).

ADVENTURERS AND THE LEAGUE

The League of Boot and Trail counts many adventurers among its members. Some of the world's most legendary adventurers recruit for their expeditions by posting offers of employment on the walls of league station common rooms. After all, anyone heading beyond the edge of the world should have some seasoned travelers along. A typical league station might have the following postings.

- Travel with Karil Minick to the mirrored ice caves of Suskana. Hiring experienced guards, scouts, healers, and arcanists. Pays 10 gp/day plus a share of treasure gained, after expenses. Assemble here at summer's end.
- MISSING: Ahn of Azath, somewhere along NW portion of Griever's Trail. 5,000 gp reward.
- Are you brave enough to enter the Valley of Mostarek? I, Duncan Sameth, offer only your fair share of glory—the chance that your name will appear in the epics sung by minstrels yet unborn. Meet me here on the 13th of Flocktime.
- AUCTION: The survivors of Vinto Uredsky's expedition to Yezelri have returned. Their treasures from this wondrous land will be auctioned here on 18 Flocktime, along with surplus expedition gear. Lots can be viewed at dawn, with bidding to begin at noon.
- Royal-commissioned explorer seeks guides and guards for one-month exploration to undisclosed location. Top wages guaranteed.

Lore of the Guild: Although the league is more interested in collecting tales of its members' recent travels than in unearthing lost lore or discovering magical treasure, plenty of legends tell of the exploits of league members. One of the most controversial claims is that Fharlanghn, the deity of travel, was a league member when he was still a mortal. But most members, including almost every follower of Fharlanghn, claim that the league was actually founded by a well-disguised avatar of Fharlanghn.

A League of Boot and Trail Campaign: Travel is an exciting challenge that many adventurers enjoy, and the League of Boot and Trail makes an excellent element of any campaign that features a great deal of overland travel. Even in campaigns with more modest amounts of travel, the league's open policies and ingrained desire to reach new places can provide an excellent rationale for introducing exotic character options such as monstrous characters, cultural prestige classes that originated in distant lands, and even new standard classes such as the ninja or the samurai.

Sample League of Boot and Trail Member

Skirna Longwalker: Female gnome scout 4; CR 4; Small humanoid; HD 4d8; hp 21; Init +3; Spd 30 ft.; AC 19, touch 14, flat-footed 19; Base Atk +3; Grp +0; Atk or Full Atk +5 melee (1d4+1, masterwork short sword) or +7 ranged (1d4+1, composite shortbow); SA skirmish +1d6/+1 AC, spell-like abilities; SQ battle fortitude +1, gnome traits, low-light vision, trackless step, trapfinding, uncanny dodge; AL CG; SV Fort +2*, Ref +7*, Will +2*; Str 12, Dex 16, Con 10, Int 10, Wis 12, Cha 13.

Skills and Feats: Climb +8, Diplomacy +3, Escape Artist +10, Gather Information +7, Hide +14, Knowledge (geography) +4, Knowledge (nature) +6, Listen +10, Sense Motive +8, Survival +8, Use Rope +3 (+5 involving bindings); Dodge, Mobility[B], Skill Focus (Gather Information).

Languages: Common, Gnome.

Skirmish (Ex): Skirna gains a +1 competence bonus to AC and deals an extra 1d6 points of damage on all attacks during any round in which she moves at least 10 feet. The extra damage applies only to attacks taken during her turn. This damage also applies to ranged attacks against targets up to 30 feet away. Creatures with concealment, creatures without discernible anatomies, and creatures immune to extra damage from critical hits are all immune to additional extra damage. Skirna loses this ability when wearing medium or heavy armor or when carrying a medium or heavy load.

Gnome Traits: Gnomes have a +1 racial bonus on attack rolls against kobolds and goblinoids. Gnomes have a +4 racial bonus to Armor Class against giants.

*Gnomes have a +2 racial bonus on saving throws against illusions.

Spell-Like Abilities: 1/day—*dancing lights, ghost sound* (DC 11), *prestidigitation, speak with animals* (burrowing mammal only, duration 1 minute).

Trackless Step (Ex): Skirna leaves no trail in natural surroundings and cannot be tracked.

Trapfinding (Ex): Skirna can find, disarm, or bypass traps with a DC of 20 or higher. She can use the Search skill to find, and the Disable Device skill to disarm, magic traps (DC 25 + the level of the spell used to create it). If her Disable Device result exceeds the trap's DC by 10 or more, she discovers how to bypass the trap without triggering or disarming it.

Uncanny Dodge (Ex): Skirna retains her Dexterity bonus to AC even when flat-footed or targeted by an unseen foe (she still loses her Dexterity bonus if paralyzed or otherwise immobile).

Possessions: +1 *mithral shirt*, masterwork short sword, composite shortbow (+1 Str bonus) with 20 masterwork arrows, 2 *potions of cat's grace.*

NIGHTSONG GUILD

The Nightsong Guild has worked within the city for as long as most people can remember—and probably a good deal longer. Its members deal in matters not entirely legal as well as those quite clearly illegal—gambling, smuggling, blackmail, and theft. The guild's reputation is one of extreme skill and competence. It is not feared as much as it is afforded the respect that it has earned. Most would refer to the Nightsong Guild as a thieves' guild, but it is actually a far more extensive group than that. Its membership includes rogues, fighters, bards, wizards, and sorcerers.

Guild members do not take part in violent activities such as extortion or murder, for the guild leadership has long maintained that if you kill or intimidate your clientele, those people cease to make money (and if they don't have money, the guild can't make money). Of course, if one or more of its members are attacked or threatened with violence, the guild is quite clearly capable of dealing with the situation.

League of Boot and Trail symbol

Illus. by C. Lukacs

Joining the Nightsong Guild: Slow to add new members, the Nightsong Guild prefers to work with those it considers potential recruits for several years before actually inviting them to join. Candidates serve as paid informants, freelance burglars, or muscle for hire for long periods of time while their competence and trustworthiness are judged. Although most of these recruits are never told explicitly that they're working for the Nightsong Guild, the group is powerful and notorious enough that most individuals guess correctly where their money comes from.

Members are required to contribute 10% of their earnings to the guild. In return, they have access to extensive resources (see below).

Character Benefits: Within the confines of its home city, the Nightsong Guild can offer its members nearly impenetrable security, well-funded political connections, and access to well-trained and loyal hirelings or followers. Members also have access to the guild's extensive library, training facilities, and workshops. Many places of business in the city offer 10% discounts on services, goods, and equipment to Nightsong Guild members.

These resources can be incredibly useful, but they come with a price. As an efficient and long-lived criminal organization, the Nightsong Guild finds a profit in every activity that it undertakes. If the guild provides a PC with access to a local baron and guarantees that the baron listens to her request, the guild requires in turn that the character undertake a dangerous mission to further cement that baron's willingness to obey the wishes of the guild.

Roleplaying Suggestions: Highly trained and supremely confident, members of the Nightsong Guild remain calm and professional even in the most intense circumstances. They work best in unified teams, and they make a habit of knowing their companions' strengths and weaknesses. They expect quick and competent action from their allies, especially in combat or on a dangerous mission. This combination of expertise and trust makes most members

reserved and stable individuals, and they rarely waste words on trivial matters or debate. When a guild team or adventuring group makes a decision, the member is likely to keep her opinion in reserve until she has heard arguments from several other members, speak up once, and then quickly act on whatever decision is reached by the leader or by consensus.

Typical Member: Most members of the Nightsong Guild are low-level rogues, experts, fighters, or warriors. The rogues and experts serve as the eyes and ears of the organization, and the best and most loyal eventually advance to become members of either the nightsong infiltrator or nightsong enforcer prestige class.

Prestige Classes: The Nightsong Guild includes members with levels in an eclectic collection of prestige classes, but most belong to the nightsong infiltrator or nightsong enforcer classes. These two prestige classes epitomize the organization of the guild itself. Two-thirds of the group, led by the nightsong infiltrators, spy on the rich and noble, ferret out secrets for use in blackmail, perform daring acts of burglary, and attempt to divert the efforts of law enforcement. The remaining one-third of the guild's membership, led by the nightsong enforcers, provides the group with the muscle that it needs to protect itself.

Lore of the Guild: Lenias D'Brule, noblewoman, adventurer, and one of the few powerful members of the Nightsong Guild who is open about her guild membership, has recently disappeared. The guild would like this problem to go away permanently. Either Lenias must be found and convinced to tone down her high-profile lifestyle, or the guild must be certain that she will never surface again. Because the guild is busy with its own interests in the city, a few representatives are quietly approaching established adventuring groups to find the noblewoman, deal with those who caused her disappearance, and then confront Lenias herself.

Nightsong Guild symbol

A Nightsong Guild Campaign: Although exceptions exist, the Nightsong Guild shouldn't become a major feature in a campaign until the player characters reach at least 3rd or 4th level. That's because until they've completed a few adventures or missions, they're not likely to attract the attention of the guild. Once they've achieved at least a small amount of success, an adventuring party could find the Nightsong Guild to be an intriguing and powerful patron—or a dangerous and resourceful enemy.

Sample Nightsong Guild Member

Alyson Adair: Female halfling rogue 1/fighter 2; CR 3; Small humanoid; HD 1d6+1 plus 2d10+1; hp 19; Init +7; Spd 20 ft.; AC 18, touch 14, flat-footed 15; Base Atk +2; Grp –1; Atk or Full Atk +7 melee (1d4+1/18–20, masterwork rapier) or +7 ranged (1d8/19–20, masterwork heavy crossbow); SA sneak attack +1d6; SQ trapfinding; AL NE; SV Fort +4, Ref +5, Will +3 (+5 against fear); Str 12, Dex 17, Con 12, Int 10, Wis 13, Cha 8.

Skills and Feats: Balance +7, Climb +9, Hide +11, Intimidate +5, Jump +2, Listen +9, Move Silently +9, Spot +3, Tumble +7; Alertness, Improved Initiative[B], Iron Will, Weapon Finesse[B].

Languages: Common, Halfling.

Sneak Attack (Ex): Alyson deals an extra 1d6 points of damage on any successful attack against flat-footed or flanked targets, or against a target that has been denied its Dexterity bonus for any reason. This damage also applies to ranged attacks against targets up to 30 feet away. Creatures with concealment, creatures without discernible anatomies, and creatures immune to extra damage from critical hits are all immune to sneak attacks. Alyson can choose to deliver nonlethal damage with her sneak attack, but only when using a weapon designed for that purpose, such as a sap (blackjack).

Trapfinding (Ex): Alyson can find, disarm, or bypass traps with a DC of 20 or higher. She can use the Search skill to find, and the Disable Device skill to disarm, magic traps (DC 25 + the level of the spell used to create it). If her Disable Device result exceeds the trap's DC by 10 or more, she discovers how to bypass the trap without triggering or disarming it.

Possessions: Mithral shirt, masterwork rapier, masterwork heavy crossbow with 20 bolts, 2 *potions of cure light wounds*, 30 gp.

ORDER OF ILLUMINATION

Evil might lie behind any door, and shadow might hide in any heart. The Order of Illumination holds this maxim close as it seeks out and destroys evil wherever necessary.

The organization has two main branches, each dedicated to fulfilling one of the order's two functions. The first is to ferret out evil wherever it hides, and it is the shadowbane stalkers who devote themselves to finding hidden evils and piercing the lies of evildoers. The second task is to confront these evils directly, and it is the shadowbane inquisitors who pick up sword and shield and take the fight to evil creatures.

Although many of its members adventure with their comrades (especially in partnerships between a stalker and an inquisitor) and with independent adventuring groups, the Order of Illumination is not an adventuring-oriented organization. The order is far more concerned with finding and combating the evils that hide within civilized communities than it is with finding lost tombs or raiding the lairs of dragons. The comrades are quick to praise such activity when it clearly serves the cause of good, but members are encouraged to look for evil closer to home whenever possible.

Joining the Order of Illumination: Becoming a member of the Order of Illumination is no easy task. A prospective member must prove his or her dedication, purity, and desire to fight evil by fasting for three days. During this trial period, paladins and clerics belonging to the order visit the candidate to pose difficult moral questions, engage in mock combat trials, and repeatedly subject the candidate to *detect evil*, *detect chaos*, and *discern lies* spells. Membership also requires an offering of 100 gp.

A potential member need not meet any specific class or level requirements, but he cannot be evil or chaotic. Although a very small number of neutral characters choose to join, the order's strict requirements and rules

Order of Illumination symbol

Illus. by C. Lukacs

mean that only lawful characters find it appealing for long. The majority of the membership is lawful good, with a significant portion being lawful neutral.

Character Benefits: The resources of the Order of Illumination are vast, but the organization is careful never to put too many of these resources into the hands of one person, however trustworthy that person may seem to be. Player characters who are members can count on shadowbane stalkers to provide a steady stream of rumors about evil or suspicious activity, and can find a safe place to rest and heal in any city that has a cathedral dedicated to the order. The order's intolerance of evil means that it is willing to combat any real threat, but it won't throw lives away needlessly just on the player characters' say-so. If the PCs need help with a particularly evil foe or opposing force, they might be able to appeal to an individual inquisitor, but the DM has the final say in any such activities.

The Order of Illumination greatly covets holy weapons, and it will pay 60% of a weapon's value if it has the holy special ability. Likewise, the order prizes the destruction of evil items and weapons and will pay 60% of the value of any such item turned in by a member. The order sees the procurement of holy items and the destruction of unholy items as among its most important duties.

Roleplaying Suggestions: Personalities vary greatly between the members of the two arms of the Order of Illumination.

Those affiliated with the shadowbane stalkers prefer unobtrusive methods of finding evil. They lace their dialogue with subtle questions, use deceit whenever they feel such behavior is warranted by the greater good, and often hide their affiliation with the order in order to better discover the true intentions of those they meet. Shadowbane stalkers are often quiet individuals who carefully watch the effects that their words and actions have on others. They are just as suspicious and reactionary as the inquisitors, but they are less open and vocal about both of these traits.

Members affiliated with the shadowbane inquisitors, on the other hand, rely on physical power and an unquestioning sense of what's right to battle evil openly. Unwavering in their devotion to what they define as law and good, the inquisitors are blunt speakers who assume guilt or hidden motives in most individuals. They are highly suspicious of others and seem driven more by zeal than by regard for the facts.

Typical Member: Most members of the Order of Illumination are low-level clerics and paladins dedicated to a deity of law, good, destruction, or war. The order's teachings blend these faiths together into a pure quest to rid the world of evil. Most members with more experience end up taking a level or two in rogue and then pursue one of the two prestige classes associated with the order. Although members of other classes join the order all the time, the group encourages new members to begin training as either a cleric or a paladin (if they haven't already done so) to prepare for entry into one of the shadowbane prestige classes. Although a typical member may be too inexperienced to enter those prestige classes, each still thinks of himself or herself as serving one of the two branches. For example, a 1st-level paladin in the service of the order probably thinks of himself as a shadowbane inquisitor-in-training even though he's several levels away from meeting the prestige class prerequisites, while a 1st-level cleric/1st-level rogue who has served the stalkers for a few years considers herself a potential shadowbane stalker even though she might never meet the requirements for the prestige class.

Prestige Classes: The two prestige classes associated with the order represent the pinnacle of the two arms of the group. The shadowbane stalkers ferret out evil, and the shadowbane inquisitors confront evil directly. Both classes require a mix of cleric and rogue (or paladin and rogue) abilities to meet the entry requirements, and these requirements shape the abilities of the bulk of the guild's membership. The order expects all its members to aspire to one of the two classes.

For some characters, the power and purity of the inquisitor is difficult to maintain, and those who fall from its demanding standards often end up becoming some of evil's most powerful and dedicated servants—blackguards. These traitors are a dark blight on the light of the order, and they are its greatest foe. What's worse, such villains often maintain the illusion that they retain their former status and operate from within the order for long periods of time before their evil is finally discovered.

Lore of the Guild: One of the order's most deadly foes, a blackguard known only by rumor and reputation, supposedly works from within the highest ranks of the organization itself. This villain has reportedly killed or subverted any member who has ever come close to discovering his true identity, yet rumors of his existence persist. The order officially denies the existence of such an individual and strictly forbids its members from discussing such rumors. However, paladin comrades use

Illus. by C. Lukacs

detect evil on the membership with surprising frequency, and it is extremely unusual for a member to refuse being the subject of such a spell.

An Order of Illumination Campaign: The Order of Illumination has a complex relationship with the evil that it fights, and a campaign that features one or more members can give the PCs a chance to explore their own definition of good in the light of the extremist stance taken by the group. Likewise, there are many rich roleplaying opportunities in a campaign that features the order as a collection of good-aligned extremists that serve as antagonists of characters who are also good-aligned but have a more tolerant outlook.

Sample Order of Illumination Member

Gabriel Silverbrow: Male human rogue 1/paladin 2; CR 3; Medium humanoid; HD 1d6 plus 2d10; hp 17; Init +1; Spd 30 ft.; AC 16, touch 11, flat-footed 15; Base Atk +2; Grp +4; Atk or Full Atk +5 melee (2d6+3, masterwork greatsword); SA smite evil 1/day, sneak attack +1d6; SQ aura of good, *detect evil*, lay on hands 4/day, trapfinding; AL LG; SV Fort +5, Ref +5, Will +3; Str 14, Dex 12, Con 10, Int 8, Wis 13, Cha 15.

Skills and Feats: Diplomacy +4, Disable Device +5, Gather Information +8, Hide +2, Intimidate +6, Knowledge (religion) +1, Listen +5, Open Lock +7, Search +5, Sense Motive +7; Cleave, Investigator, Power Attack.

Language: Common.

Smite Evil (Su): Once per day, Gabriel can attempt to smite evil with one normal melee attack. He adds +2 to his attack roll and deals 2 additional points of damage.

Sneak Attack (Ex): Gabriel deals an extra 1d6 points of damage on any successful attack against flat-footed or flanked targets, or against a target that has been denied its Dexterity bonus for any reason. This damage also applies to ranged attacks against targets up to 30 feet away. Creatures with concealment, creatures without discernible anatomies, and creatures immune to extra damage from critical hits are all immune to sneak attacks. Gabriel can choose to deliver nonlethal damage with his sneak attack, but only when using a weapon designed for that purpose, such as a sap (blackjack).

Detect Evil (Sp): Gabriel can use *detect evil* at will. See the spell, page 218 of the *Player's Handbook*.

Trapfinding (Ex): Gabriel can find, disarm, or bypass traps with a DC of 20 or higher. He can use the Search skill to find, and the Disable Device skill to disarm, magic traps (DC 25 + the level of the spell used to create it). If his Disable Device result exceeds the trap's DC by 10 or more, he discovers how to bypass the trap without triggering or disarming it.

Possessions: +1 *chain shirt*, masterwork greatsword, 2 *elixirs of hiding*, *potion of cure moderate wounds*, masterwork thieves' tools, 12 gp.

SHADOWMIND GUILD

In the dark corners of the city, an elusive group of psionic spies ply their trade with uncanny skill. The Shadowmind Guild is a tight-knit band of high-level rogue/psions who use their varied skill sets to maintain anonymity while accepting commissions from wealthy and influential patrons. The guild has no single specialty; most of its missions involve stealing something of value, using blackmail or psionic powers to influence the actions of a specific individual, or discovering a prized piece of information.

While they are willing to engage in activities such as theft and blackmail, the shadowminds are not yet wholly evil. They shy away from assassination unless they are avenging a deliberate attack, and they seldom work directly against the good of the kingdom or city in which they reside. The guild has no particular loyalty to monarch or community, but the organization's leaders are smart enough to realize that a group as small as theirs would not likely survive an attack coordinated by a powerful ruler. The guild is willing to risk the enmity of individual nobles or wealthy merchants, but not the ire of an entire kingdom or city.

Because of the guild's shadowy reputation and the fearsome combination of skills its members possess, few are willing to cross the shadowminds, and few can afford their rates. Thus, they often work on their own initiative to gather information, undertake special missions of their own design, and even adventure outside their home territory to hone their skills in different environments and open combat.

Joining the Shadowmind Guild: The exclusive Shadowmind Guild is slow to grant membership to even

Shadowmind Guild symbol

the most trusted of candidates. Membership is by invitation only, and the existing guild members take the time to be sure of the abilities and loyalty of every potential member. Since those with a predilection for both stealth and psionics are rare, the Shadowmind Guild is careful to monitor any such individuals within the city. Once a candidate's varied abilities have developed to the point where she qualifies for the shadowmind prestige class, the guild decides whether or not to extend an invitation. These decisions are complex and depend greatly on the personalities of current guild members, and the DM has a great deal of discretion when resolving such invitations.

Character Benefits: Characters who belong to the Shadowmind Guild gain a +4 bonus on Gather Information checks when in the guild's home city, and they have ready access to two or three nondescript and well-hidden safe houses within the city. These benefits are not to be taken lightly and depend on the good opinion of the other guild members. These privileges are instantly withdrawn from any member who ever openly discusses the guild with nonmembers, whether the act is committed willfully or through incompetence.

Roleplaying Suggestions: Guild members rarely reveal their affiliation with the guild and often act in disguise, making it difficult to categorize their personalities or general behavior. Members must be circumspect in their dealings and refrain from drawing suspicion to themselves as well.

Typical Member: Because its membership is so small and so skilled, the Shadowmind Guild has no typical low-level member as other guilds do. All are of high level and are highly trained, and they all possess unique and varied skill sets. Few members even manifest the same psionic powers, although abilities that enhance stealth or cloud the minds of others are common. For a sample member of the Shadowmind Guild, see Mysk on page 76.

Prestige Classes: Only one prestige class—the shadowmind—is directly associated with the guild, and all members must have at least one level in the class. Some guild members also have levels in another prestige class, typically either the shadowdancer class or a psionic class, but most pursue additional levels in the shadowmind class to the exclusion of others.

Lore of the Guild: Despite the care of individual members to keep their activities secret, a few rumors and tales of the Shadowmind Guild's exploits have reached the general populace. The most common of these describes the fate of a small-minded lord who publicly denounced the guild and devoted much of his personal wealth to finding and destroying the group. The noble not only lost his fortune to a mysterious group of thieves, but he also forgot he ever had such wealth or power. The tale holds that the noble still works peacefully in his city today as a modest tradesman, unaware that the memories he believes are his own are really the result of careful manipulation by the shadowminds.

A Shadowmind Guild Campaign: Although the Shadowmind Guild is small and exclusive, its members have incredibly varied skill sets, making the guild an interesting choice as the focus of a psionics-oriented campaign. However, it's much more likely that only one character in an adventuring party belongs to the guild, and perhaps she even conceals her involvement from most or all of her comrades. The member will have mysterious contacts and a decided advantage when gathering information in the guild's home city, which can be a great boon to a DM looking for ways to introduce adventure leads, rumors, and conflicting information to the PCs.

Because of its small, high-level membership, the Shadowmind Guild does not provide a reasonable challenge for PCs throughout the length of a campaign, and it is best used as a single high-level encounter or as a small group of experts hired by the characters' true foes.

TALESPINNERS LEAGUE

Centuries ago, some members of the College of Concrescent Lore objected on philosophical grounds to the organization's secretive approach to information. Their desire to share information with outsiders literally tore the college in two. The disaffected members formed the Talespinners League, a college devoted to the free flow of information. Since that time, league members have honed their performance skills and branched out beyond the history and arcana studies that Concrescent Lorists favor. Many Talespinners are bards, but occasional arcane spellcasters are also welcome, especially if they are members of the virtuoso prestige class.

The Talespinners League collects every kind of lore imaginable. Not as academic as the College of Concrescent Lore, Talespinners study down-to-earth topics such as the everyday traditions of various cultures. Members spend their time gathering all kinds of information. Rather than relying on academic reports to disperse it, the league embeds its lore within historical or fictitious tales. Any member is free to specialize if desired, but anyone can change specialties at a moment's notice.

The Talespinners League is based on the master-apprentice relationship. New students learn lore from masters and eventually become masters themselves. The masters in each region meet once or twice a year and make any necessary decisions by a simple majority vote. (Usually, there aren't many pressing issues, because league members tend not to involve themselves with politics.) Once that part of the meeting is over, other invited members arrive, and the gathering becomes a grand exercise in tale-swapping. Each member who attends is expected as a matter of courtesy to share (via a tale) any new lore uncovered since the last meeting. Keeping secrets is against the league's code of conduct, but the only penalty for doing so is a lack of tales to tell at the regional meeting. Secretive or troublesome Talespinners are rarely booted out of the league. They just don't get invitations to future meetings, and the rest of the college learns to ignore them.

Talespinners League symbol

The league's motto is "The heart of the tale is in the telling." Talespinners don't wear robes, but many add blue and white tassels to their clothing.

Talespinners regard the College of Concrescent Lore with contempt for "wanting to keep the most interesting things in the world locked up for their private little club." Because they travel a great deal, they are generally cordial toward members of the League of Boot and Trail. In addition, they love to quiz adventurers about the perils they have faced.

Joining the Talespinners League: Because the Talespinners League is nothing more than chains of masters and apprentices, the only prerequisite for membership is gaining a mentor. To achieve this, a candidate must tell the prospective mentor three tales, making a successful DC 25 Perform check for each. One story must be about the candidate, one about a stranger, and the third about

one of the candidate's friends. Choosing tales particularly suited to the listener provides a +2 circumstance bonus on the check. A candidate who fails to impress one mentor can try again with another if desired.

Once a candidate is accepted, his or her apprenticeship proceeds entirely at the mentor's whim. The process typically lasts for several months and involves learning hundreds of new tales and performance techniques. The apprentice earns the title Master Talespinner at the mentor's discretion. Only a Talespinner who has been a master for at least five years can take on apprentices.

The Talespinners League has no official admission fee. However, mentors have been known to hint that a suitably expensive gift speeds the application process along.

Character Benefits: The biggest benefit of membership is access to the college's treasure trove of lore. It's free for the asking, because Talespinners love nothing more than to exchange stories of far-off lands, arcane enigmas, and mysterious creatures. Unlike their academic rivals, however, they lack any organized means of cataloging their lore. Thus, an apprentice's query about a particular item might produce the following sort of reply: "A few years back, someone at the northern meeting mentioned a jade statue just like the one you're asking about. But I can't recall who it was. Kardalius over in Baselton might remember who told that tale . . ."

Talespinners travel frequently, and they eagerly swap stories and render assistance to fellow collegians, recognizing them by the blue and white tassels they wear. Clever innkeepers look for the tassels, too, and many offer discounts to members who are willing to spin yarns by the fire.

Roleplaying Suggestions: Talespinners love to talk, especially if doing so involves drawing a story that they haven't heard before out of an interesting individual. They

Illus. by C. Lukacs

are open, curious, and usually quite engaging. One who joins an adventuring party often serves as the group's primary negotiator, using his skills to smooth the group's way with local authorities, ferreting out countless adventure leads through his association with the league, and providing a wealth of information through his diverse knowledge.

Despite this common archetype, a few members go against the grain. These unusually introverted individuals approach storytelling as an art form, breaking out of their normally shy behavior only when properly prepared to tell a story. They see the exchange of information in story form as an opportunity to create and inspire. Although they are rare, they often are among the most respected storytellers in the league.

Typical Member: The typical Talespinner is a low-level bard who loves to travel and learn new stories. The membership also includes many low-level wizards (who see the organization as a way to learn of new sources of magical lore) and small numbers of other adventurers who seek knowledge for its own sake.

Prestige Classes: No single prestige class is associated with the Talespinners League, although many of the league's members pursue prestige classes related to their combat abilities rather than their involvement in the group. Many combat-oriented members strive to attain levels in the war chanter prestige class (from *Complete Warrior*), and spellcasters associated with the league often seek out prestige classes that boost their powers of divination or observation.

Lore of the Guild: The Talespinners' split with the College of Concrescent Lore is the most significant event in the League's history. It was the cause of the League's founding and the event that defined its purpose and shaped the outlook of its members.

By its very nature, the Talespinners League is rife with news of recent events, rumors of things to come, and legends of days long past. Recently, however, many members have begun to hunt for information regarding a golden book of lore rumored to have been penned over a thousand years ago. This tome, said to contain the complete history of a long-vanished empire, can supposedly cause the true version of any story that is told near it to appear on its pages. As seekers of the truth, the Talespinners are eager to locate this powerful magic item—if it really exists.

A Talespinners League Campaign: Although the Talespinners League probably serves a campaign best as a background organization to which one or two PCs at most belong, it can serve as the focus of a campaign. If most of the PCs are affiliated with the league, the campaign should feature an abundance of rumors and other information, and the characters might juggle half a dozen adventure leads, at least until they successfully complete a few adventures and focus on a particular branch of lost knowledge or special lore. Such a campaign should include a fair amount of social interaction in addition to the exploration of lost tombs and physical searches for lost tales.

Sample Talespinner

Garret Greenbarrel: Male halfling bard 3; CR 3; Small humanoid; HD 3d6+3; hp 16; Init +2; Spd 20 ft.; AC 17, touch 13, flat-footed 15; Base Atk +2; Grp –3; Atk or Full Atk +3 melee (1d6–1/19–20, masterwork longsword) or +6 ranged (1d6/19–20, masterwork light crossbow); SA spells; SQ bardic knowledge +5, bardic music 3/day (countersong, *fascinate*, inspire competence, inspire courage), halfling traits; AL CG; SV Fort +2, Ref +5, Will +3 (+5 against fear); Str 8, Dex 15, Con 12, Int 14, Wis 10, Cha 15.

Skills and Feats: Bluff +8, Climb +1, Decipher Script +8, Diplomacy +6, Gather Information +8, Jump –3, Knowledge (geography) +5, Knowledge (local) +5, Listen +8, Perform (oratory) +8, Sense Motive +6, Speak Language (Draconic, Giant, Gnome, Goblin, Orc, Sylvan); Extra Music†, Obscure Lore†.

† New feat described in Chapter 3.

Languages: Common, Halfling; Dwarven, Elven.

Bardic Music: Use bardic music three times per day. See the bard class feature, page 29 of the *Player's Handbook*.

Countersong (Su): Use music or poetics to counter magical effects that depend on sound.

Fascinate (Sp): Use music or poetics to cause one or more creatures to become fascinated with him.

Inspire Competence (Su): Use music or poetics to help an ally succeed at a task.

Inspire Courage (Su): Use music or poetics to bolster his allies against fear and improve their combat abilities.

Spells Known (3/2; caster level 3rd): 0—*dancing lights, ghost sound* (DC 12), *light, lullaby* (DC 12), *message*; 1st—*cure light wounds, inspirational boost†, swift expeditious retreat†*.

† New spell described in Chapter 5.

Possessions: Mithral shirt, masterwork longsword, masterwork light crossbow with 20 bolts, *potion of eagle's splendor*, 3 smokesticks, backpack, bedroll, waterskin, 3 days' trail rations, pack mule, 24 pp.

BUILDING AN ORGANIZATION

This section lays out a framework to help you build organizations for your DUNGEONS & DRAGONS campaign. Using a system similar to the town generation rules in the *Dungeon Master's Guide*, you can craft anything from a tiny boating partnership in the local village to a sprawling thieves' guild in your favorite metropolis, including the organization's type and size, dominant alignment, resources available, leadership, racial demographics, and class and level makeup of the entire group.

The organizations detailed earlier in this chapter don't necessarily follow this format, since most are spread across many communities. When using one of these organizations in your game, you may want to use the guidelines below to set up a particular town's or city's branch of the guild.

TABLE 6–1: ORGANIZATION TYPES

d%	Type of Organization	Typical Alignment*
01–40	Trade (roll d% for subtype)	—
01–45	Craft guild	LG, NG, LN, N, LE, NE
46–90	Profession guild	LG, NG, LN, N, LE, NE
91–00	Adventurers guild	Any
41–55	Religious (roll d% for subtype)	—
01–60	Holy order	Any
61–80	Druid shrine	NG, LN, N, CN, NE
81–90	Fringe cult	Any
91–00	Paladin order	LG
56–70	Learning (roll d% for subtype)	—
01–40	University	LG, NG, LN, N, LE, NE
41–55	Bardic college	LG, NG, CG, LN, N, CN
56–75	Monastery	LG, LN, LE
76–85	Spy network	Any
86–00	League of explorers	LG, NG, CG, LN, N, CN
71–80	Magical (roll d% for subtype)	—
01–50	Wizard college	NG, LN, N, CN, NE
51–70	Alchemists conclave	NG, LN, N, CN, NE
71–90	Arcanist academy	NG, LN, N, CN, NE
91–00	Guild of sorcery	NG, LN, N, CN, NE
81–90	Criminal (roll d% for subtype)	—
01–30	Thieves guild	N, CN, LE, NE, CE
31–40	Assassins guild	LE, NE, CE
41–50	Beggars guild	N, CN, LE, NE, CE
51–70	Street gang	N, CN, NE, CE
71–80	Crime syndicate	LN, N, CN, LE, NE, CE
81–90	Smugglers cartel	Any
91–95	Anarchist band	CG, CN, CE
96–100	Freedom fighters	CG, CN, CE
91–95	Reroll twice and combine the results	—
96–100	Other (DM's option)	Any

*See Alignment, below, and Table 6–2 for more details and options.

STEP 1: TYPE

An organization's type describes its role in society, from a simple craft guild to a sprawling crime syndicate. If you haven't already decided on the type of organization you want to create, use Table 6–1: Organization Types to randomly generate this information. The table isn't meant as an exhaustive list of the range of possibilities, but as a spur to your creativity.

STEP 2: ALIGNMENT

Every organization has a default alignment that describes the group's general outlook on moral and ethical issues. Not all members' alignments match this default, but most probably are no more than one step removed.

The alignment of an organization need not match the dominant alignment of its community, although many do. If you haven't already selected your organization's alignment, roll randomly on Table 6–2: Organization Alignment. Most organizations tend to be lawful (the most stable of alignments). Some alignments might not match well with certain organization types (see Table 6–1: Organization Types for typical alignments), but that doesn't mean you can't creatively mix these two elements to form a unique organization, so long as you can come up with a sufficiently persuasive rationale.

TABLE 6–2: ORGANIZATION ALIGNMENT

d%	Organization Alignment
01–25	Same as community's primary power center
26–30	Opposite of community's primary power center*
31–45	Lawful good
46–55	Neutral good
56–60	Chaotic good
61–73	Lawful neutral
74–80	Neutral
81–83	Chaotic neutral
84–93	Lawful evil
94–98	Neutral evil
99–100	Chaotic evil

*If the community's primary power center is neutral, roll again.

Alignment Descriptions

Lawful Good: A lawful good organization strives to help others, but tempers its kindness with devotion to the letter of the law and attention to detail and policies. Many centers of learning are lawful good.

Neutral Good: These organizations seek to help those in need with little regard toward influencing a community's power structure. Many charitable organizations are neutral good.

TABLE 6–4: MEMBERSHIP BY COMMUNITY SIZE

| Community Size | Community Population | Organization Membership[1] | | GP | |
		Minor	Medium	Major	Limit[2]
Thorp	20–80	n/a	n/a	1–2	20 gp
Hamlet	81 400	n/a	1–2	3–5	50 gp
Village	401–900	1–2	3–5	6–10	100 gp
Small town	901–2,000	3–5	6–10	11–25	400 gp
Large town	2,001–5,000	6–10	11–25	26–60	1,500 gp
Small city	5,001–12,000	11–25	26–60	61–125	7,500 gp
Large city	12,001–25,000	26–60	61–125	126–250	20,000 gp
Metropolis	25,001+	61–125	126–250	251+	50,000 gp

1 These numbers can be used to represent how many members exist in a given community; they need not represent the total number of members in the organization.

2 Halve the indicated value for minor organizations, and double it for major organizations.

Chaotic Good: An organization of this alignment works tirelessly to protect people from tyranny. Chaotic good organizations are always trying to do the right thing, but a lack of communication and forethought often causes plans to fail or members of the group to work at cross-purposes. Such a group might serve any function from peaceful protesters to freedom fighters.

Lawful Neutral: Most lawful neutral organizations exist for their own purposes as much as for that of their members. They tend toward bureaucracy and codified regulations, and they stress the need for order above all else. Many trade guilds are lawful neutral.

Neutral: Truly neutral organizations care little for the surrounding community, instead spending their time furthering their own goals. They tend to be the most welcoming of differing viewpoints. Many arcane guilds are neutral, respecting each wizard's right to her own beliefs.

Chaotic Neutral: While most chaotic neutral organizations claim to fight for personal freedoms and against the encroachment of governmental power, many simply exist for the sake of creating contention. A chaotic neutral organization might be a group of vandals, anarchists, or revolutionaries.

Lawful Evil: A lawful evil organization uses the community's laws and regulations to its own benefit, furthering its goals at the expense of those less able to exploit the rules. Perhaps ironically, lawful evil organizations can (and do) exist quite well in lawful good societies, simply because they are willing to follow the laws (unless they can get away with breaking them). Expansionist or monopolistic trade guilds might be lawful evil.

Neutral Evil: A neutral evil organization looks out for the needs of its members above all else. Most thieves guilds are neutral evil.

Chaotic Evil: Such an organization exists solely to help its individual members spread hatred, destruction, and mayhem. A murder cult is one example of a chaotic evil organization.

STEP 3: SIZE

Determine how large the organization is and where it is based. If you haven't already chosen a size based on your campaign needs, roll on Table 6–3: Organization Size. The size (minor, medium, or major) will help you determine the organization's member population.

TABLE 6–3: ORGANIZATION SIZE

d%	Organization Size
01–40	Minor[1]
41–90	Medium[2]
91–100	Major

1 Minor organizations don't exist in thorps or hamlets.

2 Medium organizations don't exist in thorps.

STEP 4: POPULATION AND RESOURCES

After determining the relative size of your organization, use the appropriate column on Table 6–4: Membership by Community Size to determine its population. If you've already decided on the membership's size and population, you can skip this step.

Just like a community, every organization has a gold piece limit to its resources based on its size and population. The gold piece limit is an indicator of the maximum amount of money the organization can afford to spend in any given week, on any one item, or in pursuit of any given objective.

The gold piece limit noted in Table 6–4 is for a medium organization. A minor organization has a gold piece limit of one-half the indicated value, while a major organization has a gold piece limit of twice the indicated value.

To determine the amount of ready cash in an organization, or the total value of any given item of equipment for sale at any given time, multiply half the gp limit by 1/10 of the organization's membership.

STEP 5: DEMOGRAPHICS

To effectively use an organization in play, you must know its composition. The following guidelines allow you to determine the most common classes and races represented and the levels of the various members belonging to the group, from the leader down to the lowest-ranking associates.

Class Demographics

The mix of classes represented in any given organization depends on whether that group is exclusive (limiting its membership almost wholly to a single occupation), mixed (with a dominant class and a small representation of other classes), or integrated (including members from a wide variety of classes).

TABLE 6 5: CLASS MIX

Exclusive	
Primary class	96%
Secondary class	2%
Tertiary class	1%
Other classes	1%
Mixed	
Primary class	79%
Secondary class	9%
Tertiary class	5%
Tertiary class	3%
Tertiary class	2%
Other classes	2%
Integrated	
Primary class	37%
Secondary class	20%
Tertiary class	18%
Tertiary class	10%
Tertiary class	7%
Tertiary class	5%
Other classes	3%

You should decide on a primary class based on the type, alignment, and location of your organization. For instance, most trade-based organizations count experts as their primary class, while religious organizations have adepts, clerics, and other divine spellcasters in the majority. Most thieves guilds are mixed, with a majority of rogues but a fair number of experts, warriors, fighters, bards, and other characters. A typical wizard academy might be exclusive (limiting its membership almost entirely to pure wizards) or mixed (with sorcerers and other arcane casters joining the assemblage). An adventurers guild is likely to be highly integrated, with members of all walks of life. Don't forget to include one or more NPC classes in your demographics, particularly warriors and experts.

Highest-Level Members

Use Table 6–6 and Table 6–7 to determine the highest-level character in the primary class of your organization. Roll the dice indicated for the class that you have determined is primary, and apply the modifier based on the size of the community found in Table 6–9.

For secondary, tertiary, and other classes, use Table 6–8 to determine the highest-level character based on the town size. For instance, in a small city, the highest-level character of the organization's secondary class will be one-half the result derived from Table 6–6 or 6–7, while the highest-level character of the organization's tertiary classes will be one-fourth the normal result. Characters of other classes will be 1st level.

TABLE 6–6: HIGHEST-LEVEL MEMBERS (PC CLASSES)

PC Class	Character Level (Primary Class)
Barbarian	1d4 + community modifier
Bard	1d6 + community modifier
Cleric	1d6 + community modifier
Druid	1d6 + community modifier
Fighter	1d8 + community modifier
Monk	1d4 + community modifier
Paladin	1d3 + community modifier
Ranger	1d3 + community modifier
Rogue	1d8 + community modifier
Sorcerer	1d4 + community modifier
Wizard	1d4 + community modifier

TABLE 6–7: HIGHEST-LEVEL MEMBERS (NPC CLASSES)

NPC Class	Character Level (Primary Class)
Adept	1d6 + community modifier
Aristocrat	1d4 + community modifier
Commoner	4d4 + community modifier
Expert	3d4 + community modifier
Warrior	2d4 + community modifier

In larger communities, there is a chance that the highest-level character in the secondary class will use the normal result from Table 6–6 or 6–7, and a chance that the highest-level character in the tertiary class will be determined just as for the secondary class. The highest-level character in all other classes will be half the result derived for the tertiary class. Round fractional results down, but treat any result of less than 1st level as 1st level.

In any organization, there is a 5% chance that a single member who doesn't belong to the group's primary, secondary, or tertiary classes will have a level equal to (or higher than) the highest-level character in your organization's primary class. This character might represent a "wild card" in the organization, a unique member, or simply a fish out of water.

TABLE 6–8: HIGHEST-LEVEL CHARACTER BY COMMUNITY SIZE

Secondary Class

Up to Small City	Large City	Metropolis
Divide Table 6–6 or 6–7 result by 2	01–75: Divide Table 6–6 or 6–7 result by 2	01–50: Divide Table 6–6 or 6–7 result by 2
	76–100: Use Table 6–6 or 6–7 result	51–100: Use Table 6–6 or 6–7 result

Tertiary Class

Up to Small City	Large City	Metropolis
Divide Table 6–6 or 6–7 result by 4	01–75: As secondary, but divide by 2	01–50: As secondary, but divide by 2
	76–100: Same as secondary	51–100: Same as secondary

*Other Class**

Up to Small City	Large City	Metropolis
Level 1	As tertiary, but divide by 2	As tertiary, but divide by 2

*There is a 5% chance that a single member of a miscellaneous class is calculated as if that character were the highest-level character in the primary class.

TABLE 6–9: COMMUNITY MODIFIERS

Community Size	Community Modifier
Thorp	–3*
Hamlet	–2*
Village	–1
Small town	+0
Large town	+3
Small city	+6
Large city	+9
Metropolis	+12

*A thorp or a hamlet has a 5% chance to add +10 to the modifier of a ranger or druid level.

Total Characters of Each Class

Use the following method to determine the levels of all the characters in an organization of any given class.

If the highest-level character of a given class indicated is 4th level or above, assume that there is one additional character of that class of half that level. If this process results in a character who is 4th level or higher, assume that there are two characters of half that character's level. Continue until the number of 2nd- or 3rd-level characters is generated. Do not generate 1st-level members in this manner.

After you have determined the number of 2nd- and 3rd-level characters of each class, divide the remaining population so that it matches the class demographics of the organization. For instance, if 37% of an organization are rogues, then 37% of the leftover membership are 1st-level rogues. Repeat for each class present in the organization.

You can also round out any organization with a few characters of classes not represented in the organization's typical mix. For instance, even if your thieves guild doesn't have a listing for wizards, you can still add one to the membership. Don't forget to include multiclass or prestige-class characters as appropriate.

Your final membership numbers—particularly the 1st-level characters of PC classes—might not match up well with the expected quantity of that class in the community, as indicated in Chapter 5 of the *Dungeon Master's Guide*. Don't worry too much about this. That book's method of determining the number of characters with PC class levels might be too conservative for your campaign, particularly if you have many cities and metropolises (which are likely to have large, powerful organizations). If you need a reason for this discrepancy, consider the possibility that the organization has drawn a great number of members from outlying towns and villages. Also, remember that many low-level characters might belong to more than one organization.

OPTION: CREATE AN ORGANIZATIONAL STATISTICS BLOCK

Once you've designed your organization, you can use this example to create a statistics block for the group. This step isn't necessary, but it helps you summarize the organization for easy reference.

Name (size): AL [alignment abbreviation]; XX gp resource limit; membership XX [racial mix: isolated, mixed, or integrated] [(race XX%, race XX%, race XX%, and so on)]. The number following each race name is a percentage of the entire membership, not the exact number of individuals of that race.

Authority Figure(s): [Name, gender, race, class, and level for each.]

Important Characters: [Name, gender, race, class, and level (title or position) for each.]

Others: [Class mix: exclusive, mixed, or integrated]; [class and level (XX), class and level (XX), and so on]. The numbers in this entry are the exact numbers of residents of each class.

Notes: Place any special notes about the organization here.

Leader of the Organization

The leader of an organization is usually the highest-level character of the primary class. Roll on Table 6–10: Organization Leader or select an appropriate character to lead the group.

TABLE 6–10: ORGANIZATION LEADER

d%	Leader
01–70	Highest-level character of primary class
71–85	Second-highest-level character of primary class
86–95	Highest-level character (regardless of class)
96–100	Other (DM's choice)

Racial Demographics

Most organizations mirror the local racial mix, though exceptions are common. Use Table 6–11: Racial Demographics, or select an appropriate racial mix for your organization.

TABLE 6–11: RACIAL DEMOGRAPHICS

d%	Demographics
01–60	Same as community[1]
61–90	More isolated than community[2]
91–100	More integrated than community[3]

1 See the Racial Mix of Communities table, page 139 of the *Dungeon Master's Guide*.
2 Use the racial mix one step toward isolated. If the community already uses the isolated racial mix, treat as isolated.
3 Use the racial mix one step toward integrated. If the community already uses the integrated racial mix, treat as integrated.

STEP 6: FLESH OUT THE DETAILS

At this point, all that's left is to breathe life into the framework you've created. Provide the organization with a name, turn your NPCs into full-fledged characters (with personalities and backgrounds as appropriate), and link the organization to your campaign history.

Now's the time to determine other crucial details about the group you've created. Is it a secretive organization whose existence is known only to its members? Even a craft guild might pride itself on secrecy and mystery. How hard or easy is it to join the group? What kind of insignias, code words, or secret handshakes does the group use? Does the group enjoy support (whether public or private) from local authorities, or is it a renegade assembly? Is the organization respected by the populace, or are its members social pariahs?

These and other details are what will transform your organization from a mere collection of numbers into a full-fledged part of your campaign.

APPENDIX: THE EPIC ADVENTURER

The *Player's Handbook* establishes 20th level as the limit of a character's power and experience. The *Dungeon Master's Guide*, however, provides rules for going beyond that limit to 21st level and higher. Such characters are called epic-level characters and use slightly modified rules to govern their interactions.

This section addresses some issues relevant to epic skill-using characters, from becoming an epic character, to advancing to epic levels in prestige classes, to new epic feats.

BECOMING AN EPIC-LEVEL ADVENTURER

The passage from everyday hero to epic hero isn't a given fact of life in all games. Every DM has his or her own opinions about how (or if) to incorporate epic-level characters into the campaign. Assuming that your campaign offers characters the opportunity to achieve 21st level, this section provides some advice for the player and DM of a rogue, ranger, bard, or similar character to use when approaching that point.

More than any other type of character, great adventurers of lore are identified with daring tasks of guile, skill, and sheer chutzpah. Jason led a band of mythic heroes on a great quest for the golden fleece. Orpheus braved the horrors of the underworld with only his musical talent to rescue his beloved Eurydice. The legendary hunter Orion claimed he could kill any animal in the world. Loki stole anything he could get his hands on, including the Golden Apples of Idun and the Necklace of Brisingamen. In order to reach 21st level, an adventurer might have to accomplish a task of such daring that even the gods take notice of his skill.

Another mark of a legendary skilled character is his talent in a particular area of expertise. While anyone with 23 ranks in a single skill might claim to be the best in the world, epic contests involving such skills are the only way of proving such a claim. Whether such a contest takes the form of a series of ever more difficult tasks (such as a set of fiendishly trapped locks that must be opened safely) or a single challenge of titanic proportions (such as swimming across an ocean), the contest must be truly memorable in its scope and difficulty.

You can, of course, use similar goals or quests even for nonepic characters. The accomplishment of a breathtaking mission or the defeat of a great opponent in a test of skill are classic achievements for adventurers of all levels.

EPIC-LEVEL PRESTIGE CLASS CHARACTERS

The *Dungeon Master's Guide* has information on advancing the standard classes beyond 20th level. You can also advance the class level of a ten-level prestige class beyond 10th level, but only if your character level is already 20th or higher. You cannot advance the class level of a class with fewer than ten levels beyond the maximum described for that class, regardless of your character level.

When your epic-level character advances a prestige class beyond 10th level, follow all the rules presented in the *Dungeon Master's Guide*. In addition, you must create an epic-level progression for your prestige class, just as the *Dungeon Master's Guide* presents epic-level progressions for the classes from the *Player's Handbook*. Many, but not all, class features continue to accumulate after 10th level. The following guidelines describe how to create an epic class progression, and are followed by a sample epic progression for the dungeon delver prestige class (see page 42).

— Your base save bonuses and base attack bonus don't increase after character level 20th. Since you can't achieve 11th level or higher in a prestige class without being at least a 21st-level character, there are no columns for base saves or base attacks for these classes beyond 10th level. Instead, use Table 6–18: Epic Save and Epic Attack Bonuses, page 206 of the *Dungeon Master's Guide*, to determine a character's epic bonus on saving throws and attacks.

— You continue to gain Hit Dice and skill points as normal beyond 10th level.

— Generally speaking, any class feature that uses class level as part of a mathematical formula, such as a shadowbane inquisitor's smite damage, continues to increase as normal by class level. However, any prestige class feature that calculates a save DC using class level (such as the ghost-faced killer's frightful attack) should add only half the character's class levels above 10th. Thus, a 14th-level ghost-faced killer's frightful attack would have a DC of 22 (10 + class level up to 10th + 1/2 class levels above 10th) + Charisma modifier. Without this adjustment, the save DCs for epic-level character prestige class abilities increase at a much greater rate than those for normal class abilities.

— For spellcasters, caster level continues to increase after 10th level at the same rate it did during the first ten levels of the prestige class. Thus, a 13th-level vigilante adds 13 to his caster level derived from another class to determine total caster level. However, spells per day don't increase after character level 20th.

— The powers of familiars, special mounts, and animal companions continue to increase as their masters gain levels, if they're based on a formula that includes the character's level.

— Any class features that increase or accumulate as part of a repeated pattern (such as a dishonorable dread pirate's sneak attack) also continue to increase or accumulate after 10th level at the same rate. An exception to this rule is any bonus feat progression granted as a class feature. If you get bonus feats as part of a class feature, these do not increase with epic levels. Instead, these classes get a new bonus feat progression (which varies from class to class; see below).

— In addition to the class features retained from non-epic levels, each class gains a bonus feat every two, three, four, or five levels after 10th. This bonus feat augments

---

BEHIND THE CURTAIN: EPIC LEVELS AND PRESTIGE CLASSES

The epic rules allow you to go beyond the normal level limit in a prestige class, but only if it is a ten-level class. Why can't you add levels to a prestige class with fewer than ten levels?

It's Too Easy: Maxing out a ten-level prestige class takes a lot of time and effort, detracting significantly from your pursuit of the core classes. Even after maxing out a prestige class with only five levels, for instance, you haven't taken more than a short detour from your main class or classes.

It's Not Significant Enough: Characters with ten levels in the assassin prestige class undoubtedly think of themselves as assassins, regardless of the fact that they also have ten levels in one or more other classes. If you've taken fewer than ten levels

in a prestige class, those levels represent a smaller fraction of your character's identity.

It's Hard to Build an Epic Progression: With only a few levels to guide you, it's hard to determine what an appropriate progression of class features would be for the class. The rate of improvement of a special ability might be too fast to extrapolate over an infinite number of levels, or there might simply be too few class features to build a unique epic progression.

That said, if your DM wants to allow a character to gain epic levels in a prestige class with fewer than ten levels in its progression, that's okay. Work together with your DM to create an epic progression for the class (see the Behind the Curtain: Building an Epic Progression sidebar, page 210 of the *Dungeon Master's Guide*).

each class's progression of class features, because not all classes otherwise improve class features after 10th level. These bonus feats are in addition to the feat that every character gets every three levels (as per Table 6–19: Epic Experience and Level-Dependent Benefits, page 206 of the *Dungeon Master's Guide*).

— You don't gain any new class features, because there aren't any new class features described for these levels. Class features with a progression that slows or stops before 10th level and features that have a limited list of options do not improve as you gain epic levels. Likewise, class features that are gained only at a single level do not improve.

SAMPLE PRESTIGE CLASS EPIC PROGRESSION: DUNGEON DELVER

If you plan on venturing into trap-infested dungeon complexes, there's no one better to take along than the epic dungeon delver.

Hit Die: d6.

Skill Points at Each Additional Level: 8 + Int modifier.

Trap Sense (Ex): An epic dungeon delver's bonus on Reflex saves to avoid traps and his dodge bonus to AC against traps increase by 1 for every three levels above 10th.

Augury (Sp): An epic dungeon delver can use *augury* one additional time per day for every three levels above 9th.

Skill Mastery (Ex): An epic dungeon delver can apply the effect of skill mastery to one additional class skill each time he attains a new level.

Blindsense (Ex): An epic dungeon delver can use blindsense one additional time per day for every five levels above 10th.

Bonus Feats: An epic dungeon delver gains a bonus feat every three levels above 10th.

Dungeon Delver

Class Level	Special
11th	Skill Mastery
12th	*Augury* 4/day
13th	Bonus feat, trap sense +5
14th	—
15th	*Augury* 5/day, blindsense 3/day
16th	Bonus feat, trap sense +6
17th	—
18th	*Augury* 6/day
19th	Bonus feat, trap sense +7
20th	Blindsense 4/day

EPIC FEATS

The feats below are available only to epic-level characters—that is, characters of at least 21st level. The versions of these feats presented here supersede any previously published versions of feats with the same name.

Augmented Alchemy [Epic]

You can create alchemical items and substances that are much more powerful than normal.

Prerequisites: Int 21, Craft (alchemy) 24 ranks.

Benefit: Whenever creating an alchemical item or substance (not including poisons), you can choose to make it more powerful than normal by adding 20 to the DC required to create it and multiplying its price by 5.

An augmented alchemical item or substance deals double normal damage (if it deals damage), has twice the normal duration (if it has a duration), adds 2 to the save DC (if it has a save DC), and affects an area twice as wide as normal (if it has an area). If the item or substance doesn't fit any of these categories, then it cannot be affected by this feat.

For example, an augmented flask of alchemist's fire deals 2d6 points of damage (or 2 points of splash damage to all targets within 10 feet) and burns for 2 additional rounds after striking the target (rather than 1). The save DC to extinguish the flames is 17.

Epic Dodge [Epic]

You are able to evade attacks with exceptional agility.

Prerequisites: Dex 25, Tumble Dodge, 30 ranks, defensive roll, improved evasion.

Benefit: Once per round, when struck by an attack from an opponent you have designated as the target of your Dodge feat, you automatically avoid all damage from the attack.

Epic Reputation [Epic]

Your reputation provides great bonuses on interactions with others.

Benefit: You gain a +4 bonus on Bluff, Diplomacy, Gather Information, Intimidate, and Perform checks.

Epic Skill Focus [Epic]

Choose a skill, such as Move Silently. You have a legendary knack with that skill.

Prerequisite: 20 ranks in the skill selected.

Benefit: You gain a +10 bonus on all skill checks with the selected skill.

Special: You can gain this feat multiple times. Its effects do not stack. Each time you take the feat, it applies to a different skill.

Special. This feat counts as Skill Focus for the purpose of qualifying for other feats, prestige classes, and the like.

Group Inspiration [Epic]

Your bardic powers can inspire more allies than normal.

Prerequisites: Perform 30 ranks, bardic music.

Benefit: The number of allies you can affect with your inspire competence, inspire greatness, or inspire heroics ability doubles. When inspiring competence in multiple allies, you can choose different skills to inspire for different allies.

Improved Skirmish [Epic]

Your combat mobility improves.

Prerequisites: Skirmish +4d6/+4 AC.

Benefit: If the bonus to AC granted when you use your skirmish ability is equal to or higher than the number of dice of extra damage granted by your skirmish ability, your extra damage on skirmish attacks increases by 1d6.

If the bonus to AC granted by your skirmish ability is less than the number of dice of extra damage granted by your skirmish ability, the bonus to AC when skirmishing increases by 1 instead.

Special: This feat may be taken multiple times. Its effects stack.

Improved Sudden Strike [Epic]

Your ability to strike unaware foes improves.

Prerequisites: Sudden strike +8d6.

Benefit: Add 1d6 to your sudden strike damage.

Special: This feat may be taken multiple times. Its effects stack.

Legendary Acrobat [Epic]

You can balance and tumble much more easily than a normal person.

Prerequisites: Dex 21, Balance 24 ranks, Tumble 24 ranks.

Benefit: You can ignore any check penalties applied for accelerated movement while balancing (see page 67 of the *Player's Handbook*), for accelerated tumbling (see page 84 of the *Player's Handbook*), or for running while balancing on a narrow surface or while tumbling (see pages 97 and 103 in this book).

Normal: Without this feat, you take a –5 penalty on Balance checks and a –10 penalty on Tumble checks when attempting to move your full speed as a move action, or a –20 penalty on Balance or Tumble checks when attempting to run while balancing on a narrow surface or while tumbling.

Legendary Climber [Epic]

You can climb rapidly much more easily than a normal person.

Prerequisites: Dex 21, Balance 12 ranks, Climb 24 ranks.

Benefit: You can ignore any check penalties applied for accelerated climbing (see page 69 of the *Player's Handbook*), rapid climbing, or combat climbing (see page 97).

Normal: Without this feat, you take a –5 penalty on Climb checks when attempting to climb half your speed as a move action, or a –20 penalty when attempting to climb your speed as a move action or to retain your Dex bonus to AC when climbing.

Legendary Leaper [Epic]

You can cover great distances with only a brief start.

Prerequisite: Jump 24 ranks.

Benefit: You need only move 5 feet in a straight line to make a running jump.

Legendary Tracker [Epic]

You can track prey across or through the water, or even through the air.

Prerequisites: Wis 25, Knowledge (nature) 30 ranks, Survival 30 ranks, Track.

Benefit: You can track creatures across water, underwater, or through the air by the minute disturbances they make and traces of their passage. This benefit adds the surfaces of water, underwater, and air to the list of surfaces found under the Track feat in the *Player's Handbook*:

Surface	DC
Water	60
Underwater	80
Air	120

Polyglot [Epic]

You can speak, read, and write all languages.

Prerequisites: Int 25, Speak Language (five languages).

Benefit: You can speak all languages. If you are literate, you can also read and write all languages (not including magical script).